THE JANISSARIES

The rebuilding of the fortress at Kars by Lala Mustafa Pasha, 1570 (British Library)

Godfrey Goodwin

THE JANISSARIES

British Library Cataloguing-in-Publication Data
A catalogue record for this book is available from the British Library

ISBN 0-86356-740-1
EAN 9-780863-567407

copyright © Godfrey Goodwin 2006

First published in hardback in 1994 by Saqi Books

All rights reserved. No part of this book may be reproduced or transmitted in any form or by any means, electronic or mechanical, including photocopying, recording or by any information storage and retrieval system, without permission in writing from the publisher.

This book is sold subject to the condition that it shall not, by way of trade or otherwise, be lent, re-sold, hired out, or otherwise circulated without the publisher's prior consent in any form of binding or cover other than that in which it is published and without a similar condition including this condition being imposed on the subsequent purchaser.

This edition published 2006

SAQI
26 Westbourne Grove
London W2 5RH
www.saqibooks.com

To Gillian

Jacques de Hay: janissary (Maggs)

Contents

List of Illustrations	8
Acknowledgements	9
Genealogy of the House of Osman	10
A Note on Pronunciation	11
Glossary	12
Introduction	17
1. The Origins of the Janissary Corps	19
2. The *Devşirme* or Christian Levy	32
3. Pillars of the Empire	55
4. The Ottoman Armed Forces	65
5. The Victorious Years	110
6. The Great Campaign	130
7. Fish Stink from the Head	143
8. Sharp Eyes and Long Legs	168
9. Tulips and Turmoil	184
10. The Auspicious Event	214
Epilogue	230
Notes	235
Bibliography	255
Index	263

Illustrations

Jacques de Hay, after Jean Baptiste van Mour: sultan and pages wearing the sleeve of Hacı Bektaş (Maggs)	cover
The rebuilding of the fortress at Kars by Lala Mustafa Pasha, 1570 (British Library)	frontispiece
Jacques de Hay: janissary (Maggs)	6
Agha of the janissaries, mounted (Pepys Library)	18
Istanbul by Hubert Sattler (Fine Art Society)	31
Hall of the Halberdiers; a typical barracks of the janissaries at Topkapısaray (Michael Thompson)	54
Emblems of the janissary *ortas* from Marsigli (G. Gardiner)	64
The Ottoman camp from a plan drawn by Marsigli, showing the enclosure of the Grand Vezir with the five tails, guns, baggage wagons, advance and rearguard tents, scouts and camels resting	109
The Ottoman army in battle array under Süleyman the Magnificent (T.S.M.)	129
The capture of Tiflis by Lala Mustafa Pasha and Ozdemiroğlu Osman Pasha, 24 August 1578 (British Library)	142
The Ottoman army: (i) camel carrying two gun barrels; (ii) pack animals and baggage wagons; (iii) water supplies; (iv) the camp: picketed horses, cooking pots and latrines; from Marsigli (G. Gardiner)	167
Jacques de Hay: *solak*, bodyguard of the sultan (Maggs)	183
Agha of the janissaries in full dress *(L)* and *şeyhülislam (R)* (Sotheby's)	213
The Nüsretiye (Victory) mosque, erected to celebrate the suppression of the janissaries	229
Jacques de Hay: *sipahi* (Maggs)	234
The janissary band (T.S.M.)	254
Jacques de Hay: *aşcıbaşı* (Maggs)	262

Acknowledgements

I have to thank my family and friends for putting up with the janissaries for so long and for their encouragement. I have also to thank Dr Richard Luckett, librarian of the Pepys Library, Professor John Carswell of Sotheby's, Hugh Bett of Magg's and Graeme Gardiner for their help with the illustrations. Once again, Jana Gough has been an indomitable editor and André Gaspard continues to be the most equitable of publishers. I must also thank the janissaries themselves, a million or two of them, without whom the great architecture of the Ottomans would never have been accomplished. The mosque of Süleyman the Magnificent is their enduring memorial.

Genealogy of the Sultans of the House of Osman

Osman I (d. 1326)
Orhan Gazi (1326–1360)
Murat I (1360–1389)
Yıldırım Bayezit I (1389–1402)

interregnum

Mehmet I (1413–1421)
Murat II (1421–1444, 1446–1451)
Fatih Mehmet II (1444–1446, 1451–1481)
Bayezit II (1481–1512)
Selim I (1512–1520)
Süleyman I (1520–1566)
Selim II (1566–1574)
Murat III (1574–1595)
Mehmet III (1595–1603)

Ahmet I (1603–1617)   Mustafa I (1617–1618, 1622–1623)
Osman II (1618–1622)   Murat IV (1623–1640)   Ibrahim I (1640–1648)
Mehmet IV (1648–1687)   Süleyman II (1687–1691)   Ahmet II (1691–1695)
Mustafa II (1695–1703)   Ahmet III (1703–1730)
Mahmut I (1730–1754)   Osman III (1754–1757)   Mustafa III (1757–1774)   Abdülhamit I (1774–1789)
Selim III (1789–1807)   Mustafa IV (1807–1808)   Mahmut II (1808–1839)
Abdülmecit I (1839–1861)   Abdülaziz (1861–1876)
Murad V (1876)   Abdülhamit II (1876–1909)   Mehmet V (1909–1918)   Mehmet VI (1918–1922)
Abdülmecit II *(caliph only)* (1922–1924)

A Note on Pronunciation

The spelling adopted here is based on modern Turkish but I have even taken liberties with that.

While the pronunciation list may be of some help, the glossary will only please the benign: it would need an extra chapter to cover all the changing nuances of the meaning of words and the nature of various office-holders' duties over 500 years.

All Turkish letters are pronounced as in English except for the following:

c pronounced *j* as in *jam*
ç pronounced *ch* as in *child*
ğ not pronounced; lengthens the preceding vowel
ı akin to the pronunciation of *u* in *radium*
ö pronounced *ö* as in the German *König*
ş akin to the *sh* in *shark*
ü pronounced *u* as in the French *tu*

Glossary

abd: slave of Allah
acemioğlan: janissary recruit; cadet
agha: general; senior post-holder
ahi: (akhi) member of thirteenth- and fourteenth-century guilds of young élite
akçe: silver coin long used in the Ottoman Empire
akıncı: light cavalry; scout; light horse
alaybey: senior officer of the *sipahis*
Albigensians: heretical sect in the Middle Ages
Alevi: Shi'ite sectarian
aşcıbaşı: senior Royal Cook
askeri: military; infantry; auxiliaries
ateşcıbaşı: Chief Cook
ayan (pl.): local chieftains
azap: infantry (later gunners); could also serve at sea

baba: head of dervish sect
bailo: Venetian ambassador to the sultan
bayram: Muslim religious holiday
bey: (originally) ruler, chieftain; (then) man of rank; (now) any man
beylerbey: 'lord of lords'; viceroy
Bogomil: Balkan follower of Albigensian heresy
bölük: 61 out of the 196 companies of the janissary corps
bölükbaşı: captain; sergeant
bostancı: gardener; division of janissaries
bostancıbaşı: pasha of the *bostancıs*
boza: drink of fermented barley

caliph: successor to the Prophet
çardak çorbacı: commandant of the Customs House
çavuş: equerry; gate-keeper; usher
cebeci: armourer
celalı: rebels made up of dervishes, disbanded soldiers, students and the dispossessed
celeb: sheep-driver

Glossary

çelebi: title of member of élite class; *baba* or master of a Bektaşi *tekke*
cemaat: 101 out of the 196 companies of the janissary corps
çorbacı: janissary colonel

defterdar: Keeper of the Account Books; Minister of Finance
deli: 'maniac' (hence shock trooper)
derbent (pl.): guardians of the passes; local recruits
dervish: member of a mystical sect
devşirme: Christian levy
divan: general council
Divan: Grand Council of State
dizdar: commandant of a fortress

Enderun Kolej: ('College Within'), Palace School
esnaf (pl.): guildsmen; traders

fetva (pl. *fetvalar*): legal ruling with the force of an edict
firman: edict; order-in-council; command

gazi: warrior fighting for Islam/for the Faith
ghulam: royal cadet; slave held by title deed
gözde: chosen girl
güreba: foreign division

hadith: sayings of the Prophet, remembered by his followers after his death
 and seen as the ordinances of Allah
hajj: pilgrimage to Mecca
hamam: Turkish bath
han: inn
hass: royal estate
hoca: teacher; tutor and chaplain
horsetails: symbols of high-ranking commanders

içoğlan: page studying at Enderun Kolej
imam: prayer leader
irade: imperial rescript, decree

jerid: sport of mounted dart-throwing
jihad: Holy War

Glossary

kadı: judge
kadıasker: military chief justice of Europe or Asia
kahya: steward
kalafat: crested headdress
kanun: code of civil law
Kanun-i-Teşrifat: Law of Ceremonies
Kanunname: volume of laws and decrees
kapıkulı (pl.): members of the imperial household
kapudan paşa: Grand Admiral
kervansaray: Turkish spelling of caravanserai
kilim: tapestry-weave rug
Kızılbaş: Red Heads; Shi'ites
konak: villa; mansion
kös (pl.): great drums
kul: slave
kul kahya: steward of the imperial household; adjutant of the janissaries, etc.

lala: tutor

medrese: religious college
mescit: small (Ottoman) mosque without a *mimber*
meydan: square; open space
millet: non-Muslim citizens; their quarter
mimber: pulpit
molla: professor; senior religious and legal dignitary
müderris: rector; professor
muezzin: crier of the Muslim call to prayer
müsellem (pl.): settled nomads performing military service in return for smallholding
müteferrika: élite company of royal guard of feudal origin

naghile: hubble-bubble pipe
Nizam i-Cedit: New Army

ocak: barracks; hearth
oda (pl. *odalar*): room; barracks; dormitory
odabaşı: lieutenant
ordu: army; camp
orta: janissary company
otak: imperial tent (lit: high dome)

Glossary

padişah: sultan
pencik: title-deed, especially to a slave; slave
peyk: foot guardsman
piyade: Anatolian foot soldier

reis efendi: foreign minister
ribat: monastery (often fortified)

şalvar (pl.): pantaloons
sancak: flag; division of a province
sancak bey: Lord of the Standard; governor of a small province
sancak şerif: Standard of the Prophet
saray: palace
sebil: fountain
seferli: recruit
seğmen: janissary in charge of hunting dogs and greyhounds, etc.
selamlık: male guests' reception rooms
serasker: commander-in-chief
serdengeçti: shock troops ('Madcaps')
şeyh: elder; head of a Muslim religious order
şeyhülislam: Grand Mufti
seyyit: descendant of the Prophet
Shi'ite: unorthodox sect of Islam (cf. Sunni)
sılıhdar: household cavalry recruited from janissaries on a quasi-feudal basis
sipahi: horseman; feudal cavalry
softa: student
solak: royal guard (from *sol*, meaning left-handed)
Sunni: orthodox sect of Islam (cf. Shi'ite)
sürücü: drover

teber: double axe (symbol of the Bektaşi dervishes); halberd
tekke: dervish convent
tımar: fief of a retired officer
topçu: gunner
tuğ: horsetail showing rank; drum

ulema (pl.): members of the judicial class; Fathers of the Law

vakfiye: deed of endowment of religious property

Glossary

vali: governor; (modern use) chief of police
Valide Sultan: Queen Mother
vezir (Turkish spelling of vizier): minister of state
voynuk: Bulgarian who reared and tended the imperial horses; groom when on campaign

yalı: mansion beside the Bosphorus
yamak: auxiliary
yaya: Anatolian foot soldier
yayabaşı: colonel
yürük: nomad; tribesman

zaviye: dervish convent
zeamet: large *tımar*
Zülfikar: cleft sword of Ali

Introduction

Ertuğrul, the father of the Ottoman dynasty, was a pastoral chieftain grazing his flocks in a small corner of northern Anatolia. His son, Osman I Gazi, died at the taking of the rich trading city of Bursa by his own son, Orhan, on 6 April 1326. From there the Ottoman armies were to invade the Balkans and reach the Danube. Constantinople was isolated and then conquered in 1453 and by 1517 Selim I had subjugated Syria and Egypt. The threat to Rome was frustrated and only foul weather prevented the capture of Vienna in 1529. The coast of North Africa came under Ottoman sway and in 1543 Turkish galleys wintered in Toulon.

These triumphs would not have been possible without a strong bureaucracy and a formidable soldiery. Trained as a standing army, the janissaries were the core of the Ottoman forces. For a time they were dreaded throughout Europe. Who were they?

This book is not a history of the janissary corps but an attempt to understand them as human beings—which they were. Their character inevitably changed over the centuries and yet, in the end, had they changed so much?

Agha *of the janissaries, mounted (Pepys Library)*

1
The Origins of the Janissary Corps

Dark Birds over Anatolia

In the year 1336 a North African traveller on a tour of the Islamic world crossed Anatolia from south to north and left us an account of his journey. Ibn Battuta[1] was known and respected then, as he is now, and so was able to journey from one emirate to the next over territory which offered every kind of refuge to bandits and rapacious nomads. The decline of Mongol authority left the country divided among chieftains whose authority nominally derived from the khan's governors, such as Eretna, but who were virtually independent. Geographically, the terrain divided naturally into regions with fertile pockets between rude mountains and goat-ravaged wastes[2] where the inhabitants of polyglot ethnic stock had cohesive local loyalties. Moreover, the old gods lingered on in their fastnesses in valley and gorge and in the hearts of a peasant population monotonously assaulted by invading bands and companies.[3] Superstition remains strong to this day, when files of women still ascend the citadel hill at Kars to perform rites to placate Cybele or woodcutters at Elmalı still alarm the townsfolk of the coastal plain when they emerge from the forest, bronzed and fiercely bearded, armed with their axes.

Long before Hellenistic or Roman times, the government of the sub-continent depended on highways although the importance of one particular route might decline or grow over time. Thus the main road from Pertek to Divriği is still the track that it always was, whereas others now

The Janissaries

have metalled highways. Beyond the roads were the people and beyond the people were the bandits; this is still true in the mountains, especially in Kurdish areas. In the view of Christian landowners under the Byzantines, an infection as grim as the plague came in the form of Türkmen raiders[4] and they were, indeed, harbingers of defeat and desolation: but also of that reorganization into Muslim emirates that Ibn Battuta was to explore.

The Türkmen (known as Karakuş or Dark Birds) were birds of ill omen all over Central Asia. Their outstanding quality as cavalry depended on their sturdy horses, which could cover some 100 kilometres a day and are said to have achieved twice the distance when pressed.[5] Their riders were equally tough and could ride twenty hours a day for an entire week. As was to be the custom in the camp of the Ottoman army, they picketed their horses outside their tents and never stabled them. Although the rider carried a whip, it was for show or use on dogs, not his horse; and no man needed a spur.[6]

Their history was one of raids and pillage, made possible by their great skill as bowmen for they let fly several arrows from the saddle, one after the other, with deadly accuracy. Their favourite and time-hallowed manoeuvre was to ride off as if in retreat and then turn to fire the Parthian shot. Türkmen had been captured and made slaves in the sense of *kul* (a term which is discussed in Chapter 2) by the Samanids for whom they formed a valued bodyguard. Later, the caliphate was to employ Turkish slaves to its cost for gradually these democratic soldiers became the rulers of the Muslim provinces.

Türkmen were the cavalry of the Seljuk army and when Anatolia became a conglomeration of rival emirates they were the foremost raiders on the frontiers, the *gazis* (warriors for the Faith) who took their faith—to which they subscribed more for martial reasons than for Allah's—into Christian territories. In Central Asia, Islam made little progress but by the tenth century Arab merchants were trading in eastern Mongolia. The region had attracted an astonishing number of missionary religions from Zoroastrianism, Buddhism and Christianity to Judaism and Manichaeism; but the original shamanist beliefs and customs were too deep-rooted to be disturbed and it was this primitive worship of the mountains and the sky that the Türkmen took south with them. The year 960 saw the first official conversion to Islam of a numerous group of Turkic people—amounting to 2,000 tents—and the rulers of established states with roughly defined frontiers also gradually became Muslims. By 1127 Aslan Khan had built a minaret 50 metres high in Bukhara.

It was in the eleventh century that the bands of Türkmen led by their *beys* (chieftains) overran Persia and descended on Mesopotamia. Some of the

The Origins of the Janissary Corps

tribes were Mongol and not Turkish in origin and they had absorbed more Chinese culture than the Türkmen; moreover, they tended to be more aristocratic in outlook. A leader such as Chingiz Khan was so contemptuous of the populace that his history is gruesome with massacres. Only a quarter of the 100,000 inhabitants of Samarkand survived its capture in 1221 and the slaughtered local craftsmen were replaced by Chinese artisans.

Out of this feudal force of Türkmen evolved the Ottoman *sipahis* (feudal cavalry), but tribes loyal to a nomadic way of life remain a source of worry for the governments of both Turkey and Iran to this day. Transoxiana never lost its political force as the original homeland of Turk and Mongol. In the sixteenth century, the emotional importance of Central Asia for the Ottomans reinforced its strategic significance and an attempt was made to build a canal from the Volga to the Don—this would have circumvented the frontiers of Persia and opened up an Ottoman trade route across Central Asia. But the uneasy Tartar Giray Khan of the Crimea sabotaged this project because he did not wish to see his nominal overlord strongly established across his frontier. The canal would have permitted an Ottoman fleet to sail into the Caspian Sea and encircle the Safavid kingdom of Persia. The call of Asia was one that the janissaries found disagreeable, since few of them were Turks until the end of the sixteenth century, and this, too, resulted in a latent dislike of the mounted *sipahis*.

Frontier, Faith and Fervour

When the Byzantine army was routed at Manzikirt in 1071, Anatolia was overrun by Asiatic tribesmen; in their wake came the creed of Muhammad, which, with its camaraderie of the frontier, appealed to soldiers above all other sections of society. There is no caste more superstitious than the military and the tribesmen were followed, as if by their shadows, by a heterogeneous throng of mystics and charlatans, inebriated from wine or drugs, and single-minded missionaries for the Faith. There were indeed dedicated men in the midst of this rabble, just as there were true Christians among the raffish monks of the later Middle Ages (or are today in the dilapidated monasteries of Mount Athos). Such men had the authority of their courage and the necessary austerity with which to order the hordes into local communities. They followed after the invading companies of Islam to fix their *tekkes* (convents) at the crossroads of the conquered territories. From these headquarters they established sufficient tranquillity for agriculture to continue to sustain the villages until their confidence and co-operation had been won. In 1261 Anatolia was infested with robbers and terrorists, corruption was rampant and landlords had fled while the great estates were broken up.[7] Seventy years later, Ibn Battuta travelled unmolested.

Many of these dervishes were of the same Turkic stock and thought the same thoughts and shared the same phantoms as the settlers. Their quasi-socialist outlook succoured the indigent peasantry just as much as it did the newcomers at a time when central authority was impotent. Moreover, these fierce frontiersmen protected and advanced their borderlands because there were brothers among them endowed with such religious fanaticism that their daring made them invincible in battle. The Ottomans were later to harness this fervour and use it as a bridge over which the janissaries could traverse the breached defences of their foes. They were not a suicide brigade, however, since their enemies usually fled and the greatest honour was awarded those who achieved the highest heap of infidel dead.

Not all dervish orders were warlike or even populist. The ascetic Mevlevi, based in Konya, had little in common with the Rifai, or Howling Dervishes, whose orgasms for the Faith rendered them impervious to knife or fire. Yet the educative work of the Mevlevi sect, who civilized the leaders of society, was less important to the stability of the emergent Ottoman state in the fourteenth century than the ability of more plebeian orders to absorb the fears and direct the aspirations of the humble. They well knew that survival depended on cunning and dissembling, not least by that pretence of stupidity that was a protective garment which proved to be a hair shirt for successive governments. In this they were akin to peasant knaves or Russian serfs, who also resorted to the mask of simplicity.

But since cunning as a humour is not altogether satisfying, the people yearned for something more than just the wit to ward off the evil day when a rapacious tax-collector, landlord or troop of horse was hungry for forage and fat hens. No man lives without a modicum of hope, even in the shadow of declining fortunes and the depopulation of Anatolia which preceded Selim I's establishment of stable government in the sixteenth century. Its survival is a tribute to its power even if this hope amounted to the wish to swap places with the tax-gatherer and to be the oppressor rather than the oppressed.

Hope in the abstract sense was kept alive by the dervish orders, who irrationally fired a faith which could never be fuelled by reason. This fanaticism also accounts for the ferocity of such sultans as Selim I, who could not overcome the heretic tribesmen of Anatolia with anything short of an ordered terrorism to outwit their own. Previously, in the fourteenth century, the small size of some emirates had brought relief from oppression

The Origins of the Janissary Corps

because the *bey* or other local overlord was easily approached—each freeborn Muslim had the right of access to his ruler. Indeed, this right may have been one reason why, some two centuries later, Süleyman I (known to the West as the Magnificent) moved his residence from the centre of Istanbul to Topkapısaray, the seat of government. Public petitioners could now no longer delay him as he rode to and from his place of work. It was a right which extended to women and which was acknowledged from the beginning of Ottoman rule.[8] The *beys,* from whose company the Ottomans emerged, were humble enough rulers: their halls and mosques were small and their towns were what we would call villages. Their summer palaces were tents by a stream in the woods or on a hillside; their wealth was worn on the body or represented by a cup or ewer, like the superb basin in the Mevlevi convent at Konya, which became a potent symbol of authority.

Such localized power could hardly degenerate into tyranny when the leading courtiers had characters as strong as their lord's. Moreover, one and all were free men dedicated to the advancement of the Standard of the Prophet *(sancak şerif)* and if ritual prayers were perfunctorily uttered by some—not least, the opportunist Byzantine converts—the unifying force of Islam was too strong for any overt expression of agnosticism.[9] Moreover, if the ruler and his *vezir* (minister of state) were named individuals, whose quirks of personality have come down to us, most men were less personages than the shadow puppets of the brotherhood.

Islam, however, was rent into sects as violently as was Christianity. The emergence of a national ruling house in Persia epitomized this in the sixteenth century: Shah Ismail represented a heterodox sect, the Shi'ites, who were at odds with the orthodox Sunni Ottomans. The Ottoman adherence to the Sunni creed was partly due to geography. Had their early wanderings led them down into central Anatolia, they might have been sucked into the Shi'ite whirlwind which stirs the dust of that plateau. But their flocks and their swords grazed northwards and their Sufi dervishes kept pace with them. There the lure of Constantinople was irresistible and they could not remain goatherds and shepherds for long.

If brotherhood belongs to shepherds and soldiers, democracy inhabits battlefields and towns. The countryman is compelled by the seasons to a passivity that the desperate may only escape by banditry, seeking perpetual refuge in the mountain fastnesses. The democracy of the towns in the time of Ibn Battuta was maintained by a free brotherhood possessing considerable sophistication and consisting of younger merchants and the sons of the rich.

Islam as a faith was divided between a military caste and the merchants who were the educated leaders of society. Wealth determined their pursuit of the law—which was also the pursuit of religion since there were no priests, only the judiciary of a republic where all laws stemmed from Allah and religion was the law. However, the Koran only covered laws which were basic to human life at tribal level so that there grew up a miscellany of less primary legislation first collected into the *hadith* (sayings of the Prophet). Interpreting divine utterances gives scope for human prejudice and imagination, and from early Islamic times the *ulema* (judicial class) contrived to amass wealth, partly from bribes. Through the *vakfiye* system (the dedication of property to religious use), charities were established with hereditary family administrators for the benefit of a man's heirs until much country and most city land was in the hands of these pious foundations. Although the accretion of wealth was immoral and deplorable, it nevertheless obliged merchants and judges to be charitable and to mitigate the worst aspects of urban poverty over and above the payment of their tithe.

Equals among Equals

In thirteenth-century Anatolia, an egalitarian reversal of the usual order of Islam grew in an astonishing manner. Its intellectual roots may be found in the socialistic beliefs of the Karmatians, whose primitive desert communism was long a threat to the learned class. Such concepts were accepted, however, in the clubs set up in many local towns by the *ahis*, who were young craftsmen and small traders. In 1355 the prisoner Gregory Palamas found the *ahis* wise and erudite.[10] They tended to be bachelors and were tolerant towards women (although they did not go so far as to treat them as equals), allowing them to form a sect of their own. Like the Quakers, the *ahis* established *zaviyes* (central meeting-houses) where they feasted and sang as well as prayed. The building was often the finest in the town, as with the *zaviye* founded by Murat I at Iznik (Nicaea) in honour of his Christian-born mother, Nilufer Sultan. These 'club houses' were used as hostels by fortunate travellers like Ibn Battuta, who remarked that there was no other comparable movement in Islam.[11] Ibn Battuta was sometimes embarrassed when two *zaviyes* competed for his patronage but he disposed of the problem by dividing his stay equally between them.[12]

Prayer, food and ritual music were not the only functions of these clubs. They were the daily meeting-places of the community leaders, the men who paid the taxes and whose skills made civilized life possible. Naturally they conversed, and equally naturally their conversation was political. They were embryonic Jacobins whose talk was not harmless gossip, for the *ahis* achieved real power and could restrain rulers who might well find their

The Origins of the Janissary Corps

views anarchic. The *ahis* even ruled in Ankara (Angora) for a time, for there was no prince.

Without written records it is difficult to trace the *ahis*' decline; it was paralleled by the rise of the Ottomans whom they supported because the family was committed in deed, as well as word, to the advancement of the *jihad* (Holy War). For an *ahi* this was the only war and, if they exerted restraint on the *beys* who enjoyed fighting each other, it was only to urge them to fight the war that was for Allah.

The *ahis* also dealt with highwaymen and bandits and were valued allies of Orhan in the capture of Bursa when his father Osman Gazi died, just as they were to be the cause of concern to Murat I when a revolt in the region of Ankara was instigated by his rival, Karaman Bey. They were later to help Cem Sultan against Bayezit II but were one reason why Mehmet I regained the throne after his father's defeat at the hands of Timur. They had close relationships with his *vezir*, Bayezit Pasha, an Albanian with possible Bogomil antecedents whose mosque at Amasya has many *zaviye* characteristics. Anarkis[13] calls the *ahis* the aggregate of all the virtues which distinguished young men of chivalry and it was this chivalry that the Ottomans were to extinguish to their cost. The *ahis* were as determined in their opposition to banditry as they were to tyranny[14] and their apprentices swore to 'serve the seven virtues, abhor the seven vices: open seven doors and close seven doors'. Nor would they admit atheists, butchers, surgeons, tax-gatherers or money-lenders to their hostels. Most significantly, they refused to shelter astrologers, foes of all rational thought and therefore of freedom, whom monarchs and *ulema* continued to cherish. They offered with this a kinder faith than that of the uncharitable legalists, permitting men to follow winding paths between hedgerows of peccadilloes which eased the passage through life for some. They argued that wine was no evil, for example. Moreover, in their pursuit of ecstasy they inevitably employed narcotics which, with their pacifying hold over the mind, became a secret political instrument within the Ottoman state.

When the Ottomans, in effect, ceased to be *gazis* and became ambitious imperialists as eager to engulf Islamic lands as Christian, the highly developed central bureaucracy could not help but be hostile to mysticism and folk socialism. The *ahi* brotherhood had to be eliminated and if some of their ideas merged with those of Sufi orders, dervishes had little political let alone economic power.

It is true that when Ibn Battuta reached the then Ottoman capital at Bursa, the town was full of dervishes and the term *zaviye* did not apply simply to their lodges. Dervish lodgings were incorporated into the major mosques,

The Janissaries

which also sheltered travellers and holy men.[15] Only with the conquest of Constantinople in 1453 and the establishment of the autocracy of Mehmet II (known as Fatih, 'the Conqueror') did inns and mosques take on lives apart in well-differentiated buildings. Now it was the *ulema* whose high council met in the mosque of the sultan with all the authority of the established orthodoxy. Dervishes were sent to backchat elsewhere in the Conqueror's complex. As for the *ahis*, despite Byzantine precedents that lingered on in 1453, no system was fully organized until late in the sixteenth century. The guilds had to grow again from new roots, taking the form of state corporations rather than free institutions. If these were eventually to become powerful, it was partly due to their infiltration by the janissaries.

From Small Acorns Great Oaks Grow

In this search for the origins of the janissary corps, with their mystique, *esprit de corps* and cookhouse terminology, it will be seen that they emerged from obscurity with some of the ideals of the past still clinging to them, however feebly. Related to their mystique was an affinity with popular religions which echoed with ghostly voices from the antique pantheon. Janissary fraternization with these polyglot gods and debased *ahi* concepts may have arisen from a subconscious emotional need but it equally contributed to the decline of the corps as a military force—an inevitable decline, as the dynasty stumbled its way into the nineteenth century.

It may seem odd to trace the history of troops that became the terror of Europe through political roots but armies, whether passively or actively, are political bodies. In the Ottoman state, moreover, the highest officers were trained in the janissaries' image. Although the palace pages formed a separate and elect body, their connection with the corps was sufficient to quell any tendency to aristocratic disdain for the janissaries. Until power faded, hereditary rank did not count for much under the sultans. Mehmet II pursued a policy of suppressing the hereditary nobility. The promotion of the common folk was pursued by subsequent sultans in face of opposition by the *ulema*. The proud jurist Ebüssu'ûd even silenced Süleyman's Grand Vezir, Sokollu Mehmet Pasha, who was a child of Christian parents and therefore a slave, by saying that his witness was inferior to that of a true-born Muslim, however humble. That he had risen to the loftiest office in the empire was of no account.[16] In this lay the essential social superiority—and higher pay—of the *sipahis* which helped foster the bitter rivalry between them and the Christian-born janissaries, a rivalry that the government exploited.

The Origins of the Janissary Corps

The early Ottoman sultans had no need of special troops, for their ambitions were modest and they were joined by adventurers and warriors who in Europe would have enlisted in the free companies of captains like Hawkwood in Italy. Such an adventurer was Köşe Mikhal ('Michael the Beardless'), who founded the Mikhaloğlu family and who had belonged to the mercenary Catalan Company before joining other disillusioned Greeks who became Muslims and helped Orhan Gazi take Bursa. Orhan, together with his brother Alaettin Pasha and Kara Halil Çandarlı, an *ahi* and an educated man, organized his army into units of tens, hundreds and thousands. The *sipahis* were placed under the command of another brilliant Greek officer from Karası, Evrenos Bey,[17] who also became Commander of the European Marches.[18] Orhan appointed his eldest son, Süleyman Pasha, as *beylerbey* ('lord of lords', or viceroy) and *serasker* (commander-in-chief) in Europe and Köşe Mikhal as commander of the *akıncıs* (scouts or light cavalry), heirs of the Türkmen raiders. Their flare and panache gave them an authority of their own and upset the wiser if less spectacular plans for gradually absorbing the conquests of Orhan's successor, Murat I.[19]

Was the janissary corps really founded by Murat I or was the janissary Konstantin Mikhailović right that it was formed by Murat II's father, Mehmet I, some thirty years before his own attachment to the corps in 1455?[20] It is likely that the first companies of a new corps were composed of captives, corralled and driven around awaiting ransoms which were unlikely to be paid. They were not only a nuisance but also a waste of talent. The anonymous Ottoman chronicle is quite specific on this point.[21] Converted to Murat's cause, they could be valuable warriors. It was a practice which had long been followed in Islam as elsewhere. The captives were sent to learn Turkish on the farms of the feudal cavalry just as janissary recruits were later to be sent—and in that toughening process found another reason to resent their *sipahi* overseers. The law of 1362 sent one in every five prisoners to spend five to seven years labouring before their transfer to Gallipoli (Gelibolu) and, after 1453, to Istanbul.[22] It is probable that the Christian captives formed the nucleus of a standing army; they may also have been the original company that was to grow into the new army, the *yeniçeri* or janissary corps. Their commanders were chosen from among the companions of the Ottoman *bey,* thus giving them the benefit of his prestige, so that by the reign of Murat I in the mid- to late-fourteenth century the detachment had its own identity.

The first mention of the enforced enrolment of Christian children[23] occurs as late as 1438, in the reign of Murat II, when Isidore Glabas, Metropolitan of Salonika (Thessalonika), wrote to protest at the kidnapping of some boys by pirate crews sent by the emirs of the Anatolian coasts, such as the Menteşe *beys*.[24] By then an embryonic Ottoman corps was certainly in existence and is likely to have recruited the sons of the defeated military caste of the new-won Balkan provinces besides Greeks from the Black Sea region. Otherwise there would have been nothing for these youths to do for by birth they were fitted for little else than carrying arms. Moreover, with the conquest of ever-increasing areas of the Balkans (Rumelia) in the second half of the fourteenth century, there was a reservoir of manhood which the Byzantines themselves had tapped. It is probable that some system of levying a toll of boys from the peninsula to come to work in Constantinople, humbly enough, had been instituted long before the Ottoman period. The capital offered these servants a foothold from which those of spirit could achieve careers which were inconceivable in their villages.[25]

The rapid expansion of Murat I's realm left little time in which to train recruits who had been forcibly abducted. However, the new lands were Christian in a different sense from those populated by Greeks for they harboured Bogomil heretics who had affinities with the free-thinking Albigensians.[26] They were easily persuaded by dervish missionaries that they had ideas in common with Sufism. This coupling with the mystique of Ali and his two-bladed sword, Zülfikar, was to trouble the janissaries, one of whose emblems it became, and early attracted them to Bektaşi ideas (see Chapter 7) as is apparent from Konstantin Mikhailović's evidence in the 1450s. The Shi'ite movements were to hold Ali in esteem and reject Ottoman orthodoxy. The interplay of secret beliefs is difficult to reconcile but that such forces were important is not in doubt. Nor were the common people the only Bogomils for in Bosnia even Stephen, king from 1444 to 1461, was one.

The Slavs were easily converted to Islam and there was no need to extend the recruitment of Christian boys into Anatolia until 1512—which indicates that there was little opposition to the system of forced levies in the Balkans. There was, however, a trade in slaves of both sexes recruited by the Tartars from the Caucasus. These slaves were shipped down the Bosphorus throughout the fourteenth and fifteenth centuries. In about 1400 Johann Schiltberger,[27] who became page to Bayezit I, reported a sale of children—the handsomest boys and the prettiest girls—from special slave ships. The trade was permitted to continue after the conquest of 1453 by Mehmet II but he forbade the transportation of Muslims.[28] Some boys were taken for the army and some girls for the harem while other youngsters were destined for the markets of Egypt. Some 7,000 Tartar, Circassian, Russian and Magyar children were sold at Alexandria when the Italian merchant

The Origins of the Janissary Corps

Tenenti was there. The Tartars fetched 130–140 ducats but the Circassians only 110–120. The barbarous Uskok pirates of the upper Adriatic were also employed as middlemen who supplied Pope Sixtus V. Two thousand such slaves were sold on the quayside at Ancona in 1599.

The establishment of a central government at Edirne, the former Adrianopolis, with alliances which extended Ottoman masterdom over most of the territories south of the Danube, was quickly achieved. A region that had been mauled by the enmities of local princes was to be unified for 400 years—partly because the well-fed and, usually, paid Ottoman army was initially to be preferred to those of the licentious and rapacious Christian knights and their vagabond hordes. Until the eighteenth century only the Dutch could afford to pay a standing army which could be drilled and made to dig. Mercenaries thought such exercises beneath them. By good discipline and payment for supplies, the loyalty of the local peasants was quickly won. In Bulgaria, for example, the choice lay between serfdom and brigandage or Ottoman order and the country remained subject from 1393 until nationalism liberated it in 1878. The brutal feudal rule of the Bulgarian barons could win no hearts. Once they had bowed their heads to the conqueror, landowners as much as their peasantry were swift to escape the poll tax by being converted to Islam, making religion subservient to economics. The government even had to discourage the proliferation of converts because of diminished revenues, as happened when Bosnia was taken in 1463 and Herzegovina in 1482. In these territories many people would have sought employment in a standing army such as existed nowhere else. Moreover, the army wore distinguishing uniforms, a discipline that was not imposed in Europe until Martinet equipped the French army in the eighteenth century.

There were recruits to hand but the development of the janissary corps was carefully planned if only because of the economics of its pay and maintenance, for which money had to be found. It was not a question of booty, as with some mercenary companies or, later, the corsairs. Tax sources had to be allocated and the money accounted for.

The ultimate consequences of the founding of the corps could not have been foreseen by Murat I or by his successor, Yıldırım ('the Thunderbolt') Bayezit. No more could Henry VII of England have foreseen that his college at Eton would furnish a procession of social leaders and house 1,400 boys. The first levy of Balkan yokels did not imagine themselves to be destined to political power but to pay and wounds. They speedily became proud of their bowmanship and, later, their musketry and the comradeship of veterans. Nor were these crack infantrymen aware of any affinities with

The Janissaries

the populace of Edirne or Istanbul. This was to come later—as if by accident but actually to fill a vacuum. For a time, they had a real place in society as the tribunes of the populace, devoid of constructive concepts though they were. It is this that makes the pursuit of the history of the janissaries a climb up the stairs of no ivory tower but a lookout post from which to watch the struggles beneath the surface of Ottoman politics, the struggles of the tumultuous majority.

At the turn of the fourteenth century Timur captured Yıldırım Bayezit and threatened the dismembered Ottoman state with extinction. With Sufi help, Mehmet I survived his brothers and unified the provinces once more.[32] In 1416 he established the *kul* (slave) system and at that date the janissary corps appears to have numbered some 6,000 men.[33] His son, Murat II, inherited mystical leanings as well as the gift of commanding men. The corps was fully established as the standing army during Murat II's reign although it was necessarily small because of the cost.

When Murat abdicated in 1444 in order to retire to a life of contemplation at Bursa and Manisa (the old Magnesia), these troops revolted against the rule of his 14-year-old son, Mehmet II; they were attempting to overthrow the *vezir*, Kara Halil Pasha of the landowning Çandarlı family, lords of the Black Sea region. Kara Halil recalled Murat to deal with the mutiny and then the Christian enemy—an insult that the deposed adolescent, Mehmet, is said never to have forgiven the *vezir*.

On the death of Murat II in 1451, Mehmet II once again became sultan. Because he needed trained soldiers if he were to achieve his ambition of capturing Constantinople, he enlarged the janissary corps and also increased the number of boys of the Christian levy. Some were selected for their good looks and intelligence to form a cadre apart. They were trained at the exacting Palace School, the Enderun Kolej,[34] to form the future military and civil leadership. Like the humbler soldiers, these élite officers were slaves even though they were converts to Islam, but they could not be bought or sold. Indeed, the term *kapıkulı* meant that they were members of the imperial family and shared their prince's great fortune in good times. They had no right of appeal, however, if their sultan found them wanting and deserving of death. Moreover, in theory at least, their estates and treasure were forfeit in the event of their death however that came about: execution, battlefield or bed. Their recruitment was of the greatest importance for they were trained to wield great authority.

Istanbul by Hubert Satler (Fine Art Society)

2
The Devşirme *or Christian Levy*

A Bumper Harvest for the Sultans

Although the recruitment of children has been regarded as shocking, it was an old concept. The Mogul rulers enlisted children taken in war and bought others from their parents in time of famine, a custom which was Hindu in origin.[1] Later, Peter the Great was to call up able-bodied Russian boys at the age of 10 in order to educate them for his army which was hamstrung by illiteracy. The Ottoman sultan was entitled to take a fifth of all prisoners-of-war and, later, half on payment to the pious foundations. Mehmet II took all young prisoners at five gold pieces each and scribes followed in the wake of his armies to enrol boys in the janissary corps. They were known as *penciks* (slaves) and could not bequeath property whereas levies from the villages could do so. The sultan selected the best youths for himself and sent the rest for training in Anatolia.

At the capture of Novo Brdo in 1455, the population was lined up in the ditch outside the walls and 340 youths, including Konstantin Mikhailović, were enrolled in the janissary corps or as auxiliaries. Nineteen, including Konstantin, escaped only to be recaptured, beaten and dragged behind horses until comrades stood surety for their future conduct. Yet another group of this sturdy batch from mining families later attempted to stab Mehmet II to death but were betrayed. They were put to death and the sultan was spared only to die of a malignant disease. Sultans also resorted to slave markets fed by Tartars from their Russian sorties or by quasi-slave families from the Caucasus. *Akıncıs* reaped in Europe and corsairs cropped the

The Devşirme or Christian Levy

Mediterranean while sultans also received gifts of intelligent and handsome youths.

The turncoats or freebooters were experienced soldiers who needed no lengthy training. They brought novel skills with them and were unlikely to defect, as the Serbian contingent demonstrated against Timur at the battle of Ankara in 1402. They joined the Ottomans because theirs was the fulcrum of victory and so they could refresh their zest and be rewarded for valour with a fair share of booty and, if a town did not surrender, rapine. They were Christian volunteers like Murat Pasha, born a Palaeologus, or the Iskenderoğlu or Mikhaloğlu houses, born Alexanders and Michaels. Their new allegiance protected their estates and gave them employment. They dared not turn conspirators. If he were a convert to Islam, not even a great general could lead a state where the *ulema* controlled justice and commerce in the security of their Muslim birthright. Nor could these Christian turncoats take their acres—their only wealth—with them if they defected to the Hungarians. Even if some among them did disobey orders in the foolhardy manner of Christian knights of their time, none was ever a traitor twice. At worst, the Mikhaloğlu overrode orders and took Balkan provinces against Murat I's wishes.

But a newly recruited caste, educated at the palace or its subsidiary colleges, was hardened and then bound to a loyalist brotherhood proud of a growing tradition. It presented a potent force which was eventually to win civil as well as military authority. The janissaries, fed by a levy which set them apart from the commonalty, might have represented a challenge to the structure of the state.[2] It is true that at times the corps possessed an intuitive sense of occasion and did not simply accept the leadership of whatever opportunist commander presented himself. The often repeated tragedy lay in their inability to think ahead constructively or to plot more than a coup or a mutiny. The janissaries were not free men like the early comrades-in-arms of the Ottomans but were enmeshed as an integral part of the structure of a corporate state in whose overthrow lay their own demise. Thus their politics were never else than those of the narrowest self-interest so that governments could fob off rebel leaders with well-paid offices and high-sounding titles. These made them figures of envy as, with growing complacency, they lolled on their divans and cut themselves off from their followers until it was easy to strip them of their robes of honour and their lives. If they had ever considered how to serve the populace as they served themselves, the sultanate would never have endured. They did not because they could not.

Had the early sultans foreseen what a jackanapes they had hoisted on

The Janissaries

their backs with the inauguration of the levy, they might well have paused. However, they could only see, correctly, the creation of a standing army in the form of a corps attached to their person, such as Franz Josef of Austro-Hungary saw, and which was totally professional in its attitude to war: too professional, as Bernard Shaw might have warned them. And so the decision to recruit by means of the levy was taken and once it was taken, with true Ottoman concern for detail, the planning was exact and strictly ordered with clear-cut regulations which no one could misunderstand.

Choosing which Seed will Grow

No child might be recruited who was converted to Islam other than by his own free will—if the choice between life and death may be called free will. (Perhaps it might be so in a period of history when religion was a passion and martyrdom willingly endured.) A less dubious stipulation forbade taking an only son from a widow or more than a certain percentage of the youth of a village. This was not entirely due to compassion but in order not to impoverish Balkan agriculture. The policy made for political tranquillity: by selecting the best of the boys, the natural leaders of a community were taken, leaving only the less spirited youths behind. No levy was imposed on towns although Athens was subjected to it on two occasions at least; but then it had declined into little more than a village by the sixteenth century. Townsfolk were needed for their skills and were regarded as 'soft' when compared with countrymen. No married men might be taken, a provision which had the obvious result that boys were frequently married at the age of 12.[3] Indeed, janissaries were forbidden to marry until they retired in order to avoid loyalties that might conflict with their dedication to the throne. Romanians were spared because they were vassals and not subjects; neither were Moldavia or Wallachia ever 'harvested'. No Jews or gypsies might be enlisted; the former were townsmen, doctors and accountants who managed the great estates of the pashas and whose faith was as tenacious as that of any Muslim, while the latter were clearly despised. At first, this veto also applied to Armenians but some were eventually admitted. No embargo was placed on the unpopular Greeks, who produced a number of outstanding pashas if not always the most attractive humanists. Eventually, the levy was extended to Anatolia but these recruits were never as greatly admired as the Slavs from the Balkans.

Some households dreaded the thought of a son being carried off to war and becoming a Muslim. This is evident from the searches for substitutes, the regulations about absentee youths and the names that vanished from the

The Devşirme *or Christian Levy*

parish registers—if the heart of the local priest had been suitably warmed. The recruiting officer was known as the horse-dealer or drover and the term was unkindly meant.

The success of the levy is clearly shown by the rise of the best recruits to the highest offices in the state. Moreover, Muslim parents and their sons soon grew jealous of these Christian converts. A trade in Muslim substitutes (which everyone involved must have contrived at, since most of these boys were already circumcised) had received recognition by the mid-sixteenth century. By the seventeenth century, the sons of the janissaries were admitted to the paternal company against the rules and freeborn Muslims enlisted ever more openly, thus changing the very nature of the corps. In 1515, 1,000 recruits from the provinces of Bosnia and Herzegovina were already Muslims but they were denied the right to total freedom because their fathers had not been Muslim-born but were examples of the rapidity of conversion in the Bogomil Balkans. In 1550 it was reported from Palestine that local fief-holders increasingly avoided military service and the local townsfolk were accepted into the local janissary corps: that is to say, they accepted their pay but persuaded their officers to let them lead private lives. However, this scandal belongs more to the growth of a system of provincial janissary service which had little connection with the fraternity in the capital. A *firman* (order-in-council) of 1564 makes clear that in Bosnia and Herzegovina *devşirme* boys might be recruited even if they were Muslim-born and already circumcised. This decree was issued in response to the petitions of Bosnians themselves and merely sanctioned practices that had been going on illegally for some years before.

The levy was supposed to follow a seven-year cycle but was more frequent in the sixteenth century since recruitment was inevitably related to the high command's hunger for heads in a period of great military activity. Ramberti, himself a janissary at that time, reports that in the first quarter of the century there was a levy every four years but this was exceptional and his evidence is imprecise. Indeed, an early sixteenth-century *firman* limited recruitment to one boy from every forty households. The total intake for 1573 was 8,000 boys from the Balkans and Anatolia. This figure shows a slight decrease compared to the numbers taken earlier in the century.

The levy of 1637 followed on a lapse of twelve years but Murat IV had limitless ambition and was engaged in reforming the janissaries. Consequently, a fresh levy was imposed the following year. Yet Evliya Çelebi, writing at this period and a man who had been intimate with Murat, says that the levy was made every seven years and that 8,000 men (they were sent straight to the *ocaks,* or barracks, and so could hardly have been youths or boys) were recruited. The last important levy was in 1663 although there was one specifically for the Enderun Kolej in 1666.[8] Another, held ten years later, was mainly confined to Greece where Köprülü Ahmet Pasha had the greatest difficulty in scraping together 3,000 boys; he even had to include jugglers and acrobats—who might be considered a leavening element in any assault battalion. When Ahmet III called for 1,000 boys in 1705, the recruits could no longer be called a levy in the original *devşirme* sense.

It is unclear what the original age limits for the recruits were, and certainly they fluctuated as do crops of apples in a good or bad season. Ramberti boldly asserts that the boys were aged between 10 and 20 but Lybyer's researches led him to state that the youngest recruits were aged 12, while Kocu says that only men of exceptional ability were enrolled if they were as old as 20.[9] Kocu was probably attempting to solve the conundrum of the architect Sinan Abdülmennan, who was probably recruited at that age. Perhaps Sinan bribed the drover since anyone would have wanted to escape from his birthplace, Agyrnas (Mimarsinanköy). Ottoman sources suggest that from 1601 the recruits were usually aged between 15 and 20; there were other permutations at various periods, suggesting that training at the Enderun Kolej started at 13 years old. It is clear that the recruitment of young boys would only take place if a long-term policy was to be followed.

The preparations for a levy were made with care and began months in advance. Each district had to supply forty boys; the *yayabaşı* (colonel) of the *sipahis* and the *sürücü* (drover) proceeded from one locality to another with a train of previously selected youngsters and also a clerk.[10] Whatever ambitions families might or might not have, it was an unhappy day when the troop trudged into the village, hungry and thirsty. The priest was ready with his baptismal rolls and so were the boys with their fathers; in theory mothers and sisters were left to weep at home. Then each of the recruits had to be examined both physically and mentally. It is a tribute to the healthiness of Balkan rural life that stout lads were so easily found. Any boy who was rejected because of some weakness discovered by the inspector was replaced by a first reserve. Intelligence was assessed by the art of phrenology practised, one imagines, with the help of experience and a shrewd eye. It is unlikely that the village idiot was recruited, however promising the ordering of the bumps on his head, while many able boys clearly were.

Once the selection process was completed, the roll was drawn up in duplicate. The *yayabaşı* kept one copy and the *sürücü* a second which he took with him. (There was a double check because the slaves were valuable and an unscrupulous drover might use a boy as if he were a letter of credit.)

The Devşirme or Christian Levy

Each Balkan *sürücü* marched his herd in batches of 100 to 120 by way of Edirne to Istanbul.[11] Now was the time for tears and some farewells must have been poignant but the boys tramped the dusty roads side by side with friends and all had the excitement of starting out on an adventure. They could dream of promotion and fortune while the peasants returned to their fields, doubtless to weep longer than their sons. At least they were secure for seven years before the next visitation.

The Entrance Examination: Jobs and Odd Jobs

At Edirne or Istanbul the naked boys were inspected from head to foot for a second time, perhaps by the *agha* (captain-general) of the janissaries himself. They were in limbo for they were neither one thing nor the other. Even their absent fathers were given new names for the purpose of their sons' enrolment and were called Abdullah (the slave of Allah) or Abdülmennan or some other name starting with *abd* (slave) to signify 'non-Muslim' while the boys themselves were given Muslim first names. They were also circumcised, thus signifying their acceptance of the Faith. Their intelligence was also examined afresh and they were finally—or almost finally since Ottoman history always had its exceptions—assigned to their destiny. In the early sixteenth century, out of some 5–6,000 recruits only 1–200 in a year were chosen for the royal schools, which were the most illustrious in the land. At one period, the very best were sent directly to the Enderun Kolej[12] within the walls of the *saray* (palace). The second order of recruits—and these might include the best of them, such as the great architect Sinan, because their skulls were devoid of illustrious hills and valleys or else they were ugly—were selected for the colleges outside the walls. Later, the students at the palace were selected after a period at Galatasaray, which acted as a preparatory college.

The students at the Enderun Kolej were known as the *içoğlans* (inside boys, or pages of the privy household). Galatasaray had some 400 pages while the great Grand Vezir Ibrahim Pasha, Süleyman's favourite, founded a third ancillary school for Bosnian and Albanian *devşirmes* in his palace on the Hippodrome, or Atmeydan, part of which survives as a museum. In 1624 Baudier reported that the great palace—Ibrahim Pasha Saray—with its 140-metre façade and its alleged 600 rooms, served for the ceremonies and solemnities, the pomp and carousels of the Ottoman princes but that it was still an academy for 400 pages who were instructed in letters, arms and other exercises. Evliya Çelebi says of these schools that the religious education was better than that found at the *medreses* (religious colleges) and that

The Janissaries

Arabic, Persian and Turkish were taught at all of them along with archery, horsemanship and skill at the *jerid* (the sport of mounted dart-throwing). Instruction even extended to conversation, the writing of prose and verse, composing and the ultimate art of calligraphy. Ibrahim Pasha Saray was temporarily closed in the mid-seventeenth century by Ibrahim I, who also cut off the funds of Galatasaray. Ibrahim Pasha Saray survived somehow, but it ceased to send its cadets into the cavalry; they simply served in the menial unit of the Halberdiers of the Tresses, or as cooks, bakers and laundrymen in the janissary barracks.

The colleges at Galata and Edirne were finally closed in the reign of Murat IV (1623-40), when the levy as a method of recruiting for the Enderun Kolej effectively ended. Well-taught as they were, the pages behaved like any other teenagers. One stole fruit from the orchard of the Maison de France and another insulted the French ambassador, for the garden of Galatasaray bordered on his and still does to this day. The ambassador's secretary reported the first incident and in the evening His Excellency was disturbed while working at his desk at an open window by screams which appeared to be coming from the college and to be caused by a beating. He could not decide whether these were the genuine cries of the guilty page or those of a good actor.

The least exalted college was at Gallipoli, which trained recruits for sea duties from the fifteenth century. At one time 2,000 of them were working on the fleet across the Dardanelles at Çanakkale and 5,000 on public works and in the Tersane (Arsenal), the shipyards of the Golden Horn, which rivalled the Arsenal at Venice. Others served as woodcutters and kitchen hands while 2,000 were distributed as *bostancıs* (gardeners) among the royal gardens, including those of the citadel at Bursa and at Manisa which possessed extensive flower and market gardens. But it should not be forgotten that one and all of the cadets were alike in that they were trained for war.

The rest of the crop of recruits were hired out at a nominal 25 *akçes* a head for from two to four years to farmers who were old soldiers. Nicolay, who was attached to the French embassy, says that these were the leftovers.[13] They were taught Turkish if they came from the Balkans and were toughened up by being made to practise weight-lifting until, allegedly, they could carry 800 pounds (360 kilogrammes) as many paces.[14] It was also laid down very reasonably that they were to be well fed. In due course they were called on to fill vacancies as *acemioğlans* (cadets). As such they were quartered in their own barracks near the mosque of Şehzade, which consisted of 31 *odalar* (dormitories) holding some 70 to 80 cadets each,

The Devşirme or Christian Levy

achieving a total capacity of some 2,500 men. A number slept in the towers along the outer walls when doing guard duty at the palace.[15] Most of these young men acted as reserves during the campaign season in order to police the city and they were kept fit by bricklaying and other tasks on waterworks, military installations and royal buildings such as the great complex of the Süleymaniye, where they supplied half the labour force.

Three hundred *acemioğlans* were lodged in bachelor quarters attached to the janissary bakery near their own barracks and the Eski Odalar (Old Barracks) beside the Şehzade mosque. Similar lodgings were given to those who were apprentice butchers in the slaughterhouse which was supplied from the janissaries' flocks. A *firman* of 1566 sent 20 to work in the gardens at Edirne and 250 to those at Topkapısaray where, ten years later, another 120 cadets were sent. In August 1573 some 150 were dispatched to Izmit (Nicomedia), along with an equal number of members of the *bostancı* corps, to cut timber for the winter. In 1577 an order sent *acemioğlans* to work in the stores and also the parterres of the *saray* and as scullions specializing in the preparation of vegetables, yoghurt and cheeses for the royal table.

A *firman* of 1586 specifically selected 20 boys from Anatolia and 25 from the Balkans for various household posts. And so it went on, with 7 recruited for the royal laundry and 10 as grooms. In 1572, 54 unfortunate lads were condemned to work on the sewers and in 1578, 50 were assigned to the Master of the Waterworks, perhaps to lay pipes. The master at the time was the redoubtable Davut Agha, nicknamed 'the Diver' because of his renown as an engineer, who laid the foundations and began the building of the Yeni Valide mosque by the Galata Bridge. At one time the janissaries had duties at the gun foundry at Tophane and there in 1587, 100 cadets were sent as foundrymen, ironsmiths, carpenters and handymen. In 1623 a total of 1,277 *acemioğlans* were distributed between the Eski Saray (Old Palace) for the relicts of sultans, and the palaces at Galata, of Ibrahim Pasha and that of the sultan himself. Among their duties were those of sweepers, water-carriers, cooks of every kind and porters in the ice-houses. Others formed a company of armed shepherds attached to the janissary flocks and still others performed the humbler barrack tasks or swept the streets before a military parade.[16]

The new life in the city certainly led to escapades. The janissaries loved taverns and a raw recruit apes his elders. It is significant that some dancing boys, whom Evliya Çelebi deemed to be so wicked but nevertheless greatly enjoyed, were dressed in the uniform of the *acemioğlans*.

The Janissaries

Crack Troops

When, in the early sixteenth century, Selim I saw that his policies would lead to campaigns in Persia and against the Mamluks in Syria and Egypt, the need for a large recruitment resulted in his sending the levy commission into Anatolia for the first time. One result was that recruits from Asia Minor had to be sent to the Balkans for 'toughening up' on the principle that no boy was ever to be posted anywhere in reach of his home. A recruit from Anatolia had no need to learn Turkish and by the sixteenth century there were numerous *sipahi* fiefs in the Balkans needing cheap labour.

The Anatolian Greeks, on whom the levy of 1512 fell hardest, were not the most favoured of the recruits. Perhaps the Albanians, who were the fiercest of all warriors and who claimed descent from the Spartans, had this honour: their temper became a catchword among the Ottomans and their eagerness to serve contrasted with that of the equally ferocious Montenegrans who, ensconced in their mountain fastnesses, defied all recruiting officers. Yet—and it is significant—there were no uprisings against the levy save for one in 1565 in Albania, a province where Ottoman rule was confined to the towns and valleys. After the Albanians, it was the Serbians, Bosnians and Croats who were the most highly regarded soldiers, leaving aside a small nucleus of Italians. Without Italian gunnery experts, there would have been no victories for Selim I over the Persians or the Mamluks. The Greeks supplied many high officers, all of whom were eclipsed by Süleyman's favourite, Ibrahim Pasha, who was the first Grand (as opposed to Chief) Vezir. The significance of this change lay in his no longer being the senior of a group of equals: he was now the sultan's deputy and responsible only to him. Ibrahim had been the bosom companion of Süleyman in his youth. He was to prove as brilliant an administrator as he was a commander in the field. That Ottoman rule lasted so long in Egypt was due to his reforms, following on the early years of maladministration after the conquest of 1517.

Great Hopes of Glory

When the ordinary recruit had finished his training, he was enrolled in his *orta* (company) and its number and symbol were tattooed on his arm and leg and, hopefully, his soul. There followed years of danger and hardship on campaign although Ottoman camp life for ordinary soldiers was luxurious by European standards. The camaraderie and the prestige of the corps compensated those who never rose to posts of responsibility. This is to leave

The Devşirme or Christian Levy

aside its usefulness as a cloak for those who stripped off their Christian underwear merely to bare their self-interest and hedonism, two clear elements in Ottoman life. In taking its recruits young and subjecting them to long training in hardship and military skills, the state could use their egotism to its advantage since singleness of purpose treats no man like a brother: when a great man fell from power, no friend was his mourner. The house of Osman was master of the life and death of a recruit to the Enderun Kolej: one and all were slaves at once of their sultan and their own ambition.

The majority who gained admission to none of the schools could look forward to retiring on a pension in their mid-40s and, later, to employment in the relaxed, uncompetitive atmosphere of Ottoman commerce. There they smoked their *naghiles* (hubble-bubble pipes) and swaggered about, as much as rheumatism and old wounds permitted, among the overtly respectful citizenry. They might even gather enough booty to enjoy more than one wife and other minor luxuries. An officer could hope for more. Some at least obtained leases of crown land for farming although this was the privilege of their rivals, the *sipahis*.[17] They held these *timars* in return for bringing a number of armed men with them on campaign according to the size of their holding. By the end of the sixteenth century, the *timar* system had decayed because a knightly caste was outmoded, particularly with the growth of a paid household cavalry brigade. (Only in Anatolia did the fiefs supporting feudal cavalry and local levies survive into the nineteenth century.) Instead, estates were leased to tax-farmers without military obligations.

Janissaries could also nurture their relatives for even if illiterate there was no reason why, with the aid of public letter-writers, they should not keep in touch with their village.[18] Albanians and Bosnians, like most Balkan-born warriors, were responsible for a pernicious growth of nepotism. Süleyman's Croat Grand Vezir Rüstem Pasha was accused of ill-temper when his relatives came to town from their far pastures and it is said that he left his father destitute in the street.[19] But he was exceptionally unpopular and one notes that his brother rose to the rank of *kapudan paşa* (Grand Admiral). By contrast, Ibrahim Pasha was much concerned for his drunken father (who would lie in the mud until his son helped him home) and he did not spurn him although he haunted the lowest taverns.[20] Other *vezirs* like the Bosnian Sokollu Mehmet Pasha found all too good employment for all too many kinsmen.[21] His nepotism eventually led to such hostility that a Bosnian dervish was recruited as his assassin in 1579. Such nepotism was not for sergeants, yet they might send for a nephew from the home village and recommend the lad to a friendly trader as an apprentice. This innocent patronage was paralleled by the sale of offices under Süleyman and Rüstem

Pasha in order to raise money with which to fight increasingly unsuccessful wars. It was also one way of taxing the wealthy *ulema* class.

Pages of the Enderun Kolej: the Elect of the Elect

Before discussing the Enderun Kolej, or 'School within the Palace Walls', the slave status of the pages should be considered. In law there was a distinction between the status of a Muslim and even so exalted a subject as a royal *kul* or *ghulam*.[22] When a janissary enlisted, his father's fictitious name made clear that he was a slave. It had to be placed after the boy's new first name of Ali, Sinan, Osman and so on because his status was influenced and diminished by that of his father.[23] He would duly earn a nickname which differentiated him from all the other Alis and Mehmets. Some of these nicknames (as with Sokollu Mehmet, 'the Mehmet from Sokol') were polite; others awarded to unpopular ministers like Rüstem ('the Louse', among other things) were not. But the boy was not a slave in the sense that applied to a black worker on an eighteenth-century plantation in Virginia because he was admitted to the family of the Shadow of God on Earth, and to be a slave of God was an honour and no disgrace. Moreover, no *kul* was addressed in humiliating terms but as 'my young man' or, in the harem, 'my young woman'.[24] However, agents in Genoa, who were buying cloth for the janissary uniforms, said that they were the sultan's servants and, being the sons of soldiers, were still of slave status although technically Turks. And slave status meant that all property, from a vegetable plot to a palace, reverted to the crown on an officer's death if he were executed or childless. Otherwise the tax was only 10 per cent.[25] His weath, after all, had derived from the state in the first place. However, Rüstem Pasha and Mihrimah Sultan, his wife, certainly hived off some of their great wealth for the benefit of their children and what they could do others less illustrious could copy. The system was simplified by the fact that defeat meant disgrace and—since reverses of fortune occur—few officers of state died peacefully in bed. It was not until 1826 that the property of a man who had been banished and who died without an immediate heir ceased to revert to the crown as the heir-general of the empire.

Seljuk Antecedents

In the eleventh century, in the days of the renowned Persian chancellor, Nizam ul-Mülk, Turkish tribes fought each other and sold their captives as slaves. An initiatory year was devoted to teaching them discipline and

The Devşirme or Christian Levy

obedience, and a second to horsemanship, but the Persian court had no school for pages although slaves became cupbearers, chamberlains and field officers. The idea of a slave institution grew up in the caliphate, where there were many Armenians, Slavs and Greeks as well as Turks although they all retained their identity as military slaves.[26] They rose to high rank and rulers like Ibn Tulun, master of Egypt in the ninth century, were of their number. From an Abbasid root, a system developed in eastern Persia under the Seljuks and Karahanids where a fief was awarded in return for military service. This eventually led to the breakdown of central government.

From these Seljuk antecedents came the recruitment of boys to be trained in the palace. This was certainly true by the reign of Bayezit I, who had a slave market outside his complex at Bursa. These *içoğlans* were probably the suggestion of the Chief Vezir, Çandarlızade Ali Pasha, who represented the old aristocracy. The boys were appointed to the households of *vezirs* as well as that of the monarch. Ali Pasha was a formidable soldier who saved Süleyman Pasha after the rout of his father, Orhan, at Ankara and escaped with him to Edirne. His death in 1407 and the loss of his generalship led to Süleyman Pasha's defeat by Mehmet I during the fratricidal war between the three sons of Bayezit in 1410. Initially there was a distinction between pages and janissaries; this was later blurred by the *devşirme* method of recruitment. Murat I had probably already enlisted the sons of the military caste of the people whom he conquered. Under Bayezit I, and on into the fifteenth century, sons of nobles were taken into the *saray* at Edirne as a privileged class when Murat II established a school as such.

This was the system that Mehmet II was to extend so considerably and to endow with a platonic ethos after the conquest of Constantinople. He aimed to train a complete administrative class and not only field-ranking officers, and he closed the palace gates on the sons of the nobility, a class that he (like Peter the Great after him) was determined to suppress. Neither his school nor the auxiliary colleges were Byzantine in origin. The secondary schools were for those who failed entry to the Enderun Kolej or Galatasaray at first. It is an endearing and enduring Turkish quality which believes in the second chance, however, so that the possibility developed of graduating from a lesser college to that within the palace.

A School Cocooned in Symbol and Ceremony

Mehmet II's *saray* in Istanbul had lodgings for the sultan from the beginning but, as we have seen, it only became the official residence in the reign of Süleyman. It grew logically into well-defined quarters for servitors

The Janissaries

and services, pages, government, Allah and royalty.[27] The Bab-ül-Hümayün (Gate of Majesty) admitted to an open area called the First Court only by courtesy. In it were the ancillary buildings such as the armoury in the former basilica of Haghia Irene (Holy Peace) and, much later, the mint. It was also known as the Janissary Court and besides the Kiosk of Justice contained the 'example stone', or execution block, to remind men of their duty. The Orta Kapı (Middle Gate) admitted to the large Second, or Divan, Court. This was open to all palace officials and to any who had business with the government which, out of the campaigning season, met in council on three or four days a week. The barracks of the halberdiers lay behind the Divan Hall and beyond that were the quarters of the Black Eunuchs and the harem, which included the court and apartments of the Valide Sultan (Queen Mother). Across the gardens with their grazing gazelles was the gate to the long kitchen court with its array of domed halls whose lofty chimneys are so noteworthy when seen from the sea.

The Third Court was entered through the Bab-ül-Sa'adet (Gate of Felicity). There the portable gold throne was set up on the sultan's accession, on holidays and *bayrams* (religious holidays) and every three months, due to the Kanun-i-Teşrifat (Law of Ceremonies), which owed something to Byzantine ritual. Here the sultan sat and received the ceremonial obeisances of his janissaries after those of the dignitaries of state. Beyond this was the audience chamber for the reception of ambassadors in the Third Court, where the buildings of the Enderun Kolej filled three sides with some half-a-dozen dormitories and apartments for the Chief White Eunuch and senior staff, besides a mosque and large halls for study and exercise. The disrobing hall of the *hamam* (bath-house) of Selim II, which was famous for its Iznik tiles, is now incorporated into the pavilion and loggia of Mehmet II to form the Treasury Museum. The Pavilion of the Sacred Relics of the Prophet connected the school with the *selamlık* (the sultan's private reception rooms), which opened onto the terrace with the pool and later the pavilions of Murat IV, erected to celebrate his victories at Erivan (Yerivan) and Baghdad. The pages had no access to such apartments except on duty, still less the walled gardens and other kiosks beneath them.

Possibly a tenth of the recruits from each levy was sent to the *saray* and the number of pages at any one time ranged from 300 under Mehmet II to 500 or even 800 in the sixteenth century. Apart from the auxiliary colleges, some pages were distributed among the households of senior officers of state in Istanbul as well as those of *beylerbeys* and governors of provinces and these formed additional schools. The school at Ibrahim Pasha Saray must have evolved from this custom.

The Devşirme or Christian Levy

Grand Vezirs and other ministers had large slave establishments. In 1537 Ayas Pasha had 600 boys, Kasım Pasha 150, Mustafa Pasha 200 and Barbaros Pasha a mere 100, yet this was a decline in numbers from those recorded three years before when Ayas Pasha allegedly boasted 2,000 boys on his roll and Kasım Pasha 1,500. At one time, Ibrahim Pasha allegedly had 6,000 in his service but one suspects the addition of a zero. When the innocent Iskender Çelebi was executed for treason in 1534, Sokollu Mehmet was transferred from his slave household to that of the sultan on the start of his remarkable ascent to the Grand Vezirate, which illustrates the flexibility of the system. There is even evidence that some officials introduced their own pages into the *saray* in order to avoid the cost of their maintenance. On his death in 1557 the Chief White Eunuch, Cafer Agha, left 156 slaves: 13 were already employed at the palace and Süleyman took in 39 more, personally allotting them to the cavalry, the workshops or his household. He was helped by the fact that the slaves were listed by race and by ability or lack of it, from capable or strong to middling and poor. One was a trumpeter who presumably went to the royal band. 'Slaves' here means cadets who would otherwise have been sold or thrown out on the street. The lists make no reference to women but they must also have been numerous since that redoubtable warrior, the Albanian Ayas Pasha, died leaving 140 young children and 40 cradles swinging.

Apart from the thirteen boys whom Cafer Agha managed to attach to his department, not all the pages in the *saray* were the product of the levy. There were many other nationalities not listed as legal harvesting for the *devşirme*. They included Bohemians, Bulgars, Circassians, French, Germans, Hungarians, Italians, Poles, Russians, Spaniards and Transylvanians. They are likely to have been prisoners of war or kidnapped by corsairs and raiders, and their selection called for close scrutiny. Indeed, all pages were subject to a process of continuous assessment because they were not only the personal servants of the sultan but were in a position to discover secrets which could be used to the detriment of the state.

Our knowledge of the Enderun Kolej derives from some of the slaves themselves, such as Johann Schiltberger who, it will be remembered, became page to Yıldırım Bayezit. He was captured along with the household by Timur at Ankara at the age of 22 and was to pass through the households of several masters before his final escape nineteen years later. Ricoldus was a slave in several Ottoman families between 1436 and 1453 while Spandugino, who was a page in the *saray* during the reign of Bayezit II, makes helpful references to the levy. Giovanni Antonio Menavino was born of wealthy Genoese parents in 1493. He was bright, well-educated and,

The Janissaries

luckily for his survival, handsome when taken by corsairs off Corsica at the age of 12. He was a suitable gift for Bayezit II and indeed the boy delighted the sultan. He was inherited by Selim I but he had the wit to escape at Trabzon (Trebizond) and make his way back to Genoa and his rejoicing family by way of Edirne and Salonika in 1517 at the age of 24. Ramberti spent six months with the *kapudan paşa*, Barbaros. Another important witness was Nicolas de Nicolay who, selected for his observant eye, was a member of the suite of the French ambassador sent to Istanbul in 1551. Indeed, with the addition of Turkish sources, there is a quantity of information (some of which is inevitably conflicting) covering the whole period of the existence of the Enderun Kolej. What follows is a general summary.

An Élite Academy

The head of the Enderun Kolej, the Chief White Eunuch, was also Keeper of the Gate, which put him in a position of great power since he could control all who came or went. He had forty white eunuchs to assist him. At the end of the sixteenth century, the Valide Sultan would gain power if her ruling son were a child or mentally unstable; by then it was the Chief Black Eunuch who kept the gate, leaving the Chief White Eunuch to his educational duties. At this time it was effectively the gate to the harem that counted and not that to the *selamlık*, which was accessible to male visitors. The Chief White Eunuch had a staff of *lalas* (tutors), to whom the pages often grew attached, and also visiting specialist teachers besides a doctor, a surgeon, musicians, astrologers, tailors, furriers and goldsmiths. The sultan's own private *hoca* (tutor and chaplain) was also the chaplain to the pages. He was assisted by two other *imams* (prayer leaders) with *muezzins* (criers of the call to prayer).

Newcomers were placed in the Küçük Oda (Little Hall or Hall for Newcomers) and in Menavino's time numbered from eighty to a hundred under four tutors, although Ramberti says that all the pages slept together in the same hall with a *lala* for every ten boys—in his day they could talk in public.[28] It seems probable, however, that the boys spent a year in each division of the school and so in their second year were mostly promoted to the Büyük Oda (Great or Old Hall), where the training became increasingly exacting. These two halls stood right and left of the Bab-ül-Sa'adet. Somewhere around the age of 20, some seventy pages were promoted to the Hall of the Hasıne Oda (Imperial Treasury), while twenty-five went to the Kiler Odaları (Privy Stores). Murat IV built the Seferli Odası (Campaign

The Devşirme or Christian Levy

Hall) beside the sumptuous *hamam* of Selim II to house the pages who served it as laundrymen, barbers, turban folders and musicians. This hall also seems to have been used for exercise and is certainly large enough. All these departments were supervised by an intendant from the Privy Chamber.

After some seven years, youths who graduated through all these stages finally reached their goal, the Hasoda (Royal Chamber),[29] which was restricted to thirty-nine pages because the sultan himself made up the sacred number—forty—with its echoes of infinity. These men were the most intimate servants of the household; after 1517 they included the two perpetual guards of the Holy Mantle, which was kept in the most splendid room of the Pavilion of the Sacred Relics, often used by the sultan to sleep in or as a living-room. Twelve of the thirty-nine, together with several assistants, were appointed to the *selamlık* and shaved, dressed and waited on their master. They were regarded as inferior to the others except for the Head Valet until he became by usage the sultan's private secretary.

The most important post was that of Agha of the Key, who was in charge of the Privy Chamber, but at various periods he was subordinate to the Chief Page, the *silahtar agha* (Sword-Bearer). This office became so illustrious that *vezirs* incorporated it into their titles. The most trusted of these graduates were appointed sentinels, one at the head and one at the foot of the royal bed, to hold lighted torches all night against assassins or ghosts. When they dressed the sultan, these pages put 500 ducats in one pocket of his kaftan and 1,000 aspers in the other for use as largesse. The money came from the sale of the produce of the kitchen garden. At night, they were allowed to keep any loose change that had escaped the sultan's munificence. Because of their close contact with their sovereign, these pages were appointed to such offices as Master of the Bedchamber (who might be deemed to be 'head boy'), Sword-Bearer, Bow-Bearer, Cup-Bearer and Slipper- and Stool-Bearer. Some began their ascent to the peerless peak of the Divan (Grand Council of State) by means of such appointments. Thus Sokollu Mehmet Pasha began his career as Grand Falconer. Most pages can only have dreamed of such an appointment.

Iron Discipline and Golden Opportunities

To reach these heights, pages had studied reading, progressing from the Koran in Arabic to Persian but their instructors appear to have regarded calligraphy as an art apart. Persian was taught along with literary and vulgar Arabic so that, on assuming senior posts, graduates could do more than merely understand their new religion. Since the laws of Islam are based on the Koran, the study of religion was also the study of justice and this helped the pages to gain an insight into the reports of judges and their administration of the law. Pages further studied the civil legal code embodied in the Kanunnames (volumes of laws and decrees) which one day some of them would have to administer. With this went studies in Turkish anecdote rather than history. They also studied mathematics and geometry besides some geography and, as did the sultan, learnt a trade against the hour of adversity or as a recreation if they ever had leisure from their duties, their hunting or their bed. Such trades included gardening (the passion of Mehmet II) and making arrows, bow-rings or gold filigree, among many other skills. But first in importance was the science of war, which meant a study of firepower both of arquebus and musket and a variety of cannon. With this went skill as archers and swordsmen and such complementary sports as athletics, wrestling and the *jerid*, which was still being played when the Rev. Colton was in Istanbul in 1836.

The large chambers or halls where the pages slept were transformed into study rooms by day. They were spacious and well-lit, with groups of ten boys assigned to a platform surrounded on three sides by low wooden partitions. The eunuchs, one old and one young, slept on similar platforms down the middle of the long room while the senior *lalas* had latticed cabinets at either end. Each group had little collective privacy unless they stood up or walked down the lanes between the platforms. Until 1960 the great hall of Ibrahim Pasha Saray still had its late-eighteenth-century system of daises laid out in a similar manner. There was always a gallery round the hall and examples survive in the Hasıne Oda (now the picture gallery) and in the late-sixteenth-century Hall of the Halberdiers, which is still extant and notably light and airy.

These halls saw much use and the pages slept partially dressed for reasons of modesty and protection. Their woollen coverlets were surmounted by rich brocade mantles; since neither could have been washed frequently, there were problems with lice and fleas, which infested one platform so much that it was inevitably reserved for newcomers. Yet the pages had well-fitted washrooms and their own *hamam* for weekly use. After the great pavilion of Murat III was built they may have had weekly access to the heated open pool in its undercroft, designed for the sultan and his women. Food was simple but good and clearly ample. The kitchens, which gave so many symbols of rank to the janissary corps, always lay at the heart of the empire since the sultans' governments were wise long before Napoleon. In the reign of Süleyman there were fifty cooks under a master and thirty more under the Confectioner Royal besides scullions and porters.

The Devşirme or Christian Levy

Just inside the Bab-ül-Hümayün there was a hospital for the pages with several rooms and a *hamam*. Its servants were assigned according to their specialist knowledge of an illness. Since wine was used as a cure for some complaints, pages were known to feign minor ailments and some were punished for drunken behaviour. When a page reported sick to his *lala*, the latter approached the senior tutor who requested the captain of the halberdiers to send a two-wheeled carriage. This was curtained in red and drawn by two of his men. When it was drawn at the double through the palace to the hospital everyone stood aside. Since all gates and doors closed at sundown, anyone taken ill in the night was treated in the drug store and if a page died he was wrapped in a kilim to be taken to the hospital at dawn. There the corpses were washed and then rowed down the Golden Horn for burial at Kasımpaşa.

Surveillance by officers and eunuchs was strict. The rule of silence was originally enforced, along with other regulations, by the use of the bastinado[30] so that the washrooms were the only places of human contact and licence. Some sultans were interested in their school and watched sports critically or even presided at examinations; several took charge of the selection of entrants and watched their progress. Murat III made the school his chief interest to the detriment of his administration. Others made nocturnal inspections of the halls out of concern for virtue and discipline and, on occasion, for less serene motives.

Whatever else derived from this ideal education, which had many quirks and prejudices that were to be shared by a generation of English nineteenth-century headmasters, it impressed its code on the hearts of the students. Spandugino admired the Ottoman grandees for their generosity as hosts who treated Christian, Jew and Turk alike and because they were great alms-givers.[31]

The pages were paid modest salaries, usually quarterly,[32] and, if some had luxuries and vices smuggled into the *saray,* most contrived to save some money against their graduation at about the age of 25 and their marriage. They had little to spend money on since they were forbidden access to the city unless they were on duty. They received scarlet garments twice a year and a white robe in summer. These were laundered weekly (lice and fleas being confined to their beds) with scented soaps if we are to believe references to the attire of the pages being fragrant as roses.

The first requirement of any page was a zeal for hard work and hard play. School began at dawn and there can have been little spare time before the afternoon siesta. They were healthy young men—although some were not so young since they did not finally graduate until they were 30.[33] It is not surprising that the strictest rules were broken in spite of surveillance. Drunken pages were usually punished by the bastinado and, although the number of strokes conformed to a liberal (or illiberal) code, it was the threat of expulsion that was most daunting for students so little prepared for an outside world where all their privileges would have been forfeited.

The school dwindled after 1826, when the janissary corps was abolished, but did not finally close until 1922, when the sultanate was truly at an end. Galatasaray became the prestigious high school which it is today. The girls left the *saray* before the First World War, but the harem had once been a school of deportment, music, poetry and other graceful accomplishments whose graduates expected to marry a page, since few could hope for the favours of their sultan. The lucky ones married men destined for the highest office, for the Grand Vezir was always married to a princess, sister or daughter of his sultan. He then had to foreswear all other wives however fond of them he might have been.

Most graduates of the principal colleges went into the household cavalry but some were appointed to the many hundreds of posts at court, according to their merit or sycophancy. There were three chief bodyguards of the sovereign. The *müteferrikas* (life guards) always surrounded him when he went to war. They were drawn exclusively from graduates of the Enderun Kolej and their number eventually swelled from 100 to 800. There were also four companies of *solaks*, veteran janissary archers under a commander who had the important duty of holding the sultan's stirrup. Half this guard had to be left-handed in order to draw their arrows since they marched on the monarch's right. The third guard were the 150 *peyks* (foot guardsmen), who had the unenviable distinction of having their spleens removed. This was a custom that Mehmet II took over from the Byzantines, quite irrationally, just as he took over the Byzantine dress of gold and silver brocade on a violet or rose ground with gilded silver helmets bearing a heron plume. Many of the *solaks* and *peyks* were second-generation Ottomans.

The post of *çavuş* (usher) varied in importance from mere flunkey to ambassador and the number greatly increased over the years. Their *agha* was also the Master of the Household and Chief Executioner at some periods. The Halberdiers of the Tresses were janissaries attached to the Inner Service to perform the menial tasks. Half were under the orders of the Sword-Bearer while the others came under those of the Chief Black Eunuch because it was their task to act as porters in the harem, carrying wood for the fires or removing rubbish of all kinds. They wore false tresses as blinkers even though the corridors and rooms were cleared of women when they went about their work, always at the double. Their hall, with its tiled court

The Devşirme or Christian Levy

and subsidiary rooms including their own *mescit* (small mosque), was situated beside the door to the Black Eunuchs' quarters leading to the harem. Their halberds were, in effect, axes for cutting down trees and splitting logs, and when not on palace duty the halberdiers were at work in the woods preparing fuel or planks for the bridging of swamps and the maintenance of highways.

Grandees beyond the Gate

This was the Inner Service of the *saray* but the Outer Service was almost as important and posts in it were much sought after by the pages. They included that of Agha of the Stirrup, whose numbers fell from seventeen under Mehmet II to a mere five in the eighteenth century. Of these the highest-ranking officer was the *mir'alem* (Standard-Bearer), who was responsible for the twice six horsetails carried before the sultan. (The horsetail flying from a pole had been a symbol of authority among the Turks from the beginning of their history in Central Asia.) He was also responsible for the military band, which was no sinecure because it was the largest in the country and had not only to play with great pomp each day but in battle had to produce that terrifying din which was an important element of Ottoman strategy. It was to be the inspiration of military bands in Europe.

According to Dr Covel, the music was much alike, whether it was for the sultan, the Grand Vezir or anyone else. Trumpets came in now and then to squeal out a loud note or two while never playing a whole tune, but a treble pipe or hautboy played continuously. The great drums, which were not metal-plated, were beaten at both ends, the top with a great stick held in the right hand and the bottom with a little stick at every small or passing note. Kettle-drums and dish-drums were both played in pairs and Covel calls the cymbals, born in Anatolia, brass platters. He makes no mention of the Jingling-Johnny, that mast of little bells, nor does Marsigli, the eighteenth-century authority on the janissary corps. Covel refers to the orchestras for pleasure. An extraordinary instrument used by these was a row of twenty to thirty pipes and twenty-two reeds, from short to long to create a scale. Each piper was trained to blow in tune with other instruments, including a form of dulcimer, lutes of four, five or eight double strings and also tambours.

Next in importance after the *mir'alem* came the *büyük mir'ahor* (Master of the Horse or Grand Equerry), who not only controlled the stables but also the many pastures, mules and muleteers. The sultan maintained 200 horses for his own use tended by 100 grooms in a long line of privy stables below the harem but the main palace stables were situated at Ahırkapı, the Stable

The Janissaries

Gate onto the Sea of Marmara below the park and gardens. The household might stable 4,000 horses with a groom for each pair outside the city walls and along the Bosphorus as well, in order to take advantage of the grazing in the meadows. A special corps of Bulgarian Christians called *voynuks* had the hereditary right to look after the strings of horses farmed out in the Balkans and Anatolia. A Vice-Master of the Horse was responsible for the pack animals and also the carriages which were mainly used for the jaunts of the harem ladies.

There were other members of the household and government, including the royal architects and artists and commissioners who were in effect junior ministers and who, like Sinan or Mehmet Agha, were former janissary officers who had not graduated from the Enderun Kolej. Thus, while the court offices were mainly filled from within the *saray*, others were filled by veteran janissaries whose services had made them known to the sultan. There was often no sharply defined division between the ranks of the pages, and no barrier to promotion from one stratum of the ruling institution to the next, save luck. In a world of slaves no man is king.

Guards of the Hoe and Oar

The ranks of the 4,000 *bostancıs* were filled by the *acemioğlans* including, in some instances, boys straight from the levy. They wore blue *şalvar* (pantaloons) and a red jacket, which was to be the uniform of Selim III's new army at the end of the eighteenth century, while their red conical cap sometimes ended in a wadded flap. Their duties were not confined to tending the great gardens of Topkapısaray, Edirne and Manisa. The vegetable gardens and orchards were for use and made a profit. The gardeners formed a royal guard besides being the royal bargees who manned the secret skiffs when the sultan travelled incognito up and down the Bosphorus or to Kağıthane. In the seventeenth century, the French traveller Galland saw them drive barques away from the vicinity of Seraglio Point when the Valide Sultan came to the kiosk to watch some French ships arrive. Their close connection with the janissaries established links between the officers of the two corps. The *bostancıs* also performed police duties in the suburbs and the forest round Istanbul and along the shores of the waterways. They only went to war when the sultan himself took the field.

The *bostancıbaşı* held an eminent rank for he was the only officer permitted to reside at the summer *saray*. At one period he was the Royal Stirrup-Holder as well as Steersman of the Royal Barge and so had the ear of his master on land and afloat. If he gained promotion, he had to shave off

The Devşirme *or Christian Levy*

the flowing beard that he alone of the palace officers was permitted to grow. He was always appointed from the *bostancı* barracks of Istanbul and never of Edirne. When, on one unfortunate occasion, Mehmet IV found too few beasts to hunt on the road from Edirne and dismissed Saban Agha in favour of Sinan Agha, the veterans refused to accept the appointment and the sultan had to give way to their protests.

As chamberlain, the *bostancıbaşı* was responsible to the janissary units attached to the palaces. He also had the privilege of feasting his sultan at Kağıthane once a year. Less exaltedly, he was in charge of the guardhouse in the fish market. This had an evil name because a dismissed Grand Vezir was sent there to await the arrival of the *bostancıbaşı*. If he was offered white sherbert it meant exile, but if red it meant death by the bow-string, a fate which might follow him down the road in any case at the hands of a special messenger. As late as 1774 Mehmet Emin Pasha, *serasker* against the Russians, was invited to the palace of the *bostancıbaşı* as if he were a guest only to be strangled there and then and have his wealth confiscated. If the *bostancıbaşı* himself were dismissed, he was either succeeded by his lieutenant or adjutant or the Captain of the Bodyguard over whom he had some authority. His inferior at Edirne was responsible for law and order there and in its vicinity, independently of the *beylerbey* of the Balkans (in whose province the city lay).

Hall of the Halberdiers; a typical barracks of the janissaries at Topkapı-saray (Michael Thompson)

3
Pillars of the Empire

The Shadow of God on Earth

In order to understand the role of the janissary corps and its extraordinary power, a brief survey of the pillars of the Ottoman state is essential. At the summit of all and everything was the sultan, or *padişah*, who was the Shadow of God on Earth, not simply the bestower of all offices but also the trustee and heir of all his peoples—all his peoples because the empire was made up of many races and tribes and a variety of religious and divisive sects. In the Islamic tradition, the major religious groups such as the Greek Orthodox and the Armenians were answerable to their Patriarchs or other senior religious leaders and grouped in *millets* (administrative districts). These communities were partially self-governing but had varying responsibilities and tax liabilities. The Christian community had to pay a poll tax in return for exemption from military duties: without this tax the government would have been bankrupt.

The first Ottoman sultans were not majestic figures removed from daily life. They ruled from the stirrup rather than the palace gate, which symbolized justice. The earliest sultans considered themselves *gazis* on the frontiers of the infidels; their task in life was to advance Islam and their own dominion into Europe. This outlook is epitomized in the inscription dated *c.* 1350 over the door of the royal mosque of Orhan at Bursa: it calls Orhan sultan, son of a sultan of the *gazis,* son of a *gazi,* Lord Marcher of the Horizon, Hero of the World. The legitimacy of the Ottomans' descent later altered this form of dedication to that of khan, son of a khan, or something similar, and named the sultan's immediate forebears. These men were heads of the family but the modernization of the army—initiated by Orhan and developed by Murat I—ended in freeing the Ottoman rulers from the hold of rival tribal *beys*. The feudal nobility were not eliminated, however, until the reign of Mehmet II, who conquered Constantinople in 1453.

In 1402 Timur had marched across Anatolia, hunting as he went; he left behind memories of grandeur to emulate and his symbol of three balls, allegedly representing the three parts of the world. These, with the waves or clouds or even tiger stripes, were taken for his own emblem by Mehmet II. He also adopted many Byzantine practices and court ceremonial besides dreaming the dream common to monarchs of his period of establishing the Empire of the World, a greater Rome from which the concept came and with which any ruler of New Rome inevitably felt an affinity.

With the Ottoman conquest of Egypt in 1517 and the transference to Istanbul of the relics of the Prophet Muhammad, who made no claim to divinity, the question of the caliphate arose to keep industrious scholars busy. Essentially, the leadership of Islam was transmitted to designated successors of Muhammad and almost immediately there were schisms of every kind. But the central orthodox line was appropriated by Selim I in the sixteenth century. It gave a certain authority to any holder who was strong enough to use it but otherwise had little significance and was often disregarded. But to be caliph was an honour comparable to that of 'Defender of the Faith', although any just ruler who maintained the ordinance of the Faith could claim to be caliph within his own lands.[1] In his efforts to prop up the dynasty in the last years of the nineteenth century, Abdülhamit II was to make a desperate attempt to glorify his position as caliph; at the same time, he restored and faked the monuments of his family's tribal days in Soğut. He planted the graveyard there with the tombstones of various early fourteenth-century heroes—the equivalent of setting up replicas of those of Arthur and Lancelot in neat rows at Glastonbury.

This mythology was far removed from the *gazi* brotherhood of kindred and equal emirs who followed a canon of rules by which the mystical life could be led. In the seventh century, the original *gazis* of Syria were more or less bound in loyalty to the then caliphate. From this derived the presentation of the ceremonial club[2] or other weapon. Later, the enthronement of the Ottomans was symbolized by the girding on of the sword of their ancestor, Osman. At one period the Mevlevi order of dervishes took part in the ceremony; but more important in the early days was the presentation of the drum, another custom inherited from the Mongols. The drum of Orhan, or a replica, hangs before his tomb in Bursa

Pillars of the Empire

today but unlike those of the Mongol khans it was not beaten until split to announce his death.[3]

Mehmet II's interest in a pantheon which would end religious rivalries was not new. In the fourteenth century, Bayezit I had had plans to achieve a union of Islam, Judaism and Christianity. He encouraged the fable that the Ottomans were descended from Priam until Pope Nicholas V hoped that he would be converted. Fisher[4] has drawn attention to the names of Bayezit's sons—Moses (Musa), Muhammad (Mehmet), Solomon (Süleyman), Ertuğrul (Turkish) and the Sufi name of Mustafa. Bayezit adopted Byzantine dress and customs such as sodomy and drinking wine and antagonized his Muslim subjects.[5] It should not be forgotten that it was his Christian vassals who stood fast beside the janissaries when he was defeated at the battle of Ankara in 1402. But only with the fall of Constantinople in 1453, which Bayezit had planned and yearned for, was there an Ottoman Empire with all the symbolism and ritual which envelope a lonely ruler over many diverse subjects. Mehmet II introduced the Kanun-i-Teşrifat so that everyone knew their exact title, place and dress.

Everybody was affected by this grandeur for all were actors in the symbolic ceremonial laid down by Mehmet II. It was considered rude even to whisper in the presence of royalty and there were officers who enforced the rule of silence on entering the Second Court of Topkapısaray.[6] A deaf and dumb language developed. The imperial house became a quasi-sacred family and this myth preserved the lives of several ultimate heirs even in periods of degeneracy. Hence also the rule that princes must be killed without shedding their blood (they had to be strangled). It was believed that their blood contained a magic force which could be used malevolently by their enemies.[7] This was a venerable Mongol and Turkish belief. It also meant that only men could transmit this divine essence which by some quirk of heaven was lodged in the quick of the family of Osman.

Osman wore his hair long in the Mongol style but in the fourteenth century hair was cut short and eventually there was a reversion to the Muslim shaved head.[8] It was, however, the old subservience to Mongol masters that resulted in the Giray khans of Crimea being the nominal heirs of the Ottomans should the family die out, as it nearly did.[9]

The Ottoman sultan had one supreme duty, which was to pay the army, while seeing that each degree of society kept to its own tasks and did not trespass on those of the others.[10] A sultan was judged by his ability and his capacity in the platonic manner; his maternal blood did not matter provided that he maintained the ideal of the Everlasting State.[11] Initially, he could marry whom he wished and dynastic ties led to many royal wives being

The Janissaries

Christians. After the reign of Mehmet II they had to be slaves,[12] like everyone else in the royal household, although they could be married to their master with full conjugal rights. But the sultan had to renounce family feelings in the interest of the state and this was the reason for Mehmet II's rule that brothers, who might seek to usurp power, were to be strangled with a silken cord because, as we have seen, royal blood might not be spilt. In the end this concept of the slave family and the slave household was to include everyone except the *ulema* and the powerless minorities.[13]

Mehmet II was ruthless in his suppression of the feudal aristocratic families because they challenged his absolute authority by right of being fellow *gazis*. For this reason even the most loyal among them were disposed of, whatever the pretext chosen. The sultan also succeeded temporarily in weakening the *ulema* as a class by attacking their wealth but they were secure in their authority as the embodiment of the law and of religion through the law and, above all, as free-born Muslims. While their devotion to self-interest was frequently manifest, without their restraint military autocrats would have wielded irresponsible power.

Keepers of the Law, the Ulema

Conservatism made the *ulema* a redoubtable political force. Moreover, they were the educated class and the possessors of divine knowledge—though not necessarily of wisdom as a result. All spiritual and legal appeals were made to a pre-ordained justice and not to evolutionary ideas or ideals because Islamic law is intransigent. Thus these traditionalists installed as *kadıs* (judges) affected the life of every citizen, giving, not formulating, decisions. The *ulema*'s orthodox training was long and monotonous and required the *softa* (student) to graduate through each of the colleges at the original university founded by Mehmet II. These colleges were known as the Eight, and there were eight preparatory colleges as well, so that a student spent at least sixteen years there before he went on to the four colleges at the Süleymaniye, first as a *softa* and then as a *lala* (tutor). Needless to say, there were short cuts for the sons of the wealthy and influential, while many students left to become *kadıs* in minor towns or superior villages rather than pursue the ambitious course which required prowess at memorizing and the ability to wear an aspect of dignified and profound seriousness without a hint of hypocrisy. They needed to acquire an instinctive understanding of the balance between the pressing requirements of the government involved in any judgment, the inclinations of the sovereign should they differ, and the existence of such popular and other forces as might intrude into the tranquil chamber of justice. A reasonably long and healthy life was also essential, preferably attested by a patriarchal beard.

A final graduate was already middle-aged. He first became a *molla* (professor) at a superior college and then, after winning acclaim at the councils of the senior judges, the aspirant might find political advancement and achieve the cherished office of *kadıasker* (rather more a military chief justice than a provost-marshal) of Rum or Anadolu, Europe or Asia. (The name Rum, of course, derives from Rome, a city never far from the minds of the sultans.) From thence, but without a seat in the Divan, the final promotion was to the office of *şeyhülislam* (Grand Mufti), who shared precedence only with the Grand Vezir himself to the extent that temporal power usually outshines spiritual. Originally, he had only been mufti of Istanbul but, in the sixteenth century, Süleyman promoted the great jurist Ebüssu'ûd to the superior office. The *şeyhülislam* alone could depose the sultan and permit the execution of princes and, since he was the supreme arbiter, his *fetvalar* (legal rulings which had the force of edicts) were needed before any major constitutional change could be effected.[14] If the Grand Vezir and he walked side by side, it was because the *şeyhülislam* was a freeborn Muslim and the chief minister usually was not.

The Grand Vezir had to pay social calls on the spiritual leader twice a week to keep him informed even when no one doubted that the statesman was the actual authority over all other. This was partly because on his appointment the *şeyhülislam* ceased to attend meetings of the Divan which he had done as *kadıasker;* this was quite apart from the later custom of government largely being conducted at the palace of the Grand Vezir. This became known as the Sublime Porte, after the appointment of Köprülü Mehmet Pasha to the office by Mehmet IV in 1656. The *kadıaskers* also lost much of their authority in the seventeenth century when the *kanuns* (codes of civil law) became all-important. The *kadıaskers* could be dismissed from office but the *şeyhülislam* could not until later in the century, when he could be disgraced. If so, he retired to loneliness because his friends were expressly forbidden to visit him for fear of intrigue until the law was abolished by Mahmut II in 1826.

The *ulema* did not only consist of judicial and religious officers since the royal physicians and surgeons were also of that caste, along with the Astrologer Royal, without whose advice the *şeyhülislam* would have been unable to determine the auspicious moment at which to lay the foundation stone of the mihrab of a new mosque or for the army to set out on campaign. The sultan himself was a hereditary *imam* and it was inconceivable that a Muslim leader should be unable to lead his people in prayer. Moreover, there were *ulema* in all the cities of the empire and, indeed, Cairo was regarded by some as the home of wisdom. In addition, there were the *seyyits* (descendants of the Prophet) in their green turbans, who were a family apart, although they did not necessarily perform any religious duties. In Egypt and Syria they were a separate political force and in Damascus and Aleppo they were formidable rivals of the janissaries whom they detested.[15] They were, indeed, hostile to the whole military establishment and only condoned it because they feared anarchy without it.[16]

The *ulema* were originally respected for their knowledge and the dignity of their lives, which passed without ostentation of dress or dwelling. They could walk the streets without the company of a servant and all would stand aside for them. They accepted presents in moderation and legal cases of importance were judged on their merits. If their sons found their way into the privileged caste, nepotism was restrained. Later, ostentation resulted from the transient prosperity that reached its peak in the reign of Süleyman, when the state required increasing sources of revenue as the currency declined in value. By the reign of Murat III (1574–95), judgments were weighed in gold and silver. It was then that passes were bought for sons at colleges until the teaching at these *medreses* declined in quality. Indeed, it is likely that the disappearance of subjects like mathematics and geography from the curriculum was as much due to lack of staff able to teach them as to their elimination for reactionary reasons. But a mob encouraged by reactionaries closed and wrecked the only observatory in Istanbul and this was the time when three learned men were executed for free-thinking and there was an interdict on the importation of books.[17]

The remarkable Kemalpaşazade exemplifies the advantages of being a member of the *ulema* for he had first intended to become a soldier and went on campaign with Bayezit II. One day, when he was in the tent of the Chief Vezir, Çandarlı Ibrahim Pasha, he noted the respect shown the *müderris* (rector) of the college at Philippopolis, Lütfi Efendi, and that the teacher was treated as the equal of Ahmet Bey, not only an officer of the first rank but the son of the heroic *gazi* Evrenos. Thus Kemalpaşazade learnt that the *ulema* were above all others in rank and so studied under Lütfi to become a professor himself at the colleges in Edirne and Üsküp (Skopje) until promotion to a term as *kadı* of Edirne. Selim I made him his official historian and he survived this honour, accompanying the sultan to Egypt. He was Süleyman's *şeyhülislam* from 1526 until his death in 1533, while continuing to be state historian. Five years later Ebüssu'ûd Efendi succeeded to an office which, because of his personality and scholarship, he was to advance to the foremost in the state. It was he who completed the reform of

Pillars of the Empire

the civil code which gave the title of Kanuni ('Lawgiver') to Süleyman.

The Divan, or Grand Council of State

The composition of the Divan varied at different periods and according to circumstance. Indeed, according to Konstantin Mikhailović, who was one of Mehmet II's janissaries, at one period under this sultan there were but two members, the Grand Vezir Mahmut Pasha and Işak Pasha. They deliberated in private but called in whomsoever they pleased for information and reports and then presented their conclusions to the sultan. In the sixteenth century, the Grand Vezir presided and the two *kadıaskers* ranked after him because the Divan was as much a court of final appeal as an administrative body. On campaign, it met in the tent of the Grand Vezir, who was also the *serasker*.[18] The four Vezirs of the Dome under his leadership rarely lacked experience as commanders in the field and had, like him, been trained in the Enderun Kolej. With these sat the *kapudan paşa* (at least intermittently after the appointment of Barbaros Pasha) and sometimes the *agha* of the janissaries attended. If he did not, the *agha* had the right to be the first to be admitted to the audience chamber after a session to hear from the Grand Vezir himself what decisions had been taken. Foreign affairs were in the often unbelievably ignorant hands of the *reis efendi* (foreign minister) and finance in those of the *defterdar* (Keeper of the Account Books). The Divan formed a public court which sat on regular days of the week; the Grand Vezir held additional meetings of his own *divan* in his residence and later in the official compound, the Sublime Porte. This, rebuilt many times, exists in a shabby state to this day with the offices of the *vali* (chief of police) of Istanbul on one part of the site.

The Divan, or those trusted members of the Grand Vezir's inner council, also met in private. Indeed, Mehmet II's two Chief Vezirs once descended to the treasure vaults in order to confer alone. The custodian rolled out a rug for them to sit on while his brother, who was paying him a secret visit in order to relieve his loneliness, had to hide behind a chest. Such meetings left no records, wherever they may have taken place, and those present might include people who could not publicly be seen to be influencing policy such as the Chief Black Eunuch, who for much of the seventeenth century was master of the harem. With him might come one of several formidable Valide Sultans, mothers of politically impotent sultans. The *agha* of the *sipahis*, as commander of the cavalry, might also attend, along with favoured members of the inner household. In a situation seemingly designed for the formation of factions and cabals, a Machiavelli always held the trumps. In the sixteenth century, the sultans finally withdrew from their place at public meetings of the Divan, but could observe them through the grilled window of a small chamber in the tower above the council hall. This public remoteness did not mean that the sultan had withdrawn from government and he could still be an active member of the inner circle.

Divan government was reflected in the administration of the many provinces of the empire. The difficulties of communication were bound to give the local governor considerable latitude and only far-reaching decisions could wait several months for a reply from the Divan. All other decisions—including how to deal with royal decrees—were taken by the governor's local council, which in modest form mirrored that of his sultan. The inclusion on the council of several local worthies and potentates, however, ensured a measure of autonomy and a general understanding of local problems—which is not to say that these problems were solved or that dissatisfaction was less in Baghdad or Damascus than it was in Istanbul itself.[19] It did mean that when the central administration was in decline local interests became increasingly dominant. By the seventeenth century, this was also due to the curtailing of large holdings, which had been granted to support the dignity of the *beylerbey* or governor. These holdings were now reduced, partly as an economy measure but also to curb the autonomy and power of local landowners.

Beys *and* Beylerbeys

Under Orhan, the old Turkish title of *bey* (with Persian antecedents) referred to the second rank of the nobility. Like all titles it was initially coveted since only two officers held it under Murat I: Lala Şahin and Timurtaş, grandson of the Ottoman prince Alaettin Pasha. Under Mehmet I in the early fifteenth century there were *beys* of Anatolia and the Balkans. By the sixteenth century there were some forty *beys* but that of the Balkans remained the foremost in the Divan. Indeed, these officers wielded viceregal powers until they lost the right to dispose of large fiefs. None the less, the *beylerbeys*, as the principal governors of the larger provinces became known, were very close to recent concepts of viceroyalty and had under them governors of *sancaks* (divisions of a province) or more modest territories. All these officers originally came from the sultan's household and had been trained in his schools, either within the *saray* or one of the superior colleges in Edirne or Istanbul. They were often former serving officers of the janissaries and soldiers by profession. Later, local magnates were to take over, as they rapidly did in Mosul. The need for policing soon resulted in the raising of

Pillars of the Empire

local and inferior janissary units which had little in common with the brotherhood in the capital. Indeed, companies were sent out from Istanbul to deal with troublesome local levies.

At first governors might stay sufficiently long to formulate policies which required time to develop, but later appointments were usually kept brief so as to prevent a governor building up a local following with a view to winning total independence. As a result, taxation was heavy in order to enrich the potentate as quickly as possible,[20] while administration was restricted to the solution of immediate problems and devoid of long-term benefits. No province suffered more from this state of affairs than Syria, which was exceptional because Damascus was the assembly point for the *hajj* (pilgrimage to Mecca). The *beylerbey* was usually the Commander of the Caravan and, although this was a lucrative post, he had to provide adequate military protection against marauding bedouin tribes. These the Ottomans never tamed and on several occasions the pilgrims were pillaged and even massacred. Nor were such provinces as Yemen ever truly subjugated: Ottoman sovereignty was nominal for the greater part of their rule there and at best was confined to the towns and fortresses. For janissaries sent to man fortresses in such inhospitable regions, double pay was barely an inducement. They had to support themselves from itinerant traders who were prepared to supply remote garrisons and who fleeced them without compunction. Although the sultan was the protector of the Holy Places, relationships with the Sherifs of Mecca were frequently uneasy because of their Shi'ite beliefs in opposition to the Sunni outlook of the Porte.

Finally, there was the fourth pillar of the state, the merchants who paid the taxes that sustained the government and its army. Each trade formed a guild which protected its members from tyranny and mitigated against hardship. But their greatest protection was the recognition of their importance by the sultan. Our wheel has come full circle.

Emblems of the janissary ortas *from Marsigli (G. Gardiner)*

4
The Ottoman Armed Forces

The Army: Mounted Magnificences and Wild Freebooters

The janissaries were never the largest contingent in the Ottoman army but their influence was pervasive, except on the *sipahis*, and no other unit achieved their strength or renown. The *sipahis* were leased three classes of fief for life in return for their services on campaign. The smallest was the *tımar*, a farm awarded to a good soldier who was expected to report with a groom and an orderly properly mounted. The *sipahis* could be recruited from among the pages but the right to a fief tended to pass from father to son. However, any attempt at achieving a hereditary foothold in a region was discouraged, at least at first, by moving the lessee from holding to holding however bad the policy might prove for husbandry. A greater estate, producing as much as five times the revenue of a *tımar*, was the *zeamet*, which required the *sipahi* to bring several men with him on campaign. A *hass*, a royal estate with a revenue in excess of 100,000 *akçes*, could supply twenty-five cavalrymen fully equipped and with spare mounts. Originally the perquisite of the Ottoman family, these royal estates were later given to the illustrious *vezirs*—who had, in many cases, begun as pages or janissaries. Along with all the holder's goods, the estate reverted to the crown on his demise.

The household cavalry were stationed in the suburbs where there was grazing for their horses. They were chiefly recruited from the janissary corps or from the pages and were permanent, paid troops.[1] In the field, their two

The Janissaries

divisions were stationed right and left of the sultan dressed in magnificent uniforms. They were expected to be incomparable horsemen in an army renowned for its equestrian grace and to be as skilled bowmen as the Türkmen had been before them. Their pride and arrogance were reflected in their gorgeous accoutrements: these were to be their ultimate undoing because they scorned firearms, which soiled them with gunpowder. The right wing of the household cavalry carried a red oriflamme given them by Mehmet II to distinguish them from the yellow flag of the left wing, which claimed to have been founded by Orhan Gazi. In peacetime the right wing guarded the treasury and escorted the revenues of certain provinces on the way to the capital. At some time they had acquired the right to sell outworn royal tents. The left wing guarded the treasure chests stacked in front of the sultan's tent when on campaign and so they dispensed his alms for him. One squadron supplied his grooms and another had the honour of erecting the twelve horsetails which were the emblem of majesty on their two poles. In addition to his pay, the trooper was allotted a small fief so that he could maintain an armed and mailed slave. If he could ride well, there was every inducement for a janissary to transfer to the cavalry with twice the pay. They were also able to get their sons enrolled. Curiously enough, there was a ban on grandchildren.

The rest of the cavalry, amounting to some 12,000 men, were divided into the 5th and 6th *sipahi* divisions of whom the *silihdars* stationed on the sultan's left were the élite and the 3rd and 4th were called the *gürebas* or foreign divisions. Until the seventeenth century the *gürebas* were made up of Muslim mercenaries from the provinces south of Anatolia. The ferocity of these Arabs, Kurds and Persian nomads was reflected politically as well as militarily, where their duties were on the wing of the army. Dressed in mail and carrying the traditional round shields, they scorned the use of guns—even after all other horse except the household cavalry had accepted their necessity—but relied on the traditional bow, scimitar and lance and also the mace. They were thus doomed to decline in importance as weaponry developed until by the eighteenth century they were like so many Don Quixotes.[2]

The *sipahi* dislike of the gun was more rational, as we have seen. Guns were dirty and the soot befouled their accoutrements but they, like the *gürebas,* thought it cowardly to shoot an enemy. Guns, as the Mamluks put it, could kill 50 men without fighting. When some 200 *sipahi*s were trained to use pistols in Persia in 1548, they were taunted by their comrades and their clothes became so filthy that they refused to fire. The senior officers of the *sipahi*s, the *alaybeys,* were the holders of a prestigious post and were

The Ottoman Armed Forces

traditionally promoted to be provincial governors.[3] Inevitably, so aristocratic a corps must have regarded the janissaries, trudging on foot and begrimed with gunpowder and mud, as their inferiors while the *sipahi*s, great Beau Brummels that they were, were reciprocally despised as dandies. In their inevitable decline, the *sipahi*s acquired lucrative properties and the monopoly of the sawmills above Izmit, below the forests which supplied Istanbul with its timber. The trade was profitable and was carried cheaply in ships, often manned by janissary recruits. Its extent is exemplified by travellers' reporting a caravan of 1,000 buffalo fully loaded.

The *akıncıs* (light horse), who were no dandies, were recruited in the Balkans and from frontier tribes.[4] Their job was to raid and loot—foraging for their pay—and to keep the enemy bewildered and so unable to discover where a real attack might be launched. They amounted to some 20,000 troublesome freebooters whose demise was decreed by the disciplinarian conqueror of Yemen, the venerable Koca Sinan Pasha, in 1595. Related to them were the *askeris,* whose work as scouts and raiders was taken over by the Tartars of Crimea.[5] But these two units had served Mehmet II better than most after the Conquest and the *akıncıs* had reached the hastily bolted gates of Vicenza in 1499. As farmers fox-hunt in the English shires, the *müsellems* fought in groups of three or four with the aid of *yamaks* (auxiliaries) in return for the remission of their taxes. The *müsellems* had evolved from being Türkmen tribesmen, many of whom remained as *yürüks* (nomads) and had to pay taxes when caught.

Infantry and Infernal Machines

There was also an Anatolian foot, the *yayas* or *piyades*. These were crofters rather than farmers and their service also exempted them from taxation. The provinces also bred the crazy Company of Guides, the Mad Guys or Riskers of their Souls, whose savagery was suicidal. They came mostly from the Balkans and although supposed to be fanatical Muslims were recent converts whose fervour was directed towards combat for its own sake. A light archery division, the *azaps* (marines), supplemented the janissary corps when garrisoning the fortresses on the frontiers of the interior, as much against sedition as an enemy. Some of them went into the navy and the others guarded the trains of camels carrying munitions and so became absorbed into the *topçus* (artillery). They were not a levy: a neighbourhood was obliged to supply a quota of young men some of whom were genuine volunteers. Local roads and crossings were guarded by a mixed assortment of Muslims and Christians living in the vicinity who were formed into small bands known as the *derbent*. They were given fiefs and the task tended to run in families although some *yürüks* joined them.[6]

In the eighteenth century a new suicidal force grew up called the *serdengeçti* ('the lost children'), which indeed they were because thoughtless and doomed to an early death. But these were volunteers recruited out of the ranks of the janissaries who were rewarded by extra pay and a distinctive cap. They emerged significantly at a time when the corps had lost prestige and as if to dissociate themselves from their former brothers. By their desperate tactics, the *serdengeçti* were meant to set an example to less courageous, or less foolhardy, comrades.

Murat II founded the *topçus*, whose principal weapon was the siege cannon. They eventually numbered 2,000 men under the command of 3 *aghas*. These gunners were responsible for making, repairing and manning the batteries which were later the product of the foundry at Tophane in Galata. Thence the gun barrels could be rolled down onto the sandy shore for loading onto caiques. Tophane was commanded by a Master Founder and the unit eventually included 3,000 gun-carriage drivers.[7] The gunners policed Beyoğlu or Pera, the European quarter of the city, above the barracks and the foundry.

The *cebecis* (armourers), who numbered 2,000 by the sixteenth century, formed an entirely independent unit which made arquebuses for the janissaries but soon these *cebecis* were themselves trained as an infantry regiment and one might suppose that they reserved their best guns for themselves. A corps of miners was responsible for tunnelling under fortress walls and blowing them up while the mortar brigade[8] had the task of making, transporting and firing grenades and bombs. These sappers were divided into companies concerned with making the mortars and refining the powder. Those who used these weapons were further divided into fortress garrisons supported by fiefs and the main body which served in the *topçus*. All the artillery units were recruited from cadets of the levy while the *cebecis* had a particular relationship with the halberdiers and so with the janissaries.

In time of war, tradesmen and artisans along with labourers were called up through their guilds, including masons, tailors and cobblers. But many of these trades were practised by the janissaries and other soldiers who were, for example, their own butchers and cooks. All the janissaries had worked as building labourers when recruits. This meant that there were few camp followers but also that the distinction between soldier and tradesman was blurred until the spirit of one entered the body of the other.

The Ottoman Armed Forces

The Janissaries: Heart of the Ottoman Army

Three-quarters of the Ottoman army has been reviewed: the janissary corps remains.[9] Its task was to form an élite infantry corps which was permanently on duty in its barracks when not on campaign or manning a fortress. For this reason marriage was forbidden.[10] The soldier was paid and when pensioned at 45 continued to wear his uniform and, if he wished, live in his barracks where he inspired or bored raw recruits with his legendary exploits of old. In the reign of Süleyman, however, Pierre Gyllius was sent by King François I of France to collect Greek manuscripts but was forgotten and had to join the corps in order to eat. Although no longer a youth, he was accepted without more ado. Later he managed to escape to Rome while on campaign in Persia. But before this he found time in which to explore Istanbul thoroughly, which indicates freedom of movement within the city walls.

Since the janissaries were professional soldiers without the snobbery of *sipahi* knights, they accepted the use of hand guns willingly as their main weapon of offence.[11] They took to flintlocks at an early date, perhaps because in 1389 they encountered those of the Huniades at Kossovo which were among the first. It was a time when Ottoman generals learnt quickly from their foes. But much later the absorption of the corps into city life as a privileged society inevitably extinguished the light of Western military innovations, which were ignored in the intellectual dark of the eighteenth century. The janissaries' dislike of pikes accounts for the constitution of a separate brigade of halberdiers or axemen. In Mehmet II's reign, the janissary was bowman, crossbowman and musketeer and also used a mortar. The janissaries were not good at standing their ground like the Swiss pikemen at Laupen or at any manoeuvre equivalent to forming a square in the manner of Waterloo.[12]

The corps was composed of 3 divisions. The *seğmen*, that of the Keeper of the Hounds, was made up of 34 *ortas* distinguished by their red boots. The second or *cemaat* division, the Assembly, numbered 101 *ortas* and garrisoned the important fortresses. The officers had the right to ride in the presence of their *agha* and wore yellow boots. Finally, there was the *bölük* division of 61 *ortas*. This made a total of 196 companies. Each began with a complement of 100 men but swelled in time to 600 or even 800, in theory, in the later seventeenth century when the corps was supposed to muster 70,000 men. Fewer than half were soldiers and many of these included their 'shadows' as separate enlistments by using fictitious names. This total was cut in half from time to time without difficulty but always returned to the

The Janissaries

mystical figure of 70,000 even if it included the dead.

In name, they were all slaves of the sultan. In theory, they were recruited exclusively from the *acemioğlans* until there were none left in the seventeenth century. Each *orta* was commanded by a colonel or *çorbaçı* (Soup Cook), whose badge was a ladle which was proudly worn but never wielded. He had a staff of six officers, a clerk and an *imam* besides his sergeants. He wore a gilded helmet and carried a white staff, while junior officers wore sheath knives in their sashes as badges of rank. His *odabaşı* (lieutenant) was commandant of the Barracks Hall and was supported by the officers in charge of the commissariat and by the *aşcıbaşı* (Cook). The latter's job was signally important because he had to ensure those regular and well-cooked meals which kept the company happy. There was no eating dry biscuits as in other armies but fresh bread daily besides the basic ration of mutton, rice and butter. The *aşcıbaşı* was also responsible for discipline in the ranks and, perhaps because he wielded the sharpest knives and was an experienced butcher, was the executioner. But he did not often kill or send culprits to prison or even put them in irons. The common punishment was to be made to act as scullion in the company kitchen, a penalty familiar to the British private soldier as 'jankers'. Each *ocak* also had its own paymaster: his role became increasingly devious and complex when corruption set in at the end of the sixteenth century and pay warrants became currency, when no actual coin was available, to circulate like cheques in the United States. By this date, married janissaries lived outside the barracks. They therefore forfeited promotion, reasonably enough, and this precipitated their growing involvement with trade and worse.

The corps was commanded by its *agha*; an *ex-officio* member of the Divan, he ranked below the four Vezirs of the Dome but above all other commanders. Under Selim I the appointment was made from the household and no longer from the corps itself. The *agha*'s palace was the Tekeli Kiosk, which was built of wood amid gardens, offices and guardrooms between the Süleymaniye complex and the Golden Horn. Besides barrack-rooms, there were also lodgings for various officers attached to his headquarters and the whole formed a very grand complex of its own—it had to be since even common barrack-rooms were bedecked with Iznik tiles and their ceilings were gilded.

The general of the *seğmen* division was the *agha*'s deputy; the *kul kahya* was adjutant-general and ranked as his lieutenant and as commander of the *bölük* division. These, with the colonels of the three senior *ocaks*, were known as the six *ocak aghas* and ranked as generals. There was also the *yeniçeri katip* (the Secretary and the *agha* of Istanbul), who commanded the

The Ottoman Armed Forces

34 cadet *ortas* from which all the *ortas* recruited their troops, making a total of 230 companies in all. The commander of the 5th *orta* ranked as sergeant-major general and registered all recruits and their punishments. The *ateşcıbaşı* (Chief Cook) was the quartermaster-general and provost marshal. He wore a black leather dalmatic, adorned with silver knobs; his girdle was hung with hooks from which dangled chains carrying spoons and a bowl and kitchen instruments including two immense carving knives. All these objects weighed so much that he had to be supported by two janissaries when he walked and propped in his saddle when he rode. One and all wore the red or white sleeve[13] of the Bektaşis, which folded high above the brow to hang down their necks, with a spoon for regimental crest.[14] The sleeve swung with panache when they walked and gave a certain swagger which was good for morale.[15]

Officers in ceremonial dress were bedecked with splendid ornaments and a *kalafat* (crested headdress). Some wore cranes' feathers for their greater glory and some herons' but the sleeve of the Bektaşis was the more significant. Like their voluminous trousers, it probably derived from the *ahis* rather than the dervishes. Once a year on the Night of Power in the month of Ramazan, the men were apportioned blue cloth,[16] supplied from Salonika, issued from a depot at the mint near the mosque of Bayezit II. The companies paraded one by one before their commanders and the intendant and colonel of the stores who had a staff of 150. They also received shirts and lengths of muslin for turbans. They took the cloth to official tailors—one situated near the royal stables and the other by the palace of the Grand Vezir—while 60 men in 10 shops in the barracks were employed on making their felt caps.

Horsetails and Oriflammes

Their *sancaks* (flags) were vital to the Ottomans, who as emirs received colours and drum as symbols of authority from the sultans of Konya. First was the *ak sancak,* which was white with an inscription embroidered in gold—the symbol of sovereignty. The cavalry had red flags and red and green flags but household janissaries had colours of red and gold. The emblem of command derived from the Mongol khans; it consisted of horsetails hung below a golden ball with the horned moon of Cybele for a crest. A miniature Koran in a silver case also hung from the top of each pole. So it came about that the governor of a small province was known as the *sancak bey* (Lord of the Standard); the number of horsetails raised before a general's tent denoted his rank, but it varied from time to time. The sultan

The Janissaries

himself was entitled to nine horsetails, and later twelve on two totem poles bearing six apiece, but on the Mohacs campaign Süleyman only claimed seven. A petty governor had only one or two, a *beylerbey* two, but Vezirs of the Dome were permitted three and the Grand Vezir five. In the eighteenth century, Emin Pasha as *serasker* had six tails; at their presentation sheep were sacrificed and given to the poor.

The flag of the janissary corps was half-yellow and half-red, with the Zülfikar significantly emblazoned in the centre.[17] Flags were lost at sea but it is alleged that the first capture of an Ottoman standard was in 1559.[18] At that time it was coloured slate, after which the official colour of the Ottomans became slate-green. But the Standard of the Prophet was green or black with age, nor could any man change this holy colour of the family whose descendants rode to battle in a separate company dressed in the green of their birthright. Not even at the siege of Vienna under Kara Mustafa Pasha in 1683 was the Prophet's sacred standard allowed to fly but only when the sultan commanded. The regimental colours of the janissaries were regarded with little less awe and given almost equal devotion. They were all different. The 1st *orta*'s flag was bedecked with a camel, the 43rd with an elephant and the 17th with a lion; the 10th *orta* flew a hawk, and the 68th a stork, while the 74th displayed a curious *mimber* (pulpit). The 84th had a mosque with twin minarets whereas that of the 30th had but one. Other emblems ranged from the candle-snuffers of the 41st to the caravel in full sail of the 56th. There were anchors, flags, massed arms, keys, the bow and arrow of the 54th *orta* and the rose of the 44th.[19] None of these symbols was necessarily symbolic of any duty allotted the company. The *agha*'s personal ensign was carried together with his horsetails under a similar ball and crescent. When a campaign ended, the colours—like those of English regiments laid up in churches—were borne to mosques and *tekkes* with due ceremony and hung on the right or left of the *mimber*.[20]

Halls Built for Heroes

The barracks of the janissaries were monumental. In the eighteenth century there were 60 *odalar* in Istanbul capable of lodging a total of 40,000 men, according to Grenville. Sanderson, in 1594, says that the janissaries were lodged like friars, which might imply a series of cells (this may have been true of the Eski Odalar at the Şehzade). Vandal reports that they consisted of a large, straight (i.e. rectangular) hall with a high gallery covered by a partially gilded ceiling. One side was clad in tiles while the other had doors onto the courtyards—this fits the form of existing examples at Topkapısaray and the plan of the *bostancı* barracks, now destroyed, attached to the palace at Kağıthane. The halberdier barracks at the *saray* also has a vestibule (with lockers for weapons) which opens onto an L-shaped yard with privies, a fountain, storerooms and a small *mescit* besides little chambers that may have served as officers' quarters.

Galland writes of long buildings covered in tiles with marble doors and window frames and galleries lit by lamps. The rooms for janissaries and their officers were commodious and he notes a great number of fountains, including some conveniently situated in the kitchens.[21] An *orta* occupied more than one hall, which might hold 100 men and possibly double the number at some periods. A hall had its emblem, like so many houses in an English boarding school, in addition to the company crest. It was an efficient arrangement which bred loyalty among small groups, a loyalty sealed by tattooing the *orta*'s insignia on the arm and leg of each janissary. Galland states that these rooms held 250 men but this is unlikely: since the year was 1672 it is probable that many were married and had moved out by then. The Eski Odalar beside the Şehzade mosque (where, until recently, streets and some ruins recorded its erstwhile existence) was soon outgrown but continued to harbour the *bölük ortas* and, at least until the nineteenth century, some officers and sergeants. The barracks was certainly refurbished from time to time if only after a fire. A huge new complex, the Yeni Odalar (New Barracks), was erected in the sixteenth century below the mosque: it occupied an area from where the City Hall now stands to Aksaray, the mosque of Murat Pasha and the Sofalar Hamam.

Uzunçarşılı gives a precise list of rooms in these two barracks.

Table 1. Number of Rooms in the Eski Odalar and Yeni Odalar

Rooms	Eski Odalar	Yeni Odalar	Total
Halls with hearths	47	368	415
Lesser chamber for the *bölük ortas*	26	–	26
Additional bed spaces	55	–	55
Hutments	21	130	151
Bedchambers	–	69	69
Drill and exercise halls	–	90	90
Pavilions	–	20	20
Tekkes	1	4	5
Stables	26	158	184

The Janissaries

The Yeni Odalar had 7 gates. The main one—the great gate behind which the janissaries made their last, futile stand in 1826—was the Ceremonial Gate onto the immense Etmeydan, or inner Parade Ground. Table 1 does not include the kitchens, storerooms, harness rooms, workshops and tradesmen's booths, the *hamams*, latrines and prisons. They must have amounted to 800 walled areas in all, which, however lofty, were basically single-storey buildings. The central open area within the walls had the Orta mosque in the centre (a simple pun since *orta* means middle as well as a janissary company). It was the meeting-place of the 8 (later, there were more) dervishes of the Bektaşi order after 1591. Nor was this all, for there were 40 rooms for *azaps* at Ibrahim Pasha Saray on the Hippodrome in addition to the barracks for *acemioğlans* beside the Eski Odalar, where a lane is still named after them. In 1800 Le Chevalier reported that no honest woman could go anywhere near these barracks with impunity, but then this was true of France and other countries too.

A factory at the *saray* gate opposite the former basilica of Haghia Sophia was assigned to making candles for the janissaries, who were also supplied from various houses with their favourite winter drink of *boza* (fermented barley). Bread came from bakeries served by 300 cadets. Biscuits were specially baked at Kirkçeşme nearby but also at Galata and as far away as Yeniköy, a village half-way down the Bosphorus on the European shore. Meat was prepared by 80 Greek butchers in 20 shops. *Celebs* (sheep-drivers) supplied mutton to both the *saray* and local butchers. It was a rewarding calling and the *askeris* had to be forbidden from deserting to it. The income from their sales was, however, taxed to pay for mutton for the janissaries but the *ulema*, as always, were exempt. The janissaries also had their own flocks but these may well have been reserved for use during a campaign.[22]

There were barracks for the other units of the army elsewhere, including those of the *bostancıs* in the precincts of the *saray*. The *cebecis* had similar halls (which held 4,000) as did the 2,000 gunners in the region between the mosque of Kılıç Ali Pasha and the present Academy of Fine Arts, located on either side of the Nüsretiye mosque. The barracks of Selim III, built for his new army, are infamous in British history as the mortuary rather than the hospital (until Florence Nightingale arrived) for the wounded of the Crimean war, but very grand. The capacious nineteenth-century barracks of Pera have now been allocated to the Technical University.

Cities of Silk and Canvas

The splendour of the Ottomans' parade uniforms was rivalled by their tents for they lodged more grandly in the field than at home. These tents were the property of the sultan and like arms and armour were only issued in times of war. On his accession, the sultan ordered a new silk *otak* (imperial tent; literally, 'high dome'), which descended from the great marquees of the khans of Central Asia but could not rival the veritable palaces such as were built by Timur. But an *otak* took several years to make, like the one set up by the Hippodrome for everyone to admire and which Galland reported seeing. Made for Mehmet IV, it was supported by sixteen poles and covered in satin. Both within and without, it was heavily embroidered with panels of stylized vegetation in the bold Ottoman tradition in predominant shades of red and green.

Campaign tents were usually less gorgeous, but the sultan's was set in a little walled castle of cloth in the Chinese style with a two-tier gate surmounted by a canopy. He also had a kiosk some 1.5 metres square, reached by fifteen steps, housing a bath and wash basins; there was also a large tent where meetings of the Divan and councils of war were held. The *otak* symbolized majesty: the Prophet, it was alleged, had sat under a cupola-crowned tent in the desert and, more spectacularly, the Sufi saints of legend had their tents in the sky. On earth, Lady Mary Wortley Montagu reports, the tents of great men were like palaces in the eighteenth century.[23] In the days of Mohacs, Kemalpaşazade refers to the red and yellow tents of the officials and the purple tent of the Grand Vezir, Ibrahim Pasha. The importance of the tent was common to all Islam—in India, the Mogul emperor's tent was red.[24] All senior members of the Divan took part in major campaigns except for a deputy who was left in charge of the capital. They not only had personal tents commensurate with their dignity but also working tents for the clerks and the records of state—these travelled with the sultan and his army since government was exercised in the field just as it was in the *saray*.

Dr Covel, who was in Istanbul in the 1670s, describes six of the sultan's tents designed for various uses. One was preceded by a canopy 2.4 metres square; inside, it was supported by four rows of seven posts and measured 15 strides by 12, some 488 square metres in all: or more than 9 x 15 metres. Its roof was low and flat and the sides were only hung when the weather was cold (since the Ottomans were hardy it would have to have been very cold). The audience chamber was round, its top supported by one central pole crested by a gold ball on top of a flower-pot, to use the doctor's words. It was 12 or 15 metres in diameter. However, the bedchamber was a mere 3.7 metres square with lattice sides such as are traditional with tribal tents. It had short poles at each corner and two in the middle. Covel also describes

The Janissaries

a curiously long tent with a sofa down the middle measuring some 35 paces, which was supported by three poles down the centre (there was a fine example at Edirne).

But even modest tents were decorated. Marsigli admired them and cannily referred to their being a precious memento of the nomadic past. At one time large round tents were issued to the *ortas* but the janissaries generally shared a low, conical tent of cloth or camel-hair between three men. They were also given a packhorse and an orderly who went on ahead to erect the tent before the arrival of the army. These orderlies were usually those *voynuks* (Christian volunteers) who were assigned such humble tasks as stable-boys or drivers in exchange for freedom from the poll tax. The tents of the sultan and his senior officers had to be duplicated so that camps could be pitched in a leap-frog manner. Soldiers were also issued with sheepskins, of which their diet produced an excess, or kilims while the officers enjoyed knotted rugs and even cushions on low sofas. Otherwise the furniture consisted of bales of cloth in which spare clothing and rugs were wrapped in nomad fashion. The larger tents could be divided by curtains and their flaps raised on poles to act as porticoes.

Ordu, the Ottoman word for both the army and its camp, was synonymous with and indicative of the good order on which Ottoman strategy was based. Writer after writer refers to the astonishing formality of these camps, with major roads and minor roads together with piazzas; their symmetry was in total contradistinction to that of their towns where everything was ordered by laws of property rather than geometry. The roads radiated out from the central tent of the monarch and those of his court, to be divided into districts in a manner reminiscent of Roman armies. Each tent was neatly aligned with its neighbour and with the line of pickets where the horses were tethered after a period of grazing before nightfall. Each group had an ablution tent and screened latrine pits were dug at intervals, each with a red lid. Many foreigners commented on Ottoman cleanliness in contrast to the stinking camps to which they were accustomed.[25] If bones were thrown to the dogs, other rubbish must have been carefully disposed of.

The company commanders had their tents pitched in the middle of their men's, like miniature sultans, and each district had its open space with cookhouses, shops for food, tailors and armourers and other craftsmen. By the sixteenth century there were also the dissolute camp followers whom strict rulers like Süleyman controlled although they could not suppress. Empty tents were erected as prisons for slaves, malefactors and prisoners-of-war and one at least as a place of execution. These last were put to use: Marsigli at Belgrade watched the bodies of rebel subjects dragged along by ropes, to be followed by their heads which were flung into the river. The camp was lit by rags soaked in oil or grease hung from long poles in iron lanterns after darkness fell.

The hasty work of the advance guard of servants who had to erect the camp before the hour of evening prayer was helped by the re-use of established areas on the long campaign roads into Europe as well as by training. The sultan's tent had to go up first as a guide point. Naturally, the details of its erection did not have to be completed until later. The march was in no way as orderly because the best roads were rough and no soldier kept in step before Macadam made this possible, or not since the Roman legions marched in formation. But the janissaries did not straggle; they could move at great speed aided by their excellent rations[26] and could, on occasion, march by night with the use of flares. Around 35 kilometres might be covered on some days, made possible by the sappers and engineers who went ahead in order to fell trees, level obstacles, fill in potholes and lay planks across marshy ground.[27] Guarded by Tartars, the baggage train followed in the rear. It not only carried munitions, food and fodder on the backs of thousands of camels, and the goods sold by camp followers, but also the treasure, the records, and robes of honour in anticipation of victory.[28]

The best horses were kept for the vanguard commanded by the Grand Vezir if the sultan went to war with his army. The members of this vanguard were often Tartars too.[29] Their mounts were unshod; each horse had a slave groom who was taught to hold onto its tail when swimming a river or risk being decapitated on the spot. These horses were headstrong and clumsy but almost tireless. Heavier mounts were bred in Bulgaria but the forerunners of the thoroughbred racehorse, the mounts from Anatolia, were a finer and swifter breed only rivalled by those from Moldavia and Poland.[30] They were served by devoted Arabs who groomed them for hours and even dyed any white hairs in mane or tail with henna. The sultan's mounts were so esteemed that they had felt-carpeted platforms for their stalls.

Strategy, Tactics and the Zone of War

All the elaboration and precision altered when the army entered enemy territory. There were no longer any rest days nor could a day's march be timed. The men were issued with their steel helmets, light armour[31] and round shields of wood and wattle covered with leather and, finally and most important, their personal arms. The cannon now moved forward from the rear and each camping place was carefully defended, not least by the

The Janissaries

crossing guy-ropes of the close-packed tents which acted as an entanglement or tripwires. The cannon, too, were chained together to frustrate any attempt by enemy cavalry to sweep up behind them and carry them away.

The heart of Ottoman tactics was to lure and to surprise. By fleeing the field, the *akıncıs* drew out the heavy Christian cavalry and while tiring their mounts also tried to lure them onto the spikes ranged before the janissary redoubts or trenches. But they would also repeatedly swoop down the flanks of the enemy cavalry and inflict damage difficult for the cumbersome knights to turn and meet. The climax always lay with the formidable firepower of the trained janissaries. It determined the set-piece battle array which ideally had the sultan and his standards on a mound fronted by a wall of earth, stakes and shields and a ditch in the centre. Behind this, janissaries had cannon, mortars and muskets at every embrasure. The cavalry and poorly trained infantry of Anatolia were ranged on the right flank and that of the Balkans on the left. This tactic was modified by Selim I, who extended his cannon beyond the centre.

Great rivers, which Süleyman and Ibrahim Pasha exploited at Mohacs, were always a problem for any attacking army. The younger Dracula—Vlad III Tepes Kazıklı ('the Impaler' or 'the Dragon')—cut off the noses of the population of Nicopolis and sent them to Hungary boasting that he had won a victory. The atrocity forced Mehmet II to depose his vassal and place his handsome hostage brother on the throne. He sent this favourite youth with 4,000 horse on ahead but Mehmet caught up with him on the banks of the Danube, where Dracula was ensconced on the farther shore. Mehmet appealed to his janissaries: they found eighty boats, rowed across in the dark, well downstream, and set up a bridgehead which successive convoys strengthened until the whole army and its guns had crossed, but the losses were considerable. Able as he was, Dracula was hopelessly outnumbered and fled to Hungary where the king wisely imprisoned him for his crimes—but not before he had attacked the Ottoman camp at night, cutting guy-ropes and slaughtering men. Many fled wildly towards the newly aroused janissaries, who had to mow them down or be trampled to death by the mob.

Unlike Kara Mustafa Pasha before the gates of Vienna in 1683, Mehmet II was always impatient and his assaults on castles and towns were costly. A system developed with experience. Mehmet attacked on Fridays in order to enlist Allah in his forces. When cannonades had pounded a breach, the day and hour of the assault were proclaimed and the rewards for acts of daring (such as planting colours on the ramparts of the enemy) were announced. The night before an attack the camp was sparkling with tallow candles and then the cannonade started so as to drive the defenders from the walls. It stopped abruptly and the infantry rushed the breach with bundles of brushwood and branches flung in the moat and carrying scaling ladders. The timing was better than that of Allied artillery in the First World War with its many thousands of dead in Flanders. If the defenders held out until noon, munitions ran out and casualties were likely to be too great for the Ottomans to continue. If they retreated, cannon were quickly loaded, tents struck and a rearguard formed. The maimed who survived were generously pensioned because Mehmet II was strict about almsgiving and the duties of the state. He was hostile to wealth and there were few rich men at his court.

At their best, Ottoman commanders were apt at improvisation. Mehmet had shown ample evidence of this when he built ships in the woods and then had buffaloes and men drag them over rollers down trenches lined with tallow-greased planks to the Golden Horn in order to defeat the Byzantine chain across the harbour mouth in 1453. His father at Varna had let his men retreat up the ravines under the cover of thick heather to lure the enemy into successive ambushes. Only one wing of the foe was victorious in the isolation of a gorge, unaware that their king was dead, and left the field unscathed.

The underlying strategy, even in conquest in the fifteenth century, was caution. Mehmet II exemplified it when he spread a large carpet and placed an apple in the middle of it. He invited his generals to pick it up without treading on the carpet. Tactfully or genuinely, his officers were unable to solve the problem. He then slowly rolled the carpet up until he could easily grasp the apple. But this caution cannot diminish the importance of his cannon. His guns daunted Uzun Hasan of the White Sheep as those of France were to daunt the cities of Italy at the turn of the century. Mehmet was also able to cast cannon in the field due to the skilled artisans whom he had recruited from abroad. During his campaign in the Peloponnese (the Morea) he besieged Corinth and took over a church as a foundry, which was supplied from the newly captured great mines of Novo Brdo. One result of this facility in replacing cannon was that the sultan was prepared to discard them if he had to retreat. They were pushed over cliffs and into rivers, rather than abandoned to the enemy—like the guns before Belgrade. Thus Mehmet's army gained speed, always his first concern.

Perhaps the Ottoman gunnery was more renowned than it deserved to be. The first use of artillery had been in Cairo in December 1366 and the first recorded use of guns by the Ottomans was sixty years later at the siege of Antalya in 1425, while the janissaries did not use the arquebus until 1465.[32] In the seventeenth century the artillery was brought up to date by Pietro

The Janissaries

Sardi for there was a long tradition of Italian gunsmiths under the Ottomans and elsewhere—although it was Turks whom Babur engaged, along with Portuguese half-castes, as instructors in the Mogul army. During the same period, Kurtoğlu ('Son of a Wolf' or, less politely, 'Son of a Bitch') Kızır Bey, with eight gunners and fifty masters-at-arms, trained the troops of Sultan Alaettin of Aci in Sumatra.

Ottoman mortars, although improved by a Venetian renegade, were of poor quality. Cannon and mortar fired stones wrapped in oiled leather or sheepskins,[33] chains and copper balls. That their mines were well laid was due to skilled Armenian masons. It was the supply of ore which made the victories of Selim I over the Mamluks so much easier. Learning from the experience of his father's campaigns, Süleyman made it a principle of Ottoman strategy to issue the janissaries with muskets.

Ottoman gun barrels, whether cannon or musket, reflected pride in weaponry. They were usually finely damascened and inlaid with niello and silver in the case of hand weapons. The chamber was divided from the barrel by a moulding and the beech-screw had a convex comb with a series of peepholes through which to line up the target. The guns had long pentagonal stocks made of wood from Adapazar with a thick butt plate set at an angle and without a trigger guard. Dragons' heads were sculpted on the muzzles of the finest guns. In the mid-seventeenth century the Catalan miquelet lock, developed in Spain and Italy, replaced the matchlock arquebus and eliminated the need for a rest as well as the slow and clumsy use of a match. The Austrians were issued with flintlocks, however, and their rapid fire underlined the routing out of the Ottomans from Hungary after their failure at Vienna in 1683.

The janissaries were also issued with pistols for use at very close range or, like a gardener, to scare the birds. These firearms were the personal possessions of the soldiers in the sense that each gun was issued to and cared for by an individual. They were kept locked up because of janissary unruliness but they were issued on state occasions when the corps paraded, somewhat fearsomely, firing volleys in salute.

The Tartars made great use of burning arrows when attacking towns, as Marsigli witnessed at Buda and Belgrade in 1693. Other hand weapons included javelins, darts and lances, swords, scimitars, daggers and a form of rapier together with maces, hatchets and an adapted, blood-chilling, form of scythe. Scaling ladders and siege engines—forty were captured after the second siege of Vienna in 1683—were dragged along as monuments to the God of War as late as the eighteenth century. The most important weapon against towns and fortresses, however, was the skilled mining of walls and

The Ottoman Armed Forces

towers so as to topple them into moats and thus create bridges.

Tactics, which should have changed to meet the increased firepower of the Ottomans' enemies, remained the same—as if change were against the nature of the Ottoman soldier. This may have been true of the *sipahis* but was certainly not so for the janissaries. Besides, the army was made up of polyglot peoples. In 1683 some 250,000 men attacked Vienna. Of these a quarter were tribesmen from Greater Syria while a little over a quarter came from Anatolia and the same proportion were *kul:* household, *sipahi* or janissary divisions. The remainder were Tartars, Transylvanians, Vlachs and Cossacks. It was not a question of national temperament but generalship. The basis of the Ottoman attack (and they attacked too often) wasted lives in a wild encircling swoop, with wave following on wave, as if the undisciplined tribesmen were in command. The best troops were still endowed with a *gazi* spirit when warfare had become a science. It was fatal.

Where Birds Feared to Fly

The Ottoman bow was related to the sacred bow of the Mongols. Every man of any status practised archery and the training was strict and long. A boy began by learning how to flex a light practice bow for some years and then spent several more years just letting the bow-string fly. This was the dangerous period of the youth's initiation since an error could ruin his bow finger, which was also his trigger finger,[34] for life: hence the rings worn as guards although the large and ornate rings seen in museums were for display. Their making was sufficiently skilled and important to be deemed a trade worthy of a sultan. It was only after this period of training that the tiro was permitted to let his first arrow fly: only then did the years' training for long flight and accuracy begin. One and all sought perfection in aim and distance and sultans often achieved genuine prowess even when skilled at nothing else. In 1798 the English ambassador, Sir Robert Ainslie, incredibly reported that Selim III shot an arrow just short of 1 kilometre. Even in the nineteenth century the Okmeydan (Archery Ground),[35] dedicated by Mehmet II with its sacred pavilion above the Golden Horn on the dockyard side, was still in use and had not lost its sanctity. Allegedly, an American ambassador who had expressed doubt about Mahmut II's ability to hit a target at 800 metres was invited to the *meydan* (open space) and there at a range of exactly 800 metres received a royal shaft between his feet. Some twenty among the former host of tall marble columns survive to celebrate record shots and one, credited to Selim I, has given its name to a fashionable quarter of the city, Nişantaş, because of the column marking the place where

The Janissaries

it landed. Of all men, the Tartars excelled at archery so that the Chinese said that birds were afraid to fly. The Ottomans practised shooting from the saddle after passing a suspended brass ball in the old manner of the steppes.

The bow itself was a work of art and time. It was made of layers of sinew from the Achilles tendon of buffalo and other animals stretched over a maple wand preferably from Kastamonu. Horn boiled until pliable formed the centre joint and grip. The more the horn and sinew, the better the reflex shape and the better the bow. The bowyers simmered the sinew until the fat and dirt on the surface were cleansed away; it was then cooked over charcoal for several days, using rain-water to replace evaporation. The glue was equally important: the best was made from resin found at the mouth of the Danube. The bow was matured for a year and fed on linseed oil after which it could be used for two centuries. Its average draw was 70 centimetres and the length of its underbelly was 112 centimetres. The horsehair bow-string became as refined as silk after saturation in five parts beeswax, five parts resin and twenty parts fish glue. The flight guides were made of tortoiseshell or ivory; the rings were fitted from a sealing-wax impression of the archer's finger for an exact fit was essential. The arrows needed equal care in their making, with their flights of swan, eagle, cormorant and other feathers. They usually had 61-centimetre shafts of pine and goat-bone tips. Cases and quivers were elaborately decorated as befitted the most noble possession a man might acquire.

There were as many problems in keeping bow-strings dry as with powder, but the care taken resulted in the bow and arrow being a more accurate weapon than the early musket—it was also swifter-firing although less devastating. For these reasons it continued to be carried by the janissaries into the seventeenth century.[36]

One other weapon was exploited to the full by the Ottoman army, but with a training calculated to produce the maximum terror in the enemy. Noise has always been a concomitant of battle; 'professional noise' had to be heard above the normal din of war but also set up rhythms of fear in much the same way that men marching in step create rhythms that demolish a bridge. (Thus there may have been a certain truth in the story of Joshua tumbling the walls and terrifying Jericho into submission.) The trenches which the janissaries dug when besieging a town or fortress might be orderly, but when they stormed a breach there could be no question of it being drill: their charge was confused and impetuous. The unholy shrieks and yells for which they were renowned were common to any man in a moment of danger but were the more terrifying because the result of trained intent. Even they were surpassed by the demoniac howls and roars of the shock troops who went before them, orchestrated by the hysteria of fanaticism.

Bellowing cannon, musket barks, the hacking cough of bullets and the wind of cannon-balls might make a prodigious din but above this came the music of the bands, outlandish to Western ears.[37] The Mehter bands were dominated by their giant drums which, like the horsetails of rank, were called *tuğs*. Cymbals (which originated in Anatolia), flutes and forms of trumpet and horn along with the kettledrums completed the band. It was ranked in accordance with the number of its instruments which, in turn, accorded with the seniority of the officer whom it honoured. The number of instruments ranged from six to nine (nine was a lucky number according to the Oğuz Turks) except for the dozen instruments that accorded with the dignity of the sultan.[38] In peacetime the bands played daily at the palaces or fortresses: in war they accompanied the army in the field to cheer on the attack and demoralize the foe. The janissary band had an impressive and sonorous slow march which sounded disagreeably menacing and was symbolic of an implacable quality that lingered on into the eighteenth century, if only musically.

To be able to put an army in the field with all its food and fodder, its armaments and tents, and even the four great *kös* (drums) that were sounded only in war, needed detailed planning. In the early years mobility was the important requirement as new territories were conquered and a system was slow to evolve. Thus the armies of Murat II in the fifteenth century were much more mobile and flexible in their deployment than those, two centuries later, of Murat IV, whose excellent supply lines were restrictive because it was not possible to deviate from the preordained route from depot to depot (although this was not important in his Baghdad or Erivan campaigns). The Ottomans could cope with the unexpected for as long as the commanders were as gifted (as they indeed proved) and little burdened with orthodoxy, either military or religious. Mehmet II could achieve brilliant if brutal improvisation.

Monsoon on the Black Sea Coast

When Mehmet set out to conquer Trabzon in 1461, neither Uzun Hasan of the White Sheep, nor the Isfendiyaroğlu, nor the emperor of Trabzon, David Comnenus, knew which of them was the true target. In fact, Hasan was to be spared for a decade and Isfendiyar was easily crushed but David was the real objective. It was a tough journey harassed by the Tartar horse whose master preferred Christian neighbours to Mehmet. The mountain passes

The Janissaries

were high and the woods thick. The relentless downpour of the Black Sea coast turned the tracks to foul morasses where the mud was sometimes waist-high. At one point Mehmet made a memorable bonfire of the baggage wagons, including 100 of his own, and had all the supplies loaded onto the backs of the 800 camels. One of these fell over a cliff and its chests broke open to scatter 60,000 gold pieces all around. These were promptly guarded by janissaries who were allowed to gather up this fortune as a reward and so the appalling march went on. The advance guard was massacred but the army reached the city, where 150 ships had set up a blockade: after six weeks of costly attacks it fell on 26 October 1461.

Mehmet's personal caravan amounted to over 400 camels and mules of which the 60 best camels carried treasure and 24 each were apportioned to the field kitchen and the tents. But most carried the guns and ammunition of the household division, some 6,000 strong. The army had to avoid damaging crops and to pay fairly for their needs down to the last chicken or they were severely punished. Christian farmers were conscripted to bring beasts loaded with supplies which were sold at a just price. However, Mehmet's forces were much smaller than the great armies of the sixteenth and seventeenth centuries which were sometimes 250,000 strong.

Supplying a Great Army

The magnitude of the organization that supported the Ottoman campaigns can be appreciated from the fact that the army was self-supporting in food and animal fodder as well as clothing and equipment. When Henry Blount at Philippopolis admired the orderliness of the Grand Vezir's stables for his 5,000 camels,[39] he was glimpsing only part of the great train of beasts needed to convoy thousands of sacks of grain for bread, bales of cloth and boxes of spare weapons, powder and lead;[40] for every 3 camels 1 more was needed to carry their own fodder. Simply to let 100,000 beasts graze at every halt was to destroy the terrain and leave a desert for the march back home: in the eighteenth century, the Russians were to do precisely this. The planning was based on routine. A system built up over the generations worked admirably along the straight roads towards Vienna or Wallachia, or to Erzerum or Damascus in Asia.

Emergencies could also be dealt with as when Süleyman, who had newly succeeded his father Selim I and needed to still a potential mutiny among the janissaries by the promise of new victories, set off to conquer Belgrade in 1521. There were 10,000 grain wagons and 3,000 camels[41] carrying ammunition, along with thousands more. The city put up a spirited defence

The Ottoman Armed Forces

and after 3 weeks a further 300 cannon were hauled up the Danube from Istanbul by way of the Black Sea. But it was foresight which won campaigns and here the permanent organization was the strength of the Ottomans, in addition to the fact that their routes largely remained constant. Herds and flocks had to be strong enough to keep up with the army. Luckily for the soldiers, this meant that sheep and goats were in their prime and the three-year-old mutton served was the best available.[42] Cannon and heavier wagons were drawn by water buffalo, as valuable as they are ill-natured; since many were leased,[43] they had to be accounted for as well as carefully groomed.

Towers, Roads and Pontoon Bridges

The army also needed as many as 500 architects, water engineers and others, including masons, miners and ironmasters, supported by a company of 250 infantrymen with tools. They maintained and even built bridges, although usually these were made up of pontoons. They rebuilt any fortresses that they themselves had damaged during a siege and which were now required to defend a conquered district. They also converted churches into mosques: this meant not only simple carpentry, replacing altars with mihrab niches and pulpits with lofty *mimbers*, but also the skilled erection of temporary wooden minarets, reusing much of the existing Christian furniture. Ferhat Pasha's expedition to Persia in the sixteenth century was accompanied by 400 master carpenters under the future Chief Architect, Davut Agha, resulting in a serious shortage of craftsmen in Istanbul.[44]

The *acemioğlans* were used as labour as a part of their training. Over 24,000 were found employment when not on campaign as a means of keeping them out of trouble. The policy did not always work for some among the 100 sent to labour on the great mosque of Selim II at Edirne were accused of going off on their own enterprises. Damascus, long a centre for craftsmen, used its local janissaries as a labour pool. But there was no question of using soldiers as bricklayers on a campaign except in an emergency. It is easy to see how the seepage of janissaries into trades came about, quite apart from their being spurred on by lack of pay. From there it was but a step to join a guild which, full circle, was required to supply craft contingents—butchers, bakers and candlestick-makers. Out of this intermeshing of interests came the fighting janissary and the tradesman; chameleon-like, their places could change.

The Janissaries

Peacetime Duties

Thus then the janissary at war but he had home duties as well and his officers held posts of civic importance. The colonel of the 56th *orta*, who was the *çardak çorbaçı* (commandant of the Customs House), assisted the *kadı* in charge of the city's food supplies. Such important officers had normally been trained in one of the colleges for cadets but they could all (and occasionally did) rise from the ranks, especially in wartime. The heavy casualties of the reign of Selim I made promotion more common than at other periods.

The *agha* of the janissaries was as powerful as any pasha and held his own *divan* in the palace below the Süleymaniye. Indeed, during the revolt of disbanded soldiers and pillaged villagers in Anatolia in 1632, the *agha* came third in order of precedence. As the chief Agha of the Stirrup, his place next to the sultan whenever he rode made him closer to his master than any other court official. It was a post which combined with his controllership of the palace kitchens as became the captain-general of a corps founded among cauldrons. This connection between soldiers and kettles derived from the same Central Asian and Mongol antecedents as those of the sacred bow and the horsetails under the influence of shamanism (with its primitive belief in the spirit forces for good and evil), which was so important a factor in dervish movements like the Bektaşis. It was the field kitchen from which the corps took its titles and emblems and not the pastry ovens of Istanbul. Nor did anyone find these emblems funny when mutinies were announced by the resounding, bowel-twisting boom of overturned tureens.

Some among the *aghas* became strong, if stubborn, Grand Vezirs and most could hope to be at least *kapudan paşa* or *beylerbey* of the Balkans apart from those who revolted and usurped the office. But in the sixteenth century the *agha* was increasingly appointed from among officers of the palace who had been trained as pages. Such men had already held other less important offices and might go on to become Vezirs of the Dome and eventually reach the highest office of all. An *agha* who could not control his unruly soldiers, or was defeated or disgraced for some other reason, would be fortunate to live to receive the governorship of a minor Aegean island as a disguise for banishment.

Each *orta* carried the name of its palace duty quite apart from that of fighting. The 64th was responsible for the hunting dogs[45] and the 69th for the greyhounds and falcons, while the 71st looked after the bearhounds. The specialist skill of the 54th *orta* was archery; they later trained men in

The Ottoman Armed Forces

musketry as well. Their commanding officer had the privilege of wearing a royal style of turban. (It was a great honour because when the sultan's turban was carried in procession before him, the janissaries saluted it with more reverence than the man who rode behind.) Such privileges were jealously guarded as part of the grand mystique of the corps. The 82nd *orta* had the right to camp beside the tents of the regimental *imams* although their renown rested on their skill as crossbowmen, who also manned the ballistas and catapults. At one time they were commanded by the greatest of Ottoman architects, Sinan Agha. Sinan was far prouder of being a janissary, and of his career from recruit through the ranks to an officer and then colonel in the royal guards, than he was of fifty years' service as Architect of the Empire. The 17th *orta* pitched their tents next to that of their sultan and linked hands to form a chain when he proceeded to and fro. The officers of the first five *ortas* were appointed to command the fortresses while the *solaks* of the bodyguard were always drawn from the 60th, 61st, 62nd and 63rd *ortas*. They necessarily camped near their sultan.

Orthodox *imams* had originally been appointed to the 84th *orta* but their influence died when eight Bektaşi dervishes were allowed to enter the corps, where they were allotted to the 99th *orta* and their senior *baba* (spiritual master) was honoured as a colonel. Although they were overly fond of preaching that martyrs went to paradise, they remained popular and were protected by the janissaries until 1826.

Drink and the Devil

Sufi dreams were not a duty, nor was drinking, but the tavern was as much a part of the janissaries' life as it was of that of Western soldiers. In the wine shops of Galata, or when they were off duty in the outer suburbs of Edirne, the janissaries enjoyed the comedy of the shadow puppets, Karagöz and his mates, and also the popular theatre. This was called the Meydan Oyunu (Theatre of the Square) since the players could act in the middle of any open ground or meadow. Significantly, one unit of the corps was called the *meydan orta*. The puppeteers were too wise to include janissary escapades in a repertory which was full of political and social comment, however elliptical. The only known theatrical reference to the corps was a piece based on an actual incident typical of their lawlessness at the end of the sixteenth century: drunken janissaries broke into a *hamam* for women with scandalous consequences which led to their trial before a *kadı*, not their own court. These intruders were not called janissaries for long. Tavern and café were where the janissary was kept aware of the multitude beneath the obedient

The Janissaries

surface of autocracy. But the members of the corps frequented taverns in order to drink and also to enjoy the notorious boys who danced dressed up as girls and made mischievous use of their veils so that they seemed equally attractive as women. It was an attraction which applied to a number of *acemioğlans*, some of whom by the eighteenth century were made to wear veils by their protectors.[46]

By the eighteenth century, the janissaries were ruffianly everywhere, and not just in taverns, because their rules had been increasingly relaxed.[47] Tradesmen skilled in such tasks as the repair of uniforms and equipment had once been forced to renounce their guild and join an *orta*: now the reverse was the case and the janissaries joined the guild. Whereas formerly they had been forbidden to admit their sons into the corps, now they did precisely that. The situation was made worse because serving soldiers who might still be on the active list could now marry: previously, they would have been pensioners for at least twenty years before their boy was enrolled. The only virtue in the midst of this decadence was the growth of a clear distinction between the artisans (who served only for the privileges) and a core of fighting janissaries (who were often brigandly but at least could and would fight for their lives). Other units also misbehaved for Galland reports great uproar due to *seferlis* (recruits) demanding money from Christians.

Policemen and Night Watchmen

However much some citizens might hate them and dread their bullying and thieving, the janissaries did maintain order in the city. In the campaign season, these police duties were taken over by the *acemioğlans*, under the Grand Vezir's deputy who was left behind as chief of police. It was the rule that senior officers should ride through the least savoury quarters of the city at night so as to impress on the local gangs and vagabonds that the sultan's rule ran throughout. (As we shall see in Chapter 10, the *agha* performed this duty for the last time on the eve of the massacre of 1826.) In this, Istanbul had an advantage over other Islamic and European cities for the janissaries were a uniformed presence carrying authority and when they patrolled the streets at night no one dared challenge them. In Syrian cities, by contrast, law and order were left to the *ulema,* who were unable to control the mob or the bands of youths who set up what amounted to a republic. Because of the janissaries' police duties, an ambivalent relationship had to develop between the soldiers and the judicial class in spite of their fundamental hatred of each other.

Janissaries were also responsible for enforcing order and fair trading in the markets and bazaars, with the right to administer summary chastisement for crooked dealing or false measures. They also guarded the city gates and manned the fortresses and prisons. The janissary, therefore, was above the law himself, unless he raped Venuses in their baths, and not just because of his privileged position as a member of the slave family of the sultan. He embodied civil authority but, although he could only be punished by his own officers, he could be beaten on the buttocks for a serious crime—unlike the *sipahis,* who could only be bastinadoed on the feet. The janissaries could also be sentenced to short terms of imprisonment in Rumeli Hısar (Rumeli Castle) half-way down the Bosphorus. For longer terms, they were sent to the grim fortress at the bleak entry to the Black Sea, where cold winds blew while the sun shone on the Sweet Waters of Asia opposite Rumeli Hısar. For a great crime they could be sentenced to death. If so, the man was first degraded and then expelled from the corps before being strangled after dark; his corpse was flung into the sea.

Although the patrolling of highways and the policing of provincial towns became the duty of local janissaries (who had little but their name in common with the true janissaries of the capital), these provincial officers were an extension of the concept of soldiers as armed and uniformed police who protected all sections of the populace. One of the weaknesses of this concept lay in the soldier's love of taverns where he could drink and gamble into the night when the house should have been shut and barred. The janissaries also had a liking for the libidinous dancing of boys and youths in such haunts and were prepared to sprinkle them with silver, if not shower them with gold like their sultan.

The police duties of the corps extended beyond the gates of the city and at times it is difficult to differentiate between a local and a metropolitan janissary on some official journey which extended into a foreign country.[48] Thus in 1674 Richard Chandler,[49] who was protected by a *firman* obtained by the English ambassador ordering all officials to help him, needed a janissary to escort him. Yet in Gülhısar the governor had Chandler and Mustafa (his janissary) locked up in a verminous hall. To make matters worse, the unfortunate Mustafa had been involved in a mutiny at Candia and had threatened to depose this self-same officer. Fortunately he was not recognized, although he was trembling all over, and the governor granted Chandler his freedom. Later poor Mustafa was in worse trouble at Denizli, where Chandler remarked on the ferocious and hostile bearing of some Turks and heard of robber bands and murderers lurking across the plain. They were advised where to camp by a blackguardly fellow who returned with armed followers and pryed into their baggage. When the *agha* was approached for protection, Mustafa had to bear gifts of coffee, sugar and money which the local lord found insufficient. The unhappy warrior was thrown into jail but was eventually allowed to return to Chandler, who was now lodged among the fleas of another disagreeable *han* (inn). Without weapons, terrified and dejected, Mustafa reported that they were among robbers and rebels and that the *agha* was determined to cut them to pieces and steal their baggage. But he was no coward for he was prevailed on to return with more money and was able to present the *firman* which the *agha* had previously haughtily refused to read. Now, unexpectedly, on finding that Chandler was going under the sultan's protection to Istanbul, where he would report to the English embassy, it was the *agha*'s turn to take fright. Fearing that a complaint would be lodged, he returned the bribes and declared himself responsible for their safe journey.

In 1634 Henry Blount was able to engage a janissary in Venice who procured him rations, coach and horses and a passage as far as Istanbul. They crossed the Adriatic together in a Venetian galley with only Turks and Jews for companions. Blount was pleased with the lodging he obtained in the *kervansarays* (caravanserais) on the road and also with the exquisite *hamams*. Previously, in 1589, the Genoese agent Lord Harry Cavendish was far less fortunate for, apart from being attacked with whips, his lodgings included a church porch and a hen-roost besides a smithy at Edirne, a peasant's cart, a haystack, and on several occasions the earth floor of a peasant's croft. All and each of these he preferred to a smelly *kervansaray*.

Fortresses and Cannonades

The Ottomans' campaigns into Europe were based on the command of a string of fortresses which provided essential support for an army operating three months' march away from its home base. But in the hands of the enemy, a castle such as Szeged (Szigeth) held up Süleyman in 1566 and he eventually died there, although his troops outnumbered those of the Emperor Maximilian many times. Thus did Monte Cassino frustrate Field Marshal Alexander's army during the Second World War. The fortress was effectively the frontier, whether a castle on its own or the citadel of a town. Sometimes a village grew up around a castle, which then became a citadel.[50] But the Ottomans were well aware of the weakness of the stone walls of Istanbul and fortress after fortress in the Balkans and elsewhere were to be reduced by them or by explosives.[51] The principle was as effective as it was monotonous: by hurling missiles from catapults or various sizes of stone balls from cannon, and by sapping operations using quantities of gunpowder, walls and towers were made to collapse into moats, effecting breach and bridge at the same time. Besides the art of counter-mining, a new system of trench warfare also developed.

At the end of the fourteenth century, Timur had taken Damascus without guns. He heated the strong walls with fire and then rapidly cooled them with vinegar so that they could easily be cracked with hammers. Cannon-balls were a free-flying development of the battering-ram of which Timur's sledge-hammers were the ultimate refinement. After 1500 no citadel could expect to last long if exposed to the full force of the sultan's batteries. City walls might withstand a siege, however, if the citizens resolutely repaired damage, a task which was impossible for a garrison in addition to their manning of walls and breaches.[52] None the less, the Ottomans not only repaired and rebuilt the strongholds which they demolished; they designed exemplary fortresses of their own.[53]

The most famous is Rumeli Hısar, built in three months during the summer before Constantinople was taken, opposite the castle which Yıldırım Bayezit had built and manned on the Asian shore. The pair of castles with their guns had but to sink one ship to prove that they controlled the straits of the Bosphorus. In principle, Rumeli Hısar was a group of formidably strong independent towers which used up extravagant quantities of stone bonded by cross shafts of marble columns. These were linked by thick curtain walls and further fortified by a barbican which extended beneath a gun platform to the water gate. The towers, too, could mount small cannon. Except on the sea side, they cap the hill crests of the undulating ground so that, elegantly but also strategically, the castle follows the rise and fall of the terrain. The towers have lost their tile caps (copied from the Galata Tower) whose eaves sheltered the marksmen in their high galleries: except that there never were marksmen for only film actors have ever attacked the castle. The cold stone towers were for use as prisons while the garrison's quarters were built of wood within the elliptical defences. It is ironic that the success of Mehmet II's heavy guns in breaching the walls of Constantinople the following May (1453) was to foredoom such castles and end an era so that the grandest was, indeed, the last. It could easily shelter 400 men but was manned by far fewer, who were jailers rather than soldiers.

The great number of frontier castles and forts besides those of the interior provinces, especially along strategic highways, means that there was probably only a nucleus of janissaries in a garrison which was largely made up of local troops. Nor would there have been many men in the two fortresses at the Black Sea mouth of the Bosphorus either; but the two

The Janissaries

formidable strongholds at Çanakkale and Gallipoli were vitally important as the main defence against the Venetian fleet. They were built of astonishingly solid masonry somewhat in the manner of Henry VIII's fortresses on the south coast of England. In the eighteenth century they were transformed by the Hungarian engineer, the Baron de Tott, who was appalled at their state of decay and the rusty guns rotting on their wooden sleepers. Luckily, no one had any idea that these great achievements of Mehmet II were mere bluff and that the Sea of Marmara was wide open to any enemy which sailed in from the Aegean.[54] Once he had strengthened and enlarged the two fortresses, Tott mounted batteries of guns on walls many metres thick—a considerable garrison of gunners was needed to fire and maintain them.[55]

Mehmet II also built Yedikule (the Castle of the Seven Towers), which incorporated the Golden Gate through which the Byzantine emperors rode to be crowned at Hebdomon past the stinking tanneries which occupy the same locality to this day. This was one reason why the neighbourhood had a bad reputation and harboured the collectors of dog dung which is employed in tanning and fetches a good price along with rotten eggs. The etoilated master plan of the castle may have pre-dated similar constructed, if not planned, examples in Italy but can be misread: the castle was not seriously directed against an attack from the Balkans but from mobs within the city. It served as a treasury which received the revenues of the mosques and also as a prison. In the Ottoman manner, the garrison lived in wooden houses and barracks inside the walls while the captives, ambassadors included, lodged in the cold stone towers. This was not always true, however, for there is evidence that some enjoyed comparative comfort in one of the wooden houses if they were on good terms with the commander—or could afford the rent.

Other castles were taken over by the Ottomans. Examples include the venerable Armenian castle at Bakras which commanded the road to Iskenderun—Süleyman refurbished it in 1551 when he gave the village a mosque and a *han*. At Payas, which controls a pass through the Amanus mountains, Selim II built a lavishly equipped *kervansaray* of monumental size and at the same time constructed a second utilitarian castle in the form of a towered rectangle (the barracks within were rebuilt of brick in the nineteenth century) in addition to an old castle by the water. In the seventeenth century the Kurdish castle at Hoşap was taken over as the gateway to the wild Hakkari mountains, more to keep the men of the mountains out than as a defence against the Persians or their allies. Farther south there were fortified *kervansarays* or *ribats* (monasteries) to defend,

The Ottoman Armed Forces

and the forts of the Hadramaut, but these were likely to be manned by local janissaries. In the Balkans, Giurgiu in what is now Romania was newly built in 1550, but Montecastro in Moldavia was an old stronghold which the janissaries merely embellished with their favourite Iznik tiles. Until altered by the Russians, the citadel of Bender was an excellent example of a stronghold built by the Ottomans on their far frontiers. It dated from 1538 but was built on older foundations. All these castles were raised on heights which made them difficult of approach and so less vulnerable to artillery and conventional assault.

The *ribats* were garrisoned with the minimal number of troops: some ten might be fortress soldiers, possibly janissaries, but the others were married musketeers who were presumably locally recruited and who remained for a number of years.[56] In Mehmet II's time a castle or a citadel was commanded by a *dizdar* (commandant) with a *kahya* (steward) under him, and *bölükbaşıs* (sergeants). The first drew a gold piece every two days, the *kahya* one every four, the *bölükbaşıs* one every eight, and ordinary soldiers one every ten days. The money was for their maintenance for they were not allowed to resort to the stores kept inside the citadel unless they were besieged. It was a policy which must have made the garrison well aware of local economic problems.

Duties included two men on guard at the gate and a proper watch kept from a tower for each period of twenty-four hours. Significantly, no wine was permitted and this was true of the army in the field. Christians were exempt from this rule, however, and could do what they pleased. Unlike European armies, including those of Prince Eugene of Savoy who were encouraged to get drunk in order to quell the hideous clamour of an Ottoman attack, the armies of the sultan fought with bellies fired solely by the spirit of the Faith. Religious observance was clearly lax, however, and some senior officers appear to have overlooked it altogether.

A fifteenth-century frontier garrison might consist of fifty janissaries and some thirty other troops or auxiliaries, but these numbers clearly varied and by the seventeenth century garrisons were often only half-strength. None the less, even this strength was sufficient to hold the citadel of Zvecaj for eight weeks (the walls were repaired day and night as they crumbled) against the king of Hungary himself. The strength of such a fortress system was twofold. It defended the frontiers against the enemy long enough for the sultan to bring his forces to the scene and frustrate an invasion: but it also defended a province against its governor because garrisons were not under his command and they could therefore keep him under surveillance.

The Janissaries

The Island Fortress at the Iron Gates

The strongest fortress on the Danube was built by the Habsburgs in 1689–90 on an island site near the Iron Gates. Ada Kale (Castle Island) was the key to the upper river. In 1690 it fell into Ottoman hands, along with the shore forts, but was little altered except possibly for the tunnel which connected the island and the shore defences. The Imperial troops had troubled to bring quantities of stone to this wooded region where even the blockhouses tended to be built of timber. For the Ottomans, Ada Kale was a great prize both as an outpost and as support for their Danube fleet. It could be used as a rallying point for raiding parties which ruffled the calm of Habsburg lands. From the historical point of view this fortress, now drowned by yet another dam, is important because its inventory—drawn up in the early eighteenth century—has been preserved. With its meticulous detail, it is proof that the Ottomans continued to plan carefully in the evening of their power and it reveals exactly how well equipped (in theory) their fortresses were.

Fixtures such as 51 reinforced doors, iron girders, pulleys and chains, the 7 iron spikes of the fortress gate, hinges, springs, spigots, screws, grilles and staircase were all listed. All the household utensils were accounted for, including 32 cauldrons and 14 saucepans, 51 water skins, 3 iron cupboards, knives, kettles, leather table covers and 100 packing needles. There were also 106 mattresses. The artillery included 94 bronze cannon and miscellaneous guns besides 6 burst iron cannon, 142 rammers, ladles, measures, powder-horns and camp needles. Gun carriages and wagons were listed with their spare parts along with 3,311 infidel muskets, including some with bayonets, and 11 cracked specimens. There were sabres, daggers, pikestaffs and lance heads besides 3,173 bombshells, 26,018 hand-grenades, 17,813 cannon-balls, boxes of bullets and grapeshot, gunpowder, quires of cartridge paper and 100 charged rockets. There were also lead moulds for making bullets, indicating a standardization of the bore of muskets. Finally came barometers, clocks, quadrants, adzes, gouges, hammers, anvils, stone masons' tools with 6,531 shovels for the sappers and equipment for gardening and fishing, leading on to surgeons' tools and naval stores besides 17 tents, tarpaulins, ropes of all kinds and 5,850 hemp bags and sacks.

Besides the tunnel, the castle was linked to the mainland by a pontoon bridge and there were pumps against flooding. The gardens of this oasis grew cherries, plums, peaches, apples, pears, various nuts, berries, 19 varieties of grape and several kinds of vegetable besides corn, rye and wheat. Sturgeon were plentiful. This was a luxurious posting compared to many, except in winter or in wartime. The number of mattresses would suggest a garrison of some 100 men while the mountains of other equipment were likely to be held in reserve for the arrival of the army on campaign. The thousands of shovels clearly awaited a division of sappers.

Janissaries were also posted to the citadels of provincial capitals in order to reinforce the authority of the local governor. In 1669 an *orta* of 400 janissaries was sent from Istanbul to Damascus to put down the disorderly local janissaries and *sipahis* among others. They accomplished the task without difficulty since the local troops were undisciplined and bad marksmen, and clearly more interested in trade. The *orta* remained to keep the city in order until they were corrupted in their turn and had to be expelled.

Frontier service was not pleasant. A series of letters from the end of the sixteenth century gives an insight into the troubles on the Hungarian border at a time when Ottoman power was weakening. The Ottoman governor repeatedly complains of breaches of the treaty of 1568 and implies that skirmishes, raids and kidnappings were daily events. The Emperor Maximilian II was required to send an annual tribute of money, cups and goblets to the governor of Estergom and to the *beylerbey*, Ferhat Pasha, who received rifles and watches as well. More modest presents (including watches) were sent to the *agha* of the janissaries while substantial sums of money were reserved for the sultan and his ministers. Since half the population of Hungary had been killed or enslaved, the country was in ruins and the pasha of Buda clearly had a hard task because the Ottomans only held small enclaves of the subjected provinces. The fief-holders were attacked and kidnapped while harvesting or even when visiting a country fair. They were unable to collect their rents, and messengers from the governor could not reach the fortresses in outlying districts in order to send troops to their assistance. The position was not helped when, from 1590 onwards, the governors of Buda were frequently changed and sometimes almost took turn and turn about. The following year, complaints flowed from both sides and clearly neither could control their men. The Archduke Ernest of Austria was said to keep captive generals in dungeons without water, food or heat and to have stopped prisoners returning home, in order to collect their ransoms, and as hostages. Ferhat Pasha had even been sent a handful of teeth extracted from the jaws of some unlucky officers. The Hungarians were further accused of courting illegal duels and had even organized a tournament, which was 'inexcusable', according to the letter. Some villagers had been threatened with impaling—that old Balkan custom taken over by the Ottomans—if they paid their taxes to the local landowners. Above all, Istanbul was impatient for a tribute which never came.

The Janissaries

The Hungarians complained equally bitterly. The tribute had not come because some janissaries and their officers had plotted to ambush the caravan, although this was indignantly denied: the janissaries had merely gathered to be reviewed by their new *agha*. But when the Archduke Ernest complained of boats being destroyed, Ferhat Pasha put several officers in prison although they protested their innocence. There was a bloody affray (with peasants busy stealing lumber) in which the Ottomans said 12 were killed but the archduke put the number at 130. It was difficult to harvest the crops that year although some millers were released in exchange for 4 Turks. Complaints about sacked villages were promised investigation: if the sultan's troops were guilty they would be punished unless they were simply extracting unpaid taxes for the *sipahis*, who had no other means of support. One detects a note of compromise on both sides but Ottoman officers now not only lost their teeth but also ears, noses and fingers—according to another Habsburg archduke, this was merely to frustrate their efforts to escape.

None the less, *beys* were dismissed for their misdeeds while middle men behaved according to their own rules, which were scarcely honest. Three merchants made off with a fortune mulcted from Jews and Muslims and found sanctuary on Hungarian territory. They were not extradited but what happened to their booty is unclear. While admitting that a large force of Ottomans had besieged a Hungarian fortress, the pasha pointed out that they did not come under his command and that the complaint should be sent to Istanbul. If three village headsmen had been executed at his command it was because they had failed to report the presence of Hungarian troops in their districts. And, indeed, Hungarian troops had made illegal attacks on some Ottoman positions.

Running throughout the pasha's letters is a theme of taxes and tribute withheld and of the danger to any Ottoman soldier who left the protection of a fortress. The murder of Ferhat Pasha led to the appointment of a more militant governor who deliberately failed to restrain the pasha of Bosnia when he went off on an illegal campaign. However, the pasha was drowned in June 1593 when crossing a disintegrating bridge symbolic of declining Ottoman standards. A son of the late Grand Vezir Rüstem Pasha was also lost. The Imperial envoy failed to mask his derision, which infuriated the pasha of Buda: Istanbul was reported to be in uproar. Although late in the season, the Grand Vezir Sinan Pasha himself mobilized and led an army to Buda. There were preparations for war but these were delayed by a promise to send a gift of flowers when it was the season for transplanting them. It is at this point in the letters that, quite exceptionally, a reference is made to the suffering of the common people.

Against such a background of events, one can understand that the inducement of extra pay was essential if a janissary were to be kept at his post: confined to a fortress with the relief of an occasional raid, an illegal tournament and a duel or two.

Fire and Mutiny

In addition to their police duties, one of the janissaries' most important tasks was fire-fighting for which they were specially trained and equipped with various appliances. These tasks were related since arson was frequent in Istanbul and the difference between it and rubbish fires, often self-combustible and common in all Islamic cities, was hard to define. In a city made of wood, warmed by braziers and with all too many crowded streets and alleyways, fire was a constant threat of which the citizens were well aware. However alert they might have been, a fire at night could gain a hold which proved impossible to break, especially in a high wind where tearing down houses in the path of the flames did not create a large enough gap. When a fire arose it was quickly spotted from the Galata Tower or the Stamboul fire tower at Bayezit Meydan beside the Eski Saray. Both were manned by a janissary watch who sounded the alarm by the beating of drums while local night-watchmen beat the pavements with iron-shod staves. The Grand Vezir and the *agha* of the janissaries were in duty bound to oversee the fire-fighters and the sultan himself assisted in person if the conflagration proved to be of importance.

In 1489 the Chief Vezir was killed when a church near the Hippodrome, which had been converted into a powder magazine, was struck by lightning on a dramatic night when a tempest fought with the flames. The explosions at the magazine hurled stones far and wide and demolished much else besides the first minister. Very soon after this disaster, in 1501, a real fire (in the sense that it arose from a spark in a wooden house) broke out on a similarly thunderous night: on this occasion the powder magazine at Galata was either hit by lightning or ignited by the flames or the heat of neighbouring buildings. The Chief Vezir Mesih Pasha and Karagöz ('Black Eyes') Pasha, the *agha* of the janissaries, were being rowed across the Golden Horn by a platoon of janissaries when the magazine exploded. The boat was hit and both dignitaries died from their wounds within a few days.[58]

It was on 2 July 1539 that the first truly extensive fire struck the city. It began in a shop that sold pitch near the Baba Cafer prison. No one

The Janissaries

concerned themselves with the hapless convicts, who all perished in the flames but the Grand Vezir, the immensely wealthy Ayas Pasha, struggled against all odds from morning until night assisted by all the *vezirs* and every janissary who could be found. The death roll was considerable and whole neighbourhoods of Istanbul were devastated while Ayas Pasha was to die of his injuries.

Fires were used by the janissaries as political weapons. Thus in 1554, when on campaign in Asia and in their quarters at Amasya, the janissaries manifested their hatred for Rüstem Pasha by setting the innocent town alight and prevented anyone from extinguishing the flames. In 1569, when a great fire in the Jewish quarter of Istanbul burnt for a day and a night, the redoubtable Sokollu Mehmet Pasha had the greatest difficulty in fighting the flames because the janissaries' *agha* was ill and no one else had the strength of will to make them work or stop looting the houses in the path of the conflagration. By this time they expected to be rewarded handsomely and not just promoted for valour. The deaths of so many pashas demonstrates the danger of their task, if performed with zeal. More was to be gained by neglecting fire-fighting for theft and eventually janissaries deliberately started fires in order to rob the helpless householders and shopkeepers. In 1588 the quarter from the Bedesten to the Horn burnt while the janissaries looted in order to demonstrate their hostility to the government of Murat III; two other areas were burnt for the same reason in 1590. In July 1591 a genuine fire broke out at Tophane near the gun foundry below Pera but when the fire force was being rowed across the Bosphorus they saw that the flames had been brought under control by the gunners. Disappointed of their bonuses, they determined to take the opportunity to be revenged on Divanı İbrahim Pasha, governor of Dıyarbekir, whom they passionately hated because he had struck and killed an insolent comrade. They set off for his *konak* (villa) near the Şehzade mosque and the Eski Odalar and set it alight, causing widespread damage to their own neighbourhood. Yet only the next year, when a fire broke out near Haghia Sophia, they worked hard and it was quickly confined and extinguished.

In September 1633 a huge fire took revenge on the janissaries for it not only consumed one fifth of the city but gutted the Eski Odalar. When the homeless sought refuge in the coffee shops, Murat IV closed them for fear of subversive subjects plotting against his government.[59] Seven years later, on a hot August evening, the brutal Kara Mustafa Pasha hastened with pumps when mutton fat threatened disaster. As the boat with the Grand Vezir approached, the factory exploded and marred the pasha's good looks for life—perhaps it was then that he became a great drunkard.

The Ottoman Armed Forces

In 1668 we find the janissaries lazy, if not cowardly, expending their courage intimidating or molesting the inhabitants while fires spread through the poorer quarters by the Horn. But in 1718 the conflagration was truly intense: it destroyed many palaces of the *vezirs* and also the rebuilt Eski Odalar and those of the *acemioğlans* besides threatening the Şehzade complex across the way. This fire precipitated reforms and in 1721, when a fire broke out near the mosque of Selim I, the Grand Vezir Ibrahim Pasha arrived with 150 trained janissaries manning new fire-pumps invented by a Frenchman named Davut (David). These sent water jets as high as minarets into the air and quickly quenched the flames. In August the pumps were in action again with equal success when a fire in the slums of Balat was brought rapidly under control—but only after the janissaries had been promised rewards for diligence and the terrified poor had been calmed.

The next year some foolhardy wretches, in a mood of predictable zenophobia, burnt down the houses of some of the staff of the Persian ambassador with whom they were on bad terms. This nationalism might have hoisted them on their own petards but for the timely arrival of the Frenchman's pumps. The Baron de Tott, writing in the 1750s, reports on the frequency of the dreadful fires. He records one which crackled along the shores of the Golden Horn and then spread up beside the park walls of Topkapısaray, being clearly visible from the Maison de France at Pera: it destroyed the palace of the Grand Vezir while melting the lead of the dome of Haghia Sophia and sending it bubbling down its gutters. The sultan was there in person and so, Tott alleges, was an entire regiment of janissaries who were busy pulling down houses. The troops were encircled by the flames and perished. Moreover, the rebuilding of these houses was not complete before a second fire took hold. The efforts of Osman III (1754–7) to widen the streets were frustrated as always by rapacious landlords, many of whom represented religious foundations. Tott states that the sultan always went to fires but that theft incited incendiaries while waggish janissaries amused themselves by turning their hoses on the crowds.

The continual outbreaks of fires in the eighteenth century were usually related to political unrest, especially after 1769 when a demoralized army seemed incapable of protecting the empire from the Russians. The great fire of 1782 brought the sultan in haste from his palace down the Bosphorus at Beşiktaş to join his ministers who were fighting a losing battle and driven from one headquarters to another. This fire also damaged both sets of janissary barracks, partly because they were denuded of their garrisons who may or may not have been out fighting the conflagration. The great fire of 1808 will be discussed in relation to the revolution of that year (Chapter 9).

The Janissaries

Fires were connected with janissary mutinies and political ambitions, a recurrent theme in Ottoman history. The unruliness that disgraced the corps in the seventeenth and eighteenth centuries was not always due to a specific injustice but could arise from crude high spirits. If the men sometimes had an aim, their brutality was frequently purposeless even if the fracas were symbolic of a deeper and more lasting malaise. Sometimes, as in 1651, malicious trouble led to a positive revolt—in this instance, in support of the guilds as institutions and the right of janissaries to belong to them. On the other hand, the mindless destruction of the Observatory at Cıhangir, set up by Sokollu Mehmet Pasha, which killed the development of science in the empire, was due to deliberate incitement by reactionary members of the *ulema* who exploited the latent pyromania of the corps.

Cavendish recorded the troubled state of the realm at the time of his visit in 1589. He stated that, about two months before his arrival, Istanbul had been burnt by the unruly janissaries, aggrieved at two of the sultan's favourites, and angry at having to pay a new subsidy and to accept an *agha* appointed by the Grand Signor. They assembled at the gate of the *saray* and demanded the heads of the three men; when these were refused them by Murat III, they fell to burning and despoiling many areas of the city. They sent word to their master that they would burn his house too and that they would fetch his son out of Asia and make him a sultan. Seeing that no gifts or persuasion would serve, Murat was obliged to sacrifice his favourites: they were tied to the tails of horses and paraded through the streets, brutally manhandled and beheaded. Then the janissaries departed, giving the people leave to put out the fires themselves. Cavendish reported the loss of 48,000 houses in the heart of the city.

From Bad to Worse

In 1717 Lady Mary Wortley Montagu arrived in Belgrade with her husband, the new English ambassador, and found it occupied by numerous janissaries commanded by a pasha or, in truth, a pasha commanded by the janissaries. His predecessor had been murdered by them and the citizens, because he had forbidden their ravaging the German frontiers, which mildness towards the traditional foe they took for treason. He was sent off to Edirne where the sultan feared to save him although he had been following the policy of the government. The janissaries dragged him before the *kadı* and the *şeyhülislam* and mutinously demanded to know why the infidel should be protected and—theme song of janissary complaints—why they should be squeezed of their money. The pasha complained of being asked too many questions at once but had only one life which had to answer for all. Before judgment could be given, scimitars promptly sliced him to bits. So the new pasha was afraid to do else but applaud the rebels.

Not surprisingly, Lady Mary and her husband were eager to depart but had to await orders while a whole company of janissaries was mustered to guard them. They eventually proceeded to Edirne, where they saw how the Ottoman Empire in its decline had lost its traditional benevolence towards its subject peoples. The Serbian woods were full of thieves prepared to attack fifty soldiers if needs be.

The English travellers realized why so many janissaries showed neither mercy nor pity but killed all the poultry and sheep that they could find; nor did the owners dare claim recompense for fear of being beaten. New-born lambs, geese, turkeys, all were massacred. It was worse when the pasha travelled because he extracted teeth money or laudatory gifts for the honour of his devouring all the food that a village could provide. At this date government was entirely in the hands of the army, and the sultan—Ahmet III—was as much a slave as any. He trembled at a janissary's frown. So much then for the Scowl of Majesty. When previously Mehmet IV fled the mob of Istanbul, that sultry city, for the fresh air of Thrace he unwittingly brought disorder with him and, losing favour with his people, gained nothing in its place. Nor did they. The city was overcrowded with humanity and vermin and while the officers escaped to their tents beside the river their men were billeted on the citizens. In February 1672 a hapless baker was killed with one blow because he refused to accept the low-grade coins given a janissary by his sovereign.

The decline of the janissary corps began before the death of Süleyman in 1566 and was not entirely due, as has been claimed, to the enrolment of lower-class Muslims (although neither Arabs nor gypsies) instead of children of the levy. Nor was it solely caused by the new relationship with the guilds or by the insidious influence of the Bektaşi dervishes who were so intimately related to the common people. The janissaries had gone on the rampage before. They had always mutinied when forced to fight too long and they had always been obsessed with money. They also drank and it was they who at the beginning of the sixteenth century forced Bayezit II to reopen the wine shops. When the strong-handed Murat IV forbade the use of tobacco he hanged some janissaries with their pipes in their mouths to set an example, but like Selim I he was an exceptional sultan. It was the janissaries in the seventeenth century who prevented the great Mehmet Köprülü from disbanding the dervish orders. In Syria and elsewhere local janissaries were equally violent and, although related only in name,

The Janissaries

aspirations and guild connections to the metropolitan corps, they were just as rapacious. The brazen ruffians had close connections with the mobs of young men common to the lower orders of all Muslim and Western towns, reflecting the janissaries' latent affinity with the proletariat of Istanbul.

Service at Sea

The lack of a navy prior to the reign of Bayezit II had troubled successive Ottoman governments. When Yıldırım Bayezit could not prevent the Emperor Sigismund (whom he had just defeated at Nicopolis in 1396) sailing through the Sea of Marmara, he insulted him by parading the grandees, whom he was holding for ransom, in tatters on the sands at Gallipoli. Mehmet II employed craftsmen, whom he had conquered, in building ships and even manning them; he was eventually able to put to sea a strong enough fleet to land troops on the islands and even the heel of Italy at Otranto. He decisively put down Venetian piracy in 1468 with a fleet of 300 but most of these boats were small and could not have faced a serious naval force.[60] The piracy, moreover, recurred.

It was Bayezit II who replaced light craft with heavier ships modelled on Venetian and Genoese galleys. In 1515, however, his son, Selim I, was nearly captured by pirates from Rhodes—the Christian Knights—when his entourage was killed about him on the coast road to Salonika.[61] Paramountcy of the seas was to come with the enlistment of the corsairs of the Barbary coast and the recognition of the indomitable Hayrettin Barbaros (known to the West as Barbarossa) as *beylerbey* of North Africa and *kapudan paşa*. This old Greek, who dripped superstition like spray all around him, had mastered the seas of the Mediterranean and exploited the coasts, and was not afraid to venture out of the sight of land unlike most sailors at the time. He made an impressive figure when he attended the Divan in Istanbul with his kaftan of honour, sword, diamonds and personal standard. It was he who organized a navy so powerful that it commanded the western as well as the eastern waters of the Mediterranean. Under his command, there were 100 archers in the dockyard (Tersane) at Galata from which time the Turks renamed the Horn the Tersane Boğazı or Arsenal Strait. Under Murat III as many as 2,364 janissaries and *acemioğlans* were stationed there.

A second important yard was maintained at Gallipoli, of which town the *kapudan paşa* was governor. But Hayrettin Barbaros Pasha was not the founder of the navy: he simply endowed it with his personal prestige, which was so great that even the renowned Genoese admiral Andrea Doria was circumspect when his galleys were in the vicinity. François I of France allied himself sagaciously with the old pirate and in 1543 let the Ottoman fleet winter at Toulon, driving the citizens out and permitting the fitting out of mosques. Extraordinarily, it is said that the inhabitants returned to find their homes unscathed and they were full of praise for the corsairs. None the less, they were relieved of all taxes for ten years, which gives cause for thought; and Maurand, who was there, states that the city was pillaged. Part of the trouble was caused by poor biscuit sent from Villefranche, which led Barbaros to demand corn with which the Ottomans could bake their own good bread. Yet Turkish influence certainly spread as a result of this visit. In addition, a great service rendered by Barbaros to his sultan was his ability to recruit able successors and to train them in war and seamanship.

Galleys and Gallstones

The return voyage from Toulon of the fleet of 80 galleys under Barbaros gives some idea of what janissary service at sea required. The voyage lasted from 23 May until 10 August 1544 and the first part was as full of battles as any land campaign. The galleys had 24 benches with 3 slaves to each oar; each ship carried a complement of 144 working slaves, 60 sailors and 18 officers. Distributed through the fleet were 1,000 *sipahis* and 6,000 janissaries. (In 1587 Hacı Pasha's galleys were to carry 200 soldiers in each, nearly twice the number.) Serving with the fleet was Barbaros' nephew and lieutenant and the *sancak bey* of Gallipoli, Cafer Agha, who spoke and probably was Italian. Besides Maurand and other French officers, the eminent English doctor Alban Hill was aboard.

When they landed at Savona the place was deserted, such was the terror caused by the name of Barbaros. There was no resistance on Elba either. At Orbetello the castle garrison closed the gates, but the castle was taken the next day at the cost of 5 Ottoman lives. The Ottomans carried off 140 men, women and children in chains. At Giglio, guns had to be landed and 30 lives were lost before the fortress was taken and burnt, the notables beheaded and 632 Christian prisoners chained. Dr Hill and the French officers had no sooner applauded this victory than Ischia was laid waste and 2,040 prisoners taken. A spectacular eruption of Vesuvius was followed by a tempest in which a galliot was lost; the fleet had to re-form off the deserted island of Policastro, which was then laid waste in its turn.

Next they met serious resistance at Lipari. Two thousand houses were burnt and Barbaros landed to direct the siege with cannon and his janissaries. It lasted 11 days with the loss of 343 Ottoman lives and the

The Janissaries

expenditure of 2,800 cannon-balls. But 10,000 slaves were taken, the town was sacked and burnt, and the elderly and decrepit were made to strip so as to have their gallstones cut out for these were prized as lucky charms. If they were not already dead, these unlucky pensioners were then killed. Barbaros sailed on to Reggio to bargain over the ransoms of his embarrassingly large stock of prisoners. Then the fleet entered Venetian waters and, since the sultan and the Serenissima were at peace, they paid a friendly visit to Zante to take on supplies before proceeding to Istanbul. They were greeted with salutes and flags but the sultan was absent on a visit to Bursa.

Fleets were often large and carried veritable divisions of soldiers. In 1554 Turgut Reis under Sinan Pasha, brother of Rüstem Pasha, commanded 103 galleys; the following season Piyale Pasha commanded a squadron of 70 vessels. In 1561 Turgut captured the Genoese freebooting Visconte Scipione Cigala who, when ransomed, left his 16-year-old son behind to seek his fortune with the Ottomans. He became a Muslim and rose to the highest offices, including a term as *agha* of the janissaries, as Çigalazade Yusuf Sinan Pasha. His family had long been resident in Messina, where Scipione had commanded a squadron of the king of Spain. When *kapudan paşa*, Sinan Pasha anchored his fleet off the city so that he might pay his respects to his mother and greet other relatives—very much a local boy made good. He was later to command the army in Persia and to be the victor of the highly romantic battle of the torches: this raged for three days and two nights, which were among the most spectacular in military history for it was possible to battle in the dark with fires and torches to differentiate friend from foe.

Another Italian admiral, Kılıç ('Sword') Ali Pasha from Licastella in Calabria, was even more distinguished for in 1571 he brought his squadron out of the débâcle off Lepanto to form the nucleus of a revived fleet. In one season this was launched reborn but the naval lesson of the victory of Don Juan of Austria was not immediately learnt by either side. The days of the galley, which could only advance head-on, firing a restricted number of guns in poop or prow, were gone. The day of the much more manoeuvrable galleon, granted a little wind, and its broadsides had come. (Kılıç Ali Pasha was later to be famous as the captor of Cervantes, who was courteously treated.)

The Ottomans were not always fortunate with their captains. When in 1554 a fleet was launched from Egypt into the Indian Ocean, with the intent of driving the Portuguese out and saving the spice trade and thus defeating the economic crisis, the commanders proved to be of poor calibre, lacking courage and any wisdom in their handling of the inhabitants of captured ports. Their excesses rivalled those of the Duke of Albuquerque, the brilliant but savagely brutal Portuguese viceroy of the Indian Ocean, a distinction that one might imagine difficult to achieve. From far-off Istanbul, it was impossible to control these officers or measure the harm that they might be doing.[62]

The riverine fleet on the Danube was another matter: with the help of a chain of small forts supported from Belgrade, this group of flat-bottomed craft, or palanders, maintained Ottoman supremacy on the waterway from the fifteenth to the eighteenth century. The headquarters were at Rusçuk (Ruse) and were commanded by the *tuna* (Danube) *kapudan*. The fleet had as many as 60 boats, all launched on the Horn. They helped transport horses and supplies for the land armies and the 300 cannon that Süleyman needed before Belgrade. As late as 1690 it was possible, as has previously been discussed, to capture Ada Kale below the Iron Gates due to the skill of Mezzomorto ('Half-Dead') Kara Hüseyn Pasha, who had previously commanded in the Mediterranean. The Novi fortress on the Sava maintained a regular shipyard for this fleet and 100 horse transports were built there in 1538–9. A regulation of 1551 refers to the mobilizing of 70 oarsmen in the Zvornik region. The ships had to be pulled upstream by horsepower because of the strong current. Commercial vessels were shoddily built because they were broken up when they reached the Black Sea and westward commerce had to be transported by road.

Manning the Fleet

Naval commanders were highly esteemed. The office of *kapudan paşa* was at various periods regarded as second only to that of Grand Vezir and the appointment was increasingly given to officers trained at the Enderun Kolej. A Pasha of the Three Lanterns ranked above a Land Pasha of the Three Tails. If many were recruited from the waves and served their cadetships on them, they were janissaries of a kind for they were as much foreign prisoners as the early janissaries had been. As many as 2,000 janissaries from Istanbul were sent to Algiers, where Hayrettin Barbaros had his headquarters; they were to become the ruling caste in North Africa. Algiers impressed visitors as the most orderly of cities under their dictatorship, in spite of a population made up largely of scoundrels and those who served their needs both afloat and ashore.

On the galleys the oarsmen were at first volunteers but the toil, if only for brief periods, was sufficiently unpleasant for their place to be taken by slaves or prisoners. Indicative of the sweat, tears and the insanitary policy

The Janissaries

of chaining the galley slaves to their benches, the presence of a galley could be detected over a kilometre away in the dark by its stench. Galleons and other sailing vessels were manned by free seamen, Greeks or Levantines or freebooting renegades, including English and Scots, whose skills were sold to any purchaser. Eventually a corps of Levents evolved whom Grenville in the eighteenth century called ferocious, debauched animals. There was also an entrepôt of cheap labour in the Bagno, a converted *hamam* which was the great prison of the Tersane. In it were chapels for most Christian denominations and the inmates numbered 4,000 or even more.[63] If life there were not all misery, even pleasures led to sorrow—in March 1672 a Sicilian was beaten to death for stealing the musical instrument of another prisoner.

The *acemioğlans* maintained the fleets at Gallipoli and Istanbul and the janissaries served at sea in order to board a prize—the great inducement to naval service. They also had to be good archers because the arquebus had a range of less than 100 metres while a bowman could pick off enemy officers and crew before the galleys grappled and the enemy was boarded. One lonely Ottoman galley was captured in July 1589, however, carrying a miscellaneous cargo looted from merchant vessels: four horses including a colt, a woman and a boy, and but one janissary who could hardly have formed a boarding party all on his own. Perhaps his comrades were dead. For there is no doubt that janissaries were employed in large numbers on the sultan's galleons which superseded the galleys. When two English ships engaged in contraband were destroyed in 1622, an Ottoman galleon was sunk and 800 janissaries drowned along with 1,000 slaves.

Piracy was rampant in the eighteenth century, with Cretans based at Side on the south coast of Anatolia and other specialists on many offshore islands. There was even a band of Blacks from Africa afloat in 1743. Greek raiders were put down by the French in that year and they defeated some Albanians, who were everyone's worst enemies, in 1765. Piracy, indeed, rebuilt Greek naval traditions and 1,000 resolute ruffians put a garrison of 8,000 janissaries to flight when they attacked Salonika. Fortunately, Russian and Ragusan pirates were also at sea and the rival fleets helped keep each other down. The greatest corsairs of all were the Knights of Rhodes and then of Malta in the sixteenth and seventeenth centuries.

The frequent appointment of a soldier as *kapudan paşa* was for political not naval reasons. He was not chosen because of his seamanship but because of his overall command when a landing was achieved. Most Ottoman campaigns at sea were directed towards landings rather than set-piece battles with an enemy fleet. Foreigners continued to be appointed to sea commands into the nineteenth century, as with Mezzomorto, and foreign models and tactics were carefully copied. In the seventeenth century, when the *kapudan paşa* was no more a sailor than a Chief Architect could build, the main influence at the Tersane was French but an English naval architect, Spurring, and some Swedes were also employed. The dry dock built there between 1703 and 1706 was a copy of the one at Toulon.

Reform: the Navy Leads the Way

Selim III's reforms of the Ottoman navy show what he might have achieved with the land army. Ever since 1718 the *kapudan paşa* had been the personification of corruption. No new developments were introduced in ship-building and navigational skills declined to the point where captains hugged the coasts and feared a squall like masters of a coracle. Because officers and men were responsible for their own rations the decks were fairgrounds of small cookhouses and, just as in the city, outbreaks of fire were inevitable. The wrong shot was ordered for cracked or poorly maintained cannon until, with the total destruction of the fleet at the battle of Çeşme in 1770, the decks were cleared at the admiralty. Hasan Pasha was appointed to create the new fleet; he called in two French architects to build new barracks at the Tersane, organized salaries and training and reduced the impressment of unsuitable riff-raff and scallywags. Conscripts were brought from along the Aegean coasts and these young men were enlisted for life with reasonable prospects of promotion and pensions on retirement. The captain was now responsible for food—this had previously been delivered to the men's homes prior to sailing.[64]

The able Baron de Tott arrived and an English convert to Islam, Kampel Mustafa Agha: together with a French officer, they were able to establish a school which later became the Engineering College. But few officers attended and bribery remained the speediest way to promotion. In 1784 the fleet consisted of 22 ships of the line and 15 frigates, not all of which were seaworthy. In 1791 its defeat in the Black Sea resulted in the dismissal of Hasan Pasha and his replacement by Küçük Hüseyn Pasha. His aide was Işak Bey, an old friend of Selim III. The new admiral was able to enforce the education of officers and insisted that they be appointed to command only those ships in a category with which they were experienced. Receipts for pay and expenses were made obligatory. New sheds were built at the top of the Golden Horn and many provincial dockyards put in order on the Black Sea and Aegean coasts as well as at Silistria on the Danube. Between 1789 and 1798, 45 fighting ships were built, modelled on French lines. In 1796 the *Selimiye* was launched, complete with 122 cannon and manned by 1,200

The Janissaries

men. The Naval College was unostentatiously training soldiers as well as sailors simply because no military training establishment existed any more. In 1804 the Ministry of the Marine was established and has a claim to be the first modern government office founded under Ottoman rule. Equally revolutionary was the opening of a naval medical school in 1806. Finally, the navy was rid of all janissary influence a generation before the 'Auspicious Event' of 1826 (see Chapter 10).

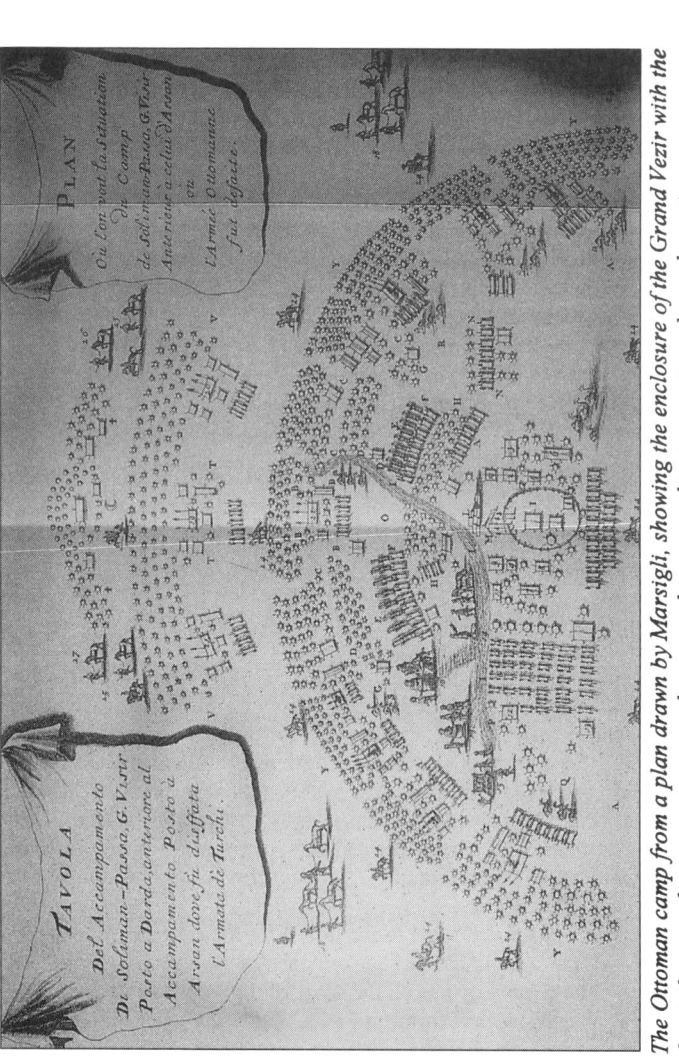

The Ottoman camp from a plan drawn by Marsigli, showing the enclosure of the Grand Vezir with the five tails, guns, baggage wagons, advance and rearguard tents, scouts and camels resting

5
The Victorious Years

Murat II, Master of Men and Mystery

The decline of the janissary corps has been dated to the end of the sixteenth century and associated with the dilution of the Christian levy and the introduction of the sons of Muslims, and even of the *ulema*, into its ranks but this infiltration had begun earlier in the century and was merely made legal in 1582. It is neither fair nor flattering to the native-born recruits to attribute the withering of Ottoman military prowess to them although the royal textbook of the time, *A Mirror for Princes*,[1] libels the Turk as only a Persian could. They are called blunt-witted, ignorant, boastful and turbulent, and devoid of a sense of justice besides being timid in the dark. Fortunately, they were also zealous, open and brave. Under such exceptional leaders as Murat IV, the janissaries continued to fight with distinction from time to time and their behaviour had always been temperamental due to their corporate pride. This matched the *esprit de corps* of Edwardians in Britain towards their old school, regiment and club. The janissaries had mutinied with or without the connivance of their senior officers from early in the days of their official existence.

When Mehmet II had come to the throne for the first time while still a boy in 1444, the jealousy and plotting of rivals led the regent, Çandarlı Halil Pasha, to order a janissary raid on the house of the boy's favourite minister, the Chief White Eunuch, Sabahıttın Pasha. With such an example set, the grumbling troops now mutinied in earnest. It was in the nature of Ottoman society until the nineteenth century that military defeat was revolutionary in

The Victorious Years

the sense that a discontented army overthrew governments; but this was done carelessly, without rational substitutes. Edirne and its bazaar were soon in flames, burning as only a wooden city can burn. Silhouetted against the flames, the soldiers gathered on the hill before the old palace of Bayezit I, where Selim II was to build the greatest of all Ottoman mosques. They boasted that they would put a supporter of the Byzantines on the throne if they did not get their arrears of pay. It was always to be pay that mattered, and quite rightly.

Mehmet's father, Murat II, had retired to a life of meditation and mysticism in Bursa. He had concluded the ten-year truce of Szeged with the Hungarians, who immediately broke it on learning of his retirement. He returned to be his son's *serasker* and, welcomed vociferously by his janissaries, won a decisive victory at Varna in 1444. He then attempted to retire to a somewhat different 'good life' at his idyllic palace in the meadows of the mountain slope at Manisa. He was not a dervish for he did not shed his possessions in his pursuit of independence of spirit. He owned a copy of *A Mirror for Princes* (as did most Muslim monarchs), which advised rulers to abdicate at the age of 40[2] when the limits of life were reached. It also advised eating only once a day, drinking at home and the enjoyment of youths in summer and women in winter. The *hamam* should be visited every other day. Hunting needed falcons, white hawks, hounds and cheetahs and the only other kingly sport was polo.

Endowed with Sufi as well as worldly wisdom, Murat was unable to illuminate the shadow cast by the death of his favourite son (who was certainly not Mehmet). His victory at Varna effaced the ignominy of his army's retreat before the Hungarian and Serbian attacks of the winter of 1442, which had deeply depressed him.

In 1446 the janissaries were disgruntled once again because their pay was six months in arrears. Indeed, Lütfi Pasha, Chief Vezir from 1429 to 1441, had only been able to pay them anything at all by debasing the currency, a recourse which became a pattern throughout Ottoman economic history and was to lead to the execution of a recent Turkish prime minister, Adnan Menderes, in 1961. The standing army only numbered 15,000 men; a third of whom were janissaries; but no other kingdom supported such an army and Murat's small state had insufficient wealth to maintain even this number. The janissary corps later multiplied to some ten times its early roll and the task became formidable. By their very existence, the troops who supported the ruling institution also threatened its stability from the beginning: even Murat II had enlisted the support of the *ulema* against the army when they favoured his brother, Mustafa.

The Janissaries

The Sacred Despot

Fickle as ever, the people and the janissaries, who in some ways represented them at the gate of power, welcomed Murat II back in 1446 with an acclamation due in part to their respect for his unostentatious mode of living but still more to their dislike of his son. Murat was the last of the democratic Ottoman sultans who spoke to any man, while Mehmet II was to become the first of the sacred despots who deliberately set themselves apart from their subjects after the conquest of Constantinople. He adopted Byzantine etiquette and ceremonial, partly because as emperor he had no other model but also because he had conquered New Rome only as a base from which to try to regain the the Old.[3] There, from a new Pantheon, he hoped to rule the world: or some of it. But this was yet to come and it was young Mehmet's precocious ill-living which earned him a contempt that, paradoxically, proved to be an asset for, when he returned to the throne in his twentieth year in 1451, the Byzantine government felt secure since they knew this licentious and profligate prince was despised by his troops.

It was a return which had not been easily accomplished. The news of the death of Murat II was suppressed by the Chief Vezir, a policy which was to become the rule when a sultan died. Halil Pasha kept his secret for a fortnight, which gave his messenger the time to summon the prince from Manisa where he had been sent as governor. When the dispatch was delivered, Mehmet rode off so precipitously that he had no time to muster his followers; most of them only caught up with him when he crossed the Sea of Marmara and landed at Gallipoli, where he felt secure enough to rest for two nights. Mehmet had travelled so fast that he had to pause for one more night on the banks of the Meriç (Maritza) river while all was made ready for his reception in his capital.

There is evidence that the Chief Vezir, the aristocrat Halil Pasha, with whom Mehmet had been at loggerheads when the former was regent, had difficulty in controlling the janissaries, who had no respect for the new sultan. Certainly Edirne was tense when Mehmet rode into the city. The officers of state were unsure of their own futures and stood apart when Mehmet was greeted by Sabahıttın Pasha, his old favourite and the enemy of Halil Pasha who had sent janissaries to sack his *konak* ten years before. However, Mehmet dissembled his dislike of the Chief Vezir, who, with the rest of the Divan, retained his post—although he headed a group of emirs who considered themselves the near equals of the sultan. When Mehmet had conquered Constantinople, it would be time to be rid of his old enemy. Işak Pasha, the idol of the army, was sent with a large force to escort the dead

The Victorious Years

Murat to the tomb prepared for him in Bursa. The pasha was also ordered to restore calm in the provinces, where several vassals had revolted, a task which fed the janissaries with hopes of loot rather than plots and mutinies.

The army was accompanied by Murat's widow. This middle-aged princess of the Iskenderoğlu family went, very properly, to inter her late husband but also, like Shakespeare's Gertrude (and on Mehmet's instructions) to marry Işak Pasha. Mehmet wanted her out of the way —perhaps in order to spare her feelings when he rid himself of his half-brother and her son, Küçük Ahmet Çelebi, who could have become a rallying-point for the many discontents. Ali Bey, son of the renegade Evrenos Pasha, strangled the boy decently with a cord of silk, not crudely with a bow-string. Ahmet's death brought to life that grim law of fratricide with which, until the seventeenth century, the Ottomans attempted to prevent family feuds and rebellions—rival brothers tending to begin the fight before their father's death.

Işak Pasha swiftly subdued the rebellious princelings in Anatolia and removed the military headquarters from Ankara to Kütahya, where it remained until the fall of the sultanate in 1923. He then marched to Bursa to meet his master. But when Mehmet arrived, new unrest broke out among the janissaries and Sabahıttın Pasha unwisely suggested that a gift of purses upon the accession of a sultan should be instituted so as to sweeten the temper of the corps. The custom proved all too popular and was to blight the Ottoman economy upon the accession of a monarch from that date onwards. Indeed, it was an incentive to overthrow their princes. Out of necessity, but with bitterness, Mehmet accepted the advice but he was so angry at his humiliation that he assaulted the commander of the insolent corps, Karancı ('Cauldron-Maker') Doğan Agha, and then dismissed him.

Mehmet proceeded to regroup the *ortas* and to swell them with pages from the palace units. These several thousand falconers and other household troops formed the original *seğmen* (keepers of the hounds and greyhounds) companies. There was no time in which to raise and train a new Christian levy, for the sultan had to garrison the frontier castles while he prepared the achievement of his overriding ambition, the conquest of Constantinople. These garrisons were independent of the local governors and subordinate only to the Divan—this ensured a check on any sedition among provincial overlords while small units of janissaries, scattered all over the empire, were unable to conspire with their comrades in the capital. As a further precaution, garrison duties were for short terms and with enhanced pay—the latter was necessary because the janissaries had to purchase all their supplies from profiteers.

The Janissaries

The *sipahis* were no less a problem than the infantry because of the lack of land to grant them as fiefs. Thus Mehmet's land policy set out to confiscate the estates of renegade landowning Byzantines and of Muslim feudal overlords and divide them into military fiefs held only for life, thus relieving the treasury of any obligation to pay its horsemen. The sultan was equally determined to break the power of the *ulema*, who had created a disguised hereditary system through the establishment of pious foundations, often with extensive property holdings to be administered in perpetuity by their heirs. Well over half the country and its towns were eventually parcelled out in this way, even if the charities discharged their functions as well as protecting the families who endowed them. As many as 2,000 officers lost and regained estates according to their reputed laxity or diligence. It was the antithesis of an aristocratic system. Mehmet eventually took over 20,000 villages, disaffecting *ulema*, dervishes and potentates alike.[4]

The reforms restored discipline in the army, however, a discipline that became enthusiastic support for a time. There were to be great victories and few defeats and the greatest victory was to be in 1453. Two years previously, Constantine XI stupidly attempted to extract a large sum from the newly reinstated Mehmet by threatening to release his captive uncle Orhan as a rival sultan. This may have precipitated the attack on Constantinople. The assault was partly disguised as a campaign against Karamania for which Rumeli Hısar, on the European side of the Bosphorus, was said to be a necessary base. The building of this castle awoke alarm among all Byzantines in 1452. Mehmet II helped carry stones, and his officers could do no less, thus creating a new respect and consequent loyalty among his janissaries. It was not long before the legend grew up of the sultan's review of the corps at Ankara when, watching his 4,000 élite infantry, he said that he would give much to have 10,000. An alert *solak* quickly said that he deserved not 10,000 but 20,000 such soldiers; the delighted Mehmet reached in his robe to give the man 100 pieces of gold as a reward.

Clamour and Catastrophe: the City Falls

The castle was completed by the end of the summer but the army did not move. It was a grey winter and in April troops massed against the city in its last pitiable spring before the fall. These, alarmingly, included young miners from Novo Brdo sent by the Christian Despot to his overlord, Mehmet II, to use their skill as sappers in destroying the walls of Constantinople.

The Victorious Years

An elaborate account of the fall of the once great city, three-quarters abandoned before its capture, is out of place here but some reference should be made to the janissaries' contribution to its conquest. In his diary of the siege, Nicolo Barbaro, the heroic surgeon from a Venetian galley, wrote of these soldiers that they came right up under the walls, none of them afraid of death, like wild beasts. When one or two were killed, more of them instantly appeared to take away the dead, carrying them on their shoulders as one would a pig, without caring how near they came to the walls. The Venetians shot at them with guns and crossbows, aiming at the one who was carrying his dead comrade, and both of them would fall; but then others came to take these victims away, none fearing death, but willing to let ten be killed rather than suffer the shame of leaving a single Ottoman corpse by the wall.

Throughout April there were heavy Ottoman assaults. On the 18th the janissaries launched a night attack with their usual cries and martial music only to lose 200 men and fall back. The continuous bombardment by the siege-cannon felled great sections of the walls whose defenders were harassed by the arquebuses of the janissaries. On 7 May an assault by 30,000 men with rams, accompanied by the usual din, was beaten back after three hours of fighting and so was an even fiercer attack at midnight on the 12th. At this point Barbaro declared the Greeks to be all cowards although their sappers had broken into the Ottoman galleries. But the Turks took four hours to build a tower which should have taken a month. It was protected by camel skins on each side and half-filled with earth. The ditch was filled, so arrows could be shot down upon the defenders. The bowmen's attack was maintained throughout 19 May along the whole length of the walls.

The noise of the great cannon firing 1,200-pound (544-kg) shot made women faint. On 22 May the moon deserted to the enemy by coming up as if but three days old, when it should have been full, in salutation to the crescent of Islam; the eclipse lasted four hours. Somewhat tactlessly, the Byzantines not only tortured two Ottoman sappers whom they had captured in order to find out where their new mines were being directed, but then removed their heads and infuriated their comrades by throwing them over the wall.

On the night of the 27th, two fires blazed before every tent in the Ottoman camp and the celebrations of the besiegers shouted the city into a state of panic. Nor did the bombardment relent once during that horrendous night which the fires made bright as day. On the 28th, the janissaries were issued with 2,000 very long ladders: when the sun set, all Mehmet's forces took up their positions for the final onslaught. The shouting went on through

The Janissaries

the night until, three hours before dawn, Mehmet ordered three separate attacks by pashas at the head of 50,000 men apiece. Two hours later, cannon fire made a great breach in the wall and the janissaries in their white headpieces, repulsed the first time, came back again through the clouds of smoke and broke into the city.

Both timing and discipline must have been superb for such a manoeuvre to succeed else the guns would have mowed down their own army. Once the Ottomans were in the city, they had nothing more to fear. Butchery and enslavement followed until midday and it is said that the sailors carried nuns off to the fleet. Men put flags over the doors of the houses which they had taken (some as many as ten) and these were respected by their comrades—if not by the Conqueror, for he had other plans which included the repopulation of his city.[5] By the end of the siege, 20,000 prisoners, 200,000 ducats and the head of the *bailo* of Venice had been taken. The loot was in no way comparable to that amassed by the Doge Enrico Dandolo and his crusaders in 1204. However, the Venetian prisoners were to pay handsome ransoms by the year's end.

Mehmet II used janissaries and also *azaps* (foot soldiers) as his assault troops against Constantinople but he later modified this tactic.[6] So as not to lose skilled, trained men when attacking a town or fortress, he made them follow up the wild assault of the expendable *delis* ('maniacs', hence shock troopers), whose fanatical and hysterical fervour carried them forward in suicidal charges. Mehmet was not always victorious. He besieged Belgrade with an army of 150,000 men from 13 June to 22 July 1456 and was wounded by an arrow in the chest. When a mine made a wide breach in the wall, the janissaries did not wait for the *delis* to lead the way but charged into the town unopposed. The reward was the first pick of the loot and the janissaries immediately devoted their energies to their favourite occupation. They were thus engaged when the defenders sprang out of hiding and drove them back in panic and total confusion to their trenches where they were assailed by flaming faggots sealed with pitch. The scorched and terrified survivors of this inferno fled in disarray to the chagrin of both their sultan and Hasan Agha, their captain-general. Hasan desperately threw himself into the fray in a deliberate search for death in battle rather than in disgrace at the hand of the executioner. Mehmet abandoned the two cannon—they were to be retaken by Süleyman when he entered Buda in 1527.

War-weariness and a Wasting Sultan

Only in 1463, when the Conqueror was himself a sick man, did his troops

The Victorious Years

weary of war. Aware of their discontent, he was compelled to rest them for two years. Moreover, his severe land and fiscal policies had aroused the hostility of the great landowners and, far worse politically, the *ulema*.[7] This hostility was exploited by his son Bayezit II, who was a religious bigot.[8] Bayezit's faith, however, was both orthodox and mystical, in the Janus-faced manner of the Ottomans, and led to no broad vista like his father's. Yet even Mehmet II had been interested in the dervish orders and had to submit with chagrin to the defiance of his *şeyhülislam* and permit his Persian favourite to be burned for heresy.

The Fight for the Throne

From his viceroyalty[9] in Amasya, where dervishes grew like poppies in the corn, Bayezit assiduously cultivated the support of both the *ulema* and the janissaries. His success at this feat of ambidexterity troubled the Chief Vezir, Karamanlı Mehmet Pasha, who knew himself to be unpopular because of the taxes he had been forced to levy in order to support successive campaigns. Moreover, he had appointed members of the *ulema* to posts which were the perquisites of the slaves of the household trained in the Enderun Kolej.

Mehmet II's death, improbably from poison, at Maltepe on the Marmara coast in May 1481 inevitably foreshadowed Mehmet Pasha's fall. The Chief Vezir was determined to make the sultan's younger son, Cem, ruler since Cem was opposed to the janissaries who supported Bayezit while cultivating his own faction of notables. The *vezir* announced that Mehmet was sick and had cancelled his campaign. Three separate messengers were sent post-haste to Bursa to summon Cem to the throne while the army returned to its camp at Üsküdar (Scutari), opposite the *saray*. There, the troops were ordered to wait while the body of Sultan Mehmet, who was supposed to be laid low by the rheumatism which had afflicted him often in the past, was rowed across the water.[10]

Unfortunately for Cem a series of mishaps prevented any of the messengers from reaching Bursa, including the impaling of one unfortunate *çavuş* by the *beylerbey* of Anatolia who read his dispatch. The army at Üsküdar soon became suspicious and restless. Rumours quickly spread and janissaries crossed the Bosphorus in any boats that they could commandeer and assailed the inner gate of the *saray*, demanding to see their sultan. When Mehmet did not appear, they broke down the doors to the Divan Court and beheld the corpse of their master lying in state before the Throne Room beyond the Bab-ül-Hümayün. Their fury rebounded on guilty and guiltless

The Janissaries

alike. The Chief Vezir died upon the spot as did the Royal Physician, an unfortunate Jew: unless he really did poison Mehmet. Their heads were stuck on lances and paraded about the city, where the janissaries fraternized with the populace and looted Jewish and Christian property with impunity. For seventy days, a janissary junta ruled Istanbul by the substitution of outrage for the law.

Işak Pasha and Sinan Agha, *agha* of the janissaries, joined forces and pacified the soldiers with promises of handsome rewards later. They discovered Bayezit's son Korkud in the the harem and paraded the boy through the streets. On 20 May his father finally arrived with 4,000 *sipahis*. As soon as he had promised that there would be no debasement of the coinage during his reign and that high office would be awarded to janissaries, Bayezit II was proclaimed sultan. It was the army that ruled.[11]

With *ahi* backing, the handsome and agreeable Cem had *himself* proclaimed sultan in the old capital, Bursa, but without a trained army to support him. The few janissaries who had rallied to his cause were bribed not to burn down the ancient city and had to be content with the murder of a few dervishes instead. These were likely to have been members of the Halveti order; its *şeyh* (elder), Hacı Çelebi, was a personal friend of Bayezit, who, with his Sufi leanings, was probably a member of the sect.[12] The *şeyh*'s considerable influence on the educated and governing class was vital in winning their support for Bayezit, whose virtues were not immediately apparent to any man.[13] Bayezit and Işak Pasha persuaded Gedik ('Toothless') Ahmet Pasha, who was an outstanding soldier and the hero of the janissaries,[14] to abandon his forthcoming campaign in Italy, which was already planned and supplied,[15] and return to Istanbul from his camp in Albania. Gedik Pasha marched into Anatolia and had no difficulty in scattering Cem's army of peasants.

Cem eventually escaped into captivity in Europe where he became a pawn sent from castle to castle and host to host, all of whom liked him, leaving behind him a respect for the Ottomans never felt before. His brother paid his expenses until his death in Capua when under papal surveillance. There was a long dispute over the return of his body but Pope Innocent VIII was rewarded with the Holy Lance and the Holy Sponge, part of the loot of 1453. On hearing of Cem's alleged murder on 25 February 1495,[16] Bayezit proclaimed the closure of all shops as a sign of mourning for the gallant brother of whom he was fond. But, as Bayezit explained, kings have no relations. As for Gedik Ahmet Pasha, his uncouth manners and soldierly predeliction for wine led to his downfall for when he was drunk he was argumentative and even insulted the sultan.[17] He was duly murdered on 18

The Victorious Years

November 1481 and his father-in-law, Işak Pasha, was finally exiled to his township of Inegöl near Bursa.

After the accession of Bayezit II in 1481, the janissary corps cherished its power as king-maker and was to use it against him when he grew old and sick and had lost their respect. But the reign was important militarily although there were no great conquests such as those achieved by his father or by his son.[18] The engine of war continued although indifferently led. The *akıncıs* kept up their unbroken assaults on the western frontiers: their motives were the capture of slaves and booty and not the establishment of new outposts. In the 1490s they attacked Transylvania[19] and in Austria they reached Villach and St Veit.[20] Gedik Ahmet Pasha's last victory was the taking of Otranto in 1491. Bayezit himself led an attack on fertile Wallachia. If the Poles succeeded in driving the Ottoman horse back from the Black Sea in 1497, the Moldavian and Tartar cavalry retaliated in force the following year. However, poor generalship and their own impetuosity led them to press on to victory too late in the season and they retreated, only to be defeated disastrously by the snows of the Carpathian mountains.

It was in Anatolia that the reverses were most serious: the province was never at rest either during Ottoman history or after. Işak Pasha had put down the last of the *beys* of Karamania early in Bayezit's reign but the Ottoman officers who succeeded the wily old warrior were alien to the region whereas the Mamluks had adherents south of the Taurus in particular, but elsewhere as well. They defeated Hersekoğlu Ahmet Pasha, who was a typical Ottoman, the son of the last Duke of Herzegovina and an able commander of the janissaries. After being sent in chains to Cairo,[21] he was released to become *serasker*, only to find himself a prisoner once again and yet again to be released. Less fortunate officers were dismissed and executed. The sending of a black kaftan to a commander signified his imminent demise, as with the venerable Albanian, Koca Davut Pasha, a lover of learning and friend of Venice, and Karagöz Pasha. None of this reversed Bayezit's ill luck. He had instituted reforms which were to be the foundations of future victories, for his ministers correctly attributed the failure of the armies sent against the Mamluks to inferior weapons and fire-power. It was Bayezit's government which set about manufacturing better arquebuses and small arms and a more mobile artillery; but it met with ill fortune when the Tersane was struck by lightning and blew up with the loss of allegedly 6,000 men including skilled craftsmen who were difficult to replace.

The death of Cem meant the end of peace with the West for the Western powers now held no hostage with whom to restrain the Ottoman war party.

The Janissaries

The Venetian party lost its dominance in the Divan as the more aggressive militarists took control of policy. War with Venice broke out in 1499, by which time the Ottoman fleet numbered 158 vessels and 15,000 crew due to the careful preparations of Bayezit's government.[22] In the Balkans, the camel trains were on the plod. Mustafa Pasha occupied the Peloponnese and Isa Pasha, followed by Firuz Bey, raided Dalmatia. Fifty galleys were built in the shipyard at Sinop in the winter of 1500–1.[23] Ottoman naval dominance in the eastern Aegean was established for 300 years. Yet the administration was to be defeated from within by the people of Anatolia.

Faith and Faction and the Death of Princes

The emergency arose from the success of Shah Ismail as leader of the resurgent Persian state due to his hereditary authority over the Shi'ites—this faction was in an overwhelming majority in Persia and had many adherents in the Ottoman provinces, which were heavily indoctrinated by Sufi mystics and hallowed pagan traditions. Ismail also had the glamour that attaches to a victorious commander: he used it to attract friends for in 1504 he took Baghdad and in 1505 he entered Mardın and Dıyarbekir. Shi'ite troubles were not new in eastern Anatolia. An earlier uprising of the Kızılbaş ('Red Heads') had been put down with some brutality by Mesih Pasha, who deported numerous rebels to Albania and Greece. But now not only Shi'ites but Bektaşis were deserting to Ismail: this was doubly serious because of the latent sense of brotherhood that this dervish sect shared with the janissaries, although the relationship was not to be officially recognized until late in the century. Yahya Pasha was sent in haste to Ankara and the ferreting out of the unorthodox was redoubled when Bayezit went to Bursa in the spring of 1508 in preparation for a Persian invasion which now appeared inevitable.

Luck was still against the sultan for in September 1509 Istanbul suffered an appalling earthquake which left 13,000 dead and a shattered city in its wake. But 60,000 men[24] rebuilt the city walls in 18 days and their workmanship on the land walls is still plain to see: evidence of the alarm that was felt that the Christians might attack while Shah Ismail was being forced out of Anatolia. The Persians did not come but the ferment in Anatolia continued and in 1511 the dreaded revolt broke out.[25] Had holiness been an attribute of the strategy, the Sufis would have won.

Instead, the rebel leader, Shah Kuli,[26] was unable to take Konya and turned to march on Afyon Karahisarı: here he defeated the *beylerbey* of Anatolia, Karagöz Pasha, who fled to his headquarters at Kütahya. Although a force of janissaries and *azaps* were stationed here, Shah Kuli's wild

The Victorious Years

tribesmen overran their defences, the town was looted and burnt and the *beylerbey* impaled. The Chief Vezir was the elderly but able eunuch Ali Pasha, who was respected for his scrupulousness and his patronage of science and letters. He now assumed command of the army and almost had Shah Kuli in his grip but the rebel escaped by the ruse of leaving his camp fires burning while he and his men crept silently away. Ali Pasha crossed the Sakarya river and, mercilessly cutting down any stragglers, pursued the rebels beyond Kayseri.[27] Shah Kuli took to the hills. The *vezir* had no wish to give his janissaries time to reflect on issues of faith and mysticism else they might have lost heart so, tired though he was, he attacked and was the first Chief Vezir to be killed in battle. Shah Kuli also died, however, and Ahmet, Bayezit II's eldest son, who arrived with reinforcements some days later, was able to complete the victory. His father, who had been ailing, now improved in health but his younger son, Selim, alarmed at Ahmet's success, rode across the steppes at the head of his Tartar cavalry from the Crimea to Edirne.

The old sultan left the city, intent on retiring to Istanbul, there to abdicate in favour of Ahmet. Indeed, the janissaries were sufficiently loyal to make a stand against Selim and he let them defeat him—since he did not wish to win their enmity.[28] But they did not want to be on the losing side and while Selim retired to the Crimea to gather a new force they did not permit Ahmet to cross the Bosphorus. Bayezit still had some hold on his troops but he could not win them over to Ahmet's side and he was hampered by very real fears that his favourite son might rally Shi'ites to his cause. It was inevitable that the helpless sultan should send for Selim, who entered his capital on 24 April 1512. Three weeks later his father, like a King Lear, departed with a large train of followers for his much-loved palace at Dimetoka (where he had been born sixty-five years before), only to die of poison or exhaustion at Çorlu on 26 May.

Selim and the Inexorable March to Greatness

Selim I, as we have seen, had taken care to cultivate the friendship of the janissaries and possessed those qualities of leadership and toughness which most appealed to them. But he was determined to avoid bowing to them as king-makers in public and entered the *saray* by a postern gate. They might have been less ready with their acclamations had they foreseen the kind of master whom they had elevated to the throne. Their training for a series of conquests began at once. There was also a special levy of the *devşirme* cadets, which might have worried more thoughtful men who realized whose

The Janissaries

deaths would necessitate these replacements in a few years' time. Moreover Selim made appointments on merit not all of whom were graduates of the Enderun Kolej.[29] The new sultan also refrained from hastily encumbering himself with a Chief Vezir to come between him and his soldiers. He began his work alone.

He first disposed of his weaker brothers, including the delicate cripple-poet Korkud and then Ahmet, called the Equivocal because he had openly donned the red cap of the Kızılbaş in his despair.[30] Selim was only hostile to Shi'ism out of political necessity but he was the ruthless adversary of the Safavid dynasty. A victorious Shah Ismail was a threat to Istanbul even when he made no open move against the Ottomans.

There was also a second, more urgent need for action. When Vasco da Gama rounded the Cape of Good Hope on 22 November 1497, it was inevitable that a Portuguese fleet should enter the Indian Ocean: this met with such success that the Levant trade was brought to a full stop. The only Asian trade that now reached Istanbul, let alone Venice, plodded along the Silk Road[31] which Persia could cut off. The Portuguese viceroy of India, the Duke of Albuquerque, was as monstrous a tyrant as he was an able admiral. Littering the Arabian coast with the noses, hands and ears of his captives and quick to blame anyone but himself when unfortunate—as when he failed to take Aden because the scaling ladders broke—he ruled the seas. Economically, the situation was disastrous for Selim I and he had no choice but to scorn the advice of any generals or advisers who lacked his foresight. It was to be a war for survival and it must have been that determination which gave him the title of 'the Grim', which might better be translated as 'the Inflexible'. He saw that a mosaic of races riven by discord in Anatolia was intolerable.

His first campaign began on 20 March 1514, which was as early in the year as the spring muds of the country permitted. It was to be his final answer to dervishes in revolt, secessionists with their pretenders to the throne, and Türkmen tribalism in general; but his ruthlessness was not witless and he made use of the advice of Idris Khan of Bitlis, who helped the sultan consolidate his power by pursuing a liberal policy towards the pugnacious Kurds. For the rest, his mercilessness was implacable. The campaign was again preceded by mass arrests and deportations, but now there were mass executions which amounted to terrorism even if the figure of 40,000 dead were exaggerated (it may not have been). Such horrors belonged to an age which began with Timur bastinadoing and scorching the citizens of Damascus hung head downwards, their nostrils stuffed with ashes, or crushing them in presses.

The Victorious Years

The army went through Anatolia with a precision that only Ottoman quartermasters could maintain.[32] When they entered Persian territory it was to find that Shah Ismail had scorched the earth before them. But the Ottomans marched with their own grain, cattle fodder and flocks, and their valuable water buffalo dragged the artillery across the roughest territory. By way of comparison, in 1472 the Duke of Milan's 18 guns needed 227 carts and 522 pairs of oxen to draw them and carry their ammunition. Even when horse later replaced oxen in Europe, 70 horses were needed to pull a gun and its ammunition cart, an impossible feat in winter weather.

The going was hard but Selim kept his army in the strictest order. The two armies met at Çaldiran on 25 August. According to Lütfi Pasha's chronicle, when the Shah watched disciplined contingent after disciplined contingent of the Ottoman army take the field when they should have been disheartened, hungry rabble, he was much more impressed than by the cannon-balls that blasted his ranks. Selim had marched so fast that the janissaries had had no time to object to fighting the unorthodox Muslims with whose views they had much in common and whose leader, the allegedly gallant Ismail, had so many adherents in Anatolia. Selim's impatience was all the greater because he was well aware that a Western army might march against him once spies reported that he was fighting in Azerbaijan.

The janissaries fought with distinction. At one point the uncouth local levies on the left flank broke and fled, but the day was saved by the gallantry of the household brigade and the fire-power of the janissaries in the centre: with cannon and 12,000 arquebuses, they achieved unprecedented success against the Shah's dumbfounded and ill-equipped forces. Selim chained his guns together so that charging cavalry were brought to their knees while hand guns killed off the helpless riders. Equally important was the hard training, matched by the care with which the supply caravans were organized. Drill and entrenchment are essential concomitants of musketry. A new strategy was born out of the janissaries' new role—not as shock troops or wandering under walls to fetch dead comrades in order to die themselves, but as a co-ordinated military machine based on the use of gunpowder but retaining the bow as a subsidiary weapon. The Persian army was out-of-date and suffered from the ill-discipline of arrogance. It was totally defeated.

The road to Tabriz was open and the city was taken in the face of autumn; there, weary with the hardships of campaigning in an alien country, the janissaries started to murmur. Selim had to establish winter quarters at Amasya, leaving garrisons in the fortresses that lay along the route. But he

The Janissaries

annexed Erzerum, which in 1523 was reported still to be an eerie, empty city, apart from the garrison of the restored fortress. In November, the sultan took Dıyarbekir, behind whose massive antique walls he founded the southern headquarters of the future. It was now possible to hope for a pan-Islamic Ottoman Empire while stability was achieved in a great area of Anatolia—even if the arrest and torture of Alevis and Kızılbaş continued and the properties of the Kalender brotherhood of dervishes were sequestrated.

In 1515 the sultan was at work training his army for the following year, aware that they were not yet fit enough to face the demands of the conquest of Syria and Egypt. Moreover, the Mamluks had a last ally in Anatolia in the fastness of Elbistan, ruled over by the Dülkadır princes. The coasts and valleys might be easy to take but the plateau was self-supporting and surrounded by high mountains. Access was restricted to two practical routes, each consisting of rough defiles that could be defended with ease. In the latter half of the century, tribes from this retreat were to devastate Karamania; in the nineteenth century, the hidden land was a citadel for innumerable bandits whom the sultan's police and troops could never ferret out. Selim's mother had been a Dülkadır but this gave him no claim to the territories of his cousin and his nephew: nor was he interested in legal niceties. The impregnable town and its hinterland were stormed and subjected and Selim divested himself of his relations. The Ottoman rear was now secure.

In 1512, at the age of 30, the future Ayas Pasha, an illiterate *devşirme* recruit, had been appointed *agha* of the janissaries. He proved to be an outstanding officer and his leadership at Çaldiran and in Elbistan fitted him for command in the coming campaign as well. Süleyman was to make him *beylerbey* of Anatolia in 1520 and later Grand Vezir from March 1536 until his death in 1539. He came from Albania, but then in the 170 years between 1453 and 1623 only 5 of the 47 Grand Vezirs were Turkish by birth.

Selim could now organize his great campaign, which was to eliminate the Mamluks. He had the supreme advantage that his slave troops were subordinate to his house whereas the Mamluk rulers were themselves slaves among slaves. Although they had defeated Selim's father, Bayezit II, the Mamluk sultan Kansuh had had to beg Bayezit for help in 1509. Timber had always been as precious as silver in Egypt and Kansuh needed a fleet with which to confront the Portuguese in the Indian Ocean. It was in the Ottoman interest to equip such an expedition, and timber for 32 ships, 150 masts and 3,000 oars was loaded on Egyptian vessels with 300 iron guns and other materials. Some of these ships and their cargo were captured by the Knights of Rhodes and the fleet, when launched, was ignominiously defeated.

The Victorious Years

Ottoman and Mamluk: the Final Reckoning

Selim began by offering Kansuh the province of Elbistan but the Mamluk sultan demanded areas of Karamania as well and the whole Mamluk army marched on Aleppo, leaving but 2,000 men to garrison Cairo. Selim's Divan still talked of peace as late as 29 July 1516 but news of the Mamluk advance showed war to be inescapable. This in no way surprised Selim. War was declared on 4 August and the Ottoman army marched the next day. All had been prepared months before July. The Mamluk envoy, shaved of hair and beard, was sent home on a lame mule and wearing a nightcap. There was no more to be said.

The first obstacle of importance was the Amanus range of mountains, but Selim encouraged his janissaries with fiery speeches while *azaps* cleared the way through the passes, for the loaded baggage trains and cannon-balls were carried on the soldiers' backs. The speed of the Ottoman march was such that on 23 August the army was camped within 16 kilometres of Aleppo, where the Mamluk governor immediately went over to Selim. The plain at Marj Dabik might have been groomed for a cup final and there on the following day a decisive battle was fought.

The two armies stood face to face: Sinan Pasha and Yunus Pasha commanded the cavalry on the right and left wings, Selim and the janissaries were in the centre and the artillery was divided into two batteries in between. It was the classic Ottoman position. The Mamluk army had at last, but too late, been equipped with a brigade of black slaves armed with arquebuses; batteries of cannon were also brought up but, immobilized in trenches, they were easily outflanked and captured. The battle, like Çaldiran, was won by superior fire-power but not immediately. Sinan Pasha's *sipahis* were repulsed, putting both wings of the Ottoman army in danger. The ablest commanders were dispatched to rally the feudal horse while Selim and his janissaries, supported by the artillery, drove back the charges of the Mamluk knights, who soon grew weary. Selim ordered his men to advance and treachery created panic in the ranks of the Mamluks. Yet the sultan cautiously held his troops back as if slow to recognize victory and it was a tribute to their discipline that they could be so restrained. There were two strokes of fortune for the Ottoman cause: Kansuh died of a hernia in the field while his men had been weakened by plague, which was endemic in sixteenth-century Egypt and its provinces to a degree unparalleled elsewhere in Islamic lands (it continued to lurk until the arrival of Napoleon). At last, the final onslaught was ordered and the Mamluk army fled helter-skelter over the corpses of the brave.

The Janissaries

Aleppo closed its gates in the face of the defeated army and Kansuh's son rode all the way back to Cairo while Yunus Pasha and his *akıncıs* rode into Aleppo followed by Selim on 28 August. The conquest of Egypt was now possible and Sinan Pasha was dispatched to besiege Damascus. Selim left Aleppo on 16 September, entered Hama on the 20th and Homs on the 22nd, to reach Damascus on 10 October. The city did not fall until 27 December, when Selim made clear that the Ottomans had come to stay—and for a long time—because looting was forbidden and even the gardens were protected whereas the uprooting of rare plants and fruit trees was habitual after an Ottoman conquest. The Christians, an important class from the standpoint of commerce, were well treated. Only the Mamluks suffered for they were hunted down, their fate made all the worse because the embittered citizens took their private revenge on their bullying rulers. They had behaved in Syria as they did in Cairo, where the court was full of pomp and luxury while merchants and everyone else dressed humbly so as to avoid savage taxation and other exactions. Only the bedouin, the desert tribes, defied the oppressor and robbed travellers with impunity. Mamluk brutality had never been worse than in the years before their fall. Many of them never bothered to learn to read or speak Arabic since they spoke Circassian among themselves. They received more support from their subject populace than they deserved for dues were collected with the bastinado, which was also the award of anyone who jostled the master race.

It was easy for Selim to cut taxes and customs dues and so appear to be the benefactor of the rich cities of Syria. However, he could not solve the problem of the warlike and lawless bedouin, who needed much but had little to sell to the townsfolk who despised them as much as they feared them. Nor could he subdue the mobs of Damascus, Aleppo or Tripoli. Mobs were endemic in Istanbul too and, like Calcutta, all these great cities had their street-sleeping lower orders, pruned by fevers. But the workers of Istanbul had a stronger sense of community than those of the Syrian towns, which had suffered a precipitous economic decline. Clashes between the janissaries and local groups of unemployed youths were frequent and bloody and continued to threaten the stability of the government until the Ottoman Empire ended. But in the last days of 1516, policing the streets had to wait on the conquest of the Nile. In Cairo the able Tuman Bey had been elected sultan.

At the turn of the year,[33] Selim marched out of Damascus into the snow, which resulted in serious losses of camels and horses. The bedouin saw no difference between Mamluk and Ottoman overlords and harassed their enemy until, at Gaza, they achieved a minor victory. Notwithstanding these

The Victorious Years

raids, Selim reached the outskirts of Cairo thirteen days later and prepared for a massive onslaught on 23 January 1517. The city was defended by ditches planted with stakes in an age-old tradition (and still used in twentieth-century tank battles), but deserters had revealed the secret and also that Tuman had mounted guns behind these defences.

Enlisting the support of the bedouin with the help of bribes, the Mamluk cavalry attacked the Ottoman wings—one defect of a Maginot Line is that defenders are as disadvantaged by the lack of a frontal attack as are the attackers. Moreover, due to the poverty that had resulted from the collapse of the Levant trade, Tuman's old and rusty cannon burst while that of the Ottomans was well-maintained by skilled Italian gunners. Ottoman gunpowder was also superior because it was mixed by Sephardic Jews, refugees from Catholic Spain. Thus when, later, the corsairs turned their broadsides on the Habsburg fleet, Jehovah was indulging in the sweetest of revenges resulting from an inexorable divine ordering of events: if only one could be sure which divinity.

The Mamluk line broke. The cavalry recoiled. The bedouin retired. Cairo was open to the final attack: it was launched on 27 January. Women and children had been called to arms and 6,000 black slaves freed. Beams were flung across the streets made dangerous by hidden holes and ditches. More stakes were beaten in to yet more pits and then resharpened. They were at their most useful as street defences; the janissaries had to struggle to get over or round these infernal devices while they were bruised and stunned by rocks hurled by Amazons and mudlarks, briefly living out the drama of a horror comic.

The janissaries replied by shooting at all windows while doors were broken down and each house in turn purged of life. After seventy-two hours of combat by day and by night, lit up by burning homes and shops, the city capitulated. It was given over, as it knew that it must be, to pillage, rape and murder. But the fight continued on the farther shores of the Nile where the last Mamluk sultan had fled across a bridge of boats. And there Tuman was taken prisoner. Selim did not execute him immediately but unrest precipitated his end and he was paraded with his hands tied behind his shoulders like an assassin, to be hanged at the city gate on 13 April. The following day, with the precision of an efficient civil service, the Ottomans demanded that the tribute revenue of Cyprus, normally paid to the Mamluks, be paid in perpetuity to Istanbul.

The Janissaries

Cancer Conquers the Conqueror

Once Selim had organized Egypt as an Ottoman province he returned to Damascus, where, on 10 January 1518, he set out with the janissaries to put down numerous bedouin rebels.[34] But they were elusive as always and there were fears of renewed war with Persia, so the sultan set off for the Horn without subduing the tribes, taking with him 500 master craftsmen whose workmanship was to embellish his son's monuments and enrich the details of the architecture of the period of Sinan. Selim left Ottoman governors in the Syrian cities, supported by janissary companies under a *beylerbey* in Damascus. Some 200,000 ducats from the revenues were lavished on the Syrian provinces, while only 100,000 were sent back to Istanbul although the treasury was empty at the end of the costly campaign. The loot that was brought back made little impression on the prodigality of war.

The companies of janissaries and *azaps,* although in no degree as aloof as the élitist Mamluks had been,[35] were also fewer and both Egypt and Syria supplied local levies for the conquest of Rhodes in 1522 and Cyprus in 1571. Lebanon was a perpetual centre of unrest because of the Druze tribes in the mountains who could muster 25,000 men when required. The most serious revolts broke out when the news of Selim's death arrived. He died of cancer in 1520 before his conquests had been consolidated. His fame had had no time to fade or the loyalty of the janissaries to waver.

The moment of accession was always the most perilous in any reign. There were internal revolts while there was a serious uprising by the Greek Ahmet Pasha in 1522 in Damascus but he received no support and was murdered in his *hamam.* Kasım Pasha put down a succession of Mamluk risings but it was Damat Ibrahim Pasha in 1524 who divided Syria into the three provinces of Damascus, Tripoli and Aleppo, which made government simpler and more immediate. He then went on, as has been stated, to pacify Egypt. There he restored the tax registers, which were in disarray, in order to raise the revenues with which to protect orphans—the inevitable undertow of war—and debtors. He won the loyalty of bedouin leaders, who were given specific duties, and let the *beys* elect a mayor for Cairo where the viceregal *divan* was to hold court four times a week, thus reflecting the central administration in Istanbul.

The Ottoman army in battle array under Süleyman the Magnificent (T.S.M.)

6
The Great Campaign[1]

Youth Has its Fling

Of all the victorious campaigns in Ottoman history the most attractive centred on Mohacs in 1526 because of the high-spirited account of it left by Kemalpaşazade, the official historian and *şeyhülislam*. His first ambition, as we have seen, was to join the army and he fought with Bayezit II in a Greek campaign but then began a career of scholarship. He progressed rapidly as a judge and teacher and held posts at Edirne and Üsküp before his appointment as chief magistrate of Edirne, the second capital. Selim I then appointed him the historian of his campaigns and his son Süleyman retained him in the post.

It was a golden moment and the chronicle records this with boyish delight. Süleyman was young and his Grand Vezir, Damat[2] İbrahim Pasha, only 26. Both were tired of peace and hankered after conquests as steadfastly as the restless janissaries. Ibrahim Pasha's youth and zest made him an irresistible hero for it was he who inspired the army and who was always in the van while Süleyman travelled after him—it was the established practice when the sultan took the field that his *vezir*, in his role as *beylerbey* of the Balkans, commanded the vanguard while the monarch held the centre from where he could control the whole army. It was a tradition which admirably suited the temperaments of these two boon companions. Kemalpaşazade pays due honour to both of them in the accepted preliminary eulogy, which is felicitous enough to ring true. When the account ends, one

The Great Campaign

does not wonder that Ibrahim had been Süleyman's chosen intimate since youth and that this *kul* was to be exalted to almost co-emperor because the sultan's duties had grown too great for one man to bear.

The janissaries received equally high praise. Mohacs was their greatest moment, summed up in their nickname, 'The Bravest of the Brave'. They were still the élite of the army and appear to have been excellent swordsmen as well as musketeers and archers. They were not shock troops for they wore no armour but instead were skilled infantrymen possessing great strength but also discipline in battle. Both they and the mounted members of the household division were to excel. This was not just due the irrepressible panache of their leaders or their own and their officers' battle experience: they had a natural preference for fighting in Europe because they loathed the long and stoney marches of Asia and because the road to Hungary led through territories native to many of them and where, in some areas, they not only spoke the language but also the local dialect. For the levy which supplied the *ocaks* of the janissary corps was still drawn mainly from the Balkans rather than Anatolia since Anatolian recruits were regarded as inferior—and not simply because they were newcomers. There were exceptions, however: one of the most distinguished commanders at Mohacs, a captain of the household cavalry who was to rise to the rank of colonel, was that Sinan from near Kayseri who has already been extolled as the greatest Ottoman architect.

Before the campaign could start, the Grand Vezir issued precise orders to the commanders at Kütahya and Dıyarbekir, Aleppo, Damascus and Cairo.[3] The officers at Jiddah, Aden and the forts along the Yemeni coast were ordered to remain vigilantly at their posts. The pilgrimage routes were to be strictly policed while the fleets in the Black Sea and the White Sea (Mediterranean) were to be prepared for action. The departure of the young sultan from his capital and the centre of communications was an invitation to rebellion and Anatolia, Syria and Egypt had all given cause for concern. All the orders made clear that divisions must stay at their posts and contain any unrest. Above all, the Türkmen tribes, with their Shi'ite leanings, were not be trusted and in this Ibrahim was right. The garrisons at Trabzon and in north-eastern Anatolia were to be prepared to fight to the death and the generals at Amasya, Tokat, Niksar and Karahısar were to equip their divisions fully and assemble on the plain of Sivas in order to go to the aid of any frontier commander who was attacked in force. This was a precaution in case of a Persian attack but also in case of trouble with local Kızılbaş, all enemies at heart.

Yet another force under the governor of Karamania was to camp in battle array on the Kayseri plain in order to cover central Anatolia and the southern coasts. There were also precise orders concerning the surveillance of the turbulent tribes of the Taurus region and the predatory nomads round the old Armenian fortress at Bakras. In short, Anatolia was put on a war footing. The *kapudan paşa* Güzelce ('Handsome') Kasım Pasha was appointed governor of Istanbul. While serious matters would be sent to the sultan in the field for a decision, the general day-to-day administration of the city would be conducted by his deputy. Kasım Pasha, who gave his name to the district round the naval dockyards, was an experienced soldier who had governed Aleppo, Egypt and Anatolia before being appointed *vezir*.

The government was optimistic that King François I of France was a reliable ally and that he could be depended on to menace a mutually hostile Holy Roman Emperor and king of Spain since the Ottoman attack on Charles V was very much in their mutual interest. The Ottoman spy network was as efficient as those of the European powers. Only when all these precautions had been taken was it possible to beat the drums, call the fief-holders to arms and assemble the forces at the imperial camp at Davutpaşa beyond the city walls. The army was made up of 12,000 janissaries, 50,000 horse and, among other units, probably some 2,000 gunners. A fine array of red and yellow tents radiated out from the central purple war pavilion of the Grand Vezir where the senior officers came to pay homage to Ibrahim. This filled the time nicely while waiting impatiently for the Royal Astrologer's announcement of the auspicious hour of the auspicious day on which the march was to begin. It turned out to be 23 April or St George's Day.

Ibrahim set out a week before his sultan at the head of the cavalry. The main body of troops followed the next Monday, preceded by the military bands with their suitably awesome wind instruments skirling above the deep and pompous booming of the great *tuğ* (drum), the throb of the kettledrums and the clash of cymbals. There followed the *vezirs* and emirs and other officers splendidly mounted and in no way resembling slaves though slaves they were. Süleyman rode in the midst of his household brigade in rose-coloured uniforms followed by torrents of dust from the hooves of packhorses, mules and camels and the cavalry of the rearguard. Gold-topped standards with horned crests, the horsetails of the generals, white, red, yellow, violet flags essential for identifying each unit individually on the march and in battle and the pennants of the lances, the glint of javelins: all provoked wild shouts from an excited populace acclaiming the departure of their sovereign.

Thus Saturn left his capital to pass the first night at Halkalüpınar, one of

The Great Campaign

the carefully spaced-out camping grounds on the route. A large army moves slowly, and when the Edirne plain was reached, several days' respite were granted the dusty men and beasts. Then Süleyman proceeded by Philippopolis to Sofia, capital and military headquarters of the Balkans, where he rested for a whole week. Ibrahim Pasha had had the imperial pavilion erected and he hastened to greet a master who might grow suspicious of a *vezir* who was so popular with the army. *A Mirror for Princes* warned its readers that a *vezir* should never be long away from his king else evil would befall him. Sofia was the rallying-point for local units and also for the contingents from Anatolia who had been ferried across the Sea of Marmara to Gallipoli with their thousands of horses and trains of mules and buffalo.[4] All arrived at the hour ordained and the vast army was reviewed by its sultan. Envoys came bearing gifts from Wallachia and the march was resumed at the appointed hour. It was a dusty tramp: dust is constantly referred to in the narrative. The weather was very hot and low clouds made it oppressive and disagreeable until light rain refreshed the army. In comforting shade, Süleyman rode protected by an umbrella, the cupola of majesty.

The Hungarians had been warned by spies of what was afoot and had sought help from Poland and Bohemia. They were able to muster 100,000 horsemen, who dug themselves in on the far banks of the Sava and Drava rivers. Ibrahim was forewarned and advanced at the head of 10,000 hand-picked janissaries with their rose-coloured oriflamme and 150 cannon pulled by buffalo. Süleyman took the highway towards Niş where he had a rendezvous with the governor of Belgrade, Balı Bey—a man famed as a skilled raider—who came with his *akıncıs*.

Ibrahim proceeded to occupy the island of Syrmie in the Sava and set his vanguard valiantly to work on a pontoon bridge, lashing the boats together with chains against the current until it was strong enough to take the weight of the army and the immense train of laden camels and baggage wagons. The work was rapidly completed and Ibrahim was able to cross the river the day before Süleyman arrived: once again a united camp radiated from the imperial pavilion. The tents of the redoubtable janissaries stood around it like a halo round the moon. The time had come to arm and the sultan supervised the issue of helmets and shields while Ibrahim Pasha put on his coat of mail. It was a war camp that could expect attack; the tents were pitched so close to each other that the guy-ropes made a wall. The soldiers slept armed: the janissaries with scimitars as well as bows and arquebuses.[5] This was indeed the zone of combat and every man a *gazi*.

There was another review of the army in battle array with its

The Janissaries

well-groomed and handsome Arab horses, its flags and its red and white bonnets like tulips in the breeze. Then the sultan set off for Slankamen to find the fortress abandoned and in ruins. He proceeded to Belgrade which he had captured in 1521. It was garrisoned with 3,000 janissaries and 200 cannon. Balı Bey and his *akıncı* squadrons were skirmishing near Peterwardein. Theirs was the honour of sending back the first prisoners in chains to the camp—those who had not been beheaded in the heat of battle. And there a message arrived from the governor of Bosnia announcing that his independent force had taken the castle at Iriğ.

The Fortresses Fall

Ibrahim Pasha marched to Peterwardein to join Balı Bey and was preparing for a siege when the defenders unexpectedly sallied forth to fight: but the Grand Vezir was prepared as always. His was the intelligence that had crushed the rebellion in Egypt in 1525, summed up the causes and cast a code of laws which was to survive for 400 years. Now he led an impetuous cavalry charge with all the bravado of a Rupert of the Rhine and drove the defenders across the river, swimming for their lives to struggle out on the far bank in disarray. A steady fusillade from the janissaries slaughtered numerous Christian troops struggling through the reeds and dispersed the survivors so that 20 men could row across in the first of 800 boats that Ibrahim Pasha had assembled for the crossing. Koca Hızır, the leader of the advance party, was just jumping ashore when a horseman rode down on him but the janissary dragged the knight from his saddle, threw him on the ground and cut off his head. The rest of the boats were already launched and the vanguard landed without casualties while the remnant of the garrison escaped within the walls.

The suburbs were promptly overrun but the defenders set fire to the city in order to win time in which to retreat into the citadel behind a wall of flames. Ibrahim mounted his batteries and assigned each man to his cannon, including himself and his staff officers. The cannon belched forth smoke like dragons until they were red hot; but the Serbians were the bravest of defenders and filled the breaches made by the terrifying cannonade. Those Ottomans not manning the batteries poured arrows and shot into the citadel, cheered on by fresh news from Hüsrev Bey of Bosnia of the fall of two other strongholds. More were to follow. Day and night, the cannon continued to smash down towers and battlements, while the sappers dug mines which blew up the rock foundations and brought down yet more of the citadel. A desperate garrison made several sorties to no effect yet they repulsed the

The Great Campaign

first assault of the Ottomans and the weary attackers were forced to retreat back on their camp. Ibrahim permitted them one night's rest and then directed a second assault, which proved to be no more glorious than the first in spite of a hurricane of shot and arrows to cover the attack. More mines were dug and the cannonade resumed, drowning the martial music. All crumbled into ruin save for one tower into which the defenders retreated. There they knew that they could fight no more and capitulated honourably, their lives spared. Peterwardein was a vital guardian of the crossing so the next day Ibrahim erected the imperial pavilion and set to work at once, not only to rebuild the fortress but to make it more formidable than ever, defending it with an immensely deep moat into which fallen towers would flounder but not make a bridge. Süleyman found the time to reward his victorious officers with kaftans and slaves.

Ibrahim waited only long enough to see the work begun and then hastened to Eszek, which was the most formidable of all the fortresses on the Danube or the Drava, and possessed a notoriously bottomless pit for a moat.[6] Deep moats made mining difficult and the answer was to drain them through trenches but at Eszek this would have taken too long. Moreover, it was defended by a strong battery of cannon. A swift foray by the Ottoman cavalry brought back some of the leading citizens, who gave the Divan valuable news of the march of the king of Hungary. Perhaps the town lacked the backbone of a Serbian contingent, unlike Peterwardein: it capitulated and its churches were turned into mosques, as was the custom. Balı Bey's ferocious *akıncıs* laid waste the countryside and the population submitted as best they could while minor castles along the banks of the river fell to the army with token resistance or none. The Ottomans resumed their march and reached Onik, where the commander of a Hungarian raiding force, the Christian equivalent of the *akıncıs*, was taken prisoner.

By the Waters of Babylon

The Drava is a formidable river and the engineers gloomily reported that it would take three months to bridge it. However, Ibrahim Pasha had a pontoon lashed together without interference from the enemy and within three days the vanguard was across it, taking every advantage of the Hungarians, who appear to have been devoid of initiative at this vulnerable moment. A week later, the entire army, and Süleyman himself, were established on the farther shore after scenes worthy of Delacroix if one thinks of the lurching of siege-cannon and water buffalo, the struggles of cameleers and muleteers with their heavily burdened beasts, the shouts, yells

The Janissaries

and bellows and no doubt the ominous splash as the bridge of boats swayed and undulated under their weight. It was to achieve successes such as these that the Ottoman army marched not only with masons and road-makers but above all with carpenters as skilled in building or adapting rafts and small boats, constructing siege-engines and repairing wagons with broken axles as in erecting *mimbers* and temporary minarets to convert churches into mosques.

Now was the moment of truth, for there on the plain of Mohacs the Hungarian army lay encamped. Its knights (of which the army largely consisted) were already celebrating their coming victory. For them the place was one of good omen for it was there that they had defeated the dreaded Tartar cavalry. King Louis of Hungary was so sure that the Ottomans had marched into a trap that he sent a raiding party to set fire to the pontoon bridge and cut off their retreat. To the Hungarians' bewilderment, Ibrahim had already had it carefully dismantled. It was a gauge thrown down and a message to the troops that they must win or die, a message that no one could misunderstand. It was all the more potent for being delivered in silence. The sight of that open, flowing river cooled the bombast and the truculence of the Magyar horse for the *akıncıs* were not idle. They ravaged the countryside full of vineyards which these knights had come to defend and reduced it to a desert. This could have little effect on the result of the battle to come but it illustrated how a commander can be trapped in his own chosen and strongly mounted position.

The Hungarian camp was built between the river Mohacs and a marsh; the open side was fortified with mounds on which innumerable batteries of cannon were installed. But whereas the marsh would bog down the heavily armoured Christian knights, the Hungarians had not realized that Ibrahim's light cavalry would find it no obstacle but an open flank when the time came. Indeed, the Hungarian generals revealed incredible ignorance of their enemy and his tactics, his strengths and weaknesses, besides a vainglorious overestimate of the capabilities of their own men.

Süleyman, khan and *gazi*, now took over supreme command from his Grand Vezir. It was 28 August 1526. The mounted pages of the household were dispatched to reinforce the vanguard under Ibrahim, who immediately marched to the edge of the battlefield where he called a halt under the midday sun. He sent for the old and experienced Balı Bey, who knew the region and the character of the enemy intimately after many raids and forays. The insight into the enemy's reactions and habits as well as the lie of the land was surely the most important loot that the *akıncıs* acquired, however much they might prefer gold and slaves. Fear none of these

Christian horsemen, the old man said, for the Hungarians like to dress in armour from head to toe, and weigh down their horses with steel, so that it is not easy to withstand their weight. He advised that neither the Ottoman foot nor cavalry should confront the knights; instead, they should open up their ranks and let the broad columns of horsemen ride through—but only so that the *akıncıs* could attack their exposed flanks before they could hope to wheel their horses round. The light Ottoman cavalry could charge right up to the knights, and their mounts turn to avoid collision while their masters struck; they should then circle round, still at the gallop, and deliver another attack before the foe could recover.

Mohacs and the Might of the Magyars

Although Ibrahim was impressed with this advice, he faced the problem that such a manoeuvre exposed the prodigious Ottoman baggage train, now halted a little way behind his forces, with its mountains of supplies, towers of grain on the backs of camels, the wagons and the gun carriages. Balı Bey was downcast while he watched Ibrahim wavering. But after pondering for a few minutes, the Grand Vezir suddenly ordered the servants to erect the camp on the spot and in all haste: with its webbing of close-set guy-ropes like nets, the knights would be caught like turbot, floundering helplessly if they dared ride into the mesh of cordage. Thus the cavalry and infantry would face battle unencumbered and with hempen defences behind them. The Hungarians watched in astonishment as the valets set up the camp, imperial pavilion and all, in what should have been the far side of the battlefield. The *aghas* of the *sipahis* were now ordered to stand ready for battle. Meanwhile 50,000 of the cream of the *akıncıs* on the best and freshest mounts were ordered to wait in ambush on the left wing until the enemy had broken through and tried to take the camp, lured on by its splendour in the brilliant sunshine. Then they were to charge with lance, battle-axe and mace.

The sultan and the main body of the army were to be heard in the distance, advancing methodically in full battle array to the clamour of the military bands, when the Hungarian cannon opened fire on the vanguard and the deadly arrows flew. The knights were formed into three mounted corps, all keeping a gap between each rider, so that their front lines were spread across the plain in a broad wave of metal. Now they could no longer be held in check partly, perhaps, because of the threat of their plate armour but also because of their ill-disciplined, tempestuous nature. They lowered their lances and charged, if not fast: indeed, at a walking pace over the first kilometre or so. Ibrahim was inspecting the troops lying in ambush when a

The Janissaries

messenger brought him news of the attack. The valets were still pitching the tents when the noise of the approaching cavalry made them redouble their efforts. Ibrahim had just enough time to mount and take his place at the head of the *sipahis* and to lead an immediate counter-charge. Both sides charged and charged again and the combat swayed this way and that. Some horsemen on both sides must have ridden through the gaps, but horses swerving to avoid crashing into each other turned the opponents away before their lances could strike—for here were no barriers, as there were at a tournament, to reassure the animals. Others may have been halted by those who had fallen and gradually the centre would appear to have been brought to a standstill after a period of the utmost confusion. Then the trap was sprung: the *akıncıs* broke cover and attacked the flank of the left wing. King Louis sent his 1st corps to scatter these pests who swept down on his right. He led the left wing in person against Ibrahim, leaving his post in the centre where the battle was becalmed. It was at that moment of trial that two great rivals, Balı Bey of Bosnia and the *bey* of Savendia, vowed to support each other to the bitter end: the last being their only miscalculation for the end was sweet.

The red bonnets of the *akıncıs* were hidden under arrows, just as oars were to hide the waves off Lepanto fifty years later. Arrows were the weapon which dominated the battle since the Hungarian cannon were marooned on their mounds and the Ottoman cannon were late in being dragged to forward positions to avoid killing their own men. So the cavalry of both armies had to push their way with shields raised, heads down and shoulders hunched through droves of bone and feather hidden in the clouds of dust. The speed of the *akıncıs* proved irresistible and the Hungarian 1st corps gave way before their reckless fury, turned cumbersomely and fled, only to be ridden down and taken prisoner.

On the left flank of King Louis' army the attack continued against Ibrahim, now supported by the janissaries of the main army whom Süleyman had sent. They waited patiently with their javelins, sheltering behind their traditional round shields. Behind them were the formidable Ottoman batteries, which would fire murderous cannonades into the attackers should the janissary lines recoil. But the king reached the Ottoman lines only to be totally repulsed and the triumphant janissaries proceeded to attack the knights with their scimitars until the weight of Christian armour drove these foot soldiers back. Ibrahim charged to their support, riding with sword aloft into the midst of the mêlée, and rallied the waverers. Louis of Hungary remained in the midst of the battle until he was almost hemmed in by his nobles, who lay felled about him. It was then that Süleyman arrived and the household division joined in the fray, followed by the infantry of the main army, fresh and unsullied by dust and sweat. Louis could fight no more; he lost hope and his dignity with it. Bleeding from three wounds, he turned and rode away.

Meanwhile Louis' left wing attacked again and was immediately engaged in a particularly bloody combat with the troops from Anatolia. Both sides were seared by arrows. When Süleyman ordered his detachment of janissaries to raise their arquebuses and fire, a single fusillade put the dispirited Christian to flight. Poles, Bohemians, Austrians, Magyars, Croats, Germans and Spaniards alike were killed or taken prisoner. Now leaderless, Louis' great army broke and fled. It is probable that the king, like many others, was drowned in the river which was meant to defend their camp. They had not learnt to be pulled across rivers by their horse's tail like the Tartars.

The Shadow of Death as Night Falls

The Hungarians left tents filled with every luxury and these were pillaged with due precision. The cords ready cut to tie up Ottoman prisoners were knotted round Christian necks instead. The field was piled with corpses of men and horses and the living fled the throat-slitting janissaries only to meet with the hungry *akıncıs*. Their coats-of-mail were the nets in which the few foot soldiers, mainly fusiliers, were trapped.

At the hour of evening prayer, the Ottomans returned to their own camp and Süleyman entered the domed pavilion of majesty. The next day the army rested except for the restless *akıncıs* who rode off in all directions to pillage and set fire until their horses' hooves met with nothing but eyes and eyelids. The prisoners numbered 10,000 knights, who were brought in fetters before the sultan and sent to execution. Their heads were neatly stacked to make an avenue of pyramids leading to his tent, which was already surrounded by 2,000 heads on poles. A festival was proclaimed. Süleyman awarded the victory to Ibrahim and implanted an imperial egret feather in his turban. Messengers were sent to post the news throughout the Islamic world: also to that faithful ally, the king of France. Every village, fortress and town celebrated; Istanbul was arrayed in splendour and no doubt the walls were whitewashed according to custom. But there was silence on the banks of the Mohacs and anywhere that the *akıncıs* rode in search of booty, eager to kill clergy and monks in particular.

The Janissaries

The Bells of Buda Silenced

The road to Buda was now open and its richer citizens packed up and fled, leaving only the humble behind to deliver the keys to Ibrahim. The Grand Vezir arrived so far in advance of the army that he was attended only by a single page when he accepted the surrender of the Hungarian capital, with all its battlements and towers, as strong a city as any if it had been defended. Ibrahim sent the keys to Süleyman, who had the treasury, armoury and palace emptied (they had been left full, so completely were the Hungarians stripped of their leaders at the battle of Mohacs). This wealth, which was first shipped down the Danube to Belgrade, included the cannon taken from Mehmet II when in 1456 he had precipitously abandoned the siege of Belgrade. Ibrahim had three classical statues of Hercules, Diana and Apollo sent to Istanbul and set up on pedestals before his palace as trophies and memorials of victory. Within a decade, they were to precipitate his downfall (and their own) at the hands of the pious mob who mistook these deities for the infidel king and his children.

Süleyman chose to reside and relax in Buda's magnificent palace before it was stripped and he proceeded to hunt down the beasts in the royal hunting ground. They included bears, panthers, wolves, boar, gazelles, jackal, foxes and hares. After two visits by the sultan with his falcons and his ounces, all these animals were dead, together with tigers, hyenas, partridges, pheasants and pigeons. Ibrahim, however, appears to have had no interest in filling an unholy stewpot. Instead he amused himself by having a new bridge thrown across the Danube. It was very long and made of chained boats stoutly anchored by the city's church bells, which were hung at bow and stern. While this work proceeded apace, for it only took one week, the Grand Vezir rode out with his cavalry to forage for beautiful girls and boys: their bodies, the chronicle records, were like lemon and water and their flesh was a brilliant white. Once the bridge was completed, Ibrahim led the janissaries and the *sipahis* across; Süleyman had to wait for the favoured hour discovered by his astrologers. It is worth noting that the Grand Vezir was not dependent on the stars, but at this stage of Süleyman's career protocol rather than superstition enforced the observance of the rituals of necromancy. Happily, the astrologers immediately discovered the fortunate minute to be at hand and the sultan was able to enter Pest in triumph. His departure from Buda was the signal for the expulsion of all the remaining artisans and merchants to Ottoman provinces. Then the splendid city, with all its irremovable monuments, was committed to the flames and destroyed—except for the palace, which a singularly courageous janissary

The Great Campaign

guard had been left to protect.[7]

Now the army marched south to Szeged, a quiet and beautiful town, which was pointlessly defended for one night before it too was pillaged and burnt, its inhabitants killed or enslaved. This was the signal for the abandonment of fortress after fortress in despair, and town after town followed this lead. They were all set on fire after they had been looted of everything including fruit trees and flowers. But the season was far advanced and the weather threatening. The Ottomans began their exultant march home, leaving desert and desolation behind them for years to come.

Passing Great to be a King

The tactics were now reversed: it was Süleyman who led his forces back across the Danube and Ibrahim who took command of the rearguard until they were back on Ottoman territory and he had rejoined the sultan at Belgrade. There the *beylerbey* of Anatolia and his troops and baggage were sent home by the road to Gallipoli and its ferries. The Balkan divisions were also discharged so that the sultan's army was now much smaller and less encumbered except for the caravans and wagon loads of loot and treasure.

The grave news of a rebellion in Anatolia which Ibrahim had foreseen was assuaged by the arrival of the heads of the rebel leaders, which were flung at Süleyman's feet. The time had come to set out for Istanbul: the sultan did not enter the city until 13 November, however, doubtless because of the floods along some of the roads due to the wretched autumn weather. Ibrahim came to meet Süleyman for he and the *vezirs* and other officers of state had arrived a day in advance to arrange their master's triumphal entry into his capital. There was rain and wind such as only that city knows in mid-November yet the whole population came out to greet him, calling the wind the street-sweeper and saying that the rain was the joyful tears of heaven for the hero of the Holy War.

The capture of Tiflis by Lala Mustafa Pasha and Özdemiroğlu Osman Pasha, 24 August 1578 (British Library)

7
Fish Stink from the Head

Shadows in the Afternoon

Süleyman the Magnificent, as he was to be called in the West, with his bosom friend Ibrahim to sustain his ambitions, opened his reign with a series of great campaigns in which the speed of the *sipahis* and *akıncı* zest were matched by the fire-power of the janissaries. The Danube was established as the frontier in Europe and was policed by a riverine fleet. The capture of Buda and the subjection of Hungary were to have been followed by the greatest of all triumphs, the capture of Vienna. But the attenuated lines of communication made that impossible just as Rome could only be a dream.

The young, well-educated sultan was an impressive figure even if his page Geuffroy found his features ill-proportioned and disliked his long red moustaches. Geuffroy did, however, note his large dark eyes while Ramberti admired his knowledge of philosophy and his reform of the laws, or their codification, which was not simply the work of able jurists but owed something to the sultan's supervision. Süleyman was faced with rebellions in Anatolia as well as the new dominions. During the campaign in Hungary there were tribal uprisings in Anatolia which continued until 1528. One of these culminated in an attack on the brutal *beylerbey*, Ferhat Pasha, by a particularly savage tribe which awarded him the greatest possible insult by cutting the guy-ropes of his tent—they were brigands rather than patriots, for the concept of patriotism did not then exist in Asia Minor. Other tribes were glad of the opportunity to plunder and murder and the commander, the able

The Janissaries

Hürrem Pasha, who was camped on the Kayseri plain, acted swiftly. But he was killed and his men fled in disorder—remembering always that disorder was a tactic in an emergency. The rebels, like the peasant rebels of fourteenth-century Europe, had not anticipated such successes and had neither military nor political plans. Valiant Türkmen leaders like Baba Zünnün or, later, Kalender Çelebi were inspired dervishes but the tribesmen were like children who, having successfully defeated authority, feared revenge: they had no illusions about their strength in the face of a victorious Ottoman host when it returned from Buda.

Their victory in 1526 indistinguishable from defeat, the tribesmen rounded up all the horses and loaded them with Hürrem Pasha's arms and treasure; then they fled to join the Kızılbaş in Azerbaijan. They were too late: although the *beylerbey* of Europe, Hüseyn Pasha, marched too hard and was killed when his janissaries faltered, the *sipahis* under Hüsrev Pasha, riding north from the winter headquarters at Dıyarbekir and from Kurdistan, charged into the midst of the triumphant rebels and cut them down without mercy.

None the less, all was not yet well. The following year Kalender Çelebi of the proscribed dervish sect proclaimed Jesus to be superior to Muhammad. Against such an intellectually confused background, the *şeyhülislam* and eminent historian Kemalpaşazade stated that the fundamental tenet of the Ottoman Empire was a wise and conservative administration of the royal estates and continual supervision of the holders of military fiefs. Such men were inscribed on the rolls for one life only and they held the country for the sultan only. The rights of the humble, their aspirations and their despair as hooves trampled down their crops, were not the subject of these canons.[1] The corpses in the shallow graves of the plateau grew roots, all the same, and Anatolia remained unquiet and unrequited.

Elsewhere the reign began auspiciously indeed. The capture of Rhodes was essential for the protection of the sea route from Turkey to Egypt.[2] Repeated successes in the west were partly due to the willingness of the janissaries to fight there rather than in the extended borderlands of Asia. Victory is sweet and there was no need to alter the ruling policy of western expansion so long as loot and prisoners were brought home or until the setback before Vienna—even that was not a defeat, but only a disengagement in the face of winter.

The successes of the 1520s were partly due to the continuing production of guns although these still had faults arising from hand-casting. Because the barrels varied in dimension, a selection of cannon-balls had to accompany each expedition and could not be standardized in the manner sought by the

Fish Stink from the Head

Ottomans. However, the renown of these guns is reflected in the surprising fact that Ottoman gunners were advising on artillery not only in India but also in Persia, enemy though that country was. It was not until Gribeauval in the eighteenth century succeeded in standardizing the artillery, making the parts interchangeable, and lightened the carriages, thus reducing the number of horses needed to pull them, that flexibility was achieved in the field in France and then, under French tutelage, in Turkey too.

Time passes and fortunes change. Ibrahim's intellect and spirit complemented Süleyman's conservative pessimism but power corrupted him and his head was forfeited with reluctance—the sultan ordered his execution in March 1536.[3] The lustre faded from Ottoman arms. As booty and slaves diminished, financial problems grew ever more serious. The number of janissary troops rose, as did the pensioners, so that the advantages of a trained, standing army were overshadowed by the costs.[4] But all the news was not bad and the regions south of the Danube were absorbed into the empire without undue friction even when Hungary was awash with local risings and retaliatory raids. But by 1547 the janissaries were war-weary and the war party in the Divan was subdued. Italy remained ill at ease and memories of *akıncı* raids led to Vicenza spending so much on the equipping of two galleys to fight under Don Juan of Austria at the battle of Lepanto that the municipality was near to bankruptcy and the Casa del Capitano was never completed.[5] They need not have feared, for the Ottoman administration was forced to look eastward. Conflict with Persia could not be avoided. The Albanian Kara Ahmet Pasha, who had been the janissaries' *agha*, rallied his men and the *sipahis* and led them to fresh victories. But these could not alleviate the economic crisis which was endemic in the empire as it was in Western Europe, a disequilibrium due more to the spewing of silver from the New World than to Ottoman extravagance.

Rüstem Pasha (nicknamed the Stinking Louse), who was appointed Grand Vezir in 1544 with the express task of controlling inflation, resorted to the debasement of the currency.[6] He paired this with a brutal fiscal policy which even levied taxes on flowers. However, his determination and his contempt for the hatred of the populace[7] refilled the treasury as well as his own purse and the troops were paid regularly. But the new prosperity of the provinces under stable Ottoman rule, which had been spectacularly restored by Selim I, slowly wilted. The farmers abandoned their land for the towns or, worse, took to the mountains and joined the bandits. Before Süleyman was dead, inflation had grown alarmingly. Rüstem Pasha was both a soldier and the most unattractive of men—except possibly to his wife Mihrimah, the sultan's daughter and the richest woman in the world. Nicolas de Nicolay

The Janissaries

accused Rüstem of leaving his uncle and nephews to beg openly in the streets of the capital. The janissaries' hatred of him led to his temporary deposition and to a plot to place Süleyman's son Mustafa on the throne because they thought their master too old to command in the field. The sultan had indeed grown superstitious and melancholy, preferring peace to war and books to carousing.[8] It was when the sultan and his army were encamped at Amasya that the crisis reached its head. The Imperial ambassador Busbecq arrived on a mission just when Mustafa had been lured there to be strangled by three mutes. He struggled fiercely in his father's tent while Süleyman waited within earshot beyond a curtain.[9] Ever since the death of Ibrahim Pasha, the sultan had had good reason to be glum and grow irascible. But he shirked no duty, not even that of executioner, and he died leading his army on campaign in Transylvania in 1566.[10]

The Aftermath of a Century of Conquests

Süleyman's death caused concern to the Grand Vezir, Sokollu Mehmet Pasha, who concealed it from the janissaries until the heir was brought post-haste from Manisa. In the last days before Selim II[11] arrived, the truth that Süleyman lay dead in his litter must have been rumoured; but the new sultan survived, if only just, his first encounter with his army. They had nothing but contempt for the fat and cheerful prince who was about to drink the horrors of kingship into oblivion. That he was fearful of the janissaries was obvious, yet he would have liked to treat them with more severity than his minister would allow. The sagacious Sokollu Mehmet Pasha was also overbearing and the command and government of army and empire were to be left to him.

Thomas Dallam, who was sent to Murat III with the gift of a water-organ combined with a clock from Queen Elizabeth, was received in audience in the Pearl Kiosk. He was so close to the sultan that he brushed his kaftan while playing. Instead of instant death, he was rewarded with Murat's applause but he preferred to go home to his family in Lancashire rather than remain in the sultan's service for a princely stipend. Dallam mentions Selim's 100 mutes with hawks and 100 dwarfs as well: a fashionable European taste which Murat, Selim's son, was to share while adding a train of freaks of other kinds and the performance of buffoonish comedies fit for the great Villa Valmarana in Vicenza or the court at Mantua.[12]

Murat was half-Venetian and Italian in his taste for splendour, which his Grand Vezir restrained for economic reasons.[13] But Sokollu Mehmet's position had been weakened by Jewish influence at court, in particular that of Joseph Nasi, the pretentious Duke of Naxos, who had supplied wine to Selim II. Sokollu's sceptical outlook had permitted the building of the Observatory at Cıhangir above Tophane, to the annoyance of the *ulema*. He had also turned Ottoman foreign policy eastwards and away from the Christian provinces where he had been born and which he fostered as he did his relatives.[14] He sent the ill-fated expedition to dig the Don to Volga canal which might have succeeded had it been possible to placate the khan of the Crimea, who feared the consequences.

It was a gamble which had to be taken for, if dug, the canal would have enabled the Ottomans to gain direct access to Central Asia and control the Silk Road; a fleet to match that of the Danube could have been established and the raids on the pilgrimage route by the new Russian Cossacks of Ivan III could have been frustrated. The khan made no overt objection to the arrival of Ottoman troops and great stocks of munitions and supplies were stored at Azov while Çerkes ('Circassian') Kasım Pasha assembled 10,000 men and 6,000 labourers at Caffa. Significantly, the khan, Devlet Giray, sent him only 3,000 Tartar cavalry. In June 1570 the expedition set out on the march while 500 men travelled with the artillery on the Don to camp at Perekop. Work on the canal began tardily at the end of August; a third had been dug when the October gales and frost arrived. Alarmed at the progress of the canal, Devlet Giray recalled his Tartars; he preferred to cope with the Cossack threat himself without the help of his overlord's troops on his own territory. His optimism was well-founded for with the coming of spring his Tartars were to reach Moscow.

Deserted by his allies, Kasım Pasha was unable to march his frightened troops on Astrakhan and there establish winter quarters. He could only bury the guns and burn the camp before disobeying the orders of the Sublime Porte and retreating to Azov. It was a bitter march. Whether Russian agents or mutinous janissaries burnt the vast arsenal there is unclear. The conflagration prevented a renewal of the expedition the following year when, with an early start, the work could have been completed. Instead 1571 was to be the year of Lepanto and the greatest of Sokollu Mehmet Pasha's dreams remained unachieved.

Süleyman's descendants lacked military skill and ambition although Selim II and Murat III were not without talent and the empire under their governments continued to expand even if at a cost. A new devaluation under Murat III severely cut purchasing power in 1584 and the janissaries, whose understanding of economics was simplicistic, overturned their cauldrons in time-honoured fashion. One of these huge cooking pots made a terrifying din, but the thundering noise of a whole battery of them was indescribable and made clear to the government that the corps was in revolt. This time, they murdered the treasurer, the *beylerbey* of Europe and the Master of the Mint. Yet the devaluation had been hastened by their own defeats in Persia due to cowardice.[15] They had behaved disgracefully, continually complaining and even murdering officers besides reversing a great Ottoman tradition and molesting the local inhabitants. On their return to Istanbul they assaulted the citizens and robbed shops as if they had taken their own capital by force of arms: both Murat III and later his son Mehmet III were forced to buy the loyalty of these mobsters.[16] Indeed, on his accession in 1595, Mehmet was lucky that his *saray* was not sacked and that he excaped alive and unmolested. Inevitably, there was uproar and disorder in the provinces as well as in the city, and bands of janissaries roamed the countryside like bandits—only they had no need to hide in the mountains. Yet, paradoxically, a number of *ortas* fought with distinction against the German princes in Europe.

The Power of the Mystic Orders

Throughout Islam the millennium of the hegira, the year of the flight of the Prophet Muhammad to Medina, was awaited with trepidation by the superstitious. It was AD 1591–2 yet nothing weird or catastrophic occurred in Istanbul. The most significant event was the official recognition of the Bektaşi connection with the janissary corps.[17] Their Grand Master was made a colonel and eight dervishes were attached to the 99th *orta* and given rooms in the Yeni Odalar below the Şehzade mosque. On state occasions, the Master in his green robe preceded the *agha* and prayed aloud for the empire and its warriors while a company of dervishes shouted the responses. Their symbol of the *teber* (double axe) became the insignia of the *orta*.

The Bektaşi dervishes are said to have attracted Christian adherents and the janissaries were well-disposed towards them since they themselves had been born Christian.[18] The Bektaşi order's corporate nature was probably valuable at a period when the guilds were reborn in Istanbul and janissary recruits and veterans alike were increasingly associated with trade. The order gave the corps a ready-made corporation with which to affiliate, with all the associated privileges and obligations. Otherwise the union would have been effected earlier when the janissaries, and not just the pages of the *saray*, were all Christian-born. Moreover, the Bektaşis attracted people unattached to any Book, Bible or Koran, but rather older, more primitive gods. Besides, when Timur crossed Anatolia it was largely depopulated save for two million goats which were as fertile as they were voracious.

Fish Stink from the Head

The rapid rebirth of towns under Süleyman, due to the temporary suppression of the forces of disorder, did not reflect a rooted growth of the rural population. The adobe hovels with their flat roofs that Busbecq described everywhere east of Bursa were not centres of agrarian reform but only of an idolatry common to any group living in perpetual fear of climate or marauders of every description. The royal estates and the farms of veterans were oases set in a wilderness of poverty and ignorance amid ever-growing desert.

The Bektaşi order was established and had its headquarters in the small town of Kırşehir after being founded by the shaman-like *babas* of Central Asia, and Horasan in particular. These Turkish-speaking Türkmen were associated with the earliest Turkish poetry and their simple symbolism had more in common with shamanism than with the developed religions. Their affinities with the more intellectual *ahi* brotherhood were expressed through ritual eating and dancing together with candles, rows of which are still encountered in primitive mosques in Anatolia. Their appeal lives on, as the size of their quasi-illegal following proves, in spite of a renewed ban on the movement by Atatürk in 1925. It took the order twenty-five years to recover from its outlawing by Mahmut II in the early nineteenth century and the same time to recover from the ban of the Republic in the twentieth.

The attraction of Bektaşi beliefs lies in the concept that no one exists but oneself, which is the soul that transmigrates the nullity that is death. Because of the order's contempt for orthodox Sunni beliefs, secrecy was essential: the authority of the *ulema* was backed by force whenever a central government was strong. But it was an open secret and the brothers—like Rotarians today—relished secrecy for its own sake. With this secrecy went taboos of all sorts inherited from shamanism, including the superstition that no one should leave his spoon on the table. From Mongolian traditions came the care taken never to step on a threshold. This tradition was also associated with *ahis* but it was a superstition with a ghostly root in forgotten rituals from before Adam. It was forbidden to eat or even look at a hare if possible and the approach of the creature was to be greeted with a sequence of turned backs. The Turkishness of the order came out in a love of giants and colossal strength which related to the sport of wrestling. Hence the long sarcophagus of the hero buried at the great convent of Seyyit Gazi beyond Eskişehir and the outsize example raised for Selim I in Istanbul.

The Bektaşis cultivated an epicurean good humour and that wit of a Nasrettin Hoca that is fertilized by the crafty innocence of peasants. They loved wine and were tolerant towards women. Their *tekke* at Kırşehir, which was under a *çelebi* (the master of the order and its wisdom), was extensive

The Janissaries

enough to include quarters for women besides the kitchen and bakery, cells, and prayer and dancing halls. Under their *babas*, all other *tekkes* were subordinate to that at Kırşehir.[19] The Bektaşis spread through Anatolia to include Osmancık and Elmalı—with its ruffianly woodmen—with the result that they were allied with many provincial rebels against the central authority. They crossed the Sea of Marmara and from Dimetoka spread through the Balkans and into Albania. Thus they had disciples all over the Christian provinces, which partly explains their relationship with the *devşirme* recruits before it was officially recognized.

The brotherhood had attracted Mehmet II until he grew alarmed at their subversive inclinations. He had some brothers burnt in the courtyard of the Üç Şerefeli mosque because of their heresies while a fanatic named Shah Ismail was burnt at Bursa in 1502.[20] Yet Bayezit II favoured the order with endowments as did the Dülkadır family of Elbistan into which Mehmet II had married. The sharp-eared Selim I, however, closed the *tekke* at Kırşehir in 1519 because of Bektaşi connections with the Türkmen tribes and it was not allowed to reopen until 1551. Even in 1577 a rebel pretending to be the fanatic, Shah Ismail, attracted followers at Malatya and there performed religious sacrifices before the tomb of Hacı Bektaş, the nominal founder of the sect. Once they were affiliated to the janissaries, the dervishes received donations from the corps, although there is only one inscription at Kırşehir. It records a contribution to the repair of the conical roof of the tomb there in 1618.[21]

One result of the union between the plebeian Bektaşi order and the janissaries was the acceptance of all and sundry who wished to join the corps. Christian fathers had openly paid forbidden gypsies, poor Muslims and Jews to take the place of their sons who were due for conscription. Murat III had imposed acrobats and jugglers on them. No wonder that by 1630 the once-exclusive janissaries included in their ranks Tartars, camel-drivers, muleteers, Laz tribesmen from the Black Sea coast and riff-raff of ports and slums in profusion. It should be remembered that lowly born recruits also filled some of the most illustrious regiments of Europe (as the Duke of Wellington recorded). Because the janissaries were politically as well as militarily important, however, the withering of the regulations, which need have done nothing to diminish their fighting power, reflected the malaise underlying the decline of a ployglot empire while also contributing to that unhappy state. Scapegoats are not always blameworthy.

Fish stink from the head, a proverb that every Turkish schoolchild knows. The sale of offices by sultan and *vezir* in the reign of Süleyman, who codified the laws, was used by his Grand Vezir, Rüstem Pasha, as a regular

Fish Stink from the Head

source of revenue. Soon the dreary sewer of peculation seeped into the nooks and crannies of imperial life. Nepotism was rife and contributed to the death of Sokollu Mehmet Pasha, whose family tree was laden with fruit, sound or maggot-ridden according to the law of averages. Officers of the imperial household with debased salaries even enrolled members of their own households in the janissary corps to avoid having to pay their salaries. Artisans joined the corps in such numbers that *ocaks* merged with craft organizations.[22] Perhaps this marriage between old enemies, since the janissaries had helped to suppress the *ahi* brotherhood, was presided over by the Bektaşi dervishes but it was the direct result of impoverishment.

Devaluation was a deliberate economic policy until the withered purchasing power of janissary pay[23] forced the officers to enrol ghosts while the men had to find jobs outside the barracks. Some increased the time given up to their trade until their one remaining military duty was to lounge on the Etmeydan on pay day, if that had not been postponed by the treasury. Barrack rooms were empty and unswept because so many men were married and had their own homes outside. The rare event of a levy after the death of Süleyman indicates how many sons were enlisted in their father's *orta* without a period of training in Anatolia. In the provinces, the recruiting of a local janissary company or brigade without connections with the corps in Istanbul was now the rule. In cities such as Baghdad the whole population allegedly consisted of this territorial army but this is certainly an exaggeration—yet one that is significant. In Damascus and Aleppo, the *ulema*, there as elsewhere the wealthy aristocracy of Islam, were at odds with the petty bourgeoisie playing at soldiers like party members in a modern autocracy. To be a janissary there was to belong to the ruder ranks if not to the thieving and murderous rabble itself.

Rival Orders on the Path to Glory

The *sipahis* also cultivated mysticism but adopted the Melameti dervish path, which had a following to rival that of the Bektaşi order. The Melameti brotherhood required the open profession of that monism which was the secret root of the dervish tree. This overt heresy led to persecution that paradoxically hastened the spread of their doctrines, especially in the provinces of Edirne and the Balkans. In 1662 the jealousy between the *ulema* and the rival dervish sects led to the execution of the venerable head of the Melameti order and forty—magic number!—of his followers at the orders of Köprülü Fazıl Ahmet Pasha. Yet, fifty years later, not only was the Grand Vezir Ali Pasha an adherent but the *şeyhülislam* himself openly belonged to the sect. Moreover the Melameti order had affinities with the Halvetis and, more significantly, the great rural confederation of the Nakşibendis, so much alive in Turkey today. It was to take over the property of the Bektaşi order in 1826 but it also gave sanctuary to many of its persecuted adherents.

In opposition to the popular dervish movements, the ruling institution and the *ulema* cultivated the aristocratic and urbane order of the Mevlevis, whose hereditary Grand Master at one time had the honour of helping gird the new sultan with the sword of Osman at Eyüp, the Ottoman equivalent of a coronation ceremony. Murat IV richly endowed the order's original *tekke* at Konya and the Mevlevis grew so powerful that they were influential in deposing his successor, the deranged Ibrahim I, and helping place Mehmet IV on the throne. Many officers of the household belonged to rival orders as if there were some irresistible spiritual drive in Ottoman society, even if Sufi mysticism flaunted every orthodox Sunni belief. It soaked up the superstitions that thrive in an age of perpetual uncertainties, alarms and excursions, and at its best exalted blind credulity to a glimpse, at least, of that light that Dante learnt to see and glorify in *Il Paradiso*.

Thus if 1591–2 (the year 1,000 of the hegira) symbolized anything, it was the ascendancy of conservatism in men's minds. Education in the *medreses*—the colleges attached to the great mosques, where once some mathematics and the elementary sciences had been taught—was stultified by religious orthodoxy. Astronomy was studied only as a prelude to the superior science of astrology and when it attracted serious scholarship the *ulema* took fright. As early as 1580, Murat III had been warned of the threat posed by the New World to Christian trade and that Europe would rule over Islam by 1625 if reforms were not effected. Later, when the prediction had proved premature, Murat IV asked a Dutch cartographer to map the empire but he refused and nobody else was approached or even available. By then, the once invincible Ottoman guns were inferior to those of Europe where swords, too, were of finer steel than even that of the forges of Damascus. The Ottoman remained a superlative bowman but this was not enough in the seventeenth century.

The Fight for Power

For a while in the last quarter of the sixteenth century there were two clearly differentiated parties in the Divan, epitomized by two remarkable soldiers, Lala Mustafa Pasha[24] and an extraordinary old man, Koca Sinan Pasha. The latter was repeatedly Grand Vezir and, although he was defeated in Persia,

Fish Stink from the Head

his military career was rewarding. Any character as overwhelming in his authority as Sinan Pasha had a hold over the janissaries and could enflame them with a victorious zeal.[25] If the province of Yemen which he temporarily subdued (taking the title of Yemeni Fatih Koca Sinan Pasha) was impossible to control from far-off Istanbul, this was the fault of geography and not his generalship. It was impossible to do more than sustain a series of loose alliances with chieftains and such eminences as the Sherifs of Mecca in a province as distant as Arabia. The empire had reached the farther limits of its communication system by sea or land.

The war policy of Sinan Pasha, an Albanian,[26] was supported by his rival, Lala Mustafa Pasha, who was a Bosnian like Sokollu Mehmet Pasha. The old admiral Piyale Pasha, son of a Croat cobbler, made the third of an uneasy triumvirate until Mustafa died. Sinan Pasha then had to contend with a succession of Grand Vezirs who, in order to be rid of him, sent him off on campaign and out of mischief. But he always contrived to return with the support of the janissaries and regain the Grand Vezirate. He died in 1596 while serving his fifth term in that office, honoured as Koca ('Grand Old Man') Sinan Pasha. Great age was no bar to advancement: one of his rivals, Mesih Pasha, was appointed at the age of 90 and still had time to build a handsome mosque. Another enemy was the unfortunate Hasan Pasha, who came into conflict with a new power which had established itself within the palace, that of the Chief Black Eunuch, Gazanfer Agha,[27] who was nourished by the rising influence of the Valide Sultans, the mothers of the sultans. These formidable dames interfered increasingly in government while their offspring were either too young to rule, deranged or obsessed.

Murat III was agreeably obsessed with learning and education: Mustafa I, in the early seventeenth century, with boys. Thus it was the venal Safiye, the Valide Sultan—to whom Queen Elizabeth I of England wrote and sent gifts—who blighted the reforms of Ibrahim Pasha and achieved his downfall. This was in spite of the fact that he had been *agha* of the janissaries, who still had influence over the appointment of *vezirs*. Janissary discontent over pay had forced Siyavuş Pasha out of office and brought about their favourite Sinan Pasha's third return to power, for his reform of the finances was directed at other forms of corruption than their own.[28] Not only did the relict of Murat III influence policy in the reign of their son, Mehmet III; she drew on state revenues for her own use as if oblivious of the suicidal nature of her interference from the viewpoint of the throne.

When Koca Sinan Pasha was recalled for the last time, in 1596, he managed to persuade Mehmet III to go on campaign and to have the preceding, venal Grand Vezir executed as an example. Koca Sinan Pasha was to die himself within four months in April. *Vezirs* continued to come and go: one such was Çigalazade Sinan Pasha, who was appointed to office for the last three months of 1596 because of his severity in dealing with janissary abuses. Meanwhile the excesses of Hasan Pasha, who achieved the nickname of Murteşi ('the Briber'), led to his execution. When Ibrahim Pasha died in 1602 while holding office a second time, he was succeeded by the Fruiterer Hasan Pasha, a successful *agha* of the janissaries in 1594, who married Ibrahim's widow and his fortune. He managed to improve the coinage before the stringencies of his policies provoked the rebellion which resulted in the execution of the odious Gazanfer Agha. Güzelce Mahmut Pasha, chosen by Safiye, cunningly set *sipahis* and janissaries against each other and contrived the execution of the reforming Hasan.

When Mehmet III died in 1603, he was succeeded by a boy and a new Valide Sultan.[29] The 13-year-old Ahmet I endured three Grand Vezirs, including the detested Dervish Mehmet who was dismissed and executed as beyond hope in December 1606. This Bosnian had been *bostancıbaşı* and was disproportionately fat, unjust and harsh. In the previous year the defeat and suicide of Çigalazade Sinan Pasha were proofs of the military decline of the empire. It was then that Kuyucu Murat Pasha became Grand Vezir and 'Baba' to the admiring Ahmet. He was nicknamed Kuyucu ('the Well-Digger') either because he fell in a well and was captured during the 1585 campaign in Persia or because he filled the wells of Anatolia with rebel corpses: or both. Here at last was a real man.

Near Anarchy in Anatolia

Forty years earlier, Süleyman had stationed household troops permanently in Anatolia during a rebellion of his son Bayezit.[30] Gradually local recruits were admitted and these broke up into rival bands.[31] Besides robbing whomsoever they wished, these ruffians collected taxes for their own support.[32] The most lawless and considerable of these bands, known as the *celalis,* terrorized whole regions of Anatolia.[33] Unable to ignore the likelihood of anarchy, Mehmet III's ministers prepared a campaign against the bands, which were still small. Hüseyn Pasha was authorized to levy recruits in central Anatolia but the lack of ready money with which to pay them drove them to join the rebels. One leader of the latent revolt was Kara Yazıcı,[34] who eventually rallied a formidable force of 20,000 followers and dominated the land, from Sivas to Elbistan, which had remained Shi'ite at heart. In 1599 Mehmet Pasha set out in Hüseyn's place determined to put an end to this rabble, which retreated south to Urfa on the Syrian border. There

Fish Stink from the Head

Kara Yazıcı resisted all attempts to win him over until 1602 when he obeyed the call to his grave.

So much is Ottoman history bound up with personalities or, rather, personifications that Yazıcı's bands dispersed. However, his brother, Deli ('Fanatic') Hasan, surrounded the headquarters of the *beylerbey* of Anatolia at Kütahya, leaving his men free to plunder and kill from Bursa[35] to Tokat. Yet they were not true brigands: their disputes over farms abandoned by villagers, who had fled to the towns for security,[36] arose from the lack of a government or an insurgent policy. The Fanatic was reasonable at heart—the offer of the rewarding office of governor of Bosnia was sufficient to recall him to his duty to his sultan.[37]

From 1603 until his death in 1611, the Grand Vezir Kuyucu Murat Pasha launched relentless attacks on the *celalıs,* always with success but never achieving that total victory which was, in any event, impossible. Counterraids became few but never ceased entirely and, tragically, the beautiful palace and terraced gardens of the sultans at Manisa were ruined and laid waste. Murat Pasha defeated both the ruler of Aleppo, Yusuf Pasha, and Kalenderoğlu, the lord of west Anatolia, before he died. In the wisdom of old age, he imposed peace by massacre: this included the deaths of local janissaries whose rump fled to Erzerum to enlist under Abaza Pasha, its governor and a formidable personality. The continuing unrest in Anatolia might seem a reversion to the logic of the Beylik period, when the house of Osman emerged from out of a platoon of warlords, the region was broken up into natural divisions and petty emirs were civilized by the *ahis.* But the reality was a travesty of this ideal.

As for fat Ahmet I, his life was devoted to hunting with his hawks, panthers and greyhounds in a country stuffed with game from pheasants to boars; to the passionate embraces of fat women; and to Allah.[38] Allah alone rewarded him by letting him live long enough to see his vast mosque below the Hippodrome completed. A boar gored him at Burgas[39] and his Jewess procuress, Madame La Quira or the Sultana Sporca, who hunted out the most Rubenesque of bedfellows, was strangled at the orders of the Grand Vezir—he had to placate the mob, which objected to the rewards heaped on her and her sons by the grateful Ahmet.[40]

The *vezir* also had the wit to admit defeat and sign the peace of Sitvatorok with Austria on 11 November 1606. Although he was rewarded with odium, peace was essential if enough troops were to be available to restore order in Anatolia. The treaty ended the myth of Ottoman supremacy, however, and its ignominy was resented by a supposedly undefeated army. While the Christian victory at Lepanto in 1571 had done no lasting damage to the Ottoman fleet, Sitvatorok penetrated the armour-plated vanity of even the *sipahis* and the janissaries. According to David Urquhart, this truth was symbolized by the first capture of a Turkish flag, which was sent to Pope Clement VII. The colour now had to be changed although the star and crescent handed down by the Byzantines, who had borrowed them from the Greeks, were retained.

The Prince of Paranoia

Kuyucu Murat Pasha's death in 1611 was followed by fresh disturbances all over Anatolia in the last years of Ahmet's reign just as there had been during the first. The sultan, who was lucky to have escaped the mob which killed his procuress, died of typhus in 1617, exhausted by a sexual appetite and an obesity that even his hours in the saddle could not deflate. In the shadow of the Chief Black Eunuch and supported by the janissaries, his brother Mustafa I succeeded because his nephew, Osman, was considered too young to rule at 13. Mustafa had twice escaped strangulation by the grace of the devil and of Ahmet's humanity. He had been hidden for ten years in a small cell above the murkiest of courtyards behind the apartments of the *gözdes* (the favourite women of the harem) because the government feared that he might become a rallying-point for the discontented. Not unnaturally, when he emerged into the sunlight he was found to be paranoic and a near idiot whose ferocious cruelty soon made him odious even to sycophants. Normal administration became impossible. After three horrendous months, Islamic respect for fools, who are incomprehensible to ordinary mortals because they talk only to Allah, turned to scorn. An unholy alliance of the *şeyhülislam*, whose *fetva* alone could depose the monarch, and the Chief Black Eunuch effected Mustafa's overthrow as soon as the Grand Vezir returned from Persia with the army. The unfortunate Osman II succeeded him.

The Janissaries Murder their Sultan

Mustafa returned to the cell which Osman II had kept warm for him and the freed boy could only feel hostile to the janissaries who had supported his uncle. He was as eager to reduce their numbers as any of those more dispassionate statesmen who, since the end of the sixteenth century, had recognized that only without the corps could stability be achieved. The policy was impossible to implement, as Kuyucu Murat Pasha knew, for, although ruthless, he had never decimated a corps on which the ultimate defence of the realm depended. Yet in 1621, commanded by the 16-year-old Osman, it fought ignobly against the Poles at Hotin. Defeat allied sultan and Grand Vezir against the janissaries and they were awarded the blame for the débâcle although it must primarily have been due to bad generalship and poor training. Osman had no minister of the calibre of Kuyucu Murat Pasha and the plot to summon a Kurdish force to put down the janissaries and take their place was absurd. It was unthinkable that an untrained horde from the mountains should be pitched against a corps armed with muskets and cohesive enough to fight ruthlessly in its own defence. It would have been equally unthinkable to have admitted wild tribesmen into the capital, which they would assuredly have looted and burnt.

A grave situation was made worse by a lack of discipline and discretion within the ruling institution itself; Osman's plot was betrayed, possibly rightly, and the prerequisite of surprise was lost. The escapade was foredoomed since the failure of the expedition to Hotin meant that there was no pay for the janissaries when they were already in a mutinous mood. The conjunction was fatal.

The young sultan was to have left his capital on a pretext—on pilgrimage, to suppress rebels at Sidon: it hardly mattered what—while his ministers courageously remained behind. Once out of Istanbul, Osman hoped to rally the *sipahis* and local troops to his standard; but the prudent janissaries guarded the gates of the *saray* and the sultan was forced to remain.

If the corps feared for its existence, the populace feared unknown horrors. Thus an alliance of tribunes and people defied the government. The palace was surrounded and after two awesome days, during which Osman defied his enemies, the Grand Vezir went out to placate the mob. When they wavered, one more brutal than his mates attacked him and the rest joined in. He was cut to pieces and, helped by the *bostancıbaşı*, Osman hid in despair. The soldiers howled for their sultan and threatened to replace him if he did not appear. They broke into the inner courts in order to ferret him out but, strangely enough, do not appear to have sacked the palace. They killed the luckless Chief Black Eunuch in the course of their rampage because he would not or could not tell them, even under duress, where Osman lay. They found Mustafa instead, starving in a vault where he was attended by two black women. They dragged the idiot out through a skylight and carried him off to the Eski Saray so that Osman could not kill him. When all was silent, Osman emerged; on hearing of his uncle's escape, he sent a secret message to the women of the Eski Saray that Mustafa was indeed to be killed. But he was saved by his guards and taken to the janissary barracks.

Young Osman did not lack courage. He dressed himself as a janissary

The Janissaries

and went to the barracks with their *agha*, Hüseyn Pasha, and twelve horseguards of his household. There he addressed the leaders of the mutiny to such purpose that they wavered and might have been won over had it not been for the uncouth tongue of the *agha*, who was surely one of the most tactless men in history. He chose that moment to rebuke his men for treason. The enraged and barbarous soldiers murdered him there and then and dragged Osman before Mustafa. The fool barely found the strength to nod when asked if the boy should be deposed. The soldiers were abetted by the Valide Sultan, Mahpeyker Kösem, in presenting the ruffianly Davut Pasha, who had served without distinction in Poland, with the seal of the Grand Vezir[41] and assured the terrified Mustafa that he was sultan once more. It was 22 May 1622 and the janissaries were established as the most important party in the state.

Osman was sent ignominiously to Yedikule, the Ottomans' Bastille. A *sipahi* swapped turbans in order to humiliate the boy but he was permitted to ride because the janissaries still bowed to the concept of a sacred dynasty. Osman could not be killed unless there was an heir, or preferably two, and unfortunately several brothers were discovered after a search of the harem. That a search was needed and its result a surprise reveals the degree of secrecy surrounding the royal family. It is unlikely that a chief minister in the West would not have known how many of the ruling house were alive, even if illegitimate. They were soon to be one less.

As soon as the continuity of the dynasty had been secured, Davut Pasha himself rode to Yedikule with three executioners. He had reason to fear an uprising in favour of young Osman since any government was preferable to his own. Wakened brusquely, the 17-year-old sultan fought for his life. His kaftan (if indeed it is his) is displayed rent and bloodstained in the museum that Topkapısaray has become. It was not until Davut took Osman's testicles in his butcher's grip that the cord could be tightened round his neck.

The insane Mustafa then ordered the Chief White Eunuch to strangle the younger brothers who were a threat to his throne; but the newly appointed Chief Black Eunuch had anticipated the murders. They would have ended the house of Osman, because Mustafa had such a passionate hatred of women that he could never have sired a son. The eunuch forewarned the pages, some of whom ran to the rescue of the princes while others killed the Chief White Eunuch with, one imagines, some pleasure since it is given few students to have a justification for killing their headmaster. Other comrades escaped by the Shawl Gate through the Chief Black Eunuch's quarters to warn the janissaries.

The assassins of the old eunuch were arrested but, before they could be tried and punished, troops poured into the Divan Court to demand pardon for the cadets who had preserved the imperial house. They were spared because no one could be found to defend the madman who had achieved dotage and impotence in early middle age. However, mercy was insufficient recompense for the janissaries, whose accession purses could not be filled. Since inflation had steadily reduced the value of their pay, this must have been a bitter blow; as a result, law and order in Istanbul were as feeble as mist on a midsummer morning. Moreover, the Persians were aware of their good fortune and were preparing to attack in force. Davut Pasha insolently blamed the *agha* of the janissaries for the turbulence of his men and ordered him and other ministers into exile in the backwaters of Anatolia where they could be conveniently strangled. But the janissaries rescued their commander, who was now resolved to place young Murat on the throne, thus substituting two lots of unfilled accession purses for one.

Abaza Disciplines the Regicides

Meanwhile, the shocking news of Osman's murder spread through the provinces. Abaza Mehmet Pasha, at his headquarters at Erzerum as Commander of the Western Marches, raised a motley army which had a core of first-class troops. He marched on Istanbul in order to punish the regicides and to depose the idiot sultan who was ruled by Davut and the Valide Sultan. Abaza saw the chance to advance himself to the Vezirate for he paused to capture Tokat, where there was a mint and therefore money with which to fill purses. His family were the rulers of the Georgians of the western Caucasus, which had once supplied eunuchs to the Byzantines. Abaza had begun his career as a rebel who, doubtless because of his good looks, was spared by the then *agha* of the janissaries, Halil. On becoming *kapudan paşa*, Halil gave Abaza command of a galley and later, as Grand Vezir, promoted him first to be governor of Maraş and then of Erzerum, a city as ever empty of honest citizens but full of troops.[42] Abaza was notoriously tough and the janissaries of the capital refused to march against him. Such ministers as had survived the holocaust of the last few weeks would gladly have been rid of Mustafa and Davut had they dared, but the Grand Vezir terrified both court and city.

Abaza marched implacably on with an ever-growing number of provincial commanders and magnates hastening to his standard. Showing how Osman might have succeeded had he been older and schemed more carefully, he slaughtered any janissary whom he encountered and the family as well. The panic-stricken corps obtained Abaza's dismissal from office but

The Janissaries

this did not halt his punitive activities or his rapid approach. In despair, they allied themselves with a deeply troubled *ulema,* who were the last reluctant supporters of the *vezir*. Deserted by one and all, Davut surrendered his seals of office on 15 June after a bare three weeks in office, which had however seemed too long. In his turn, he was immediately dragged to Yedikule, where he expiated his crimes one week later on 22 June, choosing to submit to justice on the exact spot where Osman had died. As for the miserable Mustafa, he was carried back once more to his cell, to wait quaking for the footsteps of the stranglers: they came in due course to dispose of the only threat to the accession of Murat IV, who was then but 12 years old.[43]

Janissary insolence was boundless. They and the *sipahis* refused to face certain defeat at the hands of Abaza Mehmet Pasha, claiming that it was too late in the year to go on campaign. They had the courage to demand donations, however, before they permitted the Divan to meet again. They strutted about the courts of the *saray,* demanding and obtaining lucrative offices such as the stewardships of the great mosques and other charitable foundations. Some officers became farmers of taxes and customs dues. Lawlessness inevitably extended down to the lowest ranks, who reeled drunkenly about the city demanding money from passers-by to pay for their wine and attacking any who refused. The court and the *ulema* were afraid to appear in public yet the terrified judiciary, who had most wealth to lose, merely added to their own sense of insecurity by pronouncing the new sultan to be illegally appointed. That this was partially true was the fault of the *şeyhülislam,* who spent the days of crisis in fear and trembling, seeking a way of escape. The decay of authority spread throughout the empire and janissaries in Smyrna (Izmir) attacked the foreign consuls. The government acknowledged its impotence by removing the mint from near the Bayezit mosque to the *saray* itself.

Yet Abaza Mehmet Pasha, who had ruled half Anatolia for five years, could not take the citadel at Bursa and the reverse halted his march. Murat IV's first Grand Vezir, the elderly and able Hafız Pasha, defeated Abaza before Kayseri on 26 May 1624. It was not a decisive battle since only Hafız's will-power and terror of the pasha kept the Ottoman army together. Abaza was able to retreat to Erzerum, where he agreed that a company of janissaries should be stationed in the city.

Hafız Pasha was in a hurry to reach Baghdad, which had been taken by the Persians in the preceding year and with it the control of the surrounding provinces. He besieged the city, which offered sufficient resistance to dismay the janissaries and the *sipahis* alike. They mutinied and Hafız Pasha was forced to retreat with his rabble to Dıyarbekir while fighting a fierce

Fish Stink from the Head

rearguard action all the way. Safe inside the redoubtable walls of Diyarbekir, the janissaries mutinied afresh; Hafız resigned his office, to be replaced by Halil Pasha, who was more gifted at intrigue than war. He foolishly attempted to lure Abaza from his stronghold in order to murder him but Abaza was no fool. He disposed of the pusillanimous janissaries who had been foisted on him and in the defiles of his own mountain territory he defeated Halil's force sent to capture Erzerum. So, in the autumn of 1627, Halil was forced to come in person to besiege Abaza. After two futile months, he returned in disgrace to Istanbul to be succeeded by Hüsrev Pasha. Hüsrev had the sense to offer Abaza the lucrative governorship of Bosnia—it had often been the bait with which to catch a rebel and here Abaza would be far from his followers. In 1628 the appointment was accepted: only then was it possible to restore a semblance of order to central and eastern Anatolia. Abaza protested his loyalty before Murat and warned him against the detestable janissaries, who had barbarously overthrown their sultan and killed numerous members of the *ulema* in their meeting-place, the great mosque of Fatih. Abaza became the confidential councillor of the sultan when the boy was old enough to rule. It is recorded that when angry janissaries refused to eat their soup one day, Abaza asked leave of Murat to make them eat both soup and dishes. As soon as Abaza appeared in their midst they were terrified and gobbled up their rations. Yet it was at their insistence that he was eventually executed in a white robe.

Murat IV: Laurels for a Sultan

For the present, a 12-year-old was too young to meddle in government. He wasted his restless energies on debauchery of every kind, from drunken sprees to wanton pederasty, and in the company of libidinous youths squandered everyone's respect. The dictatorship of janissary officers in alliance with the Valide Sultan, Mahpeyker Kösem, effectively continued into the spring of 1632. The ruling pashas could do nothing without these officers' consent and their own excesses deprived their men of pay, thus enraging them still further. A mulcted and frightened populace revolted against increased taxation and endless inflation. The *sipahis* were as restless as the janissaries and the Grand Vezir was driven to execute their *agha*; the unexpected result was that the janissaries perspicaciously joined with their hated rivals in a rebellion based on mutual self-interest. Stones were hurled and the *vezir* delivered into the hands of the rebels to be torn to bits. The *şeyhülislam* was deposed and his successor made to stand surety for the life of Murat's brothers, the ultimate heirs to the throne.

The Janissaries

In November 1630 Hafız Pasha was reappointed Grand Vezir but the janissaries were afraid of the stern old man and revolted in favour of the weak Hüsrev. The army in the field was recalled to Istanbul in the hope that a rest from fighting might assuage their rebelliousness, but they behaved like the conquerors that they were not, except over their own people. When they arrived on 6 February 1632, they were supported not only by the *ortas* of the garrison, the *sipahis* and the riff-raff but even the impoverished shopkeepers. This array stormed the gates of the *saray* and at the instigation of one Recep Pasha demanded, among other things, the head of the Grand Vezir.

Now a man of 23, Murat IV had the two ringleaders of the *sipahis* and the janissaries brought before him and attempted to recall them to their duty. His naturally autocratic manner enraged the two mature men, faced with this upstart of humiliatingly ill repute, and they demanded the life of the Grand Vezir. The pasha went calmly out to face the mob and fought bravely and effectively until he tired and could be stabbed to death. Murat's favourite, Musa Çelebi, was also murdered. The blood of two close friends did not move Murat to tears but to curses: the chronicler records that he recalled the advice of a military justice that the sword is the only cure for treason. The mob had no sooner departed to celebrate their success than he ordered the execution of Hüsrev Pasha.

Within a month, the Bosnian Recep Pasha had no difficulty in renewing the revolt in face of the sultan's clear threat to the power of the janissaries. The mob returned with renewed ferocity to slay their *agha*, a minister of state and yet another boon companion of Murat.[44] Worse, they openly shouted for the sultan's overthrow as if he were another Osman. He was not. On 18 May 1632 Murat mobilized his undoubted intelligence and all his virility, not to his bed but to his own defence. Recep Pasha was summoned and executed before the sultan's eyes and the white eunuchs were ordered to throw his corpse in the faces of the mutineers. Had he struck each one with his fist, the shock could not have been greater. They recoiled and slunk away. Murat was sultan at last.

Nor did he relent. His punitive policy was pursued inflexibly and punishment administered with a pitiless hand. Ahmet Agha, commander of the *sipahis*, was ordered to bring the ringleaders of sedition among his men to execution: honourably, perhaps, he refused and his own head was struck off on the spot. The watching household now stood with heads bowed and hands clasped before them as a sign of submission, not out of etiquette—that had worn thin—but before a force unleashed that they dared not defy. The soldiers who had purloined lucrative offices were dismissed. Mutineers were pursued and executed in the city and beyond the walls, week after week. Administrators, including members of the *ulema*, who had indeed much to account for, were punished for indolence as well as peculation. The *kadı* of Izmit was hanged because he had not maintained the road to Iznik in proper repair. Murat demanded and obtained an oath of loyalty from every janissary and every *sipahi* who remained inscribed on the rolls: a refusal meant death. But he went too far and too fast and a new wave of sedition spread through his capital. He prudently retired to Üsküdar, but he did not and could not put out the fires of vengeance which he had lit. When janissaries in the provinces killed their officers, the commanders responsible for discipline were sentenced to death as examples to the rest.

Murat revealed himself to be a soldier who could sleep under the stars with his saddle for a pillow. For a time he abandoned alcohol but he relinquished none of his other appetites. By 1634 he had little to fear from his army but confronted an *ulema* which had been forced to seek allies among the populace. A misguided uprising ended with the hanging of fifty ringleaders. These included a *kadı* whose death was regarded as sacrilege by the *ulema*. They indignantly met in the great mosque of Fatih. Murat had retired to Bursa but only to send for the *şeyhülislam* and his son whom he executed in their travelling clothes. A hush fell in the mosques and alleyways of Istanbul and sedition was silent. The will to rebellion was dead.

At the Davutpaşa camp, where troops trained and also assembled before setting out to fight in Europe, lightning penetrated the windows of the royal kiosk and scorched Murat's bedclothes.[45] Rumour even alleged that he had been struck on a second occasion. But once appears to have been enough, for, whether these warnings came from Allah or not, they frightened a man as superstitious as all his contemporaries. His escape could be acclaimed a miracle. Perhaps the lightning was sent to foretell victories whose real cause lay in his strict training of his janissaries, the purge he conducted of weak officers and the masterful Ottoman organization of commissariat and ordnance caravans. In 1635 he marched to Erivan and with the help of treachery took the city in eight days that August. From there, he sent the orders for the strangling of his adult brothers, Bayezit and Süleyman,[46] yet spared the weak-minded Ibrahim. This act of paranoia reveals a not unnatural sense of insecurity when a long way from the capital and, since no execution could take place without the subservient *fetva* of the *şeyhülislam*, there was no execution. All this arouses a certain curiosity concerning Murat's attitude to his house and the value of its survival.

The following year the Persians recaptured Erivan and decimated an Ottoman force. This showed that, without their sultan to lead them, the janissaries were far from the warriors of old. It also revealed the difficulty of maintaining long lines of communication when the earth had been scorched. Murat had planned the recapture of Baghdad throughout 1637 but the siege of the city was not undertaken until 1638. There the sultan dressed as a simple soldier and worked beside his men at digging trenches to surround the city, a prerequisite before taking any fortress. The work began immediately upon arrival, in defiance of the protests of his staff that his men were weary from long marches. Murat was rightly adamant and, by setting an example himself, his determination was rewarded. The day after the city fell, the trenches were flooded by torrential rains which would have put an end to the siege. On Christmas Eve a council of war deemed it possible to breach the wall. The Grand Vezir in person led the enthusiastic army to the assault only to fall with a bullet through his head. The *kapudan paşa* took over the command and a ferocious battle of the streets lasted for two days. Murat returned in triumph but was to die in 1640 either from sciatica or from his rigorous way of life, gluttony and sexual prowess.

The janissaries fought under him as well as they had ever done and were briefly worthy of their traditions. But the political climate had changed and Murat was an anachronism, brutal to excess. Yet not entirely. The orderly supply trains of his army, the camels, mules and water buffalo, together with the accurate timing of each rendezvous of supplies and army and the careful financing of the expeditions, all indicate a man who could have reformed the civil administration as well. It is probable that the *ulema* would have frustrated him, since the disestablishment of their tax-free and intellectually moribund class, full of the self-conscious pomposity of mayors in comedies, was essential for the recovery of the Ottoman state.

The Old Order and the New Classes

One class war did wither, however. The fading feudal powers of the *sipahis* foretold change even if their paid squadrons remained at full strength. The weakening of the military leasehold system meant a weakening of the sultan's control of the hinterland. Otherwise nothing but good could come of the break-up of a system that shuffled large and small estates among knights who had no hereditary interest in the fertility of their lands. Worse, they had been transferred from one fief to another until some must have hesitated before planting a rosebush which they could not hope to see bloom. With the new policy went the cutting down of the holdings of *beylerbeys* and governors, and the appointment of tax-collectors to raise money from the lessees of farms. This new cadre had to pay itself out of the monies collected; as a result, the land did not prosper but was milked by these parasites. If a hereditary element did develop among the sons of the *sipahis* it was not considerable unless allied to such commercial interests as the sawmills for the fleet in the woods above the naval base at Karamursel. None the less, farmers did become small landowners and the wiliest and most astute grew to be magnates capable of withstanding the depredations of the tax-farmers.[47] Such men could, if so inclined, protect the weak in return for their allegiance, an allegiance which brought more immediate results than any that emanated from the Porte. Among such families were janissaries who had failed to return to the capital after a campaign and their local imitators. A narrow class of petty chieftains slowly consolidated power and came to be known as the *ayan* in the seventeenth and eighteenth centuries. They were the valley lords since no one except bandits controlled the mountains or even the hills. Some families were so independent that they had to be wooed and flattered by a central government that dared not confront them. Indeed, this flattery was sometimes the only connection between the sultan and some magnate who failed to return any tribute to the capital.

These *ayan* repeated a pattern in Ottoman history. They belonged to the class of local commanders under the Mongol khans who had eventually rallied to the house of Osman or been taken in battle. Such medieval emirs as the Menteşe lords of the Meander were akin to the Çobanoğlu lords of Yozgat or the Karamanoğlu lords of Manisa in the eighteenth century. But *ayan* families did not march on Istanbul and they were too pettyfogging to think of usurping the throne; even Ali Pasha of Yanina was not so presumptuous. Some like Abaza Mehmet Pasha in the seventeenth century and Alemdar Pasha in the nineteenth might have had ideas of aggrandisement but neither attacked the dynasty; indeed, Alemdar sought to defend it. A Beylik period of petty chieftains was not reborn.

The provincial capitals of Anatolia like Amasya, Kütahya and Manisa had been dangerous centres of faction when ruled by the sultan's sons, which was why these unhappy princes came to be confined in the *saray*. Mere household officers (all *kul*) appointed in their stead held office for shorter and shorter periods until they might have one year's lease, rather than two or three, in which to fill their coffers. Although this made consistent and beneficial policies unlikely, it ensured that the ambitious had no time to rally local support against the Porte—as had happened in Mosul and Damascus until finally, in the nineteenth century, hereditary *beylerbeys* from Egypt marched on Istanbul.[48] Valley lords were rapacious but they spent their revenues in their own regions and their monuments survive at

The Janissaries

Yozgat and Doğubayezit. The pashas, on the other hand, squandered their money—extracted like teeth from their provinces until the gums were bare—on the shores of the Bosphorus. Moreover, without local roots, they had slept uneasily in their beds in the citadels and *konaks* for they were far from the court where rivals plotted their overthrow. Their fears were real: the *firman* delivered by the imperial *çavuş* and which ordered their return might be a hidden death sentence. For this reason, each pasha had his partisans who kept him informed about the day's intrigues and even enabled their master to mix in them, although at one remove.

The government also had its fears and spies[49] since a letter of recall might prompt a tough governor to revolt: and with reason. On his recall in 1655, Ibsir Pasha entered Istanbul at the head of a motley army but was quickly disposed of by the janissaries, who had no desire to share the grazing of their meadows with his rural herd. The great historian Evliya Çelebi recounts that when he (Evliya) was attached to the household of a rebellious pasha and was unable to excape, the crafty garrison commander closed the gates of the citadel of Ankara against this general but let him and his men lodge in the town; thus everybody's face was saved. The government even set one pasha against another by offering a lucrative post to the one who sent his rival's head in an appropriate velvet bag to Istanbul. Such despotism requires a certain wit, not to say a slapstick humour, which many Ottomans maintained surprisingly cheerfully through the vicissitudes of office or disgrace. In this lies one key to the understanding of the sudden quirks of behaviour, the submission to the injustices of fortune, and a willingness to serve under such monsters as Mustafa I or Ibrahim I. It must be added that all societies that depend on a blind self-interest, untempered by any capacity for self-criticism, are the playthings of ignorant chance. When they fell from power, the pashas could only console themselves with astonishment and, thus anaesthetized, submit to execution.[50]

If the empire held together, it was paradoxically due to the increasing autonomy of the regions; they became a rural federation centred on small towns and markets, interspersed with wastes created by goat and war. The spectacular increases in population of the towns of Anatolia were not sustained into the seventeenth century and the economic decline of Syria continued. Yet Osman I, Murat IV and Mehmet IV or their ministers still hoped to conquer a Europe that, since Süleyman's victory at Mohacs, had finally achieved superiority in arms, training and generalship.

The Ottoman army: (i) camel carrying two gun barrels; (ii) pack animals and baggage wagons; (iii) water supplies; (iv) the camp: picketed horses, cooking pots and latrines; from Marsigli (G. Gardiner)

8
Sharp Eyes and Long Legs

Madmen, Mothers and Minors

It was a symbolic moment when Murat IV angrily kicked the tomb of his forebear, Yıldırım Bayezit, because he had let himself be defeated by Timur. Murat's manifest hatred of his family may have been abetted by his knowledge of himself and an element of insanity in his character. Correctly, perhaps, he may have believed that a Crimean sultan—for the Giray khans were the supposed heirs to the Ottomans—or no sultan at all was preferable to his perverted brother, Ibrahim. If Muslim piety had spared Ibrahim until then, with almost his dying breath Murat ordered his execution. His rage over the deliberate delay in carrying out his order appears to have caused the stroke that killed him in 1640. As if he were the ghost of Mustafa I, Ibrahim was taken trembling from his cell, where he had long languished, not to his grave but the throne.

Frail and deformed as he was, his tastes differed from Murat's only in his choice of sex. His impassioned appetite for women was so notorious that it distorted Western concepts of the sultanate from the day that he acceded. He was obsessed with flesh for its own sake and his empire was searched for the fattest possible concubine. An Armenian woman weighing over 100 kilograms and immobile with fat was found and reigned as undisputed favourite. The Valide Sultan presented her son with a new girl of Rubenesque proportions every Friday and women were discarded from the harem like paper napkins; but the Armenian was pure damask and was never

Sharp Eyes and Long Legs

superseded. If Ibrahim needed regiments of women to satiate his gargantuan appetite, it was further stoked by quantities of aphrodisiacs. He also spent great sums on the silks and jewels with which he rewarded his darlings. His love of luxury led him to weave a net of diamonds in his beard and to monopolize the import of sables from Russia. He hung these furs as wallpaper in his voluptuous bedchamber.[1]

Ibrahim's temper was matchless. The least check to his caprice resulted in rages which grew into frenzies and were only quelled by exhaustion after a gale of injustices had stripped and uprooted those about him. When his son Mehmet was born, the Chief Black Eunuch selected a beautiful young slave from his own household to be the wet-nurse of the heir to the throne. Ibrahim fell in love with the girl and even preferred her own son to his. The boy's father is unknown but he was certainly not Sumbullu ('Hyacinth') the Eunuch, a name which can also mean either a single ear of grain or the constellation of Virgo. The scandal could not be hidden from Mehmet's mother, the redoubtable Hadıce Turhan (who was then only 16 years old), and a terrifying scene ensued. Ibrahim threatened to kill his son and allegedly threw the baby into a cistern. Sumbullu knew the tempers of both Ibrahim and Turhan and saw that several lives were in danger. He embarked on the flagship of the pilgrimage squadron with the son of his slave so as to escape royal vengeance and the anchor was weighed that same day. The fleet was attacked by the ever piratical Knights of Malta, who boarded Sumbullu Agha's vessel. The courageous eunuch fought valiantly before he was cut down and the baby captured. Ludicrously, the knights were convinced that this was the heir to the Ottoman throne and so took care of him until they reached Candia. There the Venetian governor welcomed them but rightly realized that the boy was no prince. He was brought up in Venice as a Christian and later became a monk; the credulous continued to regard the *padre Ottomano* as the son of the sultan.

When his spies informed him that the beloved boy had been taken to Candia, Ibrahim's fury was prodigious even for him: he ordered the extermination of all his Christian subjects. Fortunately the *şeyhülislam* had the courage to rescind the order and the Divan persuaded the sultan to cut the throats of all the Catholic priests instead. This decree was also suppressed but the envoys of the European monarchs were placed under house arrest. The English, Dutch and Venetian ambassadors pleaded that the Knights of Malta were all French subjects over whom they had no authority while the Grand Vezir astutely diverted Ibrahim's acts of pointless revenge into the declaration of the war he had long planned against Venice and its islands. A fleet of over 300 ships attacked Khania without warning on 24

169

The Janissaries

June 1645; 50,000 men were landed and took the town before a Venetian fleet could sail to its defence. It was an assault for janissaries to relish. The resulting conflict was quite other, for a brutal war of the islands and coasts ensued with ravages and massacres of the most senseless kind. The news was often bad enough to send Ibrahim into a predictable rage and the Christian population had only the remarkable personality of the *şeyhülislam* Abu Seyyit Efendi, which overawed the maniac, between them and extinction.

At first, Ibrahim's excesses were paid for out of the loot of Baghdad but his extravagance reached such proportions that the Grand Vezir was at his wit's end how to raise the money needed and his unpopular taxes led to his assassination.[2] Ibrahim only escaped deposition by surrendering his powers to his mother and the janissaries. In 1648 he celebrated the marriage of his 8-year-old daughter to the new Grand Vezir, Ahmet Pasha (posthumously nicknamed Hezarpare, or '1,000 Pieces', because shortly afterwards he was assassinated and hacked to bits). Ibrahim had ordered the execution of his masters, the senior officers of the janissaries, but they were forewarned and escaped to the barracks mosque where they rallied their troops and also won the *sipahis* to their side. The *ulema* allied themselves with the rebels, perhaps on the principle of kissing the hand which you cannot cut off, and the *şeyhülislam* willingly issued the *fetva* for Ibrahim's deposition since the sultan was said to have ravished the *şeyh*'s daughter. By this time Ibrahim was so demented that he might have raped his close stool. Mehmet IV, who had survived paternal hatred, was proclaimed sultan in 1648 at the age of 6. The mindless rabble was surprised when the *sipahis* reasonably argued against the reign of an infant while the ministers were terrified at the thought of a restoration. They summoned the mutes and hurried to the apartments where Ibrahim was confined. There, deaf to his frantic pleadings, the silken cord silenced him at last. He was 32 years old.

The lawlessness of the early years of Murat IV's reign was repeated under Mehmet IV. Only the individuals were different. Once again, insolent janissaries poked their noses wherever they pleased.[3] If they were checked at all it was by their hated rivals, the *sipahis*. At one point, the Anatolian brigade marched on the capital and succeeded in getting rid of a pusillanimous Grand Vezir and, more significantly, the *agha* of the janissaries. With only an army that was not an army, but a rabble, to deploy, the government quelled rebellions in Aleppo and Cairo with lavish bribes. The fleet was defeated by its own cowardice and when the janissaries went on strike the siege of Candia had to be raised because the reserves in Istanbul had stirred up the mob to scream for peace. One victim of their

Sharp Eyes and Long Legs

insubordination was the Grand Vezir of their own choosing, Sufi Mehmet Pasha, whose attempts to suppress the gathering forces of rebellion in Anatolia would have failed if the rebels had not quarrelled among themselves and betrayed each other. Money had been the underlying cause of Ibrahim's downfall and now the lack of it made Mehmet's position equally perilous. The *şeyhülislam*, the Grand Vezir and officers of state were deposed and replaced for the only constant element was the ever-increasing misery of the state. Valide Sultans, both young and old, literally fought out their rivalry to the death. Old Mahpeyker Kösem attacked the women loyal to Mehmet's Russian mother, Turhan, but her clothes were torn from her in the fight before she was dragged out of her apartment by her feet to the door of the Eunuchs' Mosque, where she was strangled with a curtain cord. Between 1651 and 1656 the young Valide Sultan set up Grand Vezirs like skittles for the janissaries to knock down and the economic situation was intolerable.[4]

Not only were new taxes invented but revenues were collected as much as two years in advance and still there was not enough coin with which to pay a rapacious army which would not fight. When new preparations were made for war, a fresh devaluation of the currency was inevitable. This could only provoke another mutiny and unite janissaries and *sipahis* with such small traders as were not already members of the corps. The Divan was powerless. In March 1656 the mutineers, dubbed the Lords of the Hippodrome, posted lists of statesmen and officers whom they had condemned to death. For seven days the city was pillaged, the *saray* attacked, ministers dismissed and the treasury looted. Mehmet was insulted.

Köprülü: a Man with a Mind at Last

It was indeed autumn in that September of 1656. The fallen Grand Vezir had been summoned the previous May from Aleppo. On his way to the capital he had requested an Albanian, Köprülü Mehmet Pasha, to come out of rural retirement on his Anatolian estates to join his service. Seeing that the minister would never solve the problems he faced, the 80-year-old pasha turned his house into a meeting-place for trusted friends and there they discussed possible solutions to the myriad stresses and strains that were deracinating the realm. This was a revolution: an intelligently formulated political programme was born and the Middle Ages were over. The cabal worked assiduously to have Köprülü raised to the Vezirate and when Turhan lost hope she had only this old man to whom she could turn. With careful timing and the way prepared, Köprülü asked for an audience with her on 13

The Janissaries

September; a secret meeting was arranged for that evening. The pasha arrived with a written contract, ready to be signed and sealed there and then.

The four basic clauses were that each and all of his requests were to be granted by the sultan, no one was to interfere with his awarding of offices, no *vezir* was to be his rival and all palace gossip and slander were to cease. Turhan was tough. Five years earlier she had defeated a coalition of janissary commanders and the old Valide Sultan by her alliance with the Chief Black Eunuch. Now, twist and turn as she might, her plots were in ruins and there were no ministers left to shuffle in and out of office. The revolt, which was plain to hear inside the palace and deafening outside, was aimed at the sultan himself. Turhan capitulated and Mehmet IV handed Köprülü Mehmet Pasha the seal of office the following morning. For 200 years the Grand Vezir had been the sultan's first deputy: now he was sultan in all but name and the 14-year-old Mehmet could hunt to his heart's delight provided he abdicated every semblance of power. Mehmet was to make Edirne his home because the chase there was so good and he understandably hated Istanbul. Moreover, Edirne was in Europe and any plans for aggrandisement were directed against the West. That the town was overcrowded to the point of being a slum where even ambassadors had difficulty in finding lodgings was subordinate to the relief of being eight days' ride away from the Horn. The boy showed no reluctance to confer powers that he did not possess on his formidable minister—at least for the present, since octogenarians do not live for ever and no one could have foreseen the Köprülü hereditary nepotism.[5]

The new master of the realm was physically fit. Taking the sultan and the other *vezirs* with him, he rode out into a seething city and dispersed the mobs and gangs terrorizing every neighbourhood. Secure in the awareness of his own authority, he rapidly impressed it on the capital and order was restored. In 1654 the Grand Vezir had obtained an official residence across the road from the Sokollu Gate to the *saray* park. Köprülü made it his seat of government and his was the Sublime Porte through which his imperial edicts flowed. He revoked the death sentence passed on his predecessor, an act of natural justice to a friend who had prepared the way for him, but proceeded with a different face against the mutineers. Hundreds, if not the alleged 4,000, janissary corpses contaminated the waters of the Marmara Sea and a clamorous army fell strangely silent.

In Danger of Dissolution

The Grand Vezir was now free to tame Anatolia. During 1657 he disciplined the janissary corps sufficiently to lead them to victory on the Konya plain in July 1658. An unruly assembly of local pashas and lords of the valleys was dispersed. Unlike his predecessors, the old man followed up his victory with reforms that reduced the burdens on the treasury and offered the helpless peasantry some protection. Both he and his son and successor, Fazıl ('Learned') Ahmet Pasha, who ruled from 1661 to 1676, steadily reduced the number of janissaries and a new corps was founded with the intention of abolishing the janissaries altogether. By now, most of the corps were tradesmen who used their tattoo to be rid of the encumbrance of civil justice: a privilege which rebounded against them since the miserable populace were jealous and no longer followed their lead. The accounts of the corps were in disarray. Not even the *agha* knew how many troops he had under his command since the detachments' colonels were issuing pay slips for pensioned veterans and even the dead. Because the treasury was often in arrears, the vouchers were negotiable and so were sold to money-lenders, among others. The corps was effectively made up of officers and sergeants and a few raw recruits.

The *sipahis* were no better and their weapons were outdated. Köprülü Mehmet Pasha weakened them still more by setting the janissaries against them in the usual manner. But his new corps failed to achieve a position of respect: perhaps because of a real decline in military ardour throughout the Ottoman lands, where the first shoots of local loyalty were reborn now that the best provincial youths were no longer carried off to become slaves of the royal family. The artillery contined to grow, however, and, after several foreign experts had been enlisted over the following 100 years, reached maturity.

In 1679 Count Marsigli arrived in Istanbul for a stay of eleven months during which time he became a considerable authority on the janissary corps. This remarkable man was to be made a prisoner and a slave during the siege of Vienna in 1683. He survived the débâcle which ended it and returned to Istanbul in 1691, where he remained until the following year and became the friend of another Grand Vezir from the Köprülü family, Amcazade ('Cousin') Hüseyn Köprülü. He studied the Ottoman army in detail and was given access to the registers and records. In his opinion, Mehmet IV and his ministers deliberately undermined the discipline of the janissaries by encouraging them to disperse and take up lucrative appointments or else to idle away their time in dissipation. They were promoted by favour, not merit or valour, and their prestige wilted to such a degree after their defeat at Niş that the Grand Vezir appointed a civilian member of his household to be their *agha*. By 1692 there were so few

The Janissaries

volunteers willing to join the corps that the government was forced to send out recruiting officers offering high pay, privileges and the right to follow a trade or a profession else the city would have been without either police or firemen and the frontier forts ungarrisoned. However, Arabs and gypsies continued to be excluded officially. Once the levy had been suspended, probably through lack of authority, the ruling institution was cut off from its roots and could not plant new ones.

In wartime the janissaries were largely replaced by volunteers who fought only during the summer months and then dwindled away. Theoretically, they were paid out of booty won in the field and so cost nothing to maintain. They did not even possess uniforms and a large number of them were Albanian mountaineers or came from other Balkan fastnesses where the diminished prosperity of the plains had reduced the spoils of banditry. They were useful only when victorious since, when outmatched, these undisciplined rascals fled home. In this they were the equals of the janissaries who, according to the Turkish proverb, had good eyes and long legs. Flight was, as we have seen, an accepted Ottoman tactic. If the volunteers ran away and abandoned guns, tents, baggage and honour, the casualties were few and there were no recruiting problems after a defeat. But brigands were no substitute for a trained, standing army which had won the Ottomans an empire.

Fazıl Ahmet Pasha, who became Grand Vezir in 1661, enlisted the best remaining *ortas* of the janissaries and established Ottoman power in Transylvania. It seemed as if a renaissance was possible and a protégé of his family, the brutal Kara Mustafa Pasha of Merzifon, who succeeded him as Grand Vezir in 1676, dreamt afresh of the conquest of the German lands. Moreover, there were successful campaigns against the Poles and Russians and an attempt to control the Cossacks of the Ukraine. These achievements were partly due to the splendid if erratic horsemen of the khan of Crimea.

The economic crisis continued to burn fitfully partly because the Ottomans, with a residual Islamic distaste for usury, stubbornly refused to follow the example of Europe and establish a national debt although the time was to come when they would revel in such a resource. Capital was gradually accumulated, however, and in 1683 there was enough ready money to equip 200,000 men. The *ulema* believed the moment to be propitious and they incited the janissaries to shout for war. Only a major conquest could recoup such an investment and this was Kara Mustafa Pasha's first objective when he marched on Vienna that year.

Sharp Eyes and Long Legs

Into the Dark: Vienna

Dark of face and dark of humour, the son of a *sipahi* who had been a palace page before enjoying the patronage of the Köprülüs, Kara Mustafa Pasha loved splendour and when he achieved his ambition and became Grand Vezir at the age of 42 he indulged his passion. At one meeting with a Prussian envoy, Mustafa was attended by 100 pages in cloth of gold over mail. His household held 1,000 slaves, 1,500 concubines, 750 eunuchs and a menagerie of horses, hounds and beasts. He drank to excess even by Christian standards.[6] His greatest misfortune—until Vienna—was the disfigurement of his good looks when fighting one of those frequent fires which blighted a wooden city where the houses, wrote the merchant Roger North, hung together like bird-cages. Kara Mustafa sulked in his apartments for three months before he was prepared to appear again in public. His campaign of 1677 did little to win him repute and so his vanity needed to be restored in every direction.

When Süleyman had besieged Vienna in 1529, the city would have been taken had not a wet summer bogged down the heavier guns on the road from Edirne and the janissaries grown mutinous as autumn approached. Kara Mustafa came within grasp of victory and this is the measure of his defeat. The emperor and his court fled the city on 7 July 1683, five days before the Ottoman camp was set up with an orderliness that astonished the defenders. The Grand Vezir had a garden planted in front of his tent and with this elegance went a certain indolence just when time could not be wasted. None the less, forty land-mines and ten counter-mines were exploded and there were eighteen Ottoman attacks.

By September many of the outworks were taken and the inner walls were crumbling but Kara Mustafa did not attack because he believed that the city was about to surrender. He may also have been cautious because the janissaries were hungry and ready to mutiny. Had Vienna been taken by assault he would have been compelled to permit the army three days and nights of looting just when the booty was desperately needed by the state. His patience was unkindly rewarded by the sudden arrival of Prince John Sobieski and his Poles; on 12 September the Polish cavalry impetuously attacked the Ottoman lines. The Grand Vezir, who had stubbornly disbelieved reports of a meeting between the prince and a force of 27,000 men under the Duke of Lorraine a week before, was taken inexplicably by surprise. By nightfall the besiegers were routed and the whole army fled, abandoning all that they possessed except for such slaves as Marsigli, who ran as fast barefoot as their booted masters ran or rode. They left behind 300

175

The Janissaries

guns, 5,000 tents, pay, provisions and all the banners and horsetails except for the sacred Standard of the Prophet. Kara Mustafa rallied his men before Buda only to be defeated in another bloody battle when his army was completely demoralized. Although he had all the fugitives shot or cut down, he could not quell the panic and his staff and his field commanders united against him.

At Edirne the defeated pasha had no friends left. Even the Valide Sultan had become his enemy. An officer met him at Belgrade with a *firman* ordering him to hand over his seal of office and to submit to execution. His head was brought back to Edirne in a velvet bag, but it did no more dead than it had done when on his shoulders to diminish the economic consequences of defeat. The revenues were depleted by the loss of rich provinces, agriculture had been disrupted by the mobilization of so many men, and the officers were as clamorous as ever in demanding their pay. Despite a campaign tax from which the indignant *ulema* were not exempt, the government could not afford to maintain military bases or even elementary supplies and in 1687 was forced to forbid all promotion as an economy measure. The army was five quarterly payments in arrears and a revolution was inevitable.[7] The Poles invaded Moldavia and the Venetians and the Russians joined in the war. All the Divan could do was appeal for help from France.

Defeat followed upon defeat. Buda fell and a new Grand Vezir, Süleyman Pasha, was routed at Mohacs among the ghosts of Ottoman glory when the janissaries fled leaving 8,000 dead and 2,000 prisoners along with baggage and artillery. His senior officers demanded Süleyman Pasha's resignation and, fearful for his own safety, Mehmet IV sent them the *vezir*'s severed head. Mutinous janissaries and *sipahis* abandoned the theatre of war and trudged towards Edirne while the Peloponnese was conquered and Count Königsmark, the German military adventurer, entered Athens. Food reached astronomic prices and there was starvation in Anatolia. It happened that the Ottomans then obtained a notable victory but did not know it. Prince Galitzine assembled a vast army of 300,000 infantry and 100,000 cavalry, supported by 1,200 guns and 1 million horses. He set forth from Moscow to roll up the Ottoman Empire like tattered linoleum. This monstrous force was too big to live off the country and the commissariat lacked all the careful planning of the Ottomans. It ran out of food for the men and fodder for the horses, and the unfortunate animals exhausted all the grazing for miles around. Thus the Russian army defeated itself and was forced to retreat in disorder through a desert of its own creation.

176

Sharp Eyes and Long Legs

Are the Ottomans Worth Keeping?

The governor, Köprülüzade Fazıl Mustafa Pasha, yet another member of the inexhaustible Köprülü clan, saved the throne by obtaining a *fetva* of deposition for its occupant on the grounds of his neglect of his royal duties. Mehmet IV accepted his fate, which he acknowledged to be the will of Allah, and on 8 November 1687 he retired to apartments set aside for him in the palace. Mehmet's half-brother, Süleyman II, had spent forty-six years in seclusion and was terrified when called upon to succeed. He was interested in religion, not government, and when faced with a mutinous army he distributed the accession purses and promoted the leaders of the revolution. He was twice to command his army in the field, at least in name, but his health was poor, not unnaturally. His janissaries saluted their new sovereign by slaughtering their *agha* and senior officers and murdering the Grand Vezir, Siyavuş Pasha. They then invaded the *vezir*'s harem, mutilated his wife and sister and paraded them shamefully through the streets.

For five months, outrage followed upon outrage until Süleyman unexpectedly roused himself, summoned a pusillanimous *ulema*, ordered them to unfurl the Standard of the Prophet and called on all true Muslims to fight the mutineers. He was responding to an emotional upsurge of disgust among the populace against a defeated rabble who had no policy except sadism and theft, let alone a long-term plan for the future. They were superstitious as well as cowardly and the sacred flag frightened them. The moment for action had come and the usually timorous Süleyman took command of his loyal units and quelled the rebels. He executed few of the ringleaders but this was sufficient to restore order to the cities: he had won the support of the tradesmen janissaries and the common folk by abolishing a number of oppressive commercial taxes.[8] All this could not save Belgrade falling to the Christians in September 1688, however, and in November Ottoman envoys arrived in Vienna and sued for peace. This was opposed by the emperor's allies, who hoped for rich rewards from a continuing conflict.

Köprülüzade Fazıl Mustafa Pasha now set about dismissing dishonest administrators. He confiscated their wealth and improved the debased state of the currency. He recruited a new army[9] and treason came to a halt—except that he was himself its chief depository. He told Marsigli in confidence that he was seriously considering putting an end to a dynasty which produced sultans like Süleyman and his successor, Ahmet II. But true power remained in the hands of the janissaries for so long as self-interest united them and the *ulema*, a curious alliance which at least prevented the government from making extravagant plans for a new campaign.

The Janissaries

Köprülüzade was regarded with awe but was also suspected of madness because, unlike normal ministers, he habitually thought out his policies. He would pace up and down a courtyard for as long as two hours while wrestling with a problem and this was regarded as a sign of an unbalanced mind. He also sought advice from experienced Westerners like Marsigli. In 1690, shortly before a merciless mischance killed him in battle, he unhappily consulted a foreign naval engineer working at the Tersane about a solution to the chronic economic crises. The foolish man suggested that one more devaluation would have to precede reforms; the inevitable unrest which followed turned into rebellion as soon as the death of Köprülüzade was known in Edirne. The engineer was arrested and beheaded in an attempt to pacify the populace. For the remaining months of Ahmet's reign, generals jostled for power and assorted Grand Vezirs handed on the seal like batons passed by the runners in a relay race. The struggle between supporters of a peace policy and those dedicated to war continued unabated between 1691 and 1695. Over both factions hung the horror nightmare of the kind of peace that would have to be accepted.

The drunken Ahmet II died of dropsy in 1695. He was succeeded by no more eminent a prince than Mustafa II, a son of Mehmet IV and the Cretan Rabia Gülnuş Ummetullah, born to the Venetian family of the Versizzi. This formidable woman was to rule from her other son Ahmet III's accession in 1703 to her death in 1715. If she did not actually sit in the Divan, as Mahpeyker Kösem allegedly did, she certainly sat on many of the members. The new sultan, Mustafa II, had spent a mere seven years in the Cage (the place of exclusion and confinement in the *saray*), which he had not entered until he was 23, whereas the miserable Ahmet II had frittered away forty-three years in seclusion. Lord Paget, the English ambassador, wrote that Mustafa was young and new and did not understand affairs, yet thought himself to be great and powerful.

Indeed, Mustafa alarmed his ministers by announcing that he would not give himself up to voluptuous living but would lead his army in the field. And this he did, to be rewarded by his capture of the great beauty Anna Sophia von Wippach (daughter of Ernst Wilhelm von Hanstein), who embellished his harem. This inconsequential conquest was followed by disaster when Prince Eugene, whose military genius depended less on astrologers and magicians, destroyed the sultan's forces at Zenta on 11 September 1697.

The first secret overtures to the emperor for a peace treaty had been made by the envoys sent to announce the accession of Süleyman II in 1687. With the assumption of power by Köprülüzade, leader of the war party, the

Sharp Eyes and Long Legs

proposal to make the river Sava the new frontier in return for Belgrade was jettisoned. The French held out hopes of an alliance and invaded the Rhineland. The English envoy William Hussey, urged on by the Levant Company, worked for peace both in Edirne and in Vienna. The economic situation in Vienna was little better than it was for the Ottomans, and the administration was as fuddled with self-importance and as narrow-minded as the Divan. The Divan was now receiving bribes from the French ambassador because Louis XIV's one instruction was to prolong the war. The task of a peacemaker was impossible since when victory was in sight, peace was no longer attractive as it had been when the enemy were losing. In 1690, for example, Köprülüzade recaptured Belgrade and Niş and with 300,000 troops in the field triumphantly talked of a third siege of Vienna. The situation was the reverse of that in 1688, when there were no funds and no recruits and troubles in Anatolia delayed the raising of a large army.

Suddenly Köprülüzade was dead at the disastrous battle of Salankmen in 1691. Resorting to a schoolboy strategy, the Imperial forces had laid a trap of felled trees. It worked because it was childish, as so often in war which, in reality, is an infernal game played by grey children in a vast nursery. Two waves of Ottomans charged against the German cannon before the death of the Grand Vezir, riding at the head of his *sipahis,* demoralized the army, which fled with the loss of 28,000 men and 150 guns. There was no money left with which to re-equip an army and empty campaigning seasons drifted by until the winter of 1695. During that year enough money had been accumulated to enable vast preparations to be made for the following year, which brought temporary gratification to Mustafa II and his equally bellicose mother. The crushing defeat of the Ottomans in August was made worse by the desertion of their French allies, who were distracted by the problems of the Spanish Succession.

Lord Paget Plods the Path to Peace

William Hussey had died of the plague in Edirne and a second English envoy, William Harbord, had also died at his post—his death was occasioned by a fit of rage due to the prevarications and delays of the Ottomans at Belgrade in July 1692. The ludicrous French ambassador, Châteauneuf, was promising the support of heavily manned and supplied, but entirely imaginary, French ships. In addition, a real contingent of French engineers were to work on the modernization of Ottoman equipment and fortifications, especially those of the straits of the Dardanelles, which were seriously threatened by Venice. Thus French influence was at its height[10] when the

The Janissaries

third English plenipotentiary arrived in Edirne in February 1693, after long delays due to foul weather. Lord Paget was not to see the sultan until March, by which time the Grand Vezir and the Divan had already rejected any idea of making peace. The articles of the proposed treaty were falsified and then read out to the janissaries by their *agha* Ismail Pasha in order to inflame them against the mediators.

By 1694 Paget was reporting on the hopelessness of negotiating with governments which came and went like fruit in season and later he commented scornfully on the feebleness of the army. Some six months later the janissaries in Sofia mutinied over their pay: pay as always. The Divan lost hope amid the disasters of 1696 for they were fearful of Persian militancy, the Russian threat and the actuality of the Venetian fleet. Popular revulsion against war matched that felt by the janissaries. Although some voices in the Divan were still bought by Châteauneuf, the silly fellow's boasts—beacons for imaginary victories—and broken promises now met with contempt. When he was approached by senior Ottoman ministers, Lord Paget had lost hope of achieving a treaty. However, he wearily consented to see the Grand Vezir, Amcazade Hüseyn Köprülü, and on informing King William III was instructed to pursue the peace.

On Christmas Day 1696, Paget had a long conversation with Amcazade Hüseyn Köprülü at Edirne and on 21 January the Divan was summoned. Among those present were the sultan, the khan of the Tartars and the *agha* of the janissaries, whose support was essential. Also present were the *reis efendi* and Mavrocordato, the intriguing ambassador extraordinary whose failures as Ottoman envoy had nearly cost him his head. Amcazade Hüseyn Köprülü was aware of the strength of the German forces for he had fought them at St Gothard and elsewhere, but he hoped to make an advantageous peace with the weaker Venetians. Paget's firmness kept at bay those ministers still on the French payroll and the Divan accepted the need for peace.

Now the problem was a warlike Poland and the visions of Peter the Great of Russia, yet he proved the easier to win over. In May 1697 the campaigning season began, with preparatory manoeuvres so as not to arouse suspicions. At the Grand Vezir's request, Paget went with him to Sofia. On 23 July the sultan allowed the envoys to leave for Vienna with Paget in spite of continued attempts by the French to continue the war. In August the long-drawn-out negotiations met with hitch after hitch but each in its turn was removed. On 11 September the Ottoman defeat at Zenta made a campaign unthinkable during the following year. Faced by Prince Eugene before Sofia, the janissaries entrenched and suffered severely before they could beat back the first attack. While the enemy regrouped, the janissaries mutinied and refused to hold the line even when their officers shot them down. The Austrians slaughtered 20,000 and 1,000 drowned in the river. The sultan, *gazi* or no *gazi*, fled to Istanbul.

The Disgrace of Karlowitz

If little happened in 1698 it was because the emperor was also war-weary and as short of money as the Porte. In September, the need for peace was conceded by his ministers and suddenly there was a hustle. A year later, the emissaries assembled at Karlowitz, a small village on the Danube, where a conference hall had to be built and suitably grandiose camps prepared. The hall was still unfinished when the conference opened on 13 November, however, and the envoys met in a tent. In spite of delays of all kinds, the pressure was maintained by the Austrians as much as by Paget and the Ottomans. After separate negotiations with Poland, Russia and the Venetians, the treaty was signed on 21 January 1699, thus ending Ottoman imperial greatness. Suddenly, everyone relaxed and the envoys entertained each other lavishly. Feasting, fireworks and fountains of wine were an agreeable change from iron rations, gunfire and fountains of blood. Needless to say, the ratifications were delayed but this was largely due to the bitterness of that inclement winter, which fortified the peace with impassable drifts of driven snow. The odium of the peace of Karlowitz had to be endured by the sultan. Although Amcazade Hüseyn Köprülü's reforms of taxation and the army were farseeing, he too was doomed.

The Divan appointed a soldier as Grand Vezir and in Daltaban ('the Barefoot or Vagabond') Pasha they found one more stupid than most. When he declared his intention of renouncing the treaty, the alliance of janissaries and *ulema* broke. The *şeyhülislam* was the notorious Feyzullah Efendi into whose keeping the sultan placed most of his authority. Feyzullah was both ambitious and inordinately greedy. Not only did he amass scandalous wealth in a time of deprivation; he was delighted to use his influence in innumerable political intrigues. He rightly saw that Daltaban Pasha was dangerous and speedily effected his downfall; for reasons of security, he had the upstart strangled. A bureaucrat was then elevated to Grand Vezir for the first time, an appointment prematurely wise.

Rami ('the Archer') Mehmet Pasha represented a new class which was utterly opposed to the unending procession of defeated soldiers in the office of first minister. Such men were often brutal as well as failures in their own trade and were unsuited to the government of an empire in transition. The

The Janissaries

new minister knew that it was essential to reform an army as barnacled with abuses as a forgotten wreck. Although his nickname Rami suggests that he was a respected bowman and therefore not without military training, Mehmet Pasha could not hope to survive a quarrel with generals. He was also opposed to the intrigues of Feyzullah Efendi, who added nepotism to his other vices and thus ensured his unpopularity at court. The *vezir* therefore fomented a riot in order to be rid of this pope. His plan succeeded. Feyzullah was arrested—his successor ignobly signed the *fetva* which alone could legalize this outrage—and the dispossessed old man was thrown to the mob. He contrived to escape and had nearly reached Varna when he was caught and dragged to Edirne, where he suffered appalling tortures in a vain attempt to draw out of him the whereabouts of his hidden treasure.[11] His sons were equally unfortunate. But the white-bearded scapegoat did not save Rami Mehmet from the deserved consequences of conjuring up the rabble and the janissaries. They marched into Edirne, imposed Ahmet Pasha as Grand Vezir and, on 22 August 1703, deposed Mustafa II, forgotten as he might be. He died of dropsy some months later.

Thus Ahmet III came to the throne in the same miserable and drearily repetitive circumstances that had become the rule, dispensing the largest accession purses in Ottoman history to rebels whom he yearned to exterminate. Fortunately, he had Feyzullah's wealth to draw on. When other troops mutinied and demanded equivalent awards, they roused no support for their rebellion. Nor was their call to put an end to the dynasty heeded. They lost cohesion and became pernicious brotherhoods of bandits, kept alive by ravaging Thrace. The future for Ahmet III was far from auspicious.

Once again, the only ally that the throne could court was the janissary corps, which had no interest other than its own survival. Although these men had, in effect, been politicians for a century they still could not draw up realistic objectives. Thus they offered no ultimate threat to the governing institution: as opposed to unlucky individual members of it. They could bully, rebel and rob. They could stack and overturn their cauldrons and make them boom because, like the janissaries themselves, they were hollow. But the *ortas* could produce no one capable of governing the country in his own right.

Jacques de Hay: solak, *bodyguard of the sultan (Maggs)*

9
Tulips and Turmoil

Ali versus Ali

Ahmet III made Istanbul the sultan's chief residence again after nearly half a century. He trusted nobody and dismissed four Grand Vezirs in three years, during which time he also rid himself of the rebels (who had jostled him onto the throne) by disgrace and banishment. It showed again how inept the janissaries were at uniting in defence of individuals. Ahmet even succeeded in ridding himself of recruits brought in by the final *devşirme* levy. He even reduced the swollen numbers of the janissary corps without arousing their overt hostility but he rightly lived in morbid terror of these revolutionaries.

In May 1706 Ali Pasha of Çorlu was given the seal of Grand Vezir. Not yet 40 years old, he was the son of a barber of Corfu who had been adopted by a member of the household, no doubt because of his good looks, and went as a cadet to the college at Galatasaray. Thence he was promoted to the Enderun Kolej and rose rapidly in the favour of Mustafa II. Unfortunately, he aroused the jealousy of the *şeyhülislam*, Feyzullah Efendi, and also of the Grand Vezir, Rami Mehmet Pasha, who ousted him from the controllership of the palace pages and expelled him to Syria as governor of Tripoli. Ahmet III remembered this comely officer, however, and recalled him as a Vezir of the Dome before making him his first minister. Ali Pasha belonged to the peace party and had very little military experience. He had married a sister of Mustafa II because it was customary for the sultan to increase a *vezir*'s commitment to the Ottoman house in this way. Although he reformed the standing army and improved the shipyards, the war party were his enemies. They were reinforced, as always, by the envious and this able minister fell from office on 10 June 1710. He was exiled as governor of Caffa in the Crimea before being transferred to Mytilene where he was executed on 11 December.

Ali Pasha of Çorlu's greatest adversary had been Damat Ali Pasha of Iznik, who was married to a daughter of Ahmet III (hence his title of Damat, or royal son-in-law). 'Coke-Seller' Ali, as he was also known, formed a secret cabinet within the *saray* consisting of himself, the meddling Valide Sultan and the Chief Black Eunuch. A village boy, Ali had been an intimate member of Ahmet II's household and there had cultivated the friendship of Ahmet III. He had distinguished himself modestly by suppressing banditry in Anatolia and a revolt in Syria. He was a self-seeking opportunist but an able minister who cut court expenditure,[1] forbade the giving of presents and reopened the pages' school at Galatasaray which had been changed into a *medrese*. He skilfully enlisted the support of both the trading and the fighting janissaries, which enabled him to overthrow the interim Grand Vezir, Koca Ibrahim Pasha. He was just in time because the old man was, very wisely, plotting his assassination. Ali Pasha achieved his life's ambition by becoming Grand Vezir on 13 April 1716. He was immediately sent to fight against Prince Eugene at Peterwardein where he was shot through the head. It was a rearguard action distinguished by lack of janissary zest. The news of his death resulted in the force which had landed on Corfu immediately embarking for home. Eugene went on from victory to victory and in 1718 the peace of Passarowitz was signed.

Too Civilized a Grand Vezir

Passarowitz was a humiliating treaty that meant the fall of the next Grand Vezir and Damat Nevşehirli Ibrahim Pasha's appointment to that office. Born in *c.* 1666, the son of a local landowner of Nevşehir, he came to Istanbul in 1698 where his patron found him a clerkship in the palace. His excellent calligraphy resulted in his appointment to the Religious Department and Ali Pasha posted him as tax-collector in Niş after an apprenticeship in the Peloponnese. These rural retreats can have given him little pleasure for he was devoted to urban luxury and the arts. Once Ahmet III made his acquaintance, they became fast friends.

Soon the sultan's confidant, Nevşehirli Ibrahim Pasha married the widow of Ali the Coke-Seller (killed at Peterwardein) in 1717 when she was only

The Janissaries

12 years old. Thus a man untrained for war became Grand Vezir after only two years' apprenticeship. One of his first actions was to send Yermisekiz ('Twenty-Six', the number of his janissary *orta*) Mehmet Seyyit Efendi as head of an embassy to France with the express purpose of bringing back plans of French palaces and other examples of Western culture. It was due to Nevşehirli Ibrahim Pasha that the languishing kilns of Iznik were refired in the ruins of the Byzantine palace known as Tekfursaray in Istanbul, porcelain was manufactured on the Bosphorus, paper mills were subsidized and the first printing press was set up. He also had textile mills built. Apart from champagne and orange trees, Yermisekiz brought back baroque plans of pavilions which were emulated at Kağıthane, the little palace among the meadows at the head of the Golden Horn. Ahmet III loathed the sea but loved easy access to the Belgrade forest, where he liked to picnic, carouse and watch girls dancing in the Elysian groves.

Of Nevşehirli Ibrahim Pasha, the Venetian *bailo* reported that he brooked no rivals but was renowned for his largesse. He enjoyed old customs and so revived the *bayram* feast at Eyüp in which he partook with the *agha* of the janissaries with whom he cultivated the best relationships in order to survive. Yet in 1723 he cut back the pay of the corps, including that of men on fortress duty, thus making them his enemies for life, which was not long. He was as devoted to the sultan whom he had civilized as Ahmet was to him. On one unprecedented occasion Ahmet spent four nights in his *vezir*'s palace, which Ibrahim—like Wolsey with Henry VIII—prudently presented to his monarch. He could follow no other policy than that of peace for the Ottoman army was shattered and demoralized and he could not lessen economic hardship while simultaneously indulging his sovereign without restraint.

It was a time of flower festivals and midnight lanterns in the *saray*, of tortoises carrying candles on their backs and candles inset in the roses. Called the Tulip Period (Lala Devri), it was also an age of water, when *sebils* (fountains) blossomed like cherry trees all over the city and throughout the provinces. The *sebils* were frequented not just for fresh water iced with the snows of Uludağ but for sherbet and other extravagances. A new dam was built for the head-waters of the Belgrade forest and canals and basins embellished the little palace at Kağıthane. Government posts went to freeborn Muslims of Nevşehirli Ibrahim Pasha's own caste since the levy had ended for ever although the janissary colleges continued.

Ahmet built a fine new library in the Third Court of the *saray* behind the Throne Room in place of the Kiosk of the Pool. A capriciously expensive programme was the reconstruction of the Byzantine wall of the city. The

Tulips and Turmoil

encouragement of books and the stocking of libraries were matched by the popularity of that other road to fiction, drugs. The *reis efendi* is said to have consumed 200 grams of opium each day.[2] One is not surprised that a perceptive French ambassador, the Marquis de Villeneuve, reported that Ahmet's throne was more fragile than any other in the world and that precipices surrounded his Grand Vezir on every side. Although Nevşehirli Ibrahim Pasha had exiled one of the sultan's favourites and had got rid of another (the Master of the Horse), his enemies within the *saray* were determined to achieve his overthrow. At first, they had no success against his cunning: but they possessed true Ottoman patience. Nevşehirli might be a great liberal but he was unfit as a leader in war and war was considered inevitable 'in the national interest'. The term was synonymous with suicide, partly because of a silver crisis caused by the flight of currency to Persia and America and partly because of the persecution of the sultan's Sunni subjects in Persia. Moreover, ministers feared that waves of rebellion there might prove contagious. When Nevşehirli Ibrahim Pasha decided to attack the Shah,[3] he had great difficulty in raking up men for the janissaries and had to take them from all over the empire. Yet in 1724 Ahmet Pasha, the commander in the field, won resounding successes and entered Hamadan after 50 days. The guns at the *saray* and the Tersane thundered their applause while the populace rejoiced in the streets for a week. Three months later Erivan fell: the city lit fireworks and illuminations and 126 volleys were fired by 2 French warships.

Twisted Fortune

Bad news followed on good, however, and the reactionaries took heart. No previous *vezir* had survived such a procession of dismal dispatches or a city hungry from inflationary prices. These were not helped by janissary meddling with commerce, for their monopoly of the okra market ruined the producers and killed the supply. False messengers were arranged to announce victory when defeat at the hands of the Russians on the Caspian could not be hidden for long. Nor was it possible to hide Nadir Shah's triumphs over the sultan's lamentable forces because of public interest in the desperate campaigns. In 1721 the Ottoman casualties were said to be 50,000. The *ulema*, who had disapproved of the occupation of Persian territory, were now openly hostile. Defeat gave them courage and for this the janissaries cannot be blamed entirely since Nevşehirli Ibrahim Pasha's refusal to allot sufficient funds for the war was far more reprehensible. Westernization was as unpopular with the mob as it was with the *ulema* and if the latter, in

187

apartments stuffy with velvet and pearls, could hardly cavil too loudly at the luxury of the court, the hungry populace had no such inhibitions.

Meanwhile, the enemy within the *saray* was quick to let the janissaries know that reforms were being planned. Finally, 1729 brought a disastrous defeat in Persia which the government hoped to reverse by raising new companies for use the next year. Indeed, the ministers were so intemperate that when a Persian envoy arrived in May he was beheaded for defending the attitude of his Shah. Both the sultan and Nevşehirli Ibrahim Pasha were kept informed of the ferment in the city and the mutinous mood of some of the janissaries but they hesitated fatally. When they tried ruthlessly to suppress the coming uprising, it was already too late. Since the janissaries employed arson as their ambassador, it was significant that in July the Venetian *bailo* reported a fire greater than any seen before, whose consequences might take 50 years to repair. He exaggerated in stating that 40,000 citizens died (the true number was probably around 5,000) and that 130 mosques were consumed by a holocaust which increased inflation by precipitating a rise in the cost of building materials.

Ibrahim continued to juggle with the news of defeats and with the economics of ruin into the autumn of 1730. On 27 September some twenty-five rebels, led by three improbable rabble-rousers who had floated to the top of the ferment, seized a tattered flag in the bazaar and called for the support of the janissaries and the populace. It was a holiday and the superior civil servants were enjoying themselves on the shores of the Bosphorus. The governor and a loyal janissary colonel failed to quell what was little more than a riot or to inform the government about a fracas among hooligans.

Ahmet III and Nevşehirli Ibrahim Pasha were in camp at Üsküdar together with the *şeyhülislam* and the household. It was from here that expeditions into Asia set forth and the monarch had come to review the army that was to campaign against Persia. The pavilion of the *agha* of the janissaries had its open flap turned symbolically eastwards; the levy of camels from Anatolia and horses from the Balkans had been effected; ships had sailed with grain and cannon to Trabzon and Iskenderun. It was intended that the vanguard should winter in Aleppo while Ahmet should proceed with reinforcements to Tokat in the spring. The dignitaries came with their plumes and their plate as well as their arms and the Koran in a royal carriage drawn by six horses and surrounded by bandsmen.

Such display of wealth was tactless. Since the peace of Karlowitz in 1699, the long flight from the land, which had begun at the end of the sixteenth century, had intensified and Istanbul was awash with peasant

Tulips and Turmoil

immigrants. The *esnaf* (traders) employed these refugees from misrule as cheap labour but took good care to exclude them from their guilds, where they would have become rivals just as the janissaries had done. Thus an embittered proletariat was created, some of whom were so impoverished that they slept in the gutters or among the ashes of the latest conflagration. When a campaign was organized, the *esnaf* had to send their quota of tradesmen, whom they supported from their funds, although the concessionaries had to pay a tax for the privilege of supplying the army. In 1730 this tax was increased although the troops remained idly at Üsküdar and so had no need of new equipment or clothing. Many of the petty traders went bankrupt and the *esnaf* as a cadre turned against the sultan. They did so at the precise moment that the *ulema* were joined by the janissaries, after months of wavering, in open opposition to the government which could not survive the union of all the elements of city and peasant society.[4]

Abdication and Misrule

When Nevşehirli Ibrahim Pasha was informed that trouble in the bazaar had spread with terrifying rapidity, he crossed the Bosphorus that same night and established himself in the *saray*. His bravery came too late and he was warned not to precipitate a massacre by shedding Muslim blood. By morning the rebels were remarkably well organized; joined by their officers as well as many other comrades, they had been able to enter the barracks to collect pots and kettles so that they could set up camp. The *agha*, the governor and the *kapudan paşa* had loyally made their way to the *saray* under cover of darkness while Ahmet III arrived in the morning after futile consultations. For two days the government attempted to reason with the mutineers but the talks were fruitless and no troops moved to save the sultan or his ministers. The rebels were reinforced by slaves from five galleys and the inhabitants of the city prisons. On Friday 29 September 1730 not only did no units rally to the government, but janissaries still on duty deserted their posts in order to avoid being accused of belonging to either side. The rebels continued cheerfully recruiting riff-raff of every kind while their orators harangued the faithful at the gates of the mosques and also sought out retired janissaries—veterans would be a misnomer—and *acemioğlans*.[5]

By evening the time for action had come, for popular support could seep away as fast as it had momentarily congealed. It was then that a high-ranking member of the *ulema* was induced to join the rebels—or was sent by the *ulema* to see that the rebellion did not falter. This professor, the illustrious Ibrahim Efendi, issued a *fetva* which legalized the revolt. (He was afterwards rewarded with the lucrative post of *kadı* of Istanbul.) Messengers could now appeal to the *sipahis*, the gunners and the Tersane, the grocers, junk-dealers and coffee-house waiters, besides the Greek, Armenian and gypsy communities. Ahmet III ordered the dispersal of this conglomeration of opposites but he was ignored and the *ulema* displayed the wisdom of duplicity when consulted in these final hours. When the rebels demanded the heads of thirty-seven members of the administration, even the *kapudan paşa* Mustafa (Ahmet III's son-in-law) went over to the enemy. His successor, Abdi Pasha, did not hesitate to follow suit.

On the morning of 30 September, the sultan sent delegates to the sprawling rebel camp before the barracks of the Etmeydan. They returned with the ultimatum that Nevşehirli Ibrahim Pasha, the *şeyhülislam* and the mullah of the Yeni Cami (New Mosque) were all to be delivered into their hands. It was soon clear that Nevşehirli and his pampered nephews would have to go and Silahtar Mehmet Pasha was appointed Grand Vezir. By evening, it was equally clear that the *ulema* were deeply involved in the uprising.[6] So it was that, on 1 October 1730, Ahmet III helplessly gave in to the demands of the victors: a Sunni sultan could not divorce himself from the *ulema* for long unless he had the support of the janissaries. To save his nearest friends from being torn to pieces, Ahmet had them strangled and their corpses given up to their enemies. The fertile flow of ideas which had been sustained by the Tulip Period was dammed and a most unenlightened triumvirate of shopkeepers, janissaries and *ulema* put and end to Western influence. Orders sent to destroy Ibrahim's extensive charitable works at Nevşehir were ignored.[7] He had prudently buried his fortune in his garden, where 3 chests containing 18 bags of 60,000 sequins were discovered along with a fourth chest filled with precious stones—not acquired from the sale of justice but the legal profits of the Anatolian silver mines. Not everyone, remarked the *bailo*, could raise such radishes (although one victim managed to leave 6 million piastres behind him). Meanwhile, Ahmet III gave up his throne in order to save his life. He retired to secluded but comfortable apartments to die six years later.

Six Wives but no Sons

Mahmut I's fresh name offered a fresh start and, weary of uproar, men of property wanted to think well of him. He was the more happily received because he could fill the accession purses from the 100 per cent death duties levied on his cousin's faithful ministers. He was 34 years old and was to reign for quarter of a century yet, in spite of six wives and numerous concubines, he left no heir.

Who were the rebel leaders? One was a fruit-vendor and another (Ali Patrona) dealt in second-hand clothes. Ali was a typical non-combatant janissary who never lived in the barracks and could neither read nor write. When the army went on campaign, he followed in order to repair or replace any clothes worn out on the march or torn in battle. When not on campaign, this Ottoman-style Danton had a stall in the flea market. Yet he was a man of personality who, if he had been educated, would have been a formidable adversary. The sultan could only woo his favour to begin with. It was at Ali Patrona's insistence that the janissary roll reached 70,000 again because of the admittance of tradesmen. The ranks of the *sipahis* and even the artillery were generously swelled with new recruits. For once there was money in the treasury due to royal stringency and confiscated fortunes and the mob was prevailed upon to disperse. Now that the first blood lust had been satiated, the *reis efendi* was dragged out of his hiding-place: he was lucky to escape to exile in Nicosia. There was a murky calm after the storm.

Popular Power but No Ideas

Ali Patrona had been disinterested and remarkably moderate in his demands immediately after his victory, although his comrades strutted in the courts of the *saray* and were given lucrative posts as fast as they demanded them from a Grand Vezir whose timidity lost him his office within two months. By then, Ali had changed his spots, for he had seen the wealth of Nevşehirli Ibrahim Pasha and discovered a kindred liking for magnificence. It was he who was vainglorious now, losing his attractive modesty in favour of boorish insolence. He was not resisted and in November 1730 one Yanak, a Greek butcher, who had lent Ali money three days before his rebellion, was rewarded with the office of Hospodar of Moldavia to please his debtor. Fortunately, the Hospodar remained at court and did not proceed to Moldavia. Meanwhile, the autocratic Ali was developing a fatal indolence. The Fruiterer, however, took the post of *kul kahya* (steward of the imperial household), which was as intimate and powerful as any in the household, only he had no idea what to do with his elevation to high office.

Meanwhile Mahmut I was at work with skill and patience, guided by a new first minister, Halil Pasha. They won over some of the janissary officers who were slighted by the arrogance of Ali Patrona, a mere rag-dealer. Moreover they had the advice of the khan of the Crimea, whose Tartar blood was as yet unthinned by good living. On 25 November, a mere seven weeks after the overthrow of Ahmet III, Mahmut I felt strong enough to invite Ali

The Janissaries

Patrona and some thirty aides and bodyguards to the Sünnet Odası (Circumcision Kiosk) for a meeting with the Divan. The sultan let it be known that Ali was about to be appointed *serasker* in Sofia, following the declaration of a new war with Persia and the dispatch of the main army there. Ali Patrona came swaggering at the thought of planting the three horsetails of a senior pasha before his tent, his vanity blinding his suspicious nature. But 400 men were concealed in the *saray*: at a sudden signal, they fell on the upstarts and cut one and all of them down. The leading janissary mutineers were also rounded up and either strangled or imprisoned.[8] The *bailo* had noted on another occasion that the public exposure of janissary heads sent from Smyrna had caused no trouble: then, as now, the rest of the corps were content with their pay and wanted no interruption to their market activities. But more ferocious rebels like the corsairs of Tripoli (North Africa) had to be assuaged with high office. One of their number even became *kapudan paşa*, but only to be quietly removed shortly afterwards.

In January 1731 yet another Grand Vezir trained under the Köprülüs worked hard to bring down inflation, but he was defeated by a fresh revolt in March when a leading mobster called the Hospodar[9] butcher was hanged. The mob, 1,500 strong, was afraid of new repression and punishment but also fixated on the hope of plunder. It was led by yet more Albanians under one Kara Ali, who drew crowds into the streets during a night of the Ramazan fast. Significantly, it was mainly Christian shops that were sacked in the early hours of the following day. The guilds now included Jews and Christians; in 1740 they were to be armed by the sultan in the face of one more rebellion. This arose from enmity between janissary guildsmen and non-Muslims and threatened the stability of the whole of Ottoman society.[10]

In November 1731 a ghastly horde once again encamped in the Hippodrome and proceeded to plunder the residence of the *agha* of the janissaries. On this occasion, the corps, cowed by Mahmut's ruthlessness, failed to rally to their cause. The *ulema* had had enough of plunder and opposed an uprising which could turn against them too. The army as a whole rallied to its prince's side but he was not allowed to lead them against the mob and had to content himself with unfurling the Standard of the Prophet at the Bab-ül-Hümayün. The Grand Vezir, the *agha* and the *kapudan paşa* proceeded to disperse the rabble, helped by popular animosity towards Albanians and Laz. In the end, 1,000 of the mob were put to death.

Soon afterwards, a curious attempt to restore Ahmet III by Nevşehirli Ibrahim Pasha's widow ended with the princess in prison and 3,000 janissaries being dispatched to the Persian war. (Still not aged 30, the princess was to die in 1733.) Coffee-houses and *hamams* were closed and

Tulips and Turmoil

the houses of ministers were put under guard. Aptullah Pasha was replaced as *agha* of the janissaries. At the *bayram* festival, the sultan went no further than the mosque of Haghia Sophia at the palace gate, and not as usual to the Fatih mosque which was the assembly hall of the *ulema;* even then he was strongly guarded. The government was right to be uneasy for food shortages worsened and inflation continued to keep the city discontented. In spite of the Grand Vezir's strong will and capacity founded on long experience, which impressed the *bailo*, when a major fire broke out on 21 July the situation blackened.

Although the Grand Vezir and the janissaries' senior officers issued orders, there was no ready cash with which to bribe the janissary firefighters and when Mahmut finally arrived at noon he was lacklustre in his leadership. Finding wine in the cellars of the wealthy, the janissaries proceeded to get drunk. Thus was the throne saved, for when the sultan and his ministers withdrew before the janissaries' threats and insults, the corps were too inebriated to act and 100 of their number were easily arrested. But discontent echoed the rumbling of falling timber and a superstitious soldier, Topal ('Lame') Osman Pasha, was hurriedly made Grand Vezir. He faced opposition from the *şeyhülislam*, the treasurer (who was Francophile) and the Chief Black Eunuch, against whom his courage and generosity were of as little use as were his clemency and total ignorance of finance. However, he successfully ordered the shops to open in order to restore life and order to the city and the fires were put out for the time being. Unfortunately, high office brought out a latent paranoia in his character: he executed anyone for the least transgression and publicly displayed that violence and choler which were so antipathetic to Ottomans. His ultimate folly was to tax food, as if inflation were not enough, and he planned a new war in Europe. For this purpose, he enlisted the services of Count Alexandre de Bonneval, also known as Ahmet Bonneval Pasha, a disaffected and hot-tempered officer of France and the Empire whose family were (and still are) proprietors in the Dordogne. Ahmet formed the bombardier corps, barracked at Üsküdar, and in 1734 opened a school of geometry. The janissaries smelt out what this General of the Two Tails was about and, fearful of any progressive measure, had the place closed. It was Ragip Pasha in 1759, however, who reopened the academy farther down the Bosphorus and in a private house.

Advisers from Western Europe

At first all went well for Topal Osman Pasha, who defeated the Persians on the Tigris and then retook Baghdad in 1733 only to meet defeat himself and

The Janissaries

his death with it. Some stability was achieved by his successor, another soldier, Hekimoğlu (so-called because he was the son of a court physician) Ali Pasha. He managed to hold office for three years for he carefully allied himself with the Valide Sultan and the Chief Black Eunuch and benefited from the unpopularity of his main opponent, the *reis efendi*. Hekimoğlu Ali Pasha even kept seditious outbreaks of fire under control, helped by the obvious moderation of his policies towards the janissaries. In addition, he was blessed with a fall in food prices and an improvement in supplies to the city, neither of which was due to his fiscal or monetary policies.

Greedy Grandees

Little had changed at court. Ambassadors were still asked for gifts of Venetian velvets, mirrors, watches, gold cloth, chandeliers and canaries as if by children. They were still splendidly received, surrounded by mounted officers and hundreds of janissaries and grooms in feathered finery. The *reis efendi* asked the new *bailo* for 1,000 large and 2,000 small pieces of glass for his *yalı* (mansion) on the Bosphorus. The Chief Dragoman, or interpreter, merely wanted panes for 20 windows and a list of small items which included 4 telescopes, an eyeglass, pistols, medicines and flowers, together with Dutch, Piacenza (Gorgonzola?) and English cheeses, fruit, vegetables, candy and chocolate. The court, said the *bailo*, was a whirlpool never filled; a special strong-room had to be built at his residence and stuffed with gifts.

Mahmut I himself, who was stable as dandelion seeds in a wind, was predictable only in his requests for gold lamé.[11] The traveller Maurand's description of the 200 horses kept at the *saray* by the sultan gives a clear picture of the brilliance of the court. The reins and stirrups were of silver and gold; most of the mounts had a gold- or silver-leaf blazon in the form of a rose in which was set a ruby, hyacinth or turquoise. Their bridles were crimson silk, embroidered in gold in the Turkish style, and these were also enriched with turquoises. The saddles were gilded too, and the cruppers covered in golden brocade or embroidered velvet, while rows of studs of gold and silk thread hung along each side. The sultan had, after all, to match the caparisoned and bedecked mounts of his 6,000 *sipahis*.

Distinguished Grand Vezirs

In 1720 plague had scurried through Istanbul and driven many of the envoys out of the city. But in 1733 it was extraordinarily enduring and reached a climax when the Grand Vezir lost his son, brother and nephew and 300 members of his household. It was also the year of Topal Osman Pasha's victories after 25,000 Tartar cavalry had joined forces with the old man against the Shah of Persia. As so often when fighting penetrates far into hostile terrain, however, the victories were indecisive even if they gave the capital cause for rejoicing with fireworks and cannonades. The army was still badly equipped because of lack of money. A new *serasker*, Aptullah Köprülü Pasha, was appointed by the new Grand Vezir because of the magic of his name and not because of his experience (he had none). Moreover, he was hated by the troops and could not even get them to leave Dıyarbekir. The navy was no better and janissary reinforcements were sent to Nauplia in a willing French bottom.

Topal Osman Pasha had chosen wisely: to Bonneval must be given the credit for reviving the janissary corps as a fighting force. He trained them hard at the price of unpopularity—he was just in time, for in 1736 Marshal Münnich launched the long-prepared Russian attack on the Crimea. The peninsula was ravaged with great brutality and only the threat to set fire to the steppes frustrated an invasion of Ottoman lands in Europe. Yet the objectives of Catherine the Great were eventually frustrated and no Russian fleet was launched in the Black Sea or given access through the Dardanelles to the Mediterranean. Indeed, a raid across the Ukraine by the Tartar horse brought in 30,000 prisoners. Although the best troops were not sent in support, the Chevalier Folard noted that the Ottoman army was as sound a fighting force as it had ever been but was handicapped by the lack of modern weapons and, in particular, bayonets. The treacherous attack of the Imperial army on Bosnia led by Field Marshal Seckendorf and the Prince of Hildberghausen, both of whom considered themselves the heir to Prince Eugene, was halted in 1737 and totally defeated in 1738. Not even the shadow of Eugene was to be seen and an advantageous peace was achieved at Belgrade.

The Ottoman government was not without talent for Ahmet III had bequeathed Mahmut I a Grand Vezir of distinction in the son of his physician, a Venetian renegade. Hekimoğlu Ali Pasha had already been victorious against the Persians when, as we have seen, he was appointed to succeed Topal Osman Pasha. He had been trained at the Enderun Kolej and thus belonged to the slave family, although technically born a Muslim. A man of liberal ideas, not without learning, he possessed a formidable temper which bowed the necks of corrupt officials for he was determined to carry out far-reaching currency reforms. Unfortunately the war with Persia was renewed without a conclusion and the *vezir* was dismissed in July 1735, just as he was beginning to succeed in his economic exercises. He survived

The Janissaries

disgrace, however, and from exile in sinister Mytilene was promoted governor of Bosnia, where he held Austrian divisions in check. He went on to defeat the Prince of Hildberghausen at Banjaluka and so preserved the silver mines for the sultan. He was sent to Egypt to put down a rising of the Mamluks and was then briefly *beylerbey* of Anatolia before becoming Grand Vezir for a second time, although only for one year due to the eternal conflict with Persia. Yet three years later he was vindicated and made *serasker* in the East and at last, in 1746, concluded an honourable peace with the Shah.

Imperial Rages

Of all *vezirs*, Hekimoğlu Ali Pasha was one of the most tenacious (or cunning) for Osman III, within two months of his accession in 1754, reappointed him Grand Vezir. Partly because of his temper, which was to kill him within three years (although it was not as bad as Osman's), and partly because of the intrigues of a young favourite, Bıyıklı ('Moustachioed') Ali Agha, Hekimoğlu was exiled, this time to Cyprus, after only fifty-three days in office: but he was rapidly sent back to rule Egypt and then Anatolia all over again until at 69 he finally retired to Kütahya. The young favourite Bıyıklı was exposed as an extortionist, fell from office and his head and moustaches were presented to Osman III on a platter.

Osman's rages even intimidated the *ulema* but in December 1756 he appointed a man of the pen and not of the sword as his first minister. Ragip Efendi, until his death seven years later, was to prove an outstanding administrator. The son of a clerk, he had served in the Divan secretariat before going as agent to various governors, including Hekimoğlu Ali Pasha, who must have taught him something of his future trade. Ragip Efendi had a brief experience of warfare before becoming *reis efendi* in 1741. He was *beylerbey* of Egypt for four years until he was ousted by the Mamluk factions in 1748, when he was given a seat in the Divan. He was a poet, historian and bibliophile who built a charming library and his term of office was a remarkably civilized interlude in a very disagreeable period. Ragip Pasha, as he became, had no reason to suppose that he would be allowed to remain in office long. His predecessors under Osman III had sometimes survived a bare fortnight because the sultan was mentally unbalanced—perhaps due to the hereditary malady which appears to have rendered both him and Mahmut I impotent. But Ragip Pasha at 57 was the same age as his master and a mature personality altogether more stable than the childish throng of courtiers. When a shortage of bread[12] led to a riot by

Tulips and Turmoil

women who were formidable enough to chase the chauvinist *agha* of the janissaries off in fear for his manhood if not for his life, the Grand Vezir went with parcels of food for the Amazons and contrived to reassure them.[13] He also managed to disarm the janissaries within the city at a period when, for example, the guard attached to the Patriarch were in the habit of cudgelling passers-by.

Wine in Excess

One prop of the janissaries had been removed when they lost French support because the French agent in Jaffa had been beaten by janissaries of the household of the *beylerbey*, Ismail al-Azam Pasha, into surrendering 60,000 *livres*. The outrage left the janissaries friendless and the government quickly asserted its authority.[14] Indeed, when Mustafa III succeeded in 1757, the corps stood with hands crossed in submission.[15] But Ragip Pasha was presented with a fresh crop of problems because the new sultan loved money to excess: his cupidity encouraged his officers to haggle over pay increases like entrenched union leaders of closed shops, while the *kapudan paşa* sold ships to the highest bidder—apart from being so ignorant of geography as to ask if Venice were not in Russia.

It was now established policy to humiliate the janissaries, in which disgrace these warriors unthinkingly assisted by their own behaviour. Volunteers were preferred to a standing army because they could be dismissed after a campaign and needed no pay or maintenance. They did not always go home obediently, however. Like the janissaries, they infested Istanbul and its suburbs in winter-time in what were effectively robber bands: thus the city only knew peace in wartime. A curious change in habits was remarked on at this period: the dervish orders took to drinking more wine but took fewer narcotics whereas the janissaries drank more coffee and less wine. It made little difference except that wine is blood to soldiers and coffee is blood to tradesmen. Wine was always a problem for the governments, which needed the revenue it brought in. However, they were taken to task by the *ulema*, who abominated wine—or said that they did—particularly when the hated Sufis, and not just the Christian army, took to consuming it.

The Baron de Tott

The military installations were in no better condition than the state troops. The Hungarian engineer the Baron de Tott found the vital castles of the

The Janissaries

Dardanelles with walls about to tumble and batteries so slowly served by poorly trained and undisciplined gunners that an enemy need not fear a second discharge. The guns were brass without carriages but simply laid on hollowed pieces of wood in the manner of the fifteenth century. Indeed, the defenders were in greater danger from their own batteries than from the enemy. Fortunately, the secret was well kept. Tott, who was contracted to reform the artillery, began by setting up workshops at Kağıthane He then remodelled the foundry at Tophane, where a company of janissaries was placed under his command.[16] He contrived to get permission for the sacred Okmeydan to be used as an artillery range but then found the sightseers so numerous that the cudgels of the household brigade could hardly clear a channel down which to fire. Six shells behaved well but the seventh fell smouldering in the midst of the throng, which refused to budge—fortunately there was no charge in it.

It was at this time that two companies of janissaries quarrelled over a 14-year-old dancing boy in a tavern. One party eventually grabbed the youth and carried him off with them. This was worse than a declaration of war and the kidnappers were chased into a mosque. When the gate was shut in their face, the rival company carried the guns off merchant ships anchored in the Golden Horn and fired at the mosque gate. By evening there were barricades at street corners and the firing went on all night. The Grand Vezir was happy to let the janissaries blast away at each other, comparing their courage at Galata with that shown (or not shown) on the Danube. However, there were fears that the trouble would spread and action had to be taken. Negotiators assured the company which held the boy that the others had no more claim on the fellow and a truce was agreed. The barricades were dismantled and the Ganymede was promptly hanged, to the satisfaction of everybody.

Janissary tempers were not improved when they discovered the good and, above all, regular pay of the new artillery companies formed by Tott. He also instituted a humane discipline which replaced fetters and bastinado with double guard duties and other light punishments, although deserters were still sent to the galleys. A Marine School was set up at the Tersane where trigonometry was taught officers with white beards and the janissaries did not feel threatened by these ancients.

Superstition still ruled, however. When Tott set about rebuilding the castles guarding the entry to the Black Sea, the Grand Vezir consulted the Chief Astrologer over the hour and the day for the laying of the first stone. The High Treasurer stood, watch in hand, awaiting the exact second ordained in order to proclaim in the name of Allah the moment when the stone was to be laid. The work progressed as did the formation of a new

Tulips and Turmoil

infantry corps, the *suracıs,* who were issued with bayonets. The artillery corps were barracked at Kağıthane. A corps of engineers, restricted to bridge-builders, was also established. But with the passing of Ragip Pasha in 1763, Mustafa III was as hamstrung by the venality of his *vezirs* as by his own stupidity and that of the *ulema.* When the sultan proposed to emulate his ancestors and lead his troops in battle, which might have given them new courage, they would not tolerate the idea and succeeded in keeping him safe at home. So the current Russian war dragged drearily on, with the illustrious and heroic Russian Marshal Suvarov winning victory after victory and the Ottomans sustaining horrendous casualties.

Humiliation at Küçük Kaynarcı

When Mustafa III died in 1774, his son (later to become Selim III) was only 13 so his brother Abdülhamit I, who was nearly 50, succeeded rather than a child ruled over by a Valide Sultan. Abdülhamit was to be the father of Mahmut II, with whom Selim III was to have such cordial relations. The new sultan inherited rebellious pashas all over his dominions, including the old rascal Ali Pasha of Yanina besides rebels in Baghdad and Albania. His first act was to free the young Selim from all constraints. He was reluctant to make peace with the ever-belligerent Russians because rioting in his capital made such a surrender impossible. He rightly decided that some sort of victory was necessary if there were to be any bargaining at all at the peace conference. But fresh defeats spread terror in the Ottoman army and, when the *reis efendi* attempted to rally the janissaries in June 1784, they murdered him. The peace of Küçük Kaynarcı had been signed on 21 July 1774 but had to be amended at Aynalı Kavak on 9 January 1784. The tsar's government had taken the Azov forts and the Crimea had been made independent to await the annexation which the treaty of Aynalı Kavak acknowledged. As if these blows were not enough, Abdülhamit, who had genuine zeal, was faced with a false Mahdi who, with Persian connivance, won over the Kurds and proceeded to capture Erzerum and then march on Sivas and Smyrna in 1785, winnowing janissaries wherever he could find them. The government was terrified and sent envoys to plead with this extraordinary man.

The Mahdi had been born Giovanni Battista Boetti in Montferrat. As a youth, his love life had exceeded all reason; repentance followed on excess, however, with the result that he entered the Dominican order. Sent as a missionary to Mosul, his intolerance and zest for converts alarmed his superiors and he was finally and fatally excommunicated by the pope. He immediately embraced Islam with that same zest with which he had first

The Janissaries

pursued lust and then the Christian mission.[17] His campaign in Anatolia had been carefully planned, the obstacles explored and spied out and arms obtained from happy Persia. Disaster faced Istanbul when, for no explicable reason, the Mahdi was persuaded by Catherine the Great to go and fight for the Russians: this he did with considerable success for four years until his capture in 1791. The prisoner was well treated and given a pension until 1798, when he retired from history into an Armenian monastery.[18] The war with Russia, which had been renewed after initial successes against the Austrians, went on as futilely as before. Meanwhile, Abdülhamit died in 1789, a year fatal for crowns, of a stroke brought on by worry and despair.

Too Civilized to Reign Long

Selim III succeeded at the age of 28, well trained by his uncle, but faced with problems which could only be solved by reforms too sweeping for the rickety state to stand. He faced a daunting economic situation, demoralized troops and the ever-increasing disdain of the provinces for the rule of Istanbul. His fleet epitomized the situation. Its navigators had to cling to the coasts because they could not read the stars, and the ships were manned by such a rabble that if several vessels were in port the shops were closed and barred. Life on board was sordid and, if the officers lived luxuriously, they could not escape the stench nor the gamut of maritime vermin that crawled up from the holds in search of human refreshment. Guns were mounted without thought for their weight and a cannonade could capsize and sink a vessel. Mercifully, the entire fleet was destroyed at the battle of Çeşme in 1770 by a small Russian squadron. The disaster hastened reforms but appointments were still bought and a new fleet was defeated in the Black Sea in 1791. It was then that Selim III succeeded in appointing Küçük Hüseyn Pasha as *kapudan paşa*, with his boyhood friend Işak Bey as deputy. Pay and book-keeping were reformed and bribery extinguished: the tragedy was that the reforms were not extended to the army.

The Balkans up in Arms

The situation in Serbia exemplified the end of Ottoman power, which was not to be blamed on one scapegoat or the other, not even the wretched janissaries. Throughout their story they reacted chameleon-like to leadership, whether in their glorious past or in the eighteenth century when they were no longer Christian-born slaves with a real personal loyalty to the ruling house. Had the sultan been abler and stronger-willed, they might have rallied to his command: even then, the lack of modern weapons would have deprived them of the firepower needed to repulse the forces of a Suvarov.[19] The venality of their officers was no worse than that of other pashas. They certainly did not squander the revenues as they were squandered by the court. But all this does not disguise the truth that, although the janissaries were not recruited like the navy from the scum of the seaboards, they were far from related to the youthful élite of old. They were now the hedonist offspring of their regions and their times.

In Serbia the Ottomans had ruled since 1459. The country estates had been taken to support the *sipahis* while the towns, including those founded and developed by the Ottomans, were the strong-points of the administration. The peasants were not ill-treated and in the first centuries of Ottoman rule the brightest sons went to serve the sultan, leaving relatively tranquil valleys behind them. Men of independent spirit were bred in the mountains but Slavs did not create the problems posed by the warlike Albanians and Montenegrans, unreachable in their free fastnesses. The common folk were not short of work because they were needed as artisans and miners apart from their hereditary commitment to the soil. With the end of the levy those youths of ability and ambition, who were once the core of the Ottoman administration, were frustrated. They could only burn their spirit by forming Serbian and other national groups which in time learnt to talk of independence.

Fighting broke out and spread as increased numbers rallied to their call in face of increasing oppression as the authorities grew more and more irresponsible. In 1789 the Serbians took Belgrade, but the Russians did not give them the support promised by their agents and the city was retaken by the janissaries. The inhabitants were left to the mercies of bandits—since fighting for freedom is difficult to differentiate from banditry—or of the janissaries, whose thirst for vengeance was heated by their inability to cope with the rebels or with bands of mercenaries who refused to go home at the end of the war. They murdered their *agha* and tyrannized over the populace, putting to death all who might become leaders of a national revolt because they had courage or wealth or came of families of repute in the city.

The lawless barbarism of their own troops frightened the Ottoman citizens as much as the Slav and they appealed for help to Selim III. With a lack of tact common to those who are despots in name but not in fact, the sultan threatened to arm the Christians; the janissaries responded by a massacre of the senior Serbian burgesses. Meanwhile, Karageorge ('Dark George'), an illiterate pig-dealer, who had become a sergeant in the Austrian army and was therefore a trained soldier, revealed remarkable talents of

The Janissaries

leadership. He rallied the peasants and the mountaineers under his banner and cleared the countryside of Ottomans, sequestrated farms and smallholdings and camped in the summer before Belgrade. There the janissaries had been driven into the citadel by the enraged populace. Although the sultan sent help, the citadel was taken and a singularly disagreeable revenge executed on the vainglorious soldiers. This was not the end of the incident because Karageorge refused to hand over the city to the governor of Bosnia, Bekir Pasha, and would have held it if the threat of Napoleon had not forced Russia to abandon support for him. It was only after the treaty of Bucharest in 1812 that Ottoman landowners could reoccupy their estates in the provinces. It was, indeed, the shadow of Napoleon rather than that of the Revolution that was preparing the Porte for change if not reform. Napoleon's landing in Egypt in 1798 was unopposed by a helpless sultan and was only brought to an end by Nelson's victory at Aboukir Bay. By this time, Selim III had sent 6,000 men to help the English land forces.[20]

Selim was delighted by the French humiliation of Austria and Russia and welcomed the help of French officers and volunteers. Küçük Hüseyn Pasha cleared the Black Sea of pirates, quelled the ruffianly marines and made it possible to exploit the virgin forests of the Anatolian coast. The janissaries did not respond to rebuilt barracks and better pay when their number was cut down to 30,000 nor did the anachronistic *sipahis:* but the artillery did, as did Tott's bombardiers, who were now 3,000 strong, and the quality of the cannon produced at Tophane was greatly improved. Unfortunately, Küçük Hüseyn Pasha died in 1803 and Selim lost in him the one minister who might have coped with the troubles to come.

The New Order and the Old Chaos

In 1792 Selim's French advisers and officers had drilled a new regiment, the Nizam ı-Cedit (the New Order or Army), which was trained and equipped in the latest European manner. The sultan had to levy new taxes on liquor, coffee, tobacco and other luxuries and these caused ill will but a new army was founded and its imprint was not to die away. The young officers were literate and educated in mathematics and Sʾlim had reason to believe that the New Army would eventually emerge as the only force in the land. However, the *ulema* were as alarmed as the janissaries at the prospect: it could only lead to the reform of their own special privileges and those of other branches of the establishment. They contrived to have the new corps partially disbanded and the republican French officers dismissed but not before units in the field had significantly distinguished themselves in a battle at Acre. Moreover, the *şeyhülislam* Velizade was unusually sagacious and supported Selim once he had found janissary officers who were prepared to impose discipline. This enabled the government to detach the gunners and bombardiers from any link with the corps and form them into auxiliary units without loyalty to the *ocaks*. It was then that the frightened janissaries saw their end approaching, mutinied at Edirne and attacked the new units. They were ably led by their formidable commander, Alemdar ('Standard-Bearer') Mustafa Pasha of Silistria, who was also *serasker* on the Danube.[21] The son of a janissary, Alemdar had served with distinction against the Russians when few others had any claim to honour. But he had become a valley lord and a quasi-independent chieftain whose loyalties extended to his sultan but were in no way attached to the government of the Porte.

The revolt was strengthened by Selim's order for the conscription of recruits. The governor of Karamania was required to call up all young men under 25 and march them to Istanbul where they were trained and paraded by Selim as if the sight of them gave him heart. But they were held back in training too long and when they reached Edirne three months later the gates were closed in their faces. They were repulsed at Babaeski and then cut off from the capital at Çorlu, driven back to Silivri and finally defeated. Selim was also defeated and dismissed his loyal youngsters at the insistence of his *vezirs*, whose intrigues were to blame for the catastrophe.[22]

The situation was compounded by an English victory at the Dardanelles, where the fortresses had again been neglected. The English fleet forced the straits amid a few splashes from spent Ottoman cannon-balls, destroyed two Turkish frigates and threatened the capital. Meanwhile the French envoy, Sebastiani, who was the corset that sustained the sultan, hurried back from a period of exile and found the *saray* in turmoil. The New Army had been sent to Anatolia; reforming ministers had been exiled like himself; and war with Russia had been insanely renewed. Istanbul might fall and with it French ascendancy at the Porte. The *agha* of the janissaries had been made Grand Vezir, symbolic of the sultan's capitulation to the implacable forces of reaction which made Metternich look liberal. The only man who might have helped was Alemdar Mustafa Pasha, who was unique in his ability to make up his own mind. He was no longer opposed to Selim's reforms of an army he found to be rotten at heart, but he could not leave his post on the Danube when the enemy was preparing an attack. Thus he was absent during the melancholy spring of 1807.

Sebastiani, epitome of European interference, was told to leave but flatly refused and the situation was further confused because both the Grand Vezir

The Janissaries

and the *şeyhülislam* had left for the European front. A reactionary governor had been appointed to safeguard their interests but the approach of the English Admiral Arbuthnott united the city. Sebastiani sought to rally the government in a palace full of screaming virgins and weeping eunuchs while the populace rose and both gunners and janissaries took to arms. There were several distinguished French officers still in Istanbul and, together with their embassy clerks and others sent by the Spanish ambassador, they mounted batteries. The sultan worked prodigiously alongside his people. It was the diplomacy of Admiral Duckworth, which wasted five days, that ensured the failure of the English expedition and Arbuthnott retired judiciously for fear of being cut off by the ill-manned batteries of the Dardanelles.

The departure brought relief but no rejoicing. The gunners sent to effect a union with the New Army in Anatolia were frustrated by the intrigues of the governor, who was newly appointed. Musa (Moses) Pasha was far worse than his predecessor, who was merely a hardened traditionalist who had fled to the Danube when it looked as if he had lost control of Istanbul. Not only did the new governor foment a revolt of the janissaries but he sought to co-ordinate their uprising in the city with a parallel revolt in Anatolia under Kabakcıoğlu ('Son of a Pumpkin-Seller') Mustafa. With his henchmen, Kabakcıoğlu was the chief rebel in the provinces and was busy stirring up the garrisons to march against Istanbul.

It was at this point that the janissary recruits in the Bosphorus forts refused to wear new uniforms (tactlessly sent at such a moment) and murdered the New Army officers who brought them. On 27 May 1807 they marched on the capital in their old attire to be joined by the janissaries themselves. Selim III's misfortunes multiplied. The *şeyhülislam* Velizade died to be replaced by the *kadıasker* of the Balkans, whose duplicity was exceptional even among conspirators in the dying empire. He was quick to advise Selim to placate the rebels. Kabakcıoğlu Mustafa killed any scattered units of the New Army who opposed him and reached the Hippodrome and also the Yeni Odalar of the janissaries. Musa Pasha made sure that the units of the New Army were kept in their barracks or in the castles down the Bosphorus. The city belonged to the rebels. Kabakcıoğlu rallied 800 janissaries to his cause and addressed the mob. He promised to punish all reformers and the New Army for violating the ancient laws of Hacı Bektaş, thus ensuring the enmity of all future reformers—from Mahmut II to Atatürk—towards that order of dervishes. The treasurer was murdered there and then and a list of like victims was proclaimed. Willingly taking on the role of hangman, the mob either slaughtered the victims in their homes or rounded them up to be put to death in the Hippodrome. Thus the heads of seventeen of the highest officers were soon displayed outside the barracks.[23]

That of the *bostancıbaşı* was missing because he was at Topkapısaray rallying the household units and preparing for a siege. On hearing the clamour of the mutineers and the howling of the mob, Selim lacked the courage to ride out at the head of his trained troops but he agreed to bar the gates and refused to sacrifice his followers in order to save his skin—unlike his cowering *vezirs*. The *bostancıbaşı* calmly requested permission to go out and die in order to save his sovereign, who finally consented, weeping and calling on the blessing of Allah. The city was given over to carnage for two days during which the government did nothing at all. In the midst of such a power vacuum, the mutineers resolved on the obvious course of deposing their sultan. They held a turbulent meeting in the Hippodrome and a deputation of janissary officers was sent to the *şeyhülislam* to ask whether a sultan who had worked against the principles of the Koran could be permitted to reign. The divine judge, with a pretty display of surprise and regret, issued the *fetva* which authorized the sultan's deposition in the interests of Islam and the Ottoman dynasty. In fact, the *fetva* was so ambiguous that it could be read however men pleased for in effect it said, 'That cannot be.' But it added the rider that Allah knew best. Armed with this document, the rebel leaders proceeded to the *saray*.

Mustafa IV, Puppet Psychopath

There, on 29 May 1807, Kabakcıoğlu Mustafa proclaimed the deposition of his master and the accession of Mustafa IV, a grandson of Ahmet III who was nearly 28 years old and would not live to see 30. The *şeyhülislam* was sent to inform Selim of this decision with a suitably lugubrious expression while Kabakcıoğlu Mustafa, his face masked by an insolent consideration for his sovereign, dwelt on the strength of the mutineers and urged Selim to submit to the will of Allah—who had never been consulted—in order to save the few who were left among his supporters. The sultan listened patiently but disdained to reply and retired by himself to the apartments reserved by now for fallen monarchs. Here he was to revenge himself on the janissaries by devoting his limitless spare time to the education of his 22-year-old cousin, the ultimate heir of all the Ottomans, the future Mahmut II.[24] Meanwhile the new sultan obediently decreed the disbandment of the New Army and appointed mutineers to senior posts, including the command of the Castles of the Bosphorus. It was by default, not merit, that the governor and the *şeyhülislam* found all power concentrated in their hands as May blossomed into June.

The Janissaries

The city was terrified and feared a general pillage but Kabakcıoğlu Mustafa did indeed possess powers of command and also knew when to bribe. Order was restored and the mutinous units were forced out of the capital. The Grand Vezir was overthrown by the combatant janissaries in favour of a creature of their choice, Çelebi Mustafa. But Kabakcıoğlu appointed his own puppet in Istanbul, taking advantage of a quarrel between the *şeyhülislam* and the governor, Musa Pasha. Nobody took account of the most overbearing personality of all: the *serasker* on the Danube, Alemdar Mustafa Pasha, was determined to restore Selim and sent his closest adviser secretly to the capital to sound out the ministers. This adviser persuaded them that his master, who was already on the road, was marching solely against Kabakcıoğlu and the *şeyhülislam* and he won the *kapudan paşa* over to his side. An executioner was sent to dispose of Kabakcıoğlu in one of his fortresses. Armed with a dagger and a *firman*, signed by the compliant Grand Vezir, the assassin, one Hacı Ali, surprised the mutineer in his harem and had no difficulty in disposing of him. He even persuaded the 100 men of the garrison to accept him as their new commander until the lamentations of the dead man's womenfolk reached such a crescendo that it changed their minds. Hacı Ali fled before the garrison and the Furies into a tower where he defended himself for three days. After tunnelling his way out at night, he escaped and fled to join Alemdar Mustafa Pasha.

On learning of the threatening situation, Mustafa IV dismissed his *vezirs* and the *şeyhülislam* and confiscated their wealth. Before he could rally his supporters, Alemdar Mustafa Pasha reached the gates of the city at the head of 16,000 of his best and most devoted troops. Having speedily put down the janissaries and their recruits on 26 July 1807, he assured Mustafa that his troops would now withdraw. Indeed, the simple-minded sultan would have left on 28 July for the pleasures of his kiosk at the Sweet Waters of Asia, Göksü, half-way down the Bosphorus, had not the Grand Vezir's spies surmised Alemdar's real intentions.

The Standard-Bearer Strikes

Nothing could now be concealed and Alemdar Mustafa Pasha acted promptly. He arrested the Grand Vezir and unfurled the sacred Standard of the Prophet, which he had carried on campaign and presciently brought back with him. The few janissaries at the Bab-ül-Hümayün offered no resistance but the *bostancıbaşı*, Master of the Household, honourably slammed the Orta Kapı in Alemdar's face and refused to open it. Preparations were being made to force it when Mustafa IV appeared in the Divan Court beyond it.

Tulips and Turmoil

The *saray* had not been surrounded because no resistance had been anticipated. The Valide Sultan had been able to send a message to her son, who immediately ordered the Chief Black Eunuch to execute Selim, and probably Mahmut too, for then Mustafa's own life would be sacrosanct since he would be the last of the dynasty. Selim was strong and, when surprised in his mother's apartment, put up a valiant fight against unequal odds until he was stabbed in the heart, a lawless and sacrilegious act since a sultan's blood might not be shed. (One might ask if the rusty, bloodstained kaftan in the palace museum today is not mislabelled as that of Osman II when it is more likely to have been Selim's.)

Alemdar Mustafa Pasha forced the gate and secured the Divan Court. The palace was his but it was too late for his sultan: Selim's cadaver was brought out and presented to Mustafa IV, who coldly ordered it to be delivered to the pasha who was so frantically looking for it. Alemdar burst upon the scene prepared to precipitate himself before his true sovereign only to be confronted by his bleeding corpse. He wept until the *kapudan paşa* asked if this fierce warrior was going to spend the day howling like a woman or would avenge his master, punish the assassins, and above all save Mahmut from being murdered too. Alemdar immediately arrested and imprisoned Mustafa IV. Mahmut was found in a closet belonging to his old nurse which was reached by a stair from the Altın Yolu (Golden Road).[25] This is the artery of the harem and the *selamlık* of the *saray*. So it was that the extraordinary 28 July ended with the proclamation of Mahmut II as sultan. Alemdar Mustafa Pasha was given the seals of office as Grand Vezir.

The murderers of Selim III and the leading rebel supporters of Mustafa IV were arrested, tortured and executed. The erstwhile Grand Vezir was beheaded and even the *kapudan paşa* was sent into exile. Alemdar Mustafa Pasha immediately set about disciplining the janissaries by calling on the senior officers of both state and army to list their vices and suggest reforms. He spoke of their capriciousness and ignorance of modern warfare of which he, who was himself a janissary and their commander in the field, was well aware. Their barracks, he said, had become the refuge of those who had neither hearth nor job and who hated work. Disorder and vice reigned there. Those janissaries who were assigned police duties ignored public security and held their neighbourhood to ransom. The senior officers were in league with usurers and the first step must be to end this venality and see that only janissaries on active service were supported and paid. While the reforms were carried out, Alemdar called upon volunteers to come forward from among the free citizens. Once the regulations were drawn up, everyone had to sign his name and none dared dissent.

The Janissaries

The arrogance of the proud Alemdar angered many people and officers were furious when he appointed commanders from the New Army over them. In particular, he enraged and frightened the *ulema* by promising to secularize the revenues of the pious foundations and by openly showing his contempt for the sacred caste. His own provincial levies, moreover, swaggered about the city like conquerors or, worse, like janissaries. His position as Grand Vezir was undermined by Mahmut's jealousy of his domineering minister. A revolt by Molla Agha, lord of Philippopolis, resulted in the dispatch of 12,000 men to put down the *ayan*, leaving barely 7,000 troops loyal to Alemdar Mustafa Pasha in Istanbul. Although his friends pleaded with him not to be so rash, he was contemptuous of his enemies and he had, perhaps, that suicidal twist in his make-up which underlies the exuberant courage of some heroes. On 14 November 1808 his men were attacked without warning when 6,000 janissaries marched on the *saray* in order to restore their creature, Mustafa IV. Alemdar and a small bodyguard were driven back into a fortified tower of the palace. There, history repeated itself when Alemdar flung the corpse of Mustafa IV at the feet of his foes.

Alemdar Mustafa Pasha then retreated to the palace of the Grand Vezir opposite the Alay Kiosk, which the mutineers immediately surrounded. They set hay alight under the Sublime Porte and burnt the great gate down. Once inside the gardens, they fired the vast wooden building, shot at those who attempted to save it and even prevented people from salvaging their possessions from the neighbouring houses. Alemdar saw that all was lost: to escape the horrors of capture, he blew up the powder magazine, killing himself, many of his own men and 300 janissaries. About 300 men of the New Army had taken refuge in their barracks at Sultan Ahmet; they fired on the janissaries in a desperate resistance which ended when barracks and neighbourhood were attacked by flames.[26] The rebels also crossed to Üsküdar where they fired the wooden barracks of the New Army in revenge.

Too late to save Alemdar Mustafa Pasha, the new *kapudan paşa* landed at the head of his marines and marched on the *saray*. At the very same moment, Kadı Pasha with 3,000 men also marched to the aid of his sultan. The *kapudan paşa* was prepared to offer the janissaries a pardon if they laid down their arms but Kadı Pasha would have none of this temerity. He ordered a general attack with cannon and drove the mutineers back at all points. They retreated in disorder to the burning palace of the Sublime Porte, where they stoked the flames still higher. Unable to force a way through the conflagration, Kadı Pasha marched on the headquarters of the *agha* below the Süleymaniye, killing anyone in his path; but fires broke out all around

Tulips and Turmoil

him and some detachments were burnt to death. Kadı Pasha was driven back and the fires spread so rapidly that the whole city was faced with destruction. Suddenly, the fury of battle died away in face of the terror of the flames. One and all turned to quenching them but by now they had spread everywhere. When they were at last brought under control and then extinguished, the body of the Grand Vezir was found in his palace. His corpse was impaled in public for three days.

The Fox Bides his Time

Mahmut II had nothing to fear in his loneliness but he could only save the rest of his ruined capital by bowing to popular fury. The *kapudan paşa* and Kadı Pasha had to be disowned but escaped. They were unable to rally support and while the former fled to St Petersburg the latter set out to seek help from Karamania only to be murdered on the road. The janissaries had triumphed for the last time. The sultan and his ministers had even been fooled into a truce when faced with defeat. The government agreed perfidiously to disband the only troops that had dared defend them when courageously led. The men of the New Army were sent home without their arms to be cut down and butchered by janissaries who had surrendered nothing.

A dreary eighteen years were to follow when defeat followed upon defeat and even the weather was hostile, its harshness only rivalled by the outbreaks of pestilence and disease. Successive administrations schemed the overthrow of the janissaries but without alienating the *ulema* or any other section of the state. The soldiers assisted in this by their behaviour until 'the Auspicious Event' (see Chapter 10) was ultimately achieved. The only extraordinary thing about 1826 is that it was so long in coming. This was surely due to the venality and egocentricity of the janissaries, who were in turn merely a mirror of the venality and egocentricity of every stratum of Ottoman society.

Mahmut II had need of patience in dealing with the enemies, both open and secret, of his single-minded policy of establishing rule by his own central autocracy. The abolition of the janissaries was but one part of this greater scheme. He also had to put an end to local despotism and the rule of men who barely bothered to pay lip-service to the Porte, let alone surrender their taxes. It was also vital to break the *ulema*'s hold on government—this could only be done by stealth for a confrontation was more likely to damage the sultanate than the rich judiciary.[27] Fortunately, the reactionary *ulema* had been seriously alarmed by the ruffianly behaviour of the janissaries and mobs such as those of 1808; their support for these soldiers was merely a mask which concealed their fear and hatred. Thus they did not stop Mahmut building up a very large artillery corps, better paid and better treated than any other section of the army. By 1826 the corps numbered 10,000 men, including 4,400 wagoners in support. In addition, there was a brigade of 1,000 gunners trained in Western methods who were intended to replace the educated and liberal officers massacred in 1808.

But the new unit, when tested under fire, was routed by the Russians in 1812. Nevertheless Mahmut was able to get rid of the *ayan* of Anatolia between 1812 and 1817, partly by force but mainly because of a fortunate series of unexpected deaths and also family quarrels.[28] In 1814 much the same mixture of luck and tactics disposed of the lords of the Balkans one by one. By 1820 Serbia was rid of them and central rule restored, although not in the mountains where bandits were free to do as they pleased. The policy reached a successful climax with the arrival at the *saray* of a sackload of heads belonging to the old arch-rebel, Ali Pasha of Yanina, and his sons. Ironically, this potentate fell only when the revolt in Greece reached critical proportions, which brought on the intervention of the European powers. In Egypt, Mehmet Seyyit Halet Efendi, who was no soldier but a leader of the *ulema*, delighted his sovereign by putting down a Mamluk uprising. As a reward he was appointed to the Divan, where he proved to be a reactionary opposed to all Mahmut's reforms. With the help of his confrères and the janissaries, however, he eased himself into the office of Grand Vezir. When the Greek revolt of 1821 fortunately called for a scapegoat, Mahmut was able to exile Halet Efendi in 1822 and have him quietly strangled.

A soldier, Silahtar Ali Pasha, was immediately appointed Grand Vezir with the express duty of having men chosen by the sultan in the most important posts while lulling the suspicions of the *şeyhülislam*. He was succeeded in 1824 by Galip Pasha, who had little difficulty in discrediting the janissary corps which by now almost gloried in its defeats. But Galip Pasha was a scribe and events were clearly moving to the moment of decision when a soldier would be needed if fighting broke out in Istanbul.

Benderli Mehmet Selim Pasha was an experienced commander who had served a two-month apprenticeship as Grand Vezir in 1821. He was to prove a good choice as leader when the Auspicious Event occurred. The steady appointment of the sultan's men as janissary officers culminated in the acceptance of Kara Hüseyn Pasha as *agha* on 26 February 1823. It was a moment of light in a bleak and bitter winter which was so cold that it killed the cholera epidemic which had been decimating the poor of the city, unchecked, since 1821. The new *agha* was so expeditious in dismissing, banishing or forcing into retirement a number of disloyal officers that he was rewarded by promotion to the rank of *vezir* and then pasha. But the janissaries were mutinous because they scented the intentions of the government. Kara Hüseyn Pasha was discreetly appointed governor of Bursa and Commander of the Castles of the Bosphorus where he would be out of sight but close at hand.

The new *agha* of the janissaries was Celalettin Mehmet, who was also of Mahmut's party. He worked more circumspectly than the old soldier Kara Hüseyn Pasha, while the corps daily added to its discredit by brigandly behaviour in the streets of the capital and the lanes of Anatolia. The *ulema* were divided among themselves and those members who continued to support the old order and the janissary corps lost many supporters. Only the dervishes were active in their alliance with the 'old women' (as some openly called the corps) who dared not face the enemy but who were happy to ruin shopkeepers, even pillaging their shops in order to sell the goods themselves. The owners of entrepôts and cargo ships alike had to pay protection money.

The fleeced shopkeepers were the most indignant and directed their venom at the men of the 56th *orta* in particular because they were responsible for checking the provisions entering Istanbul by sea and so grew rich quickly. Market gardeners had to pay tribute to janissaries who opened shops of their own which were stocked by these unfortunates to whom they paid a pittance. Coffee, chickpeas and ashes were their particular perquisite. Others overcharged wickedly for carrying loads and other services, driving away honest workmen in order to take their jobs which were performed as roughly as they chose. They would deliver 100 bricks for the price of 1,000 and made master masons build them new taverns and coffee-houses. When one of these was opened, a senior officer marched there with the insignia of the *orta* held high, surrounded by prostitute boys with cashmere shawls wound round their heads and followed by armed janissaries who beat passers-by and made anyone seated rise and salute the emblem.

The barracks were naturally the alleged scenes of fearful orgies, encouraged by the satanic dervishes who were well warmed with wine, although only officers and sergeants and a few veterans were said to live in the barracks: the rest of the corps were up to mischief on the street and in the markets. At Easter, they spread cloaks on the ground and made Christians pay to walk on them or they grabbed Christians and made them drunk on spirits forced down their throats in order to extort money from them. Many Christians and Jews were ruined by paying janissary protection money in addition to their onerous taxes, especially after the Greek rebellion.

The Janissaries

A motley crew of janissaries lounged along the route when the sultan rode to Friday prayer and they mocked great men who passed, singing ribald songs on their guitars. They robbed continuously all and everyone: even the *kadı* of Istanbul. A colonel of the sappers only just evaded a band which charged out of the *agha*'s headquarters below the Süleymaniye because he was well mounted. The men supposedly on duty guarding the streets threw lighted torches into houses before ransacking them and raping the women. They became protectors of the criminal classes, including murderers. The troops in the country were even worse than those in the city for they robbed villages like brigands and would even rob a dying comrade and bury him alive. When the corpse begged for mercy they laughed and said to a protesting officer that it was his soul talking.

The British ambassador, Lord Strangford, reported on 21 April 1821 that his wife had been beaten and insulted going to mass, though attended by three janissaries and two footmen. The state of affairs is very disgusting, he wrote, but cannot last long.[29] One must suppose that Lady Strangford was not much hurt. More significantly, but not explained in detail, is a passage in Lord Strangford's dispatch of 28 February 1823, which reads:

> The events which most commonly embellish existence at Constantinople have, during the last fortnight, been remarkably abundant and diversified. We have had several storms, an earthquake, much strangling of janissaries, various fires and not a few cases of plague . . .[30]

Who was strangling janissaries and why?

The surrender of the fort of Missolonghi brought matters to a head. The majority of the *ulema* deserted the pitiable rabble which had once been the glory of the empire. The time had come for the sultan and his government to provoke a revolt, confident in the strength of their field-guns and the exasperation of the populace. They were even supported by the students in their *medreses*.

Agha of the janissaries in full dress *(Sotheby's)*

Şeyhülislam *(Sotheby's)*

10
The Auspicious Event[1]

Keeping Secrets

The plot against the janissaries depended on far too many twists of fortune for it to succeed. The secret could hardly be kept since every important official in Istanbul had to know it.[2] Some among them doubted its wisdom and had misgivings about the consequences for themselves were it to be successful. Moreover, were it to fail there were good reasons to dread the most ghastly reprisals against all who had been privy to it together with their families. Every other attempt to be rid of the janissary corps had failed and it was only eighteen years since the sultan, Selim III, had been murdered at their instigation. Moreover, there were senior officers who were likely to be turncoats. Secrecy was impossible as tension mounted day by day and everyone held their breath—everyone except the hard-core janissaries who, in their barracks below the Şehzade mosque, were on the alert.

Mahmut II owed much to the tutelage and kindness of his uncle, Selim III, whose death he did not forgive the mutinous rabble which the once élite corps had become.[3] They were brutes whom no one could hope to reform but their popular following made it essential that their disbanding, after 500 years, should be expeditious and should be seen to be justified. They had, therefore, to be caught in open rebellion and in a rebellion which endangered every citizen from the richest to the scum of whom there were all too many in the opinion of the administration. With the rabble disposed of and the mob leaderless, the government could then re-establish its

The Auspicious Event

authority throughout the empire and, under a central autocracy, a whole series of reforms could begin at last—first and foremost in the army, which tottered from defeat to defeat such as the horrendous massacre of Turks in the Peloponnese in 1822 for which the janissaries could be blamed.

The Divan decided that reform must be tried first so that there could be no grounds for a cry of tyranny. The outward aspects of justice were to be preserved although the government must have expected that far-reaching changes would provoke a mutiny. They proposed withdrawing all veterans who had retired, all invalids and a mass of supernumeraries and hangers-on. The janissary strength in the capital was to be halved at least so that the real soldiers who remained could be drilled and disciplined. It was a paper plan that had worked several times before but it needed a strong commander to put it into effect. Such a man existed in the person of Kara ('Dark') Hüseyn Pasha, now an elderly man, who held the office of governor of the Castles of the Bosphorus. He had been a most able *agha* of the janissaries because of his formidable personality and he had ordered the execution of numerous rebellious members of the corps. In the end, he had overreached himself and had been forced to relinquish his command. He still knew the men well and those among them who could be trusted: these did not make up a large contingent. Kara Hüseyn Pasha was adamant that no one could bring order to a rabble who sat in their huge barracks plotting trouble until the place fermented like a brewery. Nor had he any greater respect for the officers, including the administrators, and clerks, whom he declared would never return to duty. There was only one thing to do, Kara Hüseyn Pasha bluntly stated, and that was to destroy them all in their barracks at a stroke.[4]

The ministers were undoubtedly alarmed by the plain-spoken old man whose courage none of them could hope to match. Most were unable to face the consequences of accepting such advice and retreated to the earlier decision to weed out the existing corps and form a new one from the better elements. With this purpose in mind, they set about bribing and flattering the senior officers and then called them in for consultation. This unprepossessing clique of dignitaries included the *agha*, Mehmetci Etin, the intendant-general, Hasan Agha, and the Chief Cook, Ibrahim Agha, who did no cooking but was quartermaster-general. The plans for reform were explained to these generals, plans which included promotion for themselves. The officers had been well prepared and agreed remarkably speedily that they would work zealously to discipline the newborn corps. The Grand Vezir, Mehmet Selim Pasha, went at once to inform his sultan, who was rightly sceptical of mere words and required a document to be drawn up for all to sign at a meeting of the Divan.

The Janissaries

The Council of the Realm

The Divan duly met on 25 May 1826 at the private house of the *şeyhülislam*[5] under the presidency of the Grand Vezir. It included the leading jurists in the state besides the ministers and senior officers. The doctors of law decided that it was the duty of Muslims to acquire the science of war and the *agha* of the janissaries said that his officers had promised their co-operation. All agreed that the proposed act was legal and a general assembly was called for three days later when the act would be proclaimed. The company then returned to the house of the *şeyhülislam* on 28 May with the addition of other officials. Among them were Kara Hüseyn Pasha and the remaining senior luminaries of the *ulema* (effectively the ruling caste), senior clerks of the treasury and numerous commanding officers.

The Grand Vezir addressed the gathering with eloquence. The eminent soldier did not spare the janissary corps any humiliation. They were the Hydra of revolt who, led by weak officers, had degenerated; a once-valiant corps was now diluted by adventurers who went to war like a rabble. Even Greeks, he said with scorn, had infiltrated its ranks. Considering the number of great Greek pashas who had been members of the corps in its illustrious past, this insult is significant of the change wrought by the Greek War of Independence. These janissaries, Mehmet Selim Pasha continued, were even opposed to wars that might destroy them. Their decadence was due to the weakening of their faith, neglect of the old laws of discipline and the death of the spirit of the *gazis*, warriors for Islam. The Grand Vezir called on the assembly to show the right road to follow, that one and all should work together for the prosperity and glory of the empire. The *reis efendi* then described the evil intentions of various European governments while the secretary of the imperial household spoke of the lousy state of the janissaries. One coward flees and the rest follow, he said, urging the assembly to begin the reform at once. Every soldier present accepted the arguments and the Grand Vezir praised them for their sincerity. When he produced the *irade* (imperial decree) to regulate the corps, the assembly rose to a man to hear it read out in the name of their sultan.

The preamble dealt with the decline of the janisssary corps and listed the battles and fortresses which they had lost. It then proposed reforms in considerable detail, the outcome of long-prepared and -discussed changes. Not only was the structure of each company outlined, together with the number of officers and sergeants to be appointed, but questions of promotion were settled. Also decided were the ever-weighty problems of pay and pensions, and medical care for sick and wounded men. The parade

The Auspicious Event

ground within the vast janissary barracks was to be used again. The stone blocks on which the senior officers stood, the decree pointed out, were still in place and training on a daily basis could begin at once. Small-arms practice would be carried out at the parade ground outside the walls at Davutpaşa or in the meadows at Kağıthane at the head of the Golden Horn. Training was to be preceded by prayers led by the regimental *imam*. The importance of this measure was that the official Sunni school of Islam was to be established within the barracks where the Bektaşi dervish order had held sway since the end of the sixteenth century. Thus the soldiery were to be recalled to orthodoxy from those Sufi paths which the *ulema* proclaimed to be the road to hell and the ministers feared as mystical and subversive. The question of rations and cookhouses was regulated, along with types of tent and the number of kilims to be issued according to rank or duties. Leave and the punishments for desertion were prescribed and an important section was concerned with arms, uniforms and equipment, including bath tents. A humane concession permitted men to choose the company in which to enlist without interference from their present officers. The decree ended with the hope that, with the help of heaven and the reorganized army, the Porte would establish for ever the superiority of the forces of Islam over all their foes.[6]

The *şeyhülislam* then read out his *fetva* that a soldier had a duty to study both military science and religion. When he asked the janissary officers present if they would undertake their new duties, they all promptly answered that they would. The Grand Vezir then proclaimed that all faithful Muslims should hasten to obey the sultan's orders and that all evil or blind men who muttered or who frustrated these reforms were to be punished. At this the *şeyhülislam* as head of the *ulema* cried out, 'Aye! And severely!' The act was then sealed by the senior ministers and the assembly broke up into animated groups but these were speedily interrupted by the Grand Vezir. He ordered the members of the *ulema* present to go in full judicial robes, with the *agha* of the janissaries, to the *agha*'s palace below the mosque of Süleymaniye overlooking the Golden Horn. There they were to address the officers and sergeants and obtain their signatures.

The Janissaries Confronted

The *ulema* set off at once in their robes of state and with every kind of pomp. They took their places nervously on the terrace before the *agha*'s personal pavilion. The decree was so falteringly read that Essat, the Chief Scribe, had to take it and read it again in loud clear tones. The *şeyhülislam* then spoke of the need for discipline and the *agha* of the need for loyalty. There was a pause that tested the nerves of the *ulema* and then the senior officers in the courtyard said that they would obey the decree and came forward to add their signatures. Others followed their lead and most officers swore to seal the *irade* with their blood: but the scramble of signatories, elbowing and pushing comrades out of their way, was clear proof of a lack of elementary discipline. The act could now be sent to the sultan and the assembly was dissolved that same evening.

There were still, however, those who had doubts about the legality of the New Army. Work began immediately but inauspiciously because the inspector-general lacked authority and had to be replaced by the Inspector of Customs and the Sultan's Kitchens, Ibrahim Seyyit Efendi. The first 5,000 men were duly enrolled but their new uniforms were distributed at Davutpaşa barracks, well outside the city, as a precautionary measure. However, with great ceremony in the presence of the senior *ulema* and field officers, 200 recruits of a token *orta* received their uniforms and arms on the Etmeydan after noon prayers on 12 June. Four instructors were present, including Davut Agha, an elderly survivor from the time of the reforms of Selim III; a colonel in the Egyptian army, already reformed, who chanced to be in Istanbul; and one unlucky fellow, Ibrahim. Scornfully, the *agha* asked Ibrahim his regiment and, although shown his tattoo, turned his back on him declaring that he was not fit to be an instructor, so only three were enrolled. The officers were then drilled while the soldiers watched.[7]

It would be interesting to know how many members of the assembly had foreseen the men's reaction to the reforms. Apparently, the sultan had done so.[8] It is inconceivable that the ministers and their advisers did not know that they were provoking a mutiny and yet the charade went on. The janissaries themselves knew that there was no more need for spies and no time to spare if the decree was to be reversed. They gathered in taverns all over the town, grumbling, not surprisingly, about the ending of pay abuses. Some officers were of a like mind, including those who had most influence with their men such as the vice-intendant Mustafa and one Yusuf the Kurd, but they hid their treachery behind fake zeal. They had indeed begun plotting on the very day that they signed the decree and the first parade had seemed to them the ideal moment for revolt. Instead, they feebly abandoned the idea because, conservative to the death, it was the tradition of the janissaries to announce a mutiny by overturning their huge cauldrons, the thunder of these sonorous cooking pots making an awesome din. There was also an unresolved debate as to whether to let their numbers grow day by day or whether the departure of veterans and camp followers would weaken them the more if they did not

The Auspicious Event

act immediately. Imbued with an Ottoman devotion to procrastination, they eventually resolved to be patient for a few days and await a more auspicious moment although it is hard to imagine what that could have been.

If the government could not keep a secret, neither could the rebels. If the rebels had spies, so had the government. The ministers' well-informed suspicions were shared by the inspector-general, who called on the *agha* ostensibly to discuss the exercises but in reality to prepare to withstand an uprising. As soon as the inspector-general had gone, the *agha*, confirmed in his own presentiment of trouble, called in his senior officers (the juniors were loyal in the main) and sought to persuade these rough, intractable characters to accept the new order. He was told that the men did not want to be drilled like infidels but to cut open bellies with their sabres and shoot until the ammunition ran out. It was obvious, without the need to study the face of Yusuf the Kurd, that unrest was not likely to lie submerged much longer. Ibrahim Seyyit Efendi even reported watching men plot openly as they moved among units and onlookers at the three subsequent drill sessions. The government was now gravely alarmed. Then the pot boiled.

The Clamour of the Cauldrons

On the night of Thursday 15 June 1826, one month after the passing of the decree, the plotters arrived in twos and threes at the Etmeydan, beyond the great gate of their barracks, except for those junior officers whom they did not trust and who were fortunate enough not to be invited. In a very short time the parade ground was filled with rebels. Their leaders sent a detachment to attack the *agha* in his residence and dispatched messengers to Hasan Agha, the intendant-general, to call on him to join them. He sent them back with the evasive answer that he would come as soon as various commandants, whom he had summoned, arrived. Although he escaped the trap laid for him, he awaited his officers with alarm.

The detachment of rebels sent against the *agha*, Mehmetci Etin, reached his mansion just as he had returned from a routine round of police inspection in the far-off and squalid quarter of Yedikule. He was preparing for bed and was, in fact, in the lavatory when the rebels arrived and so owed his life to his bowels. Supposing him still out, the janissaries began pillaging his house but realized that this pleasure must wait since the insurrection demanded their precipitous return to the Etmeydan. They contented themselves with smashing the doors and windows with their guns and then set fire to the place but, omen of failure, each fire in turn petered out and their commander escaped, unroasted.

The Janissaries

At dawn, the cauldrons were dragged out of the barracks and others were borrowed from the barracks of the armourers, and of the saddlers nearby, until an ominous pile had been stacked. At the same time, sergeants were sent to Yedikule, and kindred havens for all the city's ruffians, calling on them to join the rebellion. They spread the rumour that the Grand Vezir, the *agha* of the janissaries and all the chief officers were dead and called on the mob to pillage the helpless city. By now the crowd had overflowed from the Etmeydan and Meyvacı ('the Fruiterer') Mustafa, for such indeed was this soldier's trade, led some of them against the palace of the Grand Vezir—the Sublime Porte itself—beside the park of Topkapısaray. Another Mustafa, Sahoş ('the Drunkard'), went to seize the unpopular Egyptian instructor and also to sack the house of the agent of the pasha of Egypt whom the janissaries particularly loathed. Luckily for him, he was at his summer home on the Bosphorus at Çanlıcık. The Grand Vezir was at the royal residence at Beylerbey even farther away. His women were lucky to escape alive, owing to their courage and sagacity in hiding in a cellar or ice-house in the middle of the garden and holding their breath. Other bands of janissaries were running through the streets, crying for the blood of all who had signed the decree. They threatened to take the *ulema*'s women and children and to sell their pubescent sons for 10 piastres and their clothes for 5. They also ordered the shops to take down their shutters, promising to give a diamond in compensation for any article that was stolen. The city was more than alarmed; it had reached the farther shores of terror.

If the Grand Vezir had foreseen the event—and how could he not?—why was he half-way down the Bosphorus and why were his family left to their fate? The behaviour of the janissaries ensured that no honest citizen would regret their destruction, yet if they were deliberately being fed rope with which to hang themselves, the policy was surely irresponsible. The officers of state did not wait to be hacked to pieces but fled to join the Grand Vezir at Beylerbey and when action was taken it was swift. The Grand Vezir sent his brother and his intendant to Kara Hüseyn Pasha and to Mehmet Pasha: they were summoned to a rendezvous with all the men they could muster at the Yalı Kiosk at Seraglio Point in the summer palace below the great *saray*. Then, getting into his barque with his coffee-maker, the minister committed his soul to Allah and set off for the kiosk. There he found Kıbrıslı Mehmet Emin Pasha, intendant of the palace treasury, whom he sent to warn the sultan and ask permission to unfurl the Standard of the Prophet. He was also to beg Mahmut II to show himself to his troops. The *şeyhülislam* was also summoned and came in haste just as Kara Hüseyn Pasha and Mehmet Pasha arrived with their troops. Messages had also gone out to the *ulema* class as

The Auspicious Event

a whole, including the ubiquitous students, to rally to the defence of the throne. Similar messages were sent to senior officials and officers, including the intendant of the Tersane, the general of the artillery and the commandants of the sappers and bombardiers, ordering them to bring their forces to the palace.

Meanwhile, the intendant-general Hasan Agha proceeded to the residence of the *agha* of the janissaries, accompanied by his staff and others officers. Since the place was unaccountably deserted, including the water closet, he installed himself there and sent the Chief Scribe of the corps to ask the rebels their intentions. They shouted back that they wanted no more infidel exercises and demanded the heads of those reponsible for the decree. They were in an elated mood, convinced that their mutiny had succeeded. This was the message that Hasan Agha transmitted to the Grand Vezir and the potentates in the kiosk by the water. The *vezir* was furious and sent an immediate answer to the rebels declaring that Allah was on his side and would crush them. This reply was unanimously approved and the ministers proceeded through the *saray* vegetable gardens and out through the Bab-ül-Hümayün to the rebuilt Aslanhane (Lion House), which had once stood near the former basilica and now imperial mosque of Haghia Sophia. It made a useful rallying-point to which the *ulema* and the students came running, certain that their property would be the first to suffer from the rapacity of the mob. The Grand Vezir was further cheered by the arrival of several distinguished officers with the marines from the Tersane, a posse of mounted artillery and, most welcome of all, the intrepid Ibrahim Agha of the artillery with nine guns. The ferocity of this celebrated commander was dreaded by the army, who knew him as the Infernal Ibrahim. The one person still awaited was the sultan.

The Standard of the Prophet Unfurled

Kıbrıslı Mehmet Emin Pasha had hastened to Beşiktaş, the sovereign's summer residence, and had delivered the Grand Vezir's warning of the revolt. Mahmut II hesitated and then sent his valet de chambre in a barque which he used when travelling incognito to ask the Grand Vezir for more details. But growing impatient, and perhaps a little ashamed, the monarch embarked for the *saray*, followed by other officers in a small squadron of pleasure craft. There was no disguise now and his sword hung at his side. Landing at Seraglio Point, Mahmut proceeded immediately to the *saray* where he installed himself in the Sünnet Odası (Circumcision Kiosk) of the *selamlık,* which had a panoramic view of the city and the Golden Horn. On

The Janissaries

his way through the courts of his palace, he paused briefly to cheer on his household. Then he sent for his ministers and demanded what was to be done with the janissaries, who had been treated generously and answered only with insurrection. Ministers and *ulema* alike replied that the unjust must be fought and there was a clamorous shout of 'Victory or death!' An elderly theologian, Müderris (Professor) Abdurrahman Efendi, threw down his chaplet of beads and demanded to know what they were waiting for. 'Attack and destroy them!', he cried, waving an empty fist. The Divan then pleaded with the sultan not to fight himself but to unfurl the black standard[9] which still lay in its gold casket in the room of the Relics of the Prophet across the terrace. Mahmut agreed and criers were sent across the city, and to Galata and Pera on the opposite shores of the Horn, and to Üsküdar over the Sea of Marmara, calling on all loyal citizens to rally to their sultan's cause. Crowds were already flocking to the Bab-ül-Hümayün and more yet were to respond to the call to arms.

Meanwhile, the sultan entered the Room of the Prophet and took the standard out of its casket. He solemnly unfurled it and handed the staff to the Grand Vezir and the *şeyhülislam*. Sabres and muskets had been distributed from the palace arsenal in the former basilica of Haghia Irene, in the First or Outer Court of the *saray*, and the newly armed students escorted the sacred standard to the mosque of Sultan Ahmet, overlooking the Hippodrome. There it was unfurled afresh at the top of the *mimber* beside the large mihrab niche. At Topkapısaray, Mahmut proceeded to the Bab-ül-Hümayün above which was a viewing chamber. From here he could watch, beyond the domes of the *hamam* of Haghia Sophia, the host of loyal subjects who had come to defend their prince. Indeed, he had to sent his equerry to quell a riot in the First Court where those who had arrived too late were indignant at finding the armoury bare.

Tactics and Attack

At this moment the Grand Vezir must have been confident of victory. If the order of events had indeed been engineered, and the mutiny had been allowed to break out with government cognizance, then the policy was justified since all save the basest classes were united in opposition to the janissaries. Doubt still remains on this point. A council of war was held before the mihrab where some suggested that a plenipotentiary should be sent to parley with the rebels, the choice falling on Abdurrahman Efendi, that outspoken elder of the *ulema*. But he, with considerable haste, boldly declared the rebels to be intractable and such a mission therefore to be

The Auspicious Event

pointless. The Grand Vezir was dissuaded from leading an attack and Kara Hüseyn Pasha with Mehmet Pasha took command of the marines and the artillery.

From a corner of the Hippodrome to the mosque of Bayezit II runs the Divan Yolu, which was then 24 metres wide and still arcaded. It was the only street of any breadth within the city and commanded the approach to the *saray* from the quarters occupied by the janissaries' barracks. As soon as the first contingents of troops had marched off, the remaining company devoted twenty minutes to prayer. The ministers were heartened by the arrival of the group of janissary officers but when they begged pardon for their comrades, such as the pernicious vice-intendant Mustafa the Fruiterer, the Grand Vezir was not duped by such hypocrisy and answered them brusquely.

The crowd was clamouring for a commander who would lead them into battle—Necip Efendi, Inspector of the Powder Magazines, volunteered. Four lieutenants were appointed and the throng went off to fight the janissaries, fortunately too late to do damage to themselves. The rebels had learned of the arrival of the sultan and the unfurling of the standard and were determined to block the roads to the Etmeydan. Companies were posted at the end of Divan Yolu below the mosque of Bayezit II and in the other old Byzantine highway, the Uzunçarşı (Long Market), which descends from the bazaars to the Golden Horn.[10] They also occupied the Bayezit mosque and all approaches to the Hippodrome. As a street, the Uzunçarşı was friendly to the rebels since it was the centre of the old clothes market in which the janissaries were active traders. At the Horhor fountain, Ibrahim Agha, who, with two cannon, had been sent on in the van by the two pashas, came face to face with a company of janissaries. He had the guns manned and attacked at once. Although two artillerymen were killed, one burst of grapeshot had the rebels retreating post-haste to the Etmeydan, where their comrades rallied and, entering their barracks, closed the Great Door. This they proceeded to barricade with heavy stones. They had lost all initiative and abandoned many of their friends who were still roaming the streets. They appeared to believe that their fortress was impregnable.

Kara Hüseyn Pasha was reinforced by other units besides Necip Efendi's cheerful band and had no difficulty in encircling the barracks. He sent Ibrahim Agha to the gate to call on the mutineers to relent and regain their senses but they shouted him down, mistaking words for bullets. Mehmet Pasha had predicted the end of the story and it now fell to him to enact it: he was sent the order that the artillery were to open fire. Perhaps until then the janissaries had not believed that the army would attack itself. Some of them

The Janissaries

suggested a sortie through a postern gate in order to capture the guns from behind while secretly planning to escape together. The rest, full of a lunatic, suicidal confidence, gathered behind their Great Door—several were killed there when it was shattered by the cannonade. Mehmet Pasha advanced immediately and the heroic Gunner Mustafa (the first through the breach), who succeeded in opening what was left of the gate, was richly rewarded after the battle. Mehmet Pasha himself led the charge followed by Ibrahim Agha. The latter had rendered great service by bringing up the powder from the mosque of Sultan Ahmet and by urging on the troops. He was hit in the heel and had to retire while still encouraging his men.[11]

Retribution

Now the rebels had but one thought or hope: where could they flee? Some sought refuge in the hall of the Bektaşi dervishes situated in the middle of the Etmeydan. Others fled blindly as bats through endless corridors and deserted chambers. Each reproached the other for his plight as if the blame mattered any more. Gunner Mustafa seized a brand and set the place on fire. The flames spread with a zest which turned the barracks into hell. In it the last of the janissaries went in horror and self-pity to their deaths. Charles Addison, who visited the place a decade later, believed that 1,000 janissaries must have died there.

A horseman had ridden to the Hippodrome to announce the victory to the Grand Vezir amid scenes of great rejoicing. The news, which must by now have been self-evident, was proudly transmitted to Mahmut II. The *vezir* proceeded to the handsome chamber of the sultan's pavilion on the east side of the Sultan Ahmet mosque (which has been restored) and there assembled the officers of state. He sent messages of congratulations to the victorious pashas. Such prisoners as had been taken came trudging in ones and twos into the Hippodrome with their hands tied behind their backs and were hustled into the basement of the pavilion. An officer was sent to bring to the mosque those janissaries who had not taken part in the day's events. Their *agha*, who had hidden in disguise in a house near his own headquarters, was summarily dismissed. By 4 o'clock all the officers had reached the mosque. On being presented to the Grand Vezir, they had kissed the hem of his robe before being collected in a tent specially erected for them in the Outer Court before the pavilion. At 7 o'clock, just before sundown, the corpses of seven of the rebels who had been taken arms in hand were flung under that notorious plane tree in the Hippodrome known as the Janissary Tree because of the potentates hanged there by the corps in times past.

The Auspicious Event

The revolt was crushed. Many janissaries had been killed in the fighting. Those who had managed to escape hid, along with their adherents. The city gates were barred and guarded, as were those of Üsküdar, Kasımpaşa, Galata and Eyüp. But some with long legs had already reached the Belgrade forest, part of which was set alight in order to burn them out. Bombardiers were sent to the Women's Gallery of the Sultan Ahmet mosque to guard the standard. Sentries were posted all round the Hippodrome. The Grand Vezir and the *şeyhülislam* slept in the pavilion on both Thursday and Friday night while other ministers slept in the mosque. The pashas went to the Eski Odalar, opposite the Şehzade mosque, and routed out any of the under-officers still living there or who had escaped from the Etmeydan and had them marched off to join their comrades. They posted sentries at the barracks and then retired to rest at last at the house of the *agha* of the janissaries down the lane. On the advice of Necip Efendi, however, they crossed the road to the outer court of the Süleymaniye, where a tent had had been pitched for them. All night, officers in disguise routed out rebels from every nook and cranny in the city.

On Friday, the Grand Vezir had the leading rebels brought before him one after the other to hear his reproaches and their sentences to death. One was the captain of the firemen: he had barely time to be strangled before his hated corpse was dragged through the dust to the plane tree. Among those whom it must have given the *vezir* great pleasure to have executed were the crooked vice-intendant Mustafa and the brutal Yusuf the Kurd. In the end, more than 200 rebels were strangled in the undercroft and their corpses heaped in the Hippodrome. Kara Hüseyn Pasha presided over the execution of 120 more at the headquarters of the *agha*. Everyone accepted that the time had come to dispose of the janissaries for ever. Mahmut II gladly concurred and retired to the Zeynep mosque, below Haghia Sophia and the Sublime Porte, for the noon prayer. The Divan convened in the royal pavilion and the decision to abolish the janissary corps without a trace was agreed. Again the Outer Court of the mosque was filled with the tents of loyal officers that night and once more the leaders of the *ulema* slept within the mosque. Next day the Divan issued the *firman* of dissolution. It was sent to the sultan and approved within half an hour, with orders that it was to be executed immediately.

Messengers were sent to every province and the *firman* was read from the *mimbers* at noon prayers. At the Sultan Ahmet mosque it was the courageous secretary and chronicler Essat who mounted the stairs—standing modestly some steps short of the top—and kissed the sacred flag. Then he read out the edict of abolition and announced that the New Army was placed

The Janissaries

under the command of the illustrious *vezir* Kara Hüseyn Pasha, along with less august appointments. The pasha established his headquarters at the palace of the *agha* while the old *saray* at Bayezit was cleared of the last few relicts of dead sultans and refurbished as the Ministry of War and General Headquarters. A faded hostelry for old flames was a curiously inauspicious place from which to direct the creation of a New Army. Then the *şeyhülislam* received his special reward. Until 1826 he and his predecessors had lived in their own houses but now the former palace of the *agha* became his official residence: the victory of orthodoxy over the heterodox Sufi dervishes was complete. The *firmans* sent to the provinces carried a supplementary paragraph which instructed the *beylerbeys* and governors to take the cauldrons from all janissary units since they belonged to the state and not to the soldiers. The men themselves were to be banished across the frontiers and their name was never to be uttered again. Along with them, significantly, were to go any other potential trouble-makers. They were to be replaced by the governor's own troops. The edict was carried by the swiftest horsemen available, the Tartar cavalry.

On 17 June 1826 Kara Hüseyn Pasha was promoted governor of Yedikule, and of the fire towers at Galata and Stamboul (now the fire tower of the university), as well as *serasker*. The fear of fire in Istanbul had always been great and the abolition of the janissaries deprived the city of its trained fire-fighters. Kara Hüseyn Pasha received a magnificent cloak from the Grand Vezir and then went to his tent at the Süleymaniye. He immediately started to enrol soldiers, including Davut Agha who was promoted a colonel. Davut Agha had been dragged to the barracks but a sergeant had contrived to give him his own clothes as a disguise and he had managed to escape. Others were also rewarded, including an old officer of Selim III's who had been deprived of his captaincy by the janissaries and who was working for merchants and living in poverty.

The rebel officers confined in the tent were pardoned and, indeed, received promotion. Those retired were pensioned or given honorary appointments in the royal household so that none might gainsay the somewhat class-biased clemency of the sultan. Janissary administrators were admitted to equivalent grades of an embryonic civil service. One or two officers who had been notoriously perfidious were less well treated. The colonel of the armourers, Mehmet Agha, was exiled to Kütahya but only so that a guardsman might ride after him and execute him at Inegöl, bringing back his corpse to be exposed before the Bab-ül-Hümayün on 22 June. Kıbrıslı Mehmet Emin Pasha, who had crossed the city on the day of the revolt in order to serve his sovereign, was rewarded with the vacant

The Auspicious Event

command. Other loyalists were also promoted. Finally, the commanders of two companies were found to have been in the plot and were executed. The Yeni Odalar barracks had been totally destroyed by the fire and the Eski Odalar was demolished forthwith. Even the graves of janissaries were deprived of their tombstones bearing the symbolic headdress of the sleeve of Hacı Bektaş flowing over their shoulders.

At last the Standard of the Prophet was taken back to Topkapısaray to be received at the Bab-ül-Sa'adet, admitting to the Third Court, by Mahmut II. He kissed it and planted it in its socket before the gate, to be guarded by officers of the household. The sultan remained in uniform for several days. Because it had not been possible to prepare his apartments at short notice, he made use of a small room next to the palace mosque but frequently slipped away incognito to his summer residence at Beşiktaş to be with his family of whom he was fond. The *ulema* made a dormitory of the Great Saloon and the ministers pitched their tents in the First Court, where now no janissary camped. There was still much to do. Resistance had broken out at Edirne, Vidin and Izmit on 15 June and could spread: it did not. The government had to make sure that the units in the provinces had indeed been disbanded: they had.[12] Asiatic janissaries were merely driven out destitute. A new *beylerbey*, Kemal Bey, was later to find that one ex-janissary had survived to the age of 150 in Damascus. He lived by making walking-sticks and, when he made the usual present of one to the new governor, was amply rewarded. He had served under Abdülhamit I and remembered every historical event until 1826 but recalled nothing after that date.

Kara Hüseyn Pasha had to hurry to form a new army because the state was left defenceless in the eyes of its enemies. A new fire brigade[13] had to be recruited and some form of police force devised. The *firman* had abolished the order of Bektaşi dervishes, whom the *ulema* hated because of their popularist strength, and other sects such as the Nakşibendis took over their property. Since everyone belonged to some dervish sect or the other, it was not the Bektaşis' unorthodoxy but their liberalism that made their founder, if he ever existed, the *ulema*'s personification of the devil. Their roots were too deep in Anatolia for Mahmut II or even Atatürk, a century later, to destroy. The order is still active and influential in Turkey today.

The mosque that celebrates the victory of the Ottomans over themselves, the Nüsretiye (Divine Victory), was built below the gun foundry at Tophane and beside the Bosphorus next to the artillery barracks. The old order was ended. Topkapısaray was only to be used on a few ceremonial occasions and became itself a House of Tears for the women of past sultans. New palaces were to be erected in a Western style and with these a new era did indeed

The Janissaries

begin: only it was no more notable for its victories than the past that it had suppressed.

The Nüsretiye (Victory) mosque, erected to celebrate the suppression of the janissaries

Epilogue

There was no one left to weep for the janissaries, not even themselves. Even their tombstones were toppled and the stone caps and sleeves of Hacı Bektaş reduced to rubble. The list of their crimes, both petty and great, stretched back before living memory and was only exceeded by that of their defeats. Witness after witness could testify against them.

Why, then, were they not put down long before? However, put down they were at last. The executions, amounting to perhaps 1,000, continued at the orders of Hüsrev Pasha, Mehmet Izzat Pasha and the *bostancıbaşı*, who in his role as Grand Provost presided over the execution of high officials. The wretches were routed out of the Tersane and other retreats without compunction but, on the whole, the innocent were spared. One officer in disguise, Osman Agha, was particularly successful in hunting down the leaders. He came upon Mustafa the Fruiterer in a coffee-house and later Mustafa the Drunkard, two notable pillagers, who protested their innocence in vain. They were both hanged—the one before his shop and the other at the door of the Hasan Pasha *han*—while the assassin of a high dignitary was garrotted at Üsküdar. As for the rest—who were of little account except in the eyes of their families, perhaps—most found menial jobs for they had lost any guild status and no trade was now open to them. Some jobs were disagreeable and, of these, stoking the boilers of *hamams* was the nastiest but had the virtue that soot lost a man his identity. So many janissaries became stokers that out of the smoke and ashes arose a school of poets to keep the memory of the corps alive—it was a corps which had always been

Epilogue

proud of a poetic tradition as well as the libidinous songs which also lived on through the nineteenth century.[1] On the whole those who kept quiet were unmolested but it was unwise to drink or talk too much.

On a visit to the lunatic asylum at the Süleymaniye in the 1830s, Charles Addison found two or three madmen in each cell with leather thongs round their necks attached to rings in the wall. Their diet was bread, rice and water and the bastinado when they were outrageous. In one cell he encountered two former janissaries who had spoken too freely. That they were punished is not surprising but their presence showed either a shortage of space in the normal prisons or a very firm attitude on the part of the authorities towards any who dissented from the established policies of the state. But, if discreet, a former janissary could live the normal life of an ordinary citizen. What he could never recover were his special privileges and pay and, in particular, the right to trial in his own court.

The decree abolishing the Bektaşi dervish order on 10 July 1826 was inevitable. The parent *tekke* at Hacıbektaş had considerable control over the other convents of the order. Its income had been seriously affected by the decline in the population of central Anatolia and the village, which had maintained 837 families in 1584, now had barely 100. A cavalry officer, assisted by a clerk from the *şeyhülislam*'s office and a secretary, was appointed the administrator of the Bektaşi properties. A few of the leaders of the movement were executed while lesser lights were banished to Kayseri and other towns to be converted to orthodoxy by the Sunni doctors there.

The newer buildings of the *tekkes* were demolished but historic ones were preserved. Where possible, a *tekke* became a mosque. The mother *tekke* at Hacıbektaş was given to the Nakşibendi[2] order and its Master banished no farther than Amasya. Of the twenty-four dervishes living there, only eight were deported, the other sixteen joined the Nakşibendis and stayed at home. Their exemption from taxes, however, lapsed. Elsewhere, any who had dabbled in politics were severely punished. In Istanbul, three *babas* were arrested and imprisoned, two at Üsküdar and one at the mint within the palace walls. All three were beheaded on 19 July 1826. It is noteworthy that the decree of abolition laid stress on the heterodoxy of the order's beliefs rather than its connection with the janissaries, whose name it was already illegal to pronounce. It is not recorded what the commissioners did with the scandalous bottles of wine found in the cellars of the *tekkes* that they inspected. And it is ironic that, with the abolition of this sect, the intellectual soldier Aptullah Mehmet had to be exiled for it was due to this able, if heterodox, officer that a technical Turkish language had been evolved which was to be particularly important in the field of medicine. By their

Epilogue

subservience to the Sunni legalists, the government lost one other prop: that fatalism which travellers to Istanbul grudgingly admired was the gift of the Sufis, above all others, to the stability of conservative government and the greatest burden that reformists had to bear. No administrator is likely to be annoyed if his misgovernment is attributed to ill-fortune and so to God. The ruler rests in peace when it is blasphemy to complain.

Not with a Bang . . .

The shabby janissaries merely mirrored, after all, the society for whom they (occasionally) fought. They bequeathed a curious tradition of popular political leadership which bred the modern officer castes of the Middle East and Egypt, better educated and more idealist but also, at times, corrupted by their interest in trade. These also represent some aspirations of a new middle class in the haphazard manner of amateur governments habitually thrown up by military rule from Pakistan to Libya and beyond. The difference is that no Auspicious Event will dispose of the new castes as they rapidly become accustomed to rule.

It has been claimed that the janissaries, like the new army officers of the Islamic world, were to some extent the tribunes of the humbler citizens. Bernard Lewis[3] has suggested that they resembled a chamber of deputies which often compelled sultans to change ministers. Talented men among them who had the art of inflaming passions were sure to get good employment in order to keep them quiet. They certainly stirred up the meanest orders and the poorest when intent on trouble, but not with any idealist intention of relieving poverty

Janissary democracy was that of the bar parlour, an emotional reponse to the utterances of a tetchy and petty bourgeoisie. Heated by the irritations of the moment, their policies were only of that moment. A janissary-inspired revolt was always directed at individuals or figureheads, although not always the right ones—a *vezir* might hang in the Hippodrome as a symbol of ill-government when he himself was working to alter the policy in question. With the janissaries gone for ever, a vacuum had to be filled. This was not the intention of the men who planned the Auspicious Event, however, for it meant some echo of a voice of the populace just when Mahmut II was intent on destroying some of the dearest privileges of free men.

Islamic cities offered no more scope for democracy than those of the Byzantines which preceded them. They were ruled, more or less, but were never self-governing under royal charter. Without any form of liberal

Epilogue

education, the populace could not produce leaders capable of formulating benevolent political programmes.

Janissary democracy was that of the bar parlour until, at last, the state had had enough. The corps left behind nothing that could be of use in the twentieth century. Their years of glory had a dying fall; yet theirs was a human story. One may turn to Ziya Pasha for verses that he did not intend to be their epitaph but which may excellently serve:

> *Ziya, in the tavern of the world,*
> *the hangover weighs heavy,*
> *I have not seen much, in my brief*
> *time, worthy of admiration.*

(Ziya Pasha, 1829–80;
trans. Nermin Menemencioğlu)

Jacques de Hay: sipahi *(Maggs)*

Notes

These notes are not comprehensive but deal with relatively new information. Facts established by such famous historians as Baron Joseph von Hammer-Purgstall, Sir Hamilton Gibb, Franz Babinger and Ahmet Refik, among many others, are not referred to specifically.

Abbreviations:
EI   *Encyclopaedia of Islam*
IJMES   *International Journal of Middle East Studies*
JESHO   *Journal of Economic and Social History of the Orient*
JRAS   *Journal of the Royal Asiatic Society*
SEHME   *Studies in the Economic History of the Middle East*

Chapter 1
 1. Ibn Battuta (ed. H.A.R. Gibb), *The Travels of Ibn Battuta*, vol. II (Cambridge, 1962).
 2. H. Hookham, *Tamberlaine the Conqueror* (London, 1962), p. 258; and R.G. de Clavijo, *Embassy to Tamerlaine, 1403-1406* (London, 1925), pp. xxxix and 124: 'Truth is Safety'.
 3. W.E.D. Allen, *Problems of Turkish Power in the Sixteenth Century* (London, 1963), p. 46, n. 80.
 4. S. Vryonis Jnr, *The Decline of Medieval Hellenism in Asia Minor . . .* (Berkeley, Calif., 1971), pp. 135ff.
 5. P.H. Skrine and E. Denison Ross, *The Heart of Asia* (London, 1959), p. 277.
 6. Ibid., p. 278.
 7. G.G. Arnakis, *The Early Ottomans* (Athens, 1947), p. 237.
 8. S. Skilliter, 'Catherine de Medici's Turkish Ladies-in-Waiting', *Turcica*, vol. VII (1975), pp. 188 *et seq.*
 9. H.A.R. Gibb and H. Bowen, *Islamic Society and the West*, vol. I, part 1 (Oxford, 1950), p. 183.
 10. Arnakis, *Early Ottomans*, p. 240.
 11. Gibb and Bowen, *Islamic Society and the West*, vol. I, part 1, p. 183. Elsewhere in Islam there were the *futuwwa* bands, which were related, but they were not guilds in the *ahi* manner.
 12. Ibn Battuta (ed. Gibb), *Travels . . .* , p. 426.
 13. Anarkis, *Early Ottomans;* and 'Futuwwa Traditions in the Ottoman Empire', *Journal of Middle East Studies*, no. 4 (Oct. 1953), p. 223.

Notes

14. Gibb and Bowen, *Islamic Society and the West*, vol. I, part 1, p. 41.
15. Arnakis, *Early Ottomans*, p. 236; and Ibn Battuta (ed. Gibb), *Travels...*, pp. 450ff.
16. R.C. Repp, *The Mufti of Istanbul* (London/Oxford, 1986), pp. 269-70.
17. N. Fisher, *The Middle East, a History* (New York, 1959), p. 175. Evrenos Bey was a Greek from Karasi.
18. I. Beldiceanu-Steinherr, 'Le Règne de Selim I', *Turcica*, vol. V (1975).
19. I.H. Uzunçarşılı, *Osmanlı Devletinin Saray Teşkilatı* (Ankara, 1945), p. 41.
20. C. Cahen, 'Note sur l'Esclavage Musulman et le Devshirme Ottoman', *JESHO*, vol. XIII (1970), p. 215, prefers Orhan to Murat as founder of the janissaries.
21. B. Lewis, *Islam from the Prophet Muhammad to the Capture of Constantinople*, vol. 1 (New York, 1974), pp. 226-7.
22. H. Bowen, 'Acemioğlan', *EI*, vol. I (1960), p. 266; and H. Inalcık, *The Ottoman Empire* (London, 1973), p. 9.
23. Fisher, *Middle East...*, p. 176.
24. V. Ménage, 'Devshirme', *EI*, vol. II (1965), p. 210. He also refers to the promise of exemption if the inhabitants of Janina submit. A.H. Lybyer, *The Government of the Ottoman Empire in the Time of Süleyman the Magnificent* (Harvard, 1913), lists Schiltberger as a *kul* in 1396 when he was taken prisoner, aged 16, at Nicopolis. But the earliest *devşirme* recruit whom he records is Ricoldus, who served in Ottoman private families from 1436 to 1453. Inalcık, *Ottoman Empire*, p. 11, also refers to prisoners-of-war.
25. Cahen, 'Note sur l'Esclavage Musulman...', p. 215.
26. Allen, *Problems of Turkish Power...*', p. 48. n. 80; and N. Forbes, *A History of Serbia* (Oxford, 1915), p. 100. The Bogomils were a distinct religious movement some of whose headstones survive. The Albigensians of the south of France themselves had affinities with the mystics of Islamic Spain and so were united by the voice of the guitar, which was the voice of the troubadour.
27. Schiltberger reported a sale of children in c. 1400.
28. W. Heyd, *Histoire du Commerce du Levant au Moyen-Age*, vol. 2 (Leipzig, 1936), p. 562.
29. A. Tenenti, *Piracy and the Decline of Venice, 1580-1615* (London, 1967), p. 157, n. 1. See D. Ayalon, *Outsiders in the Lands of Islam: Mamluks, Mongols and Eunuchs* (London, 1988), *passim*, for a discussion of male slavery under Islam.
30. M. Howard, *War in European History* (Oxford, 1976), p. 54. However, Charles VII of France's Compagnies de l'Ordnance formed a standing army in the fifteenth century.
31. Inalcık, *Ottoman Empire*, p. 11.

Notes

32. Ibid., p. 193. But the Sufi poet Nesimi was flayed alive.
33. Lybyer, *Government of the Ottoman Empire* . . . , p. 47.
34. See ibid. for the platonic nature of the college and life service.

Chapter 2

1. W. Irvine, *The Army of the Indian Moghuls, its Organisation and Administration* (New Delhi, 1962), p. 11.
2. N. Fisher, *The Middle East, a History* (New York, 1959), p. 189. The levy was established in the Balkans in 1430 and culled every five years.
3. A.H. Lybyer, *The Government of the Ottoman Empire in the Time of Süleyman the Magnificent* (Harvard, 1913), p. 53; and R.E. Kocu, *Yeniçeriler* (Istanbul, 1964), p. 30.
4. E. Kovačević, 'Jedan Dokumenat o Dersirmi', *Prilozi*, no. 22 (Sarajevo, 1976), pp. 208-9.
5. U. Heyd, *Documents on Palestine, 1552-1615* (Oxford, 1960), pp. 63-4.
6. It clearly varied. See: N. de Nicolay, *Navigations and Voyages* (London, 1586), p. 69; and F.A. Geuffroy, *Briefve de la Cour du Grand Turc* (Paris, 1563). But see also V. Ménage, 'Devshirme', *EI*, vol. II (1965), p. 213.
7. B. Ramberti, 'Libro Tre delle Cose di Turchi', *Viaggi* (Venice, 1543) (London edn 1554, misprinted 1514, p. 21).
8. H.A.R. Gibb and H. Bowen, *Islamic Society and the West*, vol. I, part 1 (Oxford, 1950), p. 181.
9. Lybyer, *Government of the Ottoman Empire* . . . , p. 52; and Kocu, *Yeniçeriler*, pp. 25-6. According to Ménage, 'Devshirme', p. 212, an early *firman* states that they were to be aged 14-18; by the seventeenth century, they were to be aged 15-20 (ibid., p. 211).
10. Kocu, *Yeniçeriler*, p. 27; and Geuffroy, *Briefve de la Cour* . . . , p. 121.
11. Kocu, *Yeniçeriler*, p. 28.
12. Principal sources of information on the Enderun Kolej include: I.H. Uzunçarşılı, *Osmanlı Devletinin Saray Teskilatı* (Ankara, 1945); Lybyer, *Government of the Ottoman Empire* . . . ; Gibb and Bowen, *Islamic Society and the West*; B. Miller, *The Palace School of Muhammad the Conqueror* (Cambridge, 1941); and, most important, G. Necipoğlu, *Architecture, Ceremonial and Power. The Topkapı Palace in the 15th and 16th Centuries* (Massachusetts, 1991).
13. Nicolay, *Navigations and Voyages*, p. 69; and Djevad Bey (Ahmad Javad), *État Militaire Ottoman* . . . (Constantinople/Paris, 1882), p. 241.
14. Fisher, *Middle East* . . . , p. 199.
15. O. Bon, *Descrizione del Seraglio del Gran Signore* (Venice, 1865), p. 241.
16. Uzunçarşılı, *Osmanlı Devletinin Saray Teskilatı*, pp. 74-7 and 118-33.
17. B. Lewis, *Islam from the Prophet Muhammad to the Capture of*

Notes

Constantinople, vol. 1 (New York, 1974), p. 89.
  18. Lybyer, *Government of the Ottoman Empire* . . . , p. 52.
  19. Nicolay, *Navigations and Voyages*, p. 69.
  20. Ramberti, 'Libro Tre delle Use Turche', p. 35.
  21. C.M. Kortepeter, *Ottoman Imperialism during the Reformation* (New York, 1972), p. 214.
  22. S.J. and E.K. Shaw, *History of the Ottoman Empire and Modern Turkey* (Illinois, 1974), p. 27.
  23. Kocu, *Yeniçeriler*, p. 28.
  24. E. Schuyler (ed. G. Wheeler), *Turkestan* (New York, 1966), p. 128.
  25. Lybyer, *Government of the Ottoman Empire* . . . , p. 58.
  26. R.N. Frye, *Bukhara, the Medieval Achievement* (Oklahoma, 1965), pp. 120-1; and C. Cahen, *Pre-Ottoman Turkey* (London, 1968), p. 213.
  27. After a great fire, Murat III rebuilt the *saray* extensively. H.G. Rosedale, *Queen Elizabeth and the Levant Company* (London, 1904), p. 22, says that he adorned it with royal magnificence.
  28. Geuffroy, *Briefve de la Cour* . . . , p. 127.
  29. Lybyer, *Government of the Ottoman Empire* . . . , p. 125.
  30. Geuffroy, *Briefve de la Cour* . . . , p. 125.
  31. T. Spandugino, 'Delle Origini degli Imperatori Ottomani', *SATHAS*, Documents inédits, vol. IX (Paris, 1899).
  32. Lybyer, *Government of the Ottoman Empire* . . . , p. 77: first year, 2 aspers; second year, 3 aspers; and third year, 4 aspers.
  33. Vassif Efendi (transl. P.A. Coussin de Perceval), *Précis Historique de la Guerre des Turcs contre les Russes, 1769-1774* (Paris, n.d.), p. 47.

Chapter 3
  1. H.A.R. Gibb, 'Lutfi Pasha and the Ottoman Caliphate', *Oriens*, no. 15 (1962), pp. 287-95.
  2. P. Wittek, *The Rise of the Ottoman Empire* (London, 1938), p. 38.
  3. H. Hookham, *Tamberlaine the Conqueror* (London, 1962), p. 276.
  4. N. Fisher, *The Middle East, a History* (New York, 1959), p. 180.
  5. A.H. Lybyer, *The Government of the Ottoman Empire in the Time of Süleyman the Magnificent* (Harvard, 1913), pp. 145-6.
  6. H.G. Rosedale, *Queen Elizabeth and the Levant Company* (London, 1904), p. 32.
  7. J.P. Roux, *La Mort chez les Peuples Altaï'iques Anciens et Médiévaux* (Paris, 1963), p. 32.
  8. B. Lewis, *Islam from the Prophet Muhammad to the Capture of Constantinople*, vol. 1 (New York, 1974), p. 97.
  9. H.A.R. Gibb and H. Bowen, *Islamic Society and the West*, vol. I, part 1 (Oxford, 1950), p. 25.

Notes

10. H. Edib, *Conflict of East and West in Turkey* (Lahore, 1963), pp. 15–19.
11. Ibid., p. 187.
12. C.V. Finlay, 'The Foundation of the Ottoman Foreign Ministry', *IJMES*, vol. III (1972), p. 336. But until the Young Turks, all Turks were the slaves of the sultan.
13. D.A. Ayalon, *Le Livre de la Coronne* (Paris, 1954), p. 146. In Egypt, a Mamluk slave was often the son–and orphan–of his master because their emotional interdependence was akin to that of an ally.
14. Gibb and Bowen, *Islamic Society and the West*, vol. I, part 1, p. 151.
15. Ibid., vol. 1, part 2, p. 101.
16. J. Schacht, *An Introduction to Islamic Law* (Oxford, 1964), *passim*.
17. Gibb and Bowen, *Islamic Society and the West*, vol. I, part 1, p. 151.
18. Lybyer, *Government of the Ottoman Empire* . . . , p. 191.
19. A. Tietze, *Mustafa 'Ali's Council for Sultans, 1581* (Vienna, 1982), *passim*.
20. Ibid., R74r.

Chapter 4

1. H.A.R. and H. Bowen, *Islamic Society and the West*, vol. I, part 1 (Oxford, 1950), p. 51. B. Ramberti, 'Libro Tre delle Cose di Turchi', *Viaggi* (Venice, 1543) (London edn 1554, misprinted 1514, p. xvii), refers to janissary officers receiving *timars* as pensions.
2. See S. Purchas, *His Pilgrimage* . . . , vol. ii, Lib. ix (London, 1613), p. 1,289 for Bon's description of the Seraglio. See also H. Inalcık, *The Ottoman Empire* (London, 1973), p. 48. The *sipahi*s' roll was 87,000 in 1525, 45,000 in 1609 and 8,000 in 1630.
3. Gibb and Bowen, *Islamic Society and the West*, vol. I, part 1, pp. 70–1; and A.H. Lybyer, *the Government of the Ottoman Empire in the Time of Süleyman the Magnificent* (Harvard, 1913), p. 103.
4. M. Howard, *War in European History* (Oxford, 1976), p. 77.
5. See J. Schiltberger, *The Bondage and Travels of J. Schiltberger in Europe, Asia and Africa, 1396–1427* (J.B. Telfer, Hakluyt Society, London, 1897), p. 53, for the use of pigeon post for secrecy.
6. Inalcık, *Ottoman Empire*, p. 48. By the end of the sixteenth century, young landless villagers became *sekben* (sharpshooters) or, as *sarıca*, served provincial governors.
7. C.M. Kortepeter, *Ottoman Imperialism during the Reformation* (New York, 1972), p. 18.
8. Ibid., p. 142. See also H. Grenville (ed. A.S. Ehrenkramz), *Observations sur l'État Actuel de l'Empire Ottoman* (Michigan, 1965). The Kumbaracıs were commanded in Grenville's time by the adopted son of Bonneval Pasha, a boy from Milan.

Notes

9. Inalcık, *Ottoman Empire*, p. 48. There were 16,000 in 1520 and 37,000 in 1609.

10. Nicolay, *Navigations and Voyages* (London, 1586), p. 76. In 1550 married janissaries lived in Anatolia. Ramberti, 'Libro Tre delle Use Turche', p. xvi, refers to them in quarters of Istanbul in *c*. 1534.

11. D.A. Ayalon, *Gunpowder and Firearms in the Mamluk Kingdom* (Leiden, 1956), pp. 82 and 93–4.

12. Howard, *War in European History*, pp. 14–15. Pikes were heavy and fell into disuse after the invention of bayonets in the later seventeenth century.

13. White was the traditional colour of Ottoman infantry and the *ahis* before them.

14. Gibb and Bowen, *Islamic Society and the West*, vol. I, part 1, p. 41.

15. Howard, *War in European History*, pp. 64–5. The janissaries were far ahead of the French in wearing uniforms.

16. V. Ménage, 'The Memoirs of an Ottoman Secret Agent', *JRAS*, parts 3–4 (1965), p. 120. Until *c*. 1550 cloth was imported from Florence but manufacturing was concentrated at Salonika.

17. Djevad Bey (Ahmad Javad), *État Militaire Ottoman depuis la Fondation de l'Empire jusqu'à Nos Jours* (Constantinople/Paris, 1882), pp. 38 and 45.

18. D. Urquhart, *The Spirit of the East*, 2 vols. (London, 1838), p. 39.

19. See Purchas, *His Pilgrimage* . . . , p. 1,290, on models of elephants and other emblems carried before the *ortas*.

20. Djevad Bey, *État Militaire Ottoman* . . . , p. 181.

21. Baron de Tott, *Memoirs*, 4 parts (Amsterdam, 1785), p. 133. Only discipline was neglected.

22. According to Purchas, *His Pilgrimage* . . . , p. 128, rations on the march were rice, sugar and honey.

23. Lady Mary Wortley Montagu (ed. R. Halsband), *Letters* (London, 1968), vol. I, p. 356, mentions that the tent of Kuyuk Khan held 2,000. See also Carpini, 'The Voyage of Friar John of Pian de Carpini, 1245–1247' in M. Komroff (ed.), *Contemporaries of Marco Polo* (New York, 1928), p. 40.

24. See W. Irvine, *The Army of the Indian Moghuls, its Organisation and Administration* (New Delhi, 1962), p. 198, on the striped tents of officers.

25. O.G. Busbecq (transl. E.S. Forster), *Turkish Letters of Ogier Ghiselin de Busbequius* (Oxford, 1927), p. 243; A. Galland, *Journal d'Antoine Galland pendant son Séjour à Constantinople 1672–3* (annotated C. Schefer; Paris, 1881), p. 76; and J. Cacavelas, *Hieremias* (Kakabolus) (London, 1927), p. 123.

26. Comte L.F. de Marsigli, *Stato Militare dell'Impero Ottomano* (The Hague, 1732), p. 648.

27. Ibid.

28. Ayalon, *Livre de la Coronne*, p. 85.

29. W.E.D. Allen, *Problems of Turkish Power in the Sixteenth Century*

Notes

(London, 1963), p. 85.

30. B. Gent, 'The Warning of Ibrahim Pasha of Buda', *JRAS*, vol. XXI (Oct. 1934). Note on flyleaf: 'My father was a great rider and judge of horseflesh but had never seen anything like it. Every horse in the plough here looks fit to win the Derby.'

31. See under 'armour' in *Chamber's Encyclopaedia*, vol. 1 (London, 1950), p. 610, for a description of the lightness of Turkish armour.

32. D.A. Ayalon, *Gunpowder and Firearms in the Mamluk Kingdom* (Leiden, 1956), p. 2; Howard, *War in European History*, pp. 15–26.

33. V.J. Parry, 'Materials of War in the Ottoman Empire', *SEHME* (1970), p. 224.

34. According to Schiltberger, Timur cut off the thumbs of rebel archers at Ephesus.

35. Evliya Çelebi Efendi (transl. J. von Hammer-Purgstall), *Narrative* (London, 1846), vol. 1, p. 46, on idols from Haghia Sophia used as targets.

36. P.E. Klopsteg, *The Construction and Use of the Composite Bow by the Turks*, ms., n.d., in library of Bogazici Universitesi, ex-Robert College, Istanbul. This is the most authoritative document on the subject. See also Kortepeter, *Ottoman Imperialism . . .* , p. 172.

37. Tott, *Memoirs*, p. 140, calls it martial music of the most barbarous kind—not, however, for Mozart, whose interest in Ottoman music is well known.

38. The number of instruments increased with time.

39. See J. Jackson, *Journey from India towards England in the Year 1797* (London, 1799), p. 230. Jackson saw 1,000 buffalo at Sabunca lake carrying timber for the Tersane at Constantinople.

40. See Parry, 'Materials of War . . . ', p. 219, for a list of spoils after the Ottoman defeat at Peterwardein. See also Cacavelas, 'Sur Certaines Réformes . . . ', *JESHO*, no. 6 (1963), pp. 137–41, for a similar list.

41. N. Fisher, *The Middle East, a History* (New York, 1959), p. 219; and Cacavelas, 'Certaines Réformes . . . ', p. 51. Kara Mustafa's army against Vienna numbered 180,000 men, 30,000 labourers, 35,000 horses, 3,000 camels, 1,000 wagons and 1,500 lanterns besides Tartar cavalry.

42. B. Cvetkova, 'Les Celep', *SEHME*, pp. 172ff.

43. Parry, 'Materials of War . . . ', pp. 219ff. Wallachia (and Moldavia) supplied draught horses and oxen which came from Bulgaria and Thrace, which also supplied buffalo (as did Greece).

44. Ahmet Refik, *Istanbul Hayati* (Istanbul, 1930–5), vol. 3, no. 50, p. 24 *inter alia*; and G. Goodwin, *A History of Ottoman Architecture* (London, 1971), p. 456 and p. 487, n. 23.

45. Djevad Bey, *État Militaire Ottoman . . .* , p. 30.

46. I am indebted for this information to Dr D. Kandioti. In the nineteenth

century, wealthy parents would make their sons wear veils on the way to school.

47. See R.E. Koçu, *Yeniçeriler* (Istanbul, 1964), pp. 294 *et seq.*, for examples of decadence in the corps.

48. A. Vambery, *Travels and Adventures of the Turkish Admiral, Sidi Ali Reis, during the Years 1553-1556* (London, 1865), pp. 69-75.

49. R. Chandler, *Voyages dans l'Asie Mineure et en Grèce* (Paris, 1606), pp. 168-80.

50. D. Urquhart, *Pillars of Hercules* (London, 1848), p. 267.

51. Howard, *War in European History*, p. 35.

52. Ayalon, *Gunpowder and Firearms* . . . Cannon cracked the dome of the Sultan Hasan Medrese and twisted its *alem* (crescent finial) in 1457. This seems to have caused remarkably superficial damage. (One has visions of cannon-balls bouncing off the dome and down along the street.)

53. Howard, *War in European History*, p. 35.

54. A Persian army once camped all winter before the formidable walls of a Circassian castle made of boards plastered over to look like stone.

55. See Tott, *Memoirs*, part III, pp. 25ff on the Dardanelles.

56. U. Heyd, *Documents on Palestine, 1552-1615* (Oxford, 1960), p. 104.

57. D.M. Vaughan, *Europe and the Turk* (Liverpool, 1954).

58. M. Cezar, 'Osmanlı Devrinde Istanbul Yapılarında Tahribat Yapan Yangınlar ve Tabıı Afetler' in *Türk Sanatı Tarihi Arastırma ve Incelemeleri* (Istanbul, 1963), p. 329. In 1519 Selim I attributed a fire to his having killed a man in error a week earlier; he expressed remorse.

59. Ibid., p. 335. According to H. Blount, *A Voyage into the Levant, 1634*, in Pinkerton (ed.), *A General Collection* (London, 1918), vol. 10, 70,000 houses were destroyed. See also A. Vandal, *Les Voyages du Marquis de Nointal, 1670-1680* (Paris, 1900), p. 227.

60. See Inalcık, *Ottoman Empire*, p. 21. By 1442 there were 60 ships at Gallipoli and nearly 100 on the Danube. According to D.M. Vaughan, *Europe and the Turk* (Liverpool, 1954), pp. 94ff, galleasses were built by Greek, Genoese and Venetian shipwrights. Some had 250 rowers but their range was short.

61. J. Vasdravellis (transl. T.F. Carney), *Piracy on the Mediterranean Coast* (Salonika, 1970), p. 9.

62. G.W.F. Stripling, *The Ottoman Turks and the Arabs* (London, 1942), pp. 90-4.

63. Vandal, *Voyages* . . . , p. 75. Greeks, Latins and Russians each had their chapel in the Bagno.

64. See S.J. Shaw, 'Selim III and the Ottoman Navy', *Turcica I* (Paris, 1969), pp. 220ff, on the work of French officers in reforming the Tersane.

Notes

Chapter 5

1. Kai Ka'us ibn Iskender (transl. R. Levy), *A Mirror for Princes* (The Qābus Nāme) (London, 1957), p. ix. A Turkish translation was made for Murat II.
2. It must be remembered that 40 meant infinity and thus this advice may not have been meant to be taken literally.
3. Contrary to Muslim precept, he trimmed his beard in the Italian style.
4. B. Cvetkova, 'Sur Certaines Réformes du Régime Foncier au Temps de Mehmet II', *JESHO*, no. 6 (1963), pp. 119-20. The sequestration of *mulks* and *vakfs* led to complications when Bayezit II granted the return of property that was now the *tımar* of a *sipahi*. See I. Beldiceanu-Steinherr, 'Le Règne de Selim I', *Turcica*, vol. V (Paris, 1975), p. 35. The same applied to the estates of ex-Christian knights enlisted under Osman and Orhan.
5. H. Inalcık, *The Policy of Mehmet II towards the Greek Population of Istanbul*, Dumbarton Oaks Papers, no. 23 (1969-70), pp. 231-7. Mehmet had been unwilling to take the city by force.
6. C.W.C. Oman, *The Art of War in the Middle Ages* (Cornell, 1953), p. 72. Kossova (1389) and Nicopolis (1396) had been won by heavily armoured *sipahis*. It was not intended that janissaries should engage in hand-to-hand fighting.
7. Beldiceau-Steinherr, 'Règne de Selim I', p. 42. Sultans were forced to suppress heterodox peasants or the state would disintegrate. See Cvetkova, 'Sur Certaines Réformes . . . ', p. 120, on how the land funds of the *sipahis* were used to sustain the military system.
8. See N. Fisher, *The Middle East, a History* (New York, 1959), p. 16. Bayezit ate moderately and was a fine archer and horseman.
9. It lasted twenty-four years.
10. Fisher, *Middle East* . . . , p. 17. *Acemioğlans* were sent to repair the water courses so that the corpse could be smuggled into the palace.
11. Ibid., p. 18; and A.H. Lybyer, *The Government of the Ottoman Empire in the Time of Süleyman the Magnificent* (Harvard, 1913), p. 69. The janissaries forced the puritanical sultan to reopen the wine shops.
12. See J. von Hammer-Purgstall, *Histoire de l'Empire Ottoman*, 18 vols (Vienna, 1827-35), vol. II, pp. 347 and 399 on dervish patronage.
13. The poet Gazali of Bursa (b. 1466) was protected by Korkud from his puritanical father because of his obscene anecdotes. See the references to Kukla and Karagöz in *Turcica*, vol. III (1971), p. 9.
14. According to Fisher, *Middle East* . . . , Gedik Ahmet Pasha rose from the ranks.
15. The outspoken old man took Otranto on 11 August 1480. In this he was encouraged by the Venetian Senate, which maintained that Mehmet—as the heir of the Byzantine emperors—had a right to Otranto, Taranto and Brindisi. See

Notes

F. Babinger, *Mehmet II le Conquérant et son Temps* (Paris, 1954), p. 504.

16. Fisher, *Middle East* . . . , pp. 23 and 49, suggests that Cem died of a genuine illness related to debauchery. The wrangle over his embalmed body ended when it sailed for home in April 1499.

17. H. Inalcık, 'Gedik Ahmad Pasha', *EI*, vol. I (1960), pp. 292-3. Troops prevented Bayezit from arresting their hero. His execution resulted in tumult. There was no place for the old soldier at a notoriously effeminate court. See Hammer-Purgstall, *Histoire de l'Empire Ottoman*, vol. III, p. 100; and Fisher, *Middle East* . . . , p. 15. Gedik Ahmet Pasha criticized the sultan when he fought Uzun Hasan in 1473. See ibid., p. 27, for his outspokenness.

18. D.E. Pitcher, *An Historical Geography of the Ottoman Empire* (Leiden, 1972), p. 70, mentions the need for a period of consolidation of his father's conquests.

19. Fisher, *Middle East* . . . They attacked under Yakup Pasha, after slaves and booty, in 1493 (p. 33) and 1492 and 1493 (p. 34).

20. Beldiceau-Steinherr, 'Règne de Selim I', p. 44. There was also trouble in Thrace.

21. Fisher, *Middle East* . . . , p. 34. Ahmet Pasha had to kiss the feet of Kaitbey, the Mamluk sultan of Egypt.

22. I. Melikoff, 'Bayezit II et Venise', *Turcica*, vol. I (1969), p. 145. Between 1487 and 1502 the Ottoman fleet also faced Greek pirates who sold Turkish slaves in the Venetian market in Crete: see H.J. Kissling, *Sah Isma'il et la Nouvelle Route des Indes* (Paris, 1964), p. 137. In 1497 the pro-Venetian Davut Pasha was dismissed as Chief Vezir.

23. Kissling, *Sah Isma'il* . . . , p. 75. Bayezit introduced the composite ship, manned by forty men, with fighting tops. See also D.M. Vaughan, *Europe and the Turk* (Liverpool, 1954), p. 46.

24. Seven thousand of them were allegedly masons.

25. It broke out at Tekke (Elmalı). See V.J. Parry, 'Beyazid II', *EI* (1965); and W.E.D. Allen, *Problems of Turkish Power in the Sixteenth Century* (London, 1963), p. 12. Shah Kuli led the mystical Shi'ite revolt along the path towards the egalitarianism of the revolt of Simavi against Mehmet I.

26. R.W. Olson, *The Siege of Mosul and Ottoman-Persian Relations, 1718-1743* (Indiana, 1973), pp. 13-14. Bayezit permitted pilgrimages to Ardabil, sacred to Shi'ites. The rebels now had trained officers because the favouritism shown towards the janissaries had impoverished the *sipahi*s in Anatolia; these now joined the Kızılbaş.

27. Ibid., p. 14. The rebels fled to Persia, where the sultan (who needed Ottoman trade) put two of their leaders into cauldrons of boiling water.

28. R. Mantran, *Istanbul dans la Seconde Moitié du XVIIe Siècle* (Paris, 1962), p. 396. Ali Pasha led them ably. See Inalcık, 'Policy of Mehmet II . . . ', p. 32, on the Kızılbaş and janissary support in August 1514.

Notes

29. In 1512 the first Anatolian levy was raised in the provinces of Karaman, Trabzon, Kayseri and the Cilician shore. On Selim and outside appointments, see A. Tietze, *Mustafa 'Ali's Counsel for Sultans, 1581* (Vienna, 1982), H8v.

30. See Fisher, *Middle East* . . . , p. 203; and Beldiceneau-Steinherr, 'Règne de Selim I', p. 44. In despair, Korkud went to Egypt in search of help.

31. Olson, *Siege of Mosul* . . . , p. 15. Selim even forbade the silk trade from 1512 to 1520, to prevent the export of war materials, silver and iron. He thus became even more dependent on the Silk Road, which ran through hostile Persia. Süleyman raised the sanctions which had ruined the silk weavers of Bursa.

32. See M. Howard, *War in European History* (Oxford, 1976), p. 71, on the magazines and bases prepared along the route of the march.

33. Selim waited three months for Tuman to respond to the offer of the viceroyalty of Egypt. See G.W.F. Stripling, *The Ottoman Turks and the Arabs* (London, 1942), p. 105.

34. Selim left 500 janissaries and 5,000 horsemen to garrison Egypt. See D.A. Ayalon, *Gunpowder and Firearms in the Mamluk Kingdom* (Leiden, 1956), p. 39, n. 98.

Chapter 6

1. This account is based on that of the official historian and eye-witness, Kemalpaşazade.

2. The title Damat was carried by any man who married an Ottoman princess. It applied in particular to Grand Vezirs, who were required to renounce their own wife, however fond they might be, in order to bind them more closely to the sultan.

3. In the fourteenth century the army was recruited by criers in the villages; they called on any who wished to fight to assemble at a given place and time. Orhan began a more organized recruitment.

4. N. Fisher, *The Middle East, a History* (New York, 1959), p. 219. For the 1521 campaign, 3,000 camels with ammunition, 30,000 camels with grain and 1,000 wagons of local grain were assembled at Belgrade by the Grand Vezir, Piri Pasha.

5. Arms were carried on baggage wagons until they reached the combat zone.

6. As at the White Castle on the Welsh Marches.

7. Süleyman appointed the rebel John Zopolya, Prince of Transylvania, as his vassal ruler because he did not want to garrison Hungary.

Chapter 7

1. A. Tietze, *Mustafa 'Ali's Counsel for Sultans, 1581* (Vienna, 1982), pp. 107ff. The poor pay for all wars; the rich pay nothing. H42v. The villagers

Notes

migrated to the towns.

2. W.E.D. Allen, *Problems of Turkish Power in the 16th Century* (London, 1963), p. 13; and J.H. Kramers, 'Selim I', *EI*, vol. IV (1934), p. 214.

3. J. von Hammer-Purgstall, *Histoire de l'Empire Ottoman*, 18 vols (Vienna, 1827–35), vol. 5, p. 153. On 27 May 1533 Ibrahim boasted (with a touch of megalomania) to the Austrian ambassadors that Süleyman had built his palace for him. Within three years he had been strangled in his bedroom at the *saray*. See Gökbilgin, 'Ibrahim Pasha (Damad)', *EI*, vol. III (1965), pp. 998–9.

4. This was true in the Arab provinces, in particular. See Tietze, *Mustafa 'Ali's Counsel for Sultans*, pp. 2111h ff.

5. In 1499, 15,000 *akıncıs* appeared at the gates of Vicenza.

6. H. Sahilloğlu, 'Sivis Year Crises in the Ottoman Empire', in M.A. Cook (ed.), *SEHME* (1970), p. 239. One problem was the Sivis year. Budgets were paid out by the lunar year but taxes were perforce gathered by the solar year: one year (33) was without revenues. The conquests of Egypt, Syria, Diyarbekir and Baghdad had once covered the deficits: this was no longer true.

7. T. Bertelé, *Il Palazzo degli Ambasciatori di Venezia a Costantinopoli* (Bologna, 1937–9), p. 101. In 1553 the *bailo* Bernardo Navagero wrote of Rüstem Pasha that, although he was notoriously proud and fierce, 'I found him very sweet and gentle.'

8. B. Ramberti, 'Libro Tre delle Cose di Turchi', *Viaggi* (Venice, 1543), pp. lxi–lxii. At 50, Süleyman's face was drawn and wizened, his head was shaved except for a tuft and he had remarkably big, black eyes. O.G. Busbecq, *Turkish Letters of Ogier Ghiselin de Busbequius* (transl. Forster) (Oxford, 1927), p. 273. Süleyman ate off earthenware, not silver.

9. Busbecq, *Turkish Letters* . . . , p. 90. The janissaries set Amasya on fire by way of protest. N. Fisher, *The Middle East, a History* (New York, 1959), p. 225.

10. Hammer-Purgstall, *Histoire* . . . , vol. 6, pp. 226ff. During the siege of Szigeth, Süleyman had a propaganda war, using pamphlets in German, Hungarian and Croat to be attached to arrows shot into the citadel. See Tietze, *Mustafa 'Ali's Counsel for Sultans*, p. R22r, for the importance attached by the Ottomans to psychological warfare and (p. R42r) spies.

11. Allen, *Problems of Turkish Power* . . . , p. 58, quotes Barbarigo as saying that Selim II was jovial and much loved by his servants. He could call a halt to indulgence and take action after good advice. He was known as Sarhoş ('the Drunkard') because he assuaged the horrors of life at the *saray* with wine.

12. According to T. Dallam, 'The Diary of Master Thomas Dallam, 1599–1600' in J.T. Bent (ed.), *Early Voyages* (London, 1893), Selim II had 200 pages dressed in gold with gold caps and red Cordovan buskins.

13. E. Binney, 'A Lost Manuscript of Mehmet III', *5th Congress of Turkish Art* (Ankara), p. 191, calls Murat the greatest Turkish bibliophile. According to

Notes

Allen, *Problems of Turkish Power* . . . , p. 34, the sultan liked intellectuals, especially Italians and Hungarians, but he could be flippant and trivial and was inclined to mysticism.

14. N. Forbes, *A History of Serbia* (Oxford, 1915), p. 104. In 1567 Murat revived the Patriarchate of Peç as part of his pan-Serbian policy. The new Holiness was allegedly the Grand Vezir's brother.

15. R.W. Olson, *The Siege of Mosul and Ottoman-Persian Relations, 1718-1743* (Indiana, 1973), pp. 17-18. The economic war of 1578-90, opposed by Sokollu, ruined the Ottomans and impoverished Anatolia, resulting in the *celalı* rebellions. By 1588 there was no booty and taxes could not be gathered.

16. On the bankruptcy of the military caste and inflation, see Tietze, *Mustafa 'Ali's Counsel for Sultans*, p. R95r. Food was short in the capital due to the migration of peasants: see ibid., p. R52v.

17. See J.K. Birge, *The Bektashi Order of Dervishes* (London, 1937). In 1682 an old janissary stood up at the name of Hacı Bektaş.

18. I. Melikoff, *Le Problème Kızılbaş* (Paris), p. 66. Armenian influences in Sivas and Cilicia mingled with old Persian beliefs and with the cult of Satan, who loved Divinity too well, and so with the Yazidis.

19. S. Faroqhi, 'The Tekke of Haci Bektaş: Social Position and Economic Activities', *IJMES*, 7 (April 1976), no. 1, p. 185.

20. Tietze, *Mustafa 'Ali's Counsel for Sultans*, p. H217v. Dervishes were disreputable company.

21. Faroqhi, 'Tekke of Haci Bektaş . . . '. The janissaries' most notorious gift was the Black Kettle in which was served *asure*, a charitable sweet hotchpotch of left-overs from a rich man's table. The kettle is inscribed with the name of the first Dede *baba* after the reopening in 1551.

22. See G. Baer, 'The Administrative, Economic and Social Functions of the Turkish Guilds', *IJMES*, vol. I (1970), pp. 28ff. For their establishment, see ibid., p. 40. They were required to supply labour to the government and auxiliaries in war. See R. Mantran, *Istanbul dans la Seconde Moitié du XVIIe Siecle* (Paris, 1962), on janissaries in the guilds (p. 370) and their support for widows and orphans (p. 390).

23. H. Inalcık, *The Ottoman Empire* (London, 1973), p. 92. Equally angry at being paid in debased currency in 1588, the *sipahis*—supported by the *şeyhülislam*—obtained the lives of the Grand Vezir Mehmet Pasha and the *defterdar* (Minister of Finance).

24. According to Allen, *Problems of Turkish Power* . . . , p. 55, n. 73, Lala Mustafa Pasha came from the same village as Sokollu and it was he who had Bragadino flayed on conquering Cyprus in 1571.

25. Tiflis was taken briefly in 1578 and Georgia subjected, but extended supply lines brought this victory to nothing.

Notes

26. Sinan was a peasant from the Dibra mountains of Albania. See Allen, *Problems of Turkish Power* . . . , p. 55, n. 75.

27. Gazanfer Agha was a Hungarian friend of Murat IV. See ibid., p. 55, n. 74.

28. Between 1489 and 1616 the price of rice soared by 506 per cent, wheat by 493 per cent and pepper by 800 per cent. On average, staple foods rose by 434 per cent but gold by only 240 per cent. The worst period was between 1585 and 1605. See Olson, *Siege of Mosul* . . . , p. 22.

29. According to O. Burian, *The Letters of Lello, Third English Ambassador to the Sublime Porte* (Ankara, 1952), p. 8, the Valide Sultan was a Christian from Slavonia. A. Alderson, *The Structure of the Ottoman Dynasty* (Oxford, 1956), table xxxiii, n. 2, says that the Valide was poisoned on 26 November 1605 either by her son who disliked her advice or by a harem intrigue.

30. *Cambridge History of Islam*, vol. I (*The Central Islamic Lands*), 1970, p. 346. These troops became a privileged class in Anatolia.

31. According to Inalcık, *Ottoman Empire*, p. 48, these *sekben* (sharpshooters) were paid by the mid-sixteenth century but inflation meant that the pay was of little value. They rebelled and became the fighting core of the *celalıs* (p. 50). They posed as janissaries for nefarious reasons.

32. 'You discover the city of Antioch built upon a hill. Formerly the road ran through that city, but, the janissaries of that place exacting a piastre of every person travelling that way, the road is now disused.' Unauthenticated letter.

33. M. Howard, *War in European History* (Oxford, 1976), p. 18, compares the *celalıs* with the *écorcheurs* of fourteenth- to mid-fifteenth-century France. They were unlike the far worse disbanded soldiers of the Thirty Years War because of their relationship with the peasantry, from whom they sprang, which enabled them to dissolve and then reform in face of an attack by the central authority (ibid., p. 37). See also *Cambridge History of Islam*, vol. I, p. 347.

34. 'Yazıcı', meaning scribe, suggests that his education may have helped him to the leadership.

35. G. de Gortaut Biron, Baron de Salignac, *Ambassade en Turquie, 1605–1610* (Paris/Auch, 1888), vol. 2, p. 185, reports daily sackings of Bursa in a letter dated 23 December 1607.

36. Inalcık, *Ottoman Empire*, pp. 89–90. Peasants were not allowed to carry arms.

37. Or perhaps he was irrational: it was easier to dispose of him in the Balkans.

38. Salignac, *Ambassade en Turquie* . . . , vol. 2, p. 372.

39. He was gored at the hunting lodge of Sokollu Mehmet Pasha (ibid., p. 412).

40. Madame La Quira cured Ahmet I of smallpox (ibid., p. 182). According to Lello (Burian, *Letters of Lello* . . .), pp. 5–6, the Sultana Sporca was

Notes

lynched and eaten by dogs. Ahmet had given her revenues that were meant for the *sipahis* (ibid., p. 4).

41. Davut Pasha was a Croat. See V.S. Parry, 'Davud Pasha', *EI*, vol. II (1965), p. 183.

42. In 1591 the population was only 584 of whom two-thirds were Christians. See R. Jennings, 'Urban Population in Anatolia in the 16th Century', *IJMES*, no. 7 (Jan. 1976), p. i; and *Cambridge History of Islam*, vol. I, p. 349.

43. Evliya Çelebi Efendi (transl. J. von Hammer-Purgstall), *Narrative* (London, 1846), part I, p. 120. Instead, for the present, Murat was dispatched to the Eski Saray.

44. Ibid., part I, p. 129. Hasan Çelebi Agha was formally executed but the *defterdar* was dragged out of hiding in the Hippodrome to be hanged from the Janissary Tree.

45. Sir P. Rycault, *The History of the Turkish Empire, 1623-1677* (London, 1680), vol. I, p. 31. In 1631 Murat fainted when unattended. By way of penance, he gave up drink and dismissed his buffoons.

46. A.D. Alderson, *The Structure of the Ottoman Dynasty* (Oxford, 1956), table xxxvi, includes a third brother, Kasım, who survived until his 15th year in 1638.

47. Tietze, *Mustafa 'Ali's Counsel for Sultans*, p. H84r. Mustafa Ali states that fiefs often produced two or three times their official incomes.

48. This proved that the policy was not irrational.

49. Tietze, *Mustafa 'Ali's Counsel for Sultans*, p. 39v *inter alia*. Mustafa Ali expressly advises that all officials should be spied on.

50. Ibid., p. R26r, states that the *vezir* was the source of all evil.

Chapter 8

1. H.A.R. Gibb and H. Bowen, *Islamic Society and the West*, vol. I, part 1 (Oxford, 1950), vol. II, p. 37, n. 4. Ibrahim I also used furs to carpet the Ibrahim Pasha Saray in the Hippodrome, presented to one of his sweethearts. See M.T. Gökbilgin, 'Ibrahim', *EI*, vol. III (1965), p. 983. Ibrahim suffered from perpetual headaches and nervous prostration. Fear of his impotence and an end to the dynasty drove his mother to encourage sexual excess.

2. Gökbilgin, 'Ibrahim', p. 983, records the sultan's unforgivable execution of the *kapudan paşa*, Yusuf, on his triumphant return from the capture of Khania in January 1646. Even Evliya Çelebi Efendi (transl. J. von Hammer-Purgstall), *Narrative* (London, 1846), book 1, p. 148, cannot hide his disgust.

3. H. Inalcık, *The Ottoman Empire* (London, 1973), p. 161. In 1651 the janissaries rose in defence of the guilds, joining them in greater numbers than ever before.

4. In 1659 two pamphlets praising the Ottomans were in circulation in the London of the Regents: Thomas Campanello's *Advice to the King of Spain* and

Notes

Learn of a Turk by M.B. The janissary corps was particularly praised and recommended to the Lord Protector, Cromwell.

5. A. Tietze, *Mustafa 'Ali's Counsel for Sultans, 1581* (Vienna, 1982), R28v. The state did not collapse because of the excellent book-keeping of the civil service clerks.

6. A. Vandal, *Les Voyages du Marquis de Nointal, 1670-1680* (Paris, 1900), p. 225. Drinking was a family failing. Fazıl Ahmet died of his prescribed medicine, Polish brandy, taken—like his women—in excess. Perhaps he also died of boredom with the problems of ruling the Ottoman Empire. See R.C. Repp, 'Köprülü', *EI*, vol. III (1980), p. 1,061.

7. Writing of eighteenth-century Western society, M. Howard, *War in European History* (Oxford, 1976), p. 75, states that the nature of warfare was so bound up with the nature of society that revolution in one was bound to create revolution in the other.

8. J.H. Kramers, 'Süleyman II', *EI*, vol. IV (1936), p. 527. The uprising lasted a month and was put down by a spontaneous popular attack on the janissaries.

9. Repp, 'Köprülü', pp. 1,060-1.

10. W.D. Munson, *The Last Crusade* (Dubuque, 1969), pp. 79ff. It was also of importance that the French enjoyed more than half the foreign trade of the Ottoman Empire.

11. Seyyit Feyzullah Efendi was beheaded in the flea market. Rami Mehmet was sent as governor of Cyprus, only to die of torture on Rhodes in 1707. In six months he had reduced the number of frontier fortresses, established estates with revenues devoted to army pay, settled a number of Türkmen tribes and re-established the Jewish silk merchants of Salonika and the Greek merchants of Bursa in order to reduce imports. See E. Babinger, 'Rami Muhammed Pasha', *EI*, vol. V (1936).

Chapter 9

1. See A. Tietze, *Mustafa 'Ali's Counsel for Sultans, 1581* (Vienna, 1982), p. H41r, on the large amount of food and drink wasted in the *saray*.

2. See ibid., p. R41v, on the opium addiction (also hashish) of officials. Opium poppies grow at Afyan Karahısar. The strains of office meant that a pasha might consume more than 4 oz of very best-quality hashish a day.

3. R.W. Olson, *The Siege of Mosul and Ottoman-Persian Relations, 1718-1743* (Indiana, 1973), p. 43. This was a reversal of Ibrahim's peace policy due to reports of Persian weakness.

4. Ibid., pp. 68-9. Savage economies and taxes were imposed and Nadir Shah's victory at Tabriz was shattering.

5. S.J. Shaw and E.K. Shaw, *History of the Ottoman Empire and Modern Turkey* (Illinois, 1974), vol. I, pp. 238 *et seq.*

Notes

6. Olson, *Siege of Mosul* . . . , p. 75. The *şeyhülislam* was too discreet to show his inclinations: he was the enemy of Ibrahim, who had procured his advancement. See Shaw and Shaw, *History of the Ottoman Empire* . . . , vol. I, p. 236; C. Perry, *A View of the Levant, particularly of Constantinople, Syria, Egypt and Greece* (London, 1743), p. 73; and Olson, *Siege of Mosul* . . . , pp. 77-8.

7. Perry, *View of the Levant* . . . , p. 88. Nevşehir was Ibrahim's home town where he had laid out a new suburb with a grid of wide streets.

8. Olson, *Siege of Mosul* . . . , p. 79. The death toll due to Patrona could be counted in thousands.

9. Hospodar: a Romanian title of nobility which would seem to indicate the butcher's origin with heavy-handed irony.

10. Olson, *Siege of Mosul* . . . , p. 3. The guilds also sheltered rebels in their quarters.

11. See S.J. and E.K. Shaw, 'Selim III and the Ottoman Navy', *Turcica*, vol. I (Paris, 1969), pp. 45-6; but Gritti remarks that the Turks also gave gifts among themselves.

12. Olson, *Siege of Mosul* . . . , p. 141. Most other basic foodstuffs were also in short supply.

13. See Baron de Tott, *Memoirs*, 4 parts (Paris, 1785), part I, p. 23, for the Grand Vezir's character. See ibid., p. 29, for the riot. Osman not only suppressed cafés but all liberties permitted to women: he was reaping the whirlwind.

14. Olson, *Siege of Mosul* . . . , pp. 142-3. Shopkeepers who did not take their shutters down were hanged; *hamams* were raided for agitators, who were mercilessly killed. Some 3,000 bodies were dumped in the Black Sea, openly and by daylight.

15. Tott, *Memoirs*, part I, p. 92. The corps lined the sultan's accession route to Eyüp.

16. Vicomte de la Jonquière, *L'Histoire de l'Empire Ottoman* (Paris, 1911), pp. 321-2. Tophane was eventually to be modelled on the French system devised by Gribeauval. See also M. Howard, *War in European History* (Oxford, 1976), p. 61.

17. Cardinal de Retz recounts that in an age of adventurers, in August 1656, he encountered the Abbé de Votteville at Besançon: as a young Carthusian monk, the abbot had been guilty of a double murder and had joined the Ottoman army against the Venetians in the Peloponnese. He had then sold Ottoman military secrets to the Venetians in exchange for papal absolution from his crimes and apostasy. See J.H.M. Salmon, *Cardinal de Retz* (London, 1969).

18. Jonquière, *Histoire de l'Empire Ottoman*, pp. 315-16. The Empress Catherine of Russia took an interest in the Mahdi.

19. Ibid., p. 230. Suvarov's victories caused an uprising in Istanbul.

Notes

20. P.M. Holt, *Egypt and the Fertile Crescent, 1516-1922* (New York, 1966), p. 182, calls Napoleon's Egyptian adventure the turning-point in Ottoman history.
21. B. Lewis, *The Emergence of Modern Turkey* (Oxford, 1961), p. 73; and J.H. Kramers, 'Bayraktar Mustafa Pasha', *EI*, vol. IV (1936), p. 765.
22. Shaw and Shaw, *History of the Ottoman Empire* . . . , vol. II, p. 15. Balkan *ayans* (valley lords) feared for their independence. Jonquière, *Histoire de l'Empire Ottoman*, p. 326.
23. Lewis, *Emergence of Modern Turkey*, p. 84. The educated officers were decimated.
24. Ibid., p. 76.
25. According to Jonquière, *Histoire de l'Empire Ottoman*, Mahmut escaped over the roofs.
26. C. MacFarlane, *Constantinople in 1828* (London, 1829), p. 293. The commanding officer of the Sultan Ahmet barracks was a German renegade, Süleyman Agha, who was hacked to bits. The barracks behind Yıldız Kiosk were also razed to the ground.
27. Lewis, *Emergence of Modern Turkey*, p. 79. Without janissary support, the *ulema* would have been greatly weakened.
28. S. Faroqhi, 'The Tekke of Haçı Bektaş: Social Positions in Economic Activities', *IJMES*, no. 7 (April 1976), p. 198. The valley lords were on bad terms with the Bektaşi dervishes in particular and the Capanoğlu family of Yozgat was involved in a legal dispute which was referred to the Divan. This weakened the authority of these petty despots.
29. E.B. de Fonblanque, *Lives of the Lords Strangford* (London, 1877), p. 126.
30. Ibid., p. 132.

Chapter 10

1. Assad (Essat) Efendi, *Historiographer of the Empire* (transl. P.A. Coussin de Perceval) (Paris, 1833) is the principal source of information for this chapter.
2. C. MacFarlane, *Constantinople in 1828* (London, 1829), p. 231. Halet Efendi, a senior official, spoke of the mole working secretly in the dark.
3. Vicomte de la Jonquière, *L'Histoire de l'Empire Ottoman* (Paris, 1911), p. 414, lists examples of the janissaries' insolence.
4. H.H. Reed, 'Hüseyn Pasha (Agha)', *EI*, vol. III (1965), p. 65. Hüseyn Pasha was born in 1776 and enlisted in the janissaries near Bender. He died in 1849 after several defeats in Serbia.
5. This had only been true since the mid-sixteenth century. Previously, he was simply the Mufti of Istanbul.
6. B. Lewis, *The Emergence of Modern Turkey* (Oxford, 1961), p. 78. The Hatt-i-Şerif (imperial rescript) of 28 May 1826 also established that officers

Notes

could be neither Christians nor foreigners.

7. Assad Efendi, *Historiographer* . . . , pp. 91–5; and M. Howard, *War in European History* (Oxford, 1976), p. 54. Drill is vital to firepower. See Howard's reference to Ottoman military decline, p. 75a.

8. According to Lewis, *Emergence of Modern Turkey*, p. 78, Mahmut anticipated that the janissaries would not be persuaded.

9. I.H. Uzunçarşılı, *Osmanlı Devletinin Saray Teskilatı* (Ankara, 1945), pp. 250ff. The Sancak Şerif (Standard of the Prophet) was black with a green cover. The original always remained with the sultan, but two others were formed from a part of it: one to go with the *serasker* and one that was kept at the treasury.

10. Jonquière, *Histoire de l'Empire Ottoman*, p. 418. They also occupied the Bayezit mosque and all approaches to the Hippodrome.

11. C.G. Addison, *Damascus and Palmyra—A Journey to the East* (London, 1838), vol. I, p. 201.

12. MacFarlane, *Constantinople in 1812*, p. 321. See also Ismail Kemal Bey (ed. S. Storey), *Memoirs* (London, 1920), p. 201.

13. M. Cezar, 'Osmanlı Devrinde Istanbul Yapılarında Tahribat Yapan Yangınlar ve Tabıı Afetler', *Türk Sanatı Tarihi Arastırma ve Incelemeleri* (Istanbul, 1963), p. 370; and R.Y. Ebied and M.J.L Young, *A Nineteenth-Century Arabic Survey of the Ottoman Dynasty* (Leiden, 1976), p. 270. Janissary wives are said to have caused a great fire in Istanbul after the massacre of 1826.

Epilogue

1. Nermin Menemencioğlu, oral information. Whether the poets responsible for 'Wake up, Sultan!' (*Uyum Padişahım!*)—verses that gave the monarch intermittent gratuitous advice until the Crimean war—were ex-janissaries is not clear.

2. H.A.R. Gibb and H. Bowen, *Islamic Society and the West* (Oxford, 1950), vol. 1, part 2, p. 197. The orders had early links in Transoxiana.

3. B. Lewis, *The Emergence of Modern Turkey* (Oxford, 1961), p. 123, quoting Admiral Slade.

The janissary band (T.S.M.)

Select Bibliography

Abbreviations:
EI   Encyclopaedia of Islam
IJMES International Journal of Middle East Studies
JESHO Journal of Economic and Social History of the Orient
JRAS   Journal of the Royal Asiatic Society
SEHME Studies in the Economic History of the Middle East

Abbot, G.F., *Under the Turk in Constantinople*, London, 1920.
Addison, C.G., *Damascus and Palmyra—A Journey to the East*, vol. 1, London, 1838.
Ahmet Refik, *Istanbul Hayati*, 4 vols, Istanbul, 1930–5.
Alderson, A.D., *The Structure of the Ottoman Dynasty*, Oxford, 1956.
Allen, W.E.D., *Problems of Turkish Power in the Sixteenth Century*, London, 1963.
And, M., *A History of the Theatre and Popular Entertainment in Turkey*, Ankara, 1963.
Arnakis, G.G., *The Early Ottomans*, Athens, 1947.
——'Futuwwa Traditions in the Ottoman Empire', *Journal of Middle East Studies*, 4, Oct. 1953.
Assad (Essat) Efendi, *Historiographer of Empire*, trans. P.A. Coussin de Perceval, Paris, 1833.
Atis, I.H., *The History of the Mehter Military Band*, Istanbul, 1964.
Ayalon, D.A., *Le Livre de la Coronne*, Paris, 1954.
——*Gunpowder and Firearms in the Mamluk Kingdom*, Leiden, 1956.
——*Outsiders in the Lands of Islam: Mamluks, Mongols and Eunuchs*, London, 1988.
Ayverdi, R.H., *Avrupa'da Osmanlı Mimarı Eserleri, Rumaniye: Macarıstan*, vol. 1, books 1–2, Istanbul, 1978.
Babinger, F., 'Rami Muhammed Pasha', *EI*, V, 1936.
——*Mehmet II le Conquérant et son Temps*, Paris, 1954.
Baer, G., 'The Administrative, Economic and Social Functions of the Turkish Guilds', *IJMES*, 1, 1970.
Barbaro, N., *Diary of the Siege of Constantinople, 1453*, trans. T.R. Jones, New York, 1969.
Battuta, Ibn, ed. H.A.R. Gibb, *The Travels of Ibn Battuta*, 2 vols, Cambridge, 1962.
Beldiceanu-Steinherr, I., *Recherches sur les Actes des Règnes des Sultans*

Select Bibliography

Osman, Orhan et Murad I, Munich, 1967.
——'Le Règne de Selim I', *Turcica*, V, Paris, 1975.
Bent, J.T., ed., *Early Voyages and Travels in the Levant, II. Extracts from the Diaries of Dr John Covel, 1670-1679*, London, 1893. *See also* Dallam.
Bertelé, T., *Il Palazzo degli Ambasciatori di Venezia a Costantinopoli*, Bologna, 1937-9.
Bertrandon de la Broquière, ed. C. Schefer, *Le Voyage d'Outremer*, Paris, 1892.
Binney, E., 'A Lost Manuscript of Mehmet III', *5th Congress of Turkish Art*, Ankara.
Birge, J.K., *The Bektashi Order of Dervisches*, London, 1937.
Blount, H., 'A Voyage into the Levant, 1634' in Pinkerton, ed., *A General Collection*, vol. 10, London, 1918.
Bon, O., *Descrizione del Seraglio del Gran Signore*, Venice, 1865.
Bowen, H., 'Acemioğlan', *EI*, I, Leiden, 1960.
Burian, O., *The Letters of Lello, Third English Ambassador to the Sublime Porte*, Ankara, 1952.
Busbecq, O.G., *Turkish Letters of Ogier Ghiselin de Busbequius*, trans. E.S. Forster, Oxford, 1927.
Cacavelas, J., *Hieremias* (Kakabolus), London, 1927.
Cahen, C., *Pre-Ottoman Turkey*, London, 1968.
——'Note sur l'Esclavage Musulman et le Devshirme Ottoman', *JESHO*, XIII, 1970.
Careri, G.F.G., *Indian Travels of Thevenot*, 3 vols, New Delhi, 1949.
Cambridge History of Islamic Lands, vol. I: *The Central Islamic Lands*, Cambridge, 1970.
Carney, T.F., *see* Vasdravellis.
Carpini, 'The Voyage of Friar John of Pian de Carpini, 1245-1247' in M. Komroff, ed., *Contemporaries of Marco Polo*, New York, 1928.
Cezar, M., 'Osmanlı Devrinde Istanbul Yapılarında Tahribat Yapan Yangınlar ve Tabii Afetler', *Türk Sanatı Tarihi Araştırma ve İncelemeleri*, Istanbul, 1963.
Chandler, R., *Voyages dans l'Asie Mineure et en Grèce*, Paris, 1606.
Clavijo, R.G. de, *Embassy to Tamerlaine, 1403-1406*, London, 1925.
Colton, W., *A Visit to Constantinople and Athens*, New York, 1936.
Coussin de Perceval, P.A., *see* Assad.
Covel, Dr John, *see* Bent.
Cvetkova, B., 'Sur Certaines Réformes du Régime Foncier au Temps de Mehmet II', *JESHO*, 6, 1963.
——'Les Celep et leur Rôle dans la Vie Économique des Balkans à l'Époque Ottomane (XVe-XVIIIe Siècle)' in M.A. Cook, *SEHME*, London, 1970.
Dallam, T., 'The Diary of Master Thomas Dallam, 1599-1600' in J.T. Bent, ed., *Early Voyages and Travels in the Levant, II. Extracts from the Diaries*

Select Bibliography

of Dr John Covel, 1670–1679, London, 1893.
Dames, Longworth, 'The Portuguese and Turks in the Indian Ocean in the Sixteenth Century', *JRAS*, part I, London, 1921.
Djevad Bey (Ahmad Javad), *État Militaire Ottoman depuis la Fondation de l'Empire jusqu'à Nos Jours*, Constantinople/Paris, 1882.
Ebied, R.Y., and Young, M.J.L., *A Nineteenth-Century Arabic Survey of the Ottoman Dynasty*, Leiden, 1976.
Edib, R., *Conflict of East and West in Turkey*, Lahore, 1963.
Essat, *see* Assad.
Evliya Çelebi Efendi, *Narrative*, trans. J. von Hammer-Purgstall, London, 1846.
Faroqhi, S., 'The Tekke of Haçi Bektaş: Social Positions in Economic Activities', *IJMES*, 7, April 1976.
Finkel, C., *The Administration of Warfare: the Ottoman Military Campaigns in Hungary, 1593–1606*, Beihefte zur Wiener Zeitschrift für die Kunde des Morgenlandes, Bd. H., Vienna, Virgö, 1988.
Finlay, C.V., 'The Foundation of the Ottoman Foreign Ministry', *IJMES*, 3, 1972.
Fisher, N., *The Foreign Relations of Turkey, 1481–1512*, Urbana, 1948.
——*The Middle East, a History*, New York, 1959.
Fleischer, C.H., *Bureaucrat and Intellectual in the Ottoman Empire*, Princeton, 1986.
Fonblanque, E.B. de, *Lives of the Lords Strangford*, London, 1877.
Forbes, N., *A History of Serbia*, Oxford, 1915.
Fox, ed. A.C. Wood, 'The Journey to and from Constantinople of Mr. Harrie Cavendish, 1589', *Camden Miscellany*, XVII, Camden 3rd series, London, 1940.
Frye, R.N., *Bukhara, the Medieval Achievement*, Oklahoma, 1965.
Galland, A., *Journal d'Antoine Galland pendant son Séjour à Constantinople, 1672–3*, annotated C. Schefer, Paris, 1881.
Gent, B., 'The Warning of Ibrahim Pasha of Buda', *JRAS*, XXI, Oct. 1934.
Geuffroy, F.A., *Briefve de la Cour du Grand Turc*, Paris, 1563.
Gibb, H.A.R., 'Lutfi Pasha in the Ottoman Caliphate', *Oriens*, 15, 1962.
——and Bowen, H., *Islamic Society and the West*, vol. 1, parts I and II, Oxford, 1950.
Gökbilgin, M.T., 'Ibrahim', *EI*, III, 1965.
Goodwin, F.G., *A History of Ottoman Architecture*, London, 1971.
——*Sinan: Ottoman Architecture and its Values Today*, London, 1993.
Grenville, H., ed. A.S. Ehrenkramz, *Observations sur l'État Actuel de l'Empire Ottoman*, Michigan, 1965.
Hammer-Purgstall, J. von, *Histoire de l'Empire Ottoman*, 18 vols, Vienna, 1827–35.

Select Bibliography

Heyd, U., *Documents on Palestine, 1552-1615*, Oxford, 1960.
Heyd, W., *Histoire du Commerce du Levant au Moyen-Age*, 2 vols, Leipzig, 1936.
Holt, P.M., *Egypt and the Fertile Crescent, 1516-1923*, New York, 1966.
Hookham, H., *Tamberlaine the Conqueror*, London, 1962.
Howard, M., *War in European History*, Oxford, 1976.
Inalcık, H., *Studies and Documents in the Reign of Mehmed the Conqueror*, Ankara, 1954 (in Turkish).
——'Bursa and the Commerce of the Levant', *JESHO*, III, 2, 1960, pp. 130-58.
——'Gedik Ahmad Pasha', *EI*, I, 1960.
——'Bayezid I', *EI*, 2nd edn, V, 1, 1965.
——*The Ottoman Empire*, London, 1973.
——'Murad II', *Islam Anseklepedisi*, VIII, pp. 589-615.
——'Ottoman Methods of Conquest', *Studia Islamica*, V, ii, pp. 103-29.
——*The Policy of Mehmet II towards the Greek Population of Istanbul*, Dumbarton Oaks Papers, no. 23, 1969-70.
Iorga, N., *Les Châteaux Occidentaux en Roumanie*, Bucharest, 1929.
Irvine, W., *The Army of the Indian Moghuls, its Organisation and Administration*, New Delhi, 1962.
Iskender, Kai Ka'us Ibn, *A Mirror for Princes: the Qābus Nāme*, trans. R. Levy, London, 1957.
Ismail Kemal Bey, ed. S. Storey, *The Memoirs of*, London, 1920.
Jackson, J., *Journey from India towards England in the Year 1797*, London, 1799.
Jennings, R., 'Urban Population in Anatolia in the 16th Century', *IJMES*, 7, 1976.
Jonquière, Vicomte de la, *L'Histoire de l'Empire Ottoman*, Paris, 1911.
Kissling, H.J., *Sāh Isma'il et la Nouvelle Route des Indes*, Paris, 1964.
Klopsteg, P.E., *The Construction and Use of the Composite Bow by the Turks*, Bosphorus University Library, Istanbul, n.d.
Koçu, R.E., *Yeniçeriler*, Istanbul, 1964.
Komroff, M., ed., see Carpini.
Kortepeter, C.M., *Ottoman Imperialism during the Reformation*, New York, 1972.
——and Renda, G., *Transformation of Turkish Culture*, New York, 1987.
Kovačević, E., 'Jedan, Dokumenat o Dersirme', *Prilozi*, 22, Sarajevo, 1976.
Kramers, J.H., 'Murad II', *EI*, III, 1936.
——'Bayraktar Mustafa Pasha', *EI*, IV, 1936.
——'Osman II', *EI*, IV, 1936.
——'Selim I', *EI*, IV, 1936.
——'Süleyman II', *EI*, IV, 1936.

Select Bibliography

Kunt, I.M., 'Kullarin Kullari', *Boğazici Üniversitesi Dergesi*, III, Istanbul, 1975.

——*The Sultan's Servants: The Transformation of Ottoman Provincial Government, 1550-1560*, Columbia, 1983.

Lapidus, I.M., *Moslem Cities in the Later Middle Ages*, Cambridge, 1967.

Le Chevalier, J.B., *Voyage de la Propontine et du Pont-Euxin*, Paris, 1800.

Lestrange, A., *Don Juan of Persia*, New York, 1928.

Levy, R., *see* Iskender.

Lewis, B., *The Emergence of Modern Turkey*, Oxford, 1961.

——*Islam from the Prophet Muhammad to the Capture of Constantinople*, 2 vols, New York, 1974.

Lybyer, A.H., *The Government of the Ottoman Empire in the Time of Süleyman the Magnificent*, Harvard, 1913.

MacFarlane, C., *Constantinople in 1828*, London, 1829.

Mantran, R., 'Ahmet II', *EI*, I, 1960.

——'Hadim Ali Pasha', *EI*, I, 1960.

——*Istanbul dans la Seconde Moitié du XVIIe Siècle*, Paris, 1940.

Marsigli, Comte L.F. de, *Stato Militare dell'Impero Ottomano*, The Hague, 1732.

Maurand, J. *Itinéraire d'Antibes à Constantinople, 1544*, trans. L. Daez, Paris, 1901.

Melikoff, I., 'Bayezit II et Venise', *Turcica*, I, Paris, 1969.

Ménage, V., 'The Memoirs of an Ottoman Secret Agent in France in 1486', *JRAS*, parts 3-4, 1965.

——'Devshirme', *EI*, II, 1965.

Menemencioğlu, N., *The Penguin Book of Turkish Verse*, Harmondsworth, 1978.

Mihailoviç, K., *Memoirs of a Janissary*, trans. B. Stolz, notes by S. Soucek, Ann Arbor, 1975.

Miller, B., *The Palace School of Muhammad the Conqueror*, Cambridge, 1941.

Montagu, Lady Mary Wortley, ed. R. Halsband, *Letters*, London, 1968.

Motraye, A. de la, *Travels in Europe, Asia, and in Parts of Africa*, 3 vols, London, 1723—32.

Muhammad ibn Ahmed ibn Iyas, *An Account of the Ottoman Conquest of Egypt in the Year AH 922 (AD 1516)*, trans. W.H. Salmon, vol. III, Oriental Translation Fund, new series XXV, Royal Asiatic Society, London, 1921.

Munson, W.D., *The Last Crusade*, Dubuque, 1969.

Murphey, Rhoads, 'The Functioning of the Ottoman Army under Murad IV (1623-39/1032-49)', 3 vols, Chicago, 1979.

Necipoğlu, G., *Architecture, Ceremonial and Power, the Topkapı Palace in the 15th and 16th Centuries*, Massachusetts, 1991.

Nicolay, Nicolas de, *Navigations and Voyages*, London, 1586.

Select Bibliography

Olson, R.W., *The Siege of Mosul and Ottoman-Persian Relations, 1718-1743*, Indiana, 1973.
Oman, C.W.C., *The Art of War in the Middle Ages*, Cornell, 1953.
Palmer, J.A.B., 'The Origins of the Janissaries', *Bulletin of the Rylands Library*, XXXV, 1953, pp. 448-91.
Parry, V.J., 'Bāyāzid II', *EI*, II, 1965.
―'Davud Pasha', *EI*, II, 1965.
―'Materials of War in the Ottoman Empire', *SEHME*, 1970.
Perry, C., *A View of the Levant, particularly of Constantinople, Syria, Egypt and Greece*, London, 1743.
Pinkerton, *see* Blount.
Pitcher, D.E., *A Historical Geography of the Ottoman Empire*, Leiden, 1972.
Plumb, J.H., *The Penguin Book of the Renaissance*, Harmondsworth, 1964.
Purchas, S., *His Pilgrimage* . . . (first pub. London, 1613), 20 vols, Hakluytas Posthumus, Glasgow, 1905-7.
Ramberti, B., 'Libro Tre delle Cose di Turchi' in *Viaggi*, Venice, 1543.
Reed, H.H., 'Hüseyn Pasha', *EI*, IV, 1965.
Refik, *see* Ahmet Refik.
Repp, R.C., 'Köprülü', *EI*, III, 1980.
―*The Mufti of Istanbul*, Oxford, 1986.
Roux, J.P., *La Mort chez les Peuples Altai'iques Anciens et Médiévaux*, Paris, 1963.
Rosedale, H.G., *Queen Elizabeth and the Levant Company*, London, 1904.
Rycault, Sir P., *The History of the Turkish Empire, 1623-1677*, London, 1680.
Sahilloğlu, H., 'Sivis Year Crises in the Ottoman Empire', *SEHME*, 1970.
Salignac, G. de Gortaut Biron, Baron de, *Ambassade en Turquie, 1605-1610*, Paris/Auch, 1888.
Salmon, W.H., *An Account of the Ottoman Conquest of Egypt* . . . , AH 922, Oriental Translation Fund, Royal Asiatic Society, London, 1921.
Sanderson, J., ed. E.S. Forster, *The Travels of* . . . , London, 1931.
Sandys, G., *Travels (1610)*, 5th edn, London, 1652.
Scanlon, G. T., *A Muslim Manual of War: Tafrīj al-Kurūb fī Tadbīr al-Hurūb* by 'Umar ibn Ibrahim al-Awsī al-Ansari, *flor. 1400 (Prisoner of Timur)*, Cairo, 1961.
Schacht, J., *An Introduction to Islamic Law*, Oxford, 1964.
Schiltberger, J., *The Bondage and Travels of J. Schiltberger in Europe, Asia and Africa, 1396-1427*, trans. K.F. Neumann, notes by P. Bruun, J.B. Telfer (Hakluyt Society), London, 1897.
Schütz, E., *An Armeno-Kipchik Chronicle on the Polish-Turkish Wars in 1620-21*, Budapest, 1968.
Schuyler, E., and Wheeler, G., *Turkestan*, New York, 1966.
Shaw, S.J., and Shaw, E.K., 'Selim III and the Ottoman Navy', *Turcica*, I,

Select Bibliography

Paris, 1969.

——*History of the Ottoman Empire and Modern Turkey*, Illinois, 1974.

Skilliter, S., 'Catherine de Medici's Turkish Ladies-in-Waiting', *Turcica*, VII, Paris, 1975.

Skrine, P.H., and Denison Ross, E., *The Heart of Asia*, London, 1959.

Slade, A., *Records of Travels in Turkey*, 2 vols, London, 1833.

Sonyel, D.S.R., 'The Protégé System in the Ottoman Empire and its Abuses', *Belletin*, LV, Ankara, Jan. 1991.

Spandugino, T., 'Delle Origini degli Imperatori Ottomani', *SATHAS, Documents inédits*, IX, Paris, 1899.

——'La Cronaca Italiana di Theodore Spandugino' in C. Villain-Grandossi, *La Méditerranée aux XII–XVIe Siècles*, London, 1983.

Stripling, G.W.F., *The Ottoman Turks and the Arabs*, London, 1942.

Storey, S., *see* Ismail Kemal Bey.

Tenenti, A., *Piracy and the Decline of Venice, 1580–1615*, London, 1967.

Tietze, A., *Mustafa 'Ali's Counsel for Sultans, 1581*, 2 vols, Vienna, 1982.

Tott, Baron de, *Memoirs of...*, 4 parts, Amsterdam, 1785.

Turan, O., 'Anatolia in the Period of the Seljuks and Beyliks' in *Cambridge History of Islam*, Cambridge, 1970.

Turkish Art, 5th Congress of, Budapest, 1976.

Urquhart, D., *The Spirit of the East*, 2 vols, London, 1838.

——*Pillars of Hercules*, London, 1848.

Uzunçarşılı, I.H., *Osmanlı Devletinin Saray Teskilatı*, Ankara, 1945.

Vambery, A., *Travels and Adventures of the Turkish Admiral, Sidi Ali Reis, during the Years 1553–1556*, London, 1865.

Vandal, A., *Les Voyages du Marquis de Nointal, 1670–1680*, Paris, 1900.

Vasdravellis, J., *Piracy on the Mediterranean Coast*, trans. T.F. Carney, Salonika, 1970.

Vassif Efendi (Ahmad Klican Wasef Efendi), *Précis Historique de la Guerre des Turcs contre les Russes, depuis l'Année 1769 jusqu'à l'Année 1774, Tiré des Annales de Vassif Efendi par P.A. Coussin de Perceval*, Paris, n.d.

Vaughan, D.M., *Europe and the Turk*, Liverpool, 1954.

Vryonis Jnr., S., *The Decline of Medieval Hellenism in Asia Minor and the Process of Islamization from the Eleventh through the Fifteenth Century*, Berkeley, 1971.

Wittek, P., *The Rise of the Ottoman Empire*, London, 1938.

Wood, A.C., *see* Fox.

Woodhead, C., *Ta'liki-Zade's Şehname-i Hümayun: A History of the Ottoman Campaign into Hungary, 1593–94*, Freiburg, 1983.

Wortley Montagu, *see* Montagu.

Jacques de Hay: aşcıbaşı *(Maggs)*

Index

Individuals are listed under their nickname if they have one: thus Kara Ahmet Pasha is indexed at K, but Ahmet Pasha is indexed at A.

Abaza Mehmet Pasha 155, 159-61, 165
Abbasid dynasty 43
Abdi Pasha, traitor 190
Abdülhamit I, Ottoman sultan 199, 200, 227
Abdülhamit II, Ottoman sultan 56
Abdurrahman Efendi 222
Aboukir Bay, battle of 202
Abu Seyyit Efendi, *şeyhülislam* 170
acemioğlans 38-9, 52, 70, 85, 88, 99, 102, 106, 189; quarters 38-9
Acre 203
Ada Kale (Castle Island), fortress 94, 105
Adapazar 80
Addison, Charles 224, 231
Aden 122, 131
Adrianopolis *see* Edirne
Adriatic Sea 29, 90
Aegean Sea 86, 92, 107, 120
Afyon Karahısarı 120
Agyrnas (Mimarsinanköy) 36
Ahırkapı 51
ahis 25-7, 71, 118, 149, 151, 155; nationality of 25
Ahmet I, Ottoman sultan 154, 155, 156
Ahmet II, Ottoman sultan 177-8, 185
Ahmet III, Ottoman sultan 36, 101, 178, 182, 184-92 *passim*, 195, 205; seclusion 190; Westernization policy of 190
Ahmet Agha, commander of *sipahis* 162
Ahmet Bey (Evrenoszade) 60
Ahmet Bonneval Pasha (Count Alexandre de Bonneval) 193, 195
Ahmet Pasha, rebel 128
Ahmet Pasha, *serasker* 187
Ahmet Pasha, Grand Vezir 182
Ahmet Şehzade, son of Bayezit II 121, 122
Ainslie, Sir Robert, ambassador 81

Index

akıncıs 27, 32, 67, 78, 119, 126, 133–9 *passim*, 143, 145
Aksaray 73
Alaettin of Aci, Sultan 80
Alaettin Pasha 27, 62
Alay Kiosk 208
Albania 40, 118, 120, 124, 150, 199
Albanian: ferocity 40; levy 37; mountaineers 174
Albigensian heresy 28
Albuquerque, Duke of 105, 122
Alemdar Mustafa Pasha of Silistria 165, 203, 206–8; arrogance of 208
Aleppo 60, 125, 126, 128, 131, 132, 151, 155, 170, 171, 188
Alevis 124
Alexandria 28
Algiers 105
Ali, the Caliph 28
Ali Bey, strangler 113
Ali Pasha, eunuch and Chief Vezir 121
Ali Pasha of Çorlu 151, 184, 185
Ali Pasha of Iznik ('Coke-Seller' Ali) 185
Ali Pasha of Yanina 165, 199, 210
Ali Patrona, rag-dealer 191–2
Amanus mountains 92, 125
Amasya 25, 98, 117, 123, 131, 146, 165, 231; dervishes 117
Amcazade Hüseyn Pasha *see* Köprülüzade Amcazade Hüseyn Pasha
America 187
Anatolia (Anadolu) 17, 19–24, 28, 32, 35, 39, 51, 52, 62, 66, 77, 78, 81, 83, 86, 106, 113, 117–20, 133, 139, 143, 144, 148–51, 156, 159–61, 165, 171, 176, 179, 185, 188, 196, 200, 203, 204, 210, 211, 227, 231; autonomy 166; *celalı* uprisings 154–5; dervishes and 22; feudalism 41; geography of 19; levy in 34, 40; Mohacs preparation of 131–2; no rest for 119; order restored 161; overrun 21; Selim I stabilizes 122–4; tamed 172–3; Timur in 56; troops in 154
Ancona 29
Angora *see* Ankara
Ankara (Angora) 25, 33, 43, 45, 57, 113, 114, 120, 166
Antalya 79
Aptullah Mehmet, intellectual 231
Aptullah Pasha, *agha* of janissaries 193
Arabia 153
Arbuthnott, Admiral 204
archery 81–2
Archery Ground *see* Okmeydan

Index

Armenian: community 190; masons 80
Arsenal *see* Tersane
Asia 59, 84, 100, 131, 144, 188; Central Asia 20, 21, 40, 51, 75, 98, 147, 149
askeris 67, 74
Aslan Khan 20
Assad Efendi *see* Essat Efendi
Astrakhan 147
Atatürk (Mustafa Kemal) 149, 204, 227
Athens 34, 176
Athos, Mount 21
Atmeydan *see* Hippodrome
Auspicious Event 108, 209, 210, 214 *et seq.*
Austria 95, 104, 119, 145, 155, 202
ayan 165-6, 173; abolished 210
Ayas Pasha 45, 98; outstanding *agha* 124
Aynalı Kavak 199
azaps 67, 74, 116, 120, 125, 128
Azerbaijan 123, 144
Azov, Sea of 147, 199

Bab-ül-Hümayün (Gate of Majesty) 44, 49, 117, 192, 206, 221, 222, 226
Bab-ül-Sa'adet (Gate of Felicity) 44, 46, 227
Baba Cafer prison 97
Baba Zünnün 144
Babaeski 203
Babur, Emperor 80
Baghdad 44, 62, 83, 120, 151, 160, 164, 170, 193, 199
Bagno prison 106
bailo 116, 186, 188, 190, 192-4
Bakras, Armenian castle 92, 132
Balat 99
Balı Bey of Bosnia 133-8
Balkans (Rumelia) 17, 28, 34, 35, 38-40, 52, 53, 62, 67, 78, 86, 90, 92, 93, 120, 130, 131, 133, 150, 151, 188, 200, 204, 210
bandits: control mountains 165
Banjaluka 196
Barbaro, Nicolo 115
Barbaros Pasha (Barbarossa) *see* Hayrettin Barbaros Pasha
Barbarossa *see* Hayrettin Barbaros Pasha
Barbary coast 102
Baudier, M. 37
Bayezit I, Yıldırım, Ottoman sultan 28, 29, 30, 43, 45, 57, 91, 102, 111, 168

Index

Bayezit II, Ottoman sultan 25, 45, 46, 60, 71, 101, 102, 117, 118–21, 124, 130, 150, 223; Halveti dervish 118
Bayezit, brother of Murat IV 163
Bayezit, son of Süleyman I 154
Bayezit Meydan 97
Bayezit mosque 160, 223
Bayezit Pasha 25
bedouin 63, 126–8; defy Selim I 126, 128; Ibrahim Pasha and 128
Bekir Pasha 202
Bektaşi order of dervishes 28, 71, 86, 87, 101, 120, 148–52, 217, 224, 227, 231; and Yeni Odalar 74; attraction of 149
Belgrade 76, 79, 80, 84, 100, 105, 116, 133, 134, 140, 141, 176, 177, 179, 186, 195, 201, 202, 225
Belgrade forest 186, 225
Bender, citadel 93
Benderli Mehmet Selim Pasha, Grand Vezir 210
Beşiktaş 99, 221, 227
Beylerbey palace 220
beylerbeys 27, 53, 62, 63, 72
Beylik period 155, 165
Beyoğlu 68
Bitlis 122
Bıyıklı Ali Pasha, Grand Vezir 196
Black Sea 28, 30, 83–5, 89, 91, 105, 107, 119, 131, 150, 195, 200, 202; castles 198
Blount, Henry 84, 90
Boetti, Giovanni Battista, false Mahdi 199–200
Bogomils 25, 28, 35
Bohemia 133
bölüks 69, 70, 73
Bonneval, Count Alexandre de *see* Ahmet Bonneval Pasha
Bosnia 28, 29, 35, 96, 134, 138, 155, 161, 195, 196, 202
Bosphorus 28, 52, 74, 89, 91, 98, 99, 114, 117, 121, 166, 186, 188, 189, 193, 194, 204–6, 211, 215, 220, 227
bostancıs 38–9, 72, 74; employment 52–3
bridges, pontoon 85, 133, 136, 140
Bucharest 202
Buda(pest) 80, 95, 96, 116, 140, 143, 144, 176
Buddhism 20
Bukhara 20
Bulgaria 29, 77
Burgas 155

Index

Bursa 17, 25, 27, 30, 38, 43, 55, 56, 104, 111, 113, 117–20, 149, 150, 155, 160, 163, 211
Busbecq, O.G. 146, 149
Byzantines 20, 28, 50, 111, 114, 115, 156, 159, 232

Cafer Agha 45, 103
Caffa 147, 185
Cairo 60, 79, 119, 125–8, 131, 170
Calabria 104
Çaldıran, battle of 123–5
Çanakkale 38, 92
Çandarlı Ali Pasha, Chief Vezir 43
Çandarlı Halil Pasha, Chief Vezir 110, 112
Çandarlı Ibrahim Pasha, Chief Vezir 60
Çandarlı Kara Halil Pasha, Chief Vezir 27, 30
Candia 89, 169, 170
Çanlıcık 220
Capua 118
Caravan, Commander of the 63
Carpathian mountains 119
Casa del Capitano, Vicenza 145
Caspian Sea 21, 187
Castle Island *see* Ada Kale
Castles of the Bosphorus 205, 211, 215; *see also* Rumeli Hısar
Catalan Company 27
Catherine the Great 195, 200
Caucasus 28, 32, 159
Cavendish, Lord Henry 90, 100
cebecis 68, 74
Celalettin Mehmet Agha 211
celalıs 154, 155
Çelebi Mustafa 206
Cem Sultan 25, 117–19
cemaat 69
Central Asia *see under* Asia
Çerkes Kasım Pasha 147
Cervantes (Saavedra): prisoner 104
Çeşme, fleet destroyed at 107, 200
Chandler, Richard 89–90
Charles V, Emperor 132
Châteauneuf, French ambassador 179, 180
Chief Black Eunuch 46, 50, 61, 153, 156–8, 172, 185, 193, 194, 207; and *padre*

Index

Ottomano 169–70
Chief White Eunuch 44–6, 110, 158; as Keeper of the Gate 46; murdered 158; as tutors 46
Chinese: culture 21; style 75
Chingiz Khan 21
Christian knights 29, 33, 136; *see also* Malta, Knights of; Rhodes, Knights of
Christianity 20, 23, 57
Christians 21, 52, 58, 67, 88, 93, 120, 126, 177, 192, 201, 211
Çigalazade Yusuf Sinan Pasha, *agha* of janissaries 104, 154
Cıhangir *see* Observatory
Circumcision Kiosk *see* Sünnet Odası
Clement VII, Pope 156
Çobanoğlu family 165
Colton, Rev. W. 48
Comnenus, Emperor David 83
Constantine XI, Emperor 114
Constantinople, siege of 112–14, 115–16; *see also* Istanbul
Corfu 184, 185
Corinth 79
Çorlu 121, 184, 203
corsairs 29, 32, 45, 46, 102, 103, 106, 127, 192; kidnap boys 28, 33
Corsica 46
Cossacks 81, 147, 174
Covel, Dr John 51, 75
Crimea 21, 57, 67, 121, 147, 174, 185, 191, 195, 199; Crimean war 74
currency debased 111, 145, 147
Cyprus 127, 128, 196

Dalbatan Pasha, Grand Vezir 181
Dallam, Thomas 146
Dalmatia 120
Damascus 60, 62, 63, 84, 85, 91, 95, 122, 126, 128, 131, 151, 152, 165, 227
dancing boys *see* taverns
Dandolo, Doge Enrico 116
Dante 152
Danube, river 17, 29, 78, 82, 84, 94, 107, 135, 140, 141, 143, 145, 147, 181, 198, 203, 204, 206; fleet 105
Dardanelles 38, 179, 195, 203, 204; castles 198
Davut Agha, architect 39, 85
Davut Agha 218; escape of 226
Davut Pasha, Grand Vezir 158, 159, 160
Davutpaşa barracks 132, 163, 217, 218

Index

defterdar 61
Deli Hasan 155
delis 116
Denizli 89
derbent 68
Dervish Mehmet Pasha, Grand Vezir 154
dervishes *see* Bektaşi, Halveti, Kalender, Melameti, Mevlevi, Nakşibendi, Rifai orders; revolt 122; satanic 211
Devlet Giray Khan 147
devşirme 27, 29-30, 32-53 *passim*, 121, 124, 150, 184; Selim I and 121; suspended 174
Dimetoka 121, 150
Divan (Grand Council of State) 44, 47, 59, 61-2, 70, 75, 86, 102, 112, 113, 117, 120, 125, 128, 135, 145, 152, 159, 160, 169, 171, 176, 178-81, 192, 196, 206, 207, 210, 215, 216, 222, 223, 225; bribed 179; power of 61
Divanı Ibrahim Pasha, governor of Dıyarbekir 98
Divriği 19
Dıyarbekir 98, 120, 124, 131, 144, 160, 161, 195
Doğubayezit 166
Don-Volga canal 21, 147
Dordogne 193
Doria, Andrea, Admiral 102
Dracula, the younger (Vlad III Tepes Kazıklı) 78
Drava, river 133, 135
Druze: unrest 128
Duckworth, Admiral 204
Dülkadır family 124, 150

Ebüssu'ûd, *şeyhülislam* 26, 59, 60
Edirne (Adrianopolis) 29, 30, 37, 38, 39, 43, 46, 52, 53, 60, 62, 76, 85, 87, 90, 100, 101, 111, 112, 121, 130, 133, 151, 172, 175, 176, 178, 179, 180, 182, 203, 227
egalitarianism 24, 26
Egypt 17, 28, 40, 43, 56, 60, 104, 124-6, 128, 131, 132, 134, 144, 165, 196, 202, 210, 220, 232; Egyptian army 218
Elba 103
Elbistan 124, 125, 150, 154
Elizabeth I, Queen of England 146, 153
Elmalı 19, 150
Enderun Kolej (Palace School) 30, 36-8, 41-6, 50, 52, 61, 105, 117, 122, 184, 195
England 29, 92, 153

Index

Eretna 19
Erivan (Yerivan) 44, 83, 163, 187
Ernest von Habsburg, Archduke 95–6
Ertuğrul Bey 17, 57
Erzerum 84, 124, 155, 159–61, 199
Eski Odalar (Old Barracks) 39, 72–4, 98, 99, 225, 227
Eski Saray (Old Palace) 39, 97, 157
Eskişehir 149
Essat (Assad) Efendi, Chief Scribe 217, 225
Estergom 95
Eszek 135
Etmeydan (Parade Ground) 74, 151, 190, 218–20, 223–5
Eugene, Prince, of Savoy 93, 178, 180, 185, 195
eunuchs 49; antecedents 43; discipline 49–50; *see also* Chief Black Eunuch; Chief White Eunuch
Eunuchs' Mosque 171
Europe 27, 32, 123, 152, 174, 193, 195; campaigns into 90; Cem Sultan in 118; Danube frontier 143; dread of janissaries in 17, 26; economic crisis 145; janissaries prefer 131; *kadiasker* of 59; military bands 51; Ottoman designs on 55, 166, 172; prisoners from 28; recruits in 150; roads into 77; uniforms in 29
Evliya Çelebi 35, 37, 39, 166
Evrenos Bey 27, 60, 113
Eyüp 152, 186, 225

fanatics 67, 83, 116
Fatih mosque 161, 163, 193
Ferhat Pasha, *beylerbey* of Hungary 85, 95–6
Ferhat Pasha: insulted 143
Feyzullah Efendi, *şeyhülislam,* 181, 182, 184
Firuz Bey 120
Flanders 79
Folard, Chevalier 195
France 38, 69, 74, 79, 99, 103, 132, 139, 145, 176, 186, 193
François I, King of France 69, 103, 132
Franz Josef, Emperor 34
frontier fortresses 90–5

Galata 38, 39, 68, 74, 87, 97, 102, 198, 222, 225, 226
Galata Bridge 39
Galata Tower 91, 97
Galatasaray college 37, 38, 43, 50, 184, 185
Galip Pasha, Grand Vezir 210

Index

Galitzine, Prince 176
Galland, Antoine 52, 73, 75, 88
galleys 102 *et seq.*
Gallipoli (Gelibolu) 27, 92, 102, 103, 106, 112, 133, 141; and levy 38
gallstones 104
Gama, Vasco da 122
Gate of Felicity *see* Bab-ül-Sa'adet
Gate of Majesty *see* Bab-ül-Hümayün
Gaza 126
Gazanfer Agha, Chief Black Eunuch 153, 154
Gedik Ahmet Pasha 118, 119
Gelibolu *see* Gallipoli
Genoa 42, 46
Geuffroy, Antoine 143
Giglio 103
Giray khan: and Don-Volga canal 21; Ottoman heir 168; Giray khans 57, 147, 168
Giurgiu, fortress 93
Glabas, Isidore, Metropolitan of Salonika 27
Göksü 206
Golden Gate 92
Golden Horn 38, 49, 70, 79, 81-3, 97-9, 102, 105, 107, 128, 172, 186, 198, 217, 221-3
Golden Road 207
Grand Council of State *see* Divan
Grand Vezir *(sadrazam)*, first 40; *and see under individual entries*
Greater Syria 81
Greece 36, 120, 210
Greek Orthodox Church 55
Greek War of Independence 210, 216
Grenville, Henry 72, 106
Gribeauval, military engineer 145
guilds: and janissaries 101, 192; growth of 26; non-Muslims join 192; taxation 63; war service 68
Guides, Company of 67
guitars 212
Gülhısar 89
Gunner Mustafa 224
gürebas 66
Güzelce Kasım Pasha, *kapudan paşa* 132
Güzelce Mahmut Pasha, Grand Vezir 154
Gyllius, Pierre Gilles 69

Index

gypsies 34, 101, 150, 174, 190

Habsburgs 94, 96, 127
Hacı Ali, assassin 206
Hacı Bektaş 150, 204, 227, 230
Hacı Çelebi, *şeyh,* 118
Hacıbektaş 231
Hadıce Turhan *see* Turhan, Hadıce
Hadramaut 93
Hafız Pasha, Grand Vezir 160, 161, 162
Haghia Irene, church 44, 222
Haghia Sophia, basilica 74, 98, 99, 193, 221, 222, 225
Hakkari mountains 92
Halberdiers of the Tresses 38, 50; Hall of the 48, 50–1
Halil Pasha, Grand Vezir 161
Halkalüpınar 132
Halveti order of dervishes 118, 152; Bayezit II, member of 118
Hama 126
Hamadan 187
Hanstein, Ernst Wilhelm von 178
Harbord, William 179
Hasan, *agha* of janissaries 116
Hasan Agha, intendant-general 215, 219, 221
Hasan Pasha, Grand Vezir 154
Hasan Pasha (Murteşi) 153–4
Hasan Pasha, *han* 230
Hasan Pasha, *kapudan paşa* 107
Hawkwood, Sir John 27
Hayrettin Barbaros Pasha (Barbarossa) 45, 46, 61, 102–5
Hebdomon 92
Hekimoğlu Ali Pasha, Grand Vezir 194–6
Henry VII, King of England 29
Henry VIII, King of England 92, 186
Hersekoğlu Ahmet Pasha (Duke of Herzegovina) 119
Herzegovina 29; levy 35
Herzegovina, Duke of (Hersekoğlu Ahmet Pasha) 119
Hezarpare Ahmet Pasha, Grand Vezir 170
highways *see* supply roads
Hildberghausen, Prince of 195, 196
Hill, Dr Alban 103
Hindu recruitment 32
Hippodrome (Atmeydan) 37, 74, 75, 97, 155, 171, 192, 204, 205, 222–5, 232
Holy Mantle, guards of the 47

Index

Holy Places 63
Homs 126
Horasan 149
Horn *see* Golden Horn
horses: royal stables 51–2; Türkmen 20; vanguard 77
Hoşap 92
Hotin 157
Howling Dervishes *see* Rifai
Hungary 34, 78, 80, 93, 95, 131, 135, 136, 138, 143, 145
Hürrem Pasha 144
Hüseyn Pasha, *agha* of the janissaries 158
Hüseyn Pasha, *beylerbey* of Europe 144, 154
Hüsrev Bey 134
Hüsrev Pasha, Grand Vezir 144, 161, 162
Hüsrev Pasha: executes janissaries 230
Hussey, William 179

Ibn Battuta 19, 20, 22–5
Ibn Tulun, sultan 43
Ibrahim I, Ottoman sultan 38, 152, 163, 166, 168–70
Ibraham Agha, quartermaster 215
Ibrahim Agha (Infernal) 221, 223, 224
Ibrahim Efendi 189–90
Ibrahim Pasha, Damat, Grand Vezir 37, 41, 45, 99, 141, 143; as young commander 130; at Mohacs 75, 78, 130–41 *passim*; bridges on Danube 140; fall of 140, 145, 146; first Grand Vezir 40; in Syria and Egypt 128; purple tent of 75
Ibrahim Pasha, Grand Vezir, reforms of 153–4
Ibrahim Pasha Saray 37–8, 39, 44, 48, 74
Ibrahim Seyyit Efendi 218, 219
Ibsir Pasha 166
içoğlans 37–8, 43
Idris Khan 122
India 75, 122, 145
Indian Ocean 104, 105, 122, 124
Inegöl 119, 226
Inner Service 50–1; *see also* Outer Service
Innocent VIII, Pope 118
Iran 21; *see also* Persia
Iriğ 134
Iron Gates 94, 105
Isa Pasha 120
Işak Bey 107, 200

Index

Işak Pasha 61, 112, 113, 118, 119
Ischia 103
Isfendiyaroğlu family 83
Iskender Çelebi 45
Iskenderoğlu family 33, 113
Iskenderun 92, 188
Islam 21, 23, 24, 27–30, 33, 34, 47, 55–7, 75, 107, 115, 148, 151, 152, 199, 205, 216, 217; Turks converted to 20; *see also* Muslims
Ismail, Shah of Persia 23, 120, 122, 123
Ismail, Shah, fanatic 150
Ismail al-Azam Pasha 196–7
Ismail Pasha, *agha* of janissaries 180
Istanbul (Constantinople) 23, 27, 30, 37, 44, 46, 48, 53, 56, 63, 67, 69, 72, 75, 85–6, 90, 95, 101–2, 104–6, 122, 126–8, 132, 139–41, 149, 151, 153, 157, 159, 161, 165–6, 170–1, 173, 181, 184–6, 197, 200, 203, 206, 210, 214, 218, 226, 231; *agha* of 70; conquest of 112–16; Constantinople 17, 57; earthquake (1509) 120; fires 97–100, 208–9; janissaries in 148, 188–90, 204, 211–12; Korkud paraded in 118; mobs 105, 172, 188; order in 88; sedition 163; walls 91; whitewashed 139
Italy 27, 79, 80, 92, 102, 118, 145; Italian gunnery 40
Ivan III 147
Izmir *see* Smyrna
Izmit (Nicomedia) 39, 67, 163, 227
Iznik (Nicaea) 24, 44, 70, 93, 163, 185, 186

Jacobins 24
Jaffa 197
janissary corps *passim;* Abaza and 160; accession purses of 113, 177, 190; *see acemioğlans;* archery 81–2; Baghdad campaign 163–4; barracks 39, 44, 53, 69–70, 72–4, 98–9, 149, 151, 190, 204, 207, 211, 215, 218–20, 223–5, 227; Bektaşi influence 101, 123, 148; butcher New Army 209; camp 76–7; cauldrons 86, 147–8, 182, 218, 220, 226; caution 79; coffee 197; cowardice 216; decline 110; divisions *see ortas;* dress 70–1, 204; *esprit de corps* 26, 110; flags and insignia 71–2; Ganymede and 198; garrisons 93–4, 113; marching 132–6; marriages 34; massacre of 181; military machine 123; mobsters 148, 160, 177, 198–9, 209, 211; mutineers 24, 86, 100–1, 147–8, 157–8, 160–2, 170–2, 175, 177, 181, 189–90, 200–6, 215 *et seq.;* origins 211; *ortas* 69 *et seq.;* pay 97–8, 153, 180, 192, 212, 218; phrenology 36; pleasures 39, 87–9, 198, 211; poets 230; policing 88–90; proletariat and 102; protection money 211; rape 89, 212; recruitment unrestricted 150; retirement 40; rival *ortas* 154; sadism 177; self-interest 33, 41, 204; shopkeepers 191; stokers 230; strangled 212; *see* taverns and dancing boys; tattooing 40, 73, 211; thinking 33; treason 158; tribunes 30, 112, 157, 232

274

Index

Janissary Tree 224
Jericho 82
Jesus 144
Jews 34, 49, 90, 96, 118, 127, 146, 150, 155, 192, 211; *see also* Judaism
Jiddah 131
Joshua 82
Juan, Don, of Austria 104, 145
Judaism 20, 57; *see also* Jews

Kabakcıoğlu Mustafa 204–6
Kadı Pasha 208–9
Kağıthane 52, 53, 73, 186, 198, 199, 217
Kalender order of dervishes 124
Kalender Çelebi: and Jesus 144
Kalenderoğlu, *celalı* leader 155
Kampel Mustafa Agha, English convert 107
Kansuh, Mamluk sultan 124, 125
Kanun-i-Teşrifat (Law of Ceremonies) 44, 57
kapudan paşa 41, 46, 61, 86, 102, 104–7, 132, 159, 164, 189, 190, 192, 197, 200, 206–9
Kara Ahmet Pasha, Grand Vezir 145
Kara Ali, thug 192
Kara Hüseyn Pasha, *agha* of janissaries 210–11, 215–16, 220, 223, 225–7
Kara Mustafa Pasha of Merzifon 72, 78, 98, 174–6
Kara Yazıcı Pasha, *celalı* leader 154, 155
Karageorge, patriot 201–2
Karagöz, shadow puppet 87
Karagöz Pasha 97, 119, 120
Karahanid dynasty 43
Karahısar 131
Karakuş (Türkmen) 20
Karaman Bey 25
Karamania 114, 119, 124, 125, 131, 203, 209
Karamanlı Mehmet Pasha, Chief Vezir 117
Karamanoğlu family 165
Karamursel 165
Karancı Doğan Agha 113
Karası 27
Karlowitz, peace of 181, 188
Karmatians 24
Kars 19
Kasım Pasha 45, 128, 132

Index

Kasımpaşa 49, 225
Kastamonu 82
Kayseri 121, 131, 132, 144, 160, 231
Kemal Bey 227
Kemalpaşazade, *şeyhülislam*, 60, 75, 130, 144
Khania 169
Kıbrıslı Mehmet Emin Pasha, *serasker*, six tails 53, 72, 220, 221, 226
Kılıç Ai Pasha, *kapudan paşa* 74, 104
Kirkçeşme 74
Kırşehir 149, 150
Kızılbaş (Red Heads) 120, 122, 124, 131, 144
Koca Davut Pasha 119
Koca Hızır 134
Koca Ibrahim Pasha, Grand Vezir 185
Koca Sinan Pasha, Yemeni Fatih 67, 96, 152-3
Kocu 36
Königsmark, Count Graf von 176
Konya 22, 23, 71, 120, 152, 173
Köprülü Aptullah Pasha 195
Köprülü family 172, 173, 175
Köprülü Fazıl Ahmet Pasha, Grand Vezir 36, 151, 173, 174
Köprülü Mehmet Pasha, Grand Vezir 59, 101, 170, 173; revolution 171-2
Köprülüzade Amcazade Hüseyn Pasha 173, 180, 181
Köprülüzade Fazıl Mustafa Pasha, Grand Vezir 177-9
Koran 24, 47-8, 148, 188, 205; hung on standards 71
Korkud, Sultan, son of Bayezit II 118, 122
Köşe Mikhail, adventurer 27
Kossovo 69
Küçük Ahmet Çelebi 113
Küçük Hüseyn Pasha 107, 200, 202
Küçük Kaynarcı, peace of 199
kul 20, 30, 42, 81, 131, 165
Kurdistan 144
Kurtoğlu Kızır Bey 80
Kütahya 113, 120, 131, 155, 165, 196, 226
Kuyucu Murat Pasha 154-7

La Quira, Madame (Sultana Sporca) 155
Lala Devri *see* Tulip Period
Lala Mustafa Pasha, Grand Vezir 152, 153
Lala Şahin Bey 62
Laupen, battle of 69

Index

Laz 150, 192
Lebanon 128
Lepanto, battle of 104, 138, 145, 147, 155
Levant 122, 127
Levant Company 179
Levents 106
levy, rules of 34
Lewis, Bernard 232
Libya 232
Licastella 104
Lipari 103
Lorraine, Duke of 175
Louis, King of Hungary 136, 138-9
Louis XIV, King of France 179
Lütfi Efendi 60
Lütfi Pasha, Chief Vezir 111, 123
Lybyer 36

Maginot Line 127
Magnesia *see* Manisa
Mahdi, false *see* Boetti, Giovanni Battista
Mahmut I, Ottoman sultan 191-6 *passim*
Mahmut II, Ottoman sultan 59, 81, 149, 199, 204, 205, 207-11 *passim*, 214, 220-2, 224, 225, 227, 232
Mahmut Pasha, Grand Vezir 61
Mahpeyker Kösem, Valide Sultan 158, 161, 171, 178
Maison de France 38, 99
Malatya 150
Malta, Knights of 106, 169
Maltepe 117
Mamluk dynasty 40, 66, 80, 119, 124-8, 196, 210
Manichaeism 20
Manisa (Magnesia) 30, 38, 52, 111, 112, 146, 155, 165
Mantua 146
Manzikirt, battle of 21
Maraş 159
Mardın 120
Marine School 198
Maritza *see* Meriç
Marj Dabik, battle of 125
Marmara, Sea of 52, 92, 102, 112, 117, 133, 150, 172, 222
Marsigli, Count 51, 76, 80, 173, 175, 177, 178

Index

Martinet, General 29
Maurand, J. 103, 194
Mavrocordato, ambassador 180
Maximilian, Emperor 90, 95
Meander, river 165
Mecca 63, 153
Medina 148
Mediterranean Sea 33, 102, 105, 131, 195
Mehmet I, Ottoman sultan 25, 27, 30, 43, 57, 62
Mehmet II, Fatih, Ottoman sultan 26, 28, 32, 43, 44, 48, 50–1, 56–7, 61, 66, 67, 69, 78–9, 81, 83–4, 91–3, 102, 110–18, 140, 150; despot 112; feudalism and 58, 114; impatience of 78; insulted 30
Mehmet III, Ottoman sultan 148, 153, 154
Mehmet IV, Ottoman sultan 53, 59, 75, 101, 152, 166, 169–73 *passim*, 176–7, 178; deposed 177; surrenders power 172
Mehmet Agha, architect 52
Mehmet Agha, colonel of the armourers: exiled 226
Mehmet Izzat Pasha 220, 223, 224, 230
Mehmet Selim Pasha, Grand Vezir 210, 215, 216
Mehmet Seyyit Halet Efendi, Grand Vezir 210
Mehmetci Etin, *agha* of the janissaries 215, 219
Mehter band 83
Melameti order of dervishes 151–2
Menavino, Giovanni Antonio 45, 46
Menderes, Adnan 111
Menteşe *beys* 28
Menteşe family 165
Meriç (Maritza), river 112
Merzifon 174
Mesih Pasha, Chief Vezir 97, 120
Mesih Pasha, Grand Vezir 153
Mesopotamia 20
Messina 104
Metternich, Prince 203
Mevlevi order of dervishes 22, 23, 56, 152
Mezzomorto Kara Hüseyn Pasha 105, 106
Middle Gate *see* Orta Kapı
Mihrimah Sultan 42, 145
Mikhailović, Konstantin 27, 28, 32, 61
millet system 55
Mimarsinanköy *see* Agyrnas
Ministry of the Marine 108

Index

Mirror for Princes, A 110, 111, 133
Missolonghi, surrender of 212
Moguls 32, 75, 80
Mohacs: campaign 72, 75, 78, 130–41, 166; defeat 176
Moldavia 34, 77, 93, 176, 191
Molla Agha 208
Mongolia 20
Montagu *see* Wortley Montagu
Montecastro 93
Morea *see* Peloponnese
Moscow 147, 176
Moses 204
Mosul 62, 165, 199
Muhammad, the Prophet 21, 23–4, 44, 56–7, 60, 72, 75, 144, 148, 176–7, 192, 206, 220–2, 227; relics 56; *see also* Standard of the Prophet
Münnich, Marshal 195
Murat I, Ottoman sultan 24, 25, 27, 28, 29, 33, 43, 56, 62
Murat II, Ottoman sultan 27, 30, 43, 83, 110–13; and Sufis 111; *topçus* founded 68
Murat III, Ottoman sultan 48, 49, 60, 98, 100, 102, 147–8, 150, 152; character of 146; education and 153
Murat IV, Ottoman sultan 38, 44, 46, 83, 98, 101, 110, 152, 159, 160–2, 166, 168, 170; janissary reform 35, 162–3
Murat Pasha, Palaeologus 33
Murteşi Hasan Pasha, Grand Vezir 154
Musa, son of Bayezit I 57
Musa Çelebi 162
Musa Pasha 204, 206
music: martial 83, 132; ritual 24
Muslims 20, 27, 28, 35, 58, 67, 96, 101, 110, 123, 150, 177, 186, 192, 216, 217; *see also* Islam
Mustafa I, Ottoman sultan 153, 156–60, 166, 168
Mustafa II, Ottoman sultan 178, 179, 182, 184
Mustafa III, Ottoman sultan 197, 199
Mustafa IV, Ottoman sultan 205–8
Mustafa, Chandler's janissary 89–90
Mustafa, Gunner 224
Mustafa, son of Bayezit I 57
Mustafa, vice-intendant 218, 225
Mustafa the Drunkard (Sahoş) 220, 230
Mustafa the Fruiterer (Meyvacı), rebel 191, 220, 223, 230
Mustafa Kemal *see* Atatürk

Index

Mustafa Pasha 45, 120
Mustafa Pasha, *kapudan paşa* and son-in-law of Ahmet III 190
Mustafa Şehzade: brother of Murat II 111; son of Süleyman I 146
Mytilene 185, 196

Nadir Shah 187
Nakşibendi order of dervishes 152, 227, 231
Napoleon 48; in Egypt 125, 202
narcotics 21, 187, 197
Nasi, Joseph, Duke of Naxos 146–7
Nasrettin Hoca 149
Nauplia 195
Naval College 108
Naxos, Duke of *see* Nasi, Joseph
Necip Efendi 223, 225
Nelson, Horatio 202
nepotism 151
Nevşehir 185, 190
Nevşehirli Ibrahim Pasha, Damat 185–92 *passim*; peace policy of 186; war policy of 187
New Army (Nizam ı-Cedit) 27, 52, 74, 202–5, 208, 209, 218, 225–7
New Barracks *see* Yeni Odalar
New Mosque *see* Yeni Cami
Nicaea *see* Iznik
Nicholas V, Pope 57
Nicolay, Nicolas de 38, 46, 145
Nicomedia *see* Izmit
Nicopolis, battle of 78, 102
Nicosia 191
Nightingale, Florence 74
Niksar 131
Nile, river 126, 127
Nilufer Sultan 24
Niş 133, 173, 179, 185
Nişantaş 81
Nizam ı-Cedit *see* New Army
Nizam ul-Mülk, Persian chancellor 42
nomadic life 21
North, Roger 175
Novi, fortress 105
Novo Brdo 32, 79, 114
Nüsretiye mosque 74, 227

Index

Observatory, Istanbul 60, 100, 147
Oğuz Turks 83
Okmeydan (Archery Ground) 81, 198
Old Barracks *see* Eski Odalar
Old Palace *see* Eski Saray
Onik 135
Orbetello 103
Orhan Çelebi, uncle of Mehmet II 114
Orhan Gazi, Ottoman sultan 17, 25, 27, 43, 55–6, 62, 66; drum of 56; mosque of at Bursa 55
Orta Kapı (Middle Gate) 44, 206
Orta mosque 74
Osman I, Gazi, Ottoman sultan 17, 25, 56, 57, 166; sword of 56, 152
Osman II, Ottoman sultan 156–60 *passim*, 162, 207
Osman III, Ottoman sultan 99, 196
Osman Agha 230
Osmancık 150
Otranto 102, 119
Outer Service 51; *see also* Inner Service

Paget, Lord, ambassador 178–81
Pakistan 232
Palace School *see* Enderun Kolej
Palamas, Gregory 24
Palestine 35
Parade Ground *see* Etmeydan
Passarowitz, peace of 185
Payas 92
Peloponnese (Morea) 79, 120, 176, 185; massacre of Turks 215
Pera 68, 74, 98, 99, 222
Perekop 147
Persia 20, 21, 23, 40, 43, 66, 69, 85, 104, 120, 122, 128, 145, 148, 152, 154, 156, 187, 188, 192, 195, 196, 200; *see also* Iran
Pertek 19
Pest *see* Buda(pest)
Peter the Great 32, 43, 180
Peterwardein 134, 135, 185
Philippopolis 60, 84, 133, 208
Piacenza 194
pious foundations 114, 208
piracy *see* corsairs
Piyale Pasha 104, 153

281

Index

Poland 77, 133, 158, 180, 181
Policastro 103
Porte *see* Sublime Porte
Priam 57
Privy Chamber 47
Prophet Muhammad *see* Muhammad, the Prophet

Quakers 24

Rabia Gülnüş Ummetullah, Valide Sultan 178
races, mixed 45
Ragip Pasha, Grand Vezir 193, 196–7, 199; civilized 196
Ramberti 35, 36, 46, 143
Rami Mehmet Pasha, Grand Vezir 181–2, 184; civilian bureaucrat 181
Recep Pasha 162
Red Heads *see* Kızılbaş
Reggio 104
reis efendi 61, 180, 187, 191, 194, 196, 199, 216
Rhine 134
Rhineland 179
Rhodes 102, 128, 144; Knights of 106, 124
Ricoldus, slave 45
Rifai order of dervishes (Howling Dervishes) 22
ritual 24
Romania 93
Rome 17, 56, 59, 69, 112, 143
Rumeli Hısar (Rumeli Castle) 89, 91, 114
Rumelia *see* Balkans
Rusçuk (Ruse) 105
Ruse *see* Rusçuk
Russia 169, 180, 181, 197, 200, 202, 203
Rüstem Pasha, Grand Vezir 42, 96, 98, 104, 150; hated 41, 146; rapacious 145

Sabahıttın Pasha, Chief White Eunuch 110, 112, 113
Saban Agha, *bostancıbaşı* 53
Safavid dynasty 21, 122
Safiye, Valide Sultan 153, 154; venal 153
St Gothard 180
St Petersburg 209
St Veit 119
Sakarya, river 121
Salankmen, battle of 179

Index

Salonika (Thessalonika) 27, 46, 71, 102, 106
Samanid dynasty 20
Samarkand 21
sancak şerif see Standard of the Prophet
Sardi, Pietro, gunsmith 79-80
Sava, river 105, 133, 179
Savendia 138
Savona 103
Savoy 93
Schiltberger, Johann 28, 45
Scowl of Majesty 101
Scutari *see* Üsküdar
Sebastiani, French ambassador 203-4
Seckendorf, Marshal 195
seğmen 69, 70, 113
Şehzade mosque 38, 39, 72, 73, 98, 99, 148, 214, 225
Selim I, Ottoman sultan 17, 22, 40, 46, 56, 60, 70, 78, 80, 81, 84, 86, 99, 101, 102, 121-8, 130, 145, 149, 150; ferocity of 22, 122
Selim I mosque, Istanbul 99
Selim II, Ottoman sultan 85, 92, 111, 146, 147; *hamam* of 44, 47
Selim III, Ottoman sultan 74, 81, 107, 199-207 *passim*, 214, 218, 226; barracks 74; conscription 203; revenged 205; stabbed 207
Selimiye mosque, Edirne 85
Selimiye, ship 107
Seljuk dynasty 20, 42, 43
Sephardic Jews 127
Seraglio Point 52, 220, 221
serasker 27, 61, 72, 111, 119, 192, 195, 196, 203, 206, 226
Serbia 200, 201, 210
serdengeçti 68
Seven Towers *see* Yedikule
şeyhülislam 59, 60, 100, 117, 130, 144, 151, 156, 160, 161, 163, 169-71, 181, 184, 188, 190, 193, 203-6, 210, 216, 217, 220, 222, 225, 226
Seyyit Gazi, *tekke* 149
Shah Kuli, *celalı* rebel 120, 121
shamanism, influence of 20, 86, 149
Sherifs of Mecca 63, 153
Shi'ism; Shi'ites 23, 28, 63, 120, 121, 122, 131, 154
Sidon 157
Sigismund, Emperor 102
Silahtar Ali Pasha, Grand Vezir 210
Silahtar Mehmet Pasha, Grand Vezir 190

Index

silihdars 66
Silistria 107, 203
Silivri 203
Silk Road 122, 147
Sinan Abdülmennan, architect 36, 37, 52, 87, 128, 131
Sinan Agha, *agha* of janissaries 118
Sinan Pasha, cavalry commander 125-6
Sinan Pasha, Grand Vezir 96
Sinan Pasha, *kapudan paşa* 104
Sinop 120
sipahis 21, 26, 27, 36, 40-1, 61, 65-7, 69, 81, 89, 95, 96, 103, 114, 118, 125, 137, 138, 140, 143-5, 151, 154, 156, 157, 158, 160-5, 170, 171, 173, 175, 176, 179, 190, 191, 194, 201, 202; estates of 65; power fades 164
Sitvatorok, treaty of 155-6
Sivas 131, 154, 199
Sixtus V, Pope 29
Siyavuş Pasha 153, 177
Skopje *see* Üsküp
Slankamen 134
slaves 20, 28; *kapıkulı* and *kul* 30-42, 58, 70, 195; markets 32
Smyrna (Izmir) 160, 192, 199
Sobieski, Prince John 175
Sofalar Hamam 73
Sofia 133, 180, 192
Soğut 56
Sokollu Gate 172
Sokollu Mehmet Pasha, Grand Vezir 26, 42, 45, 47, 98, 100, 146, 147, 151, 153; nepotism 41
Spain 80, 104, 127, 132; Spanish Succession 179
Spandugino, T.C. 45, 49
Stamboul fire tower 97, 226
Standard of the Prophet *(sancak şerif)* 23, 72, 176, 177, 192, 206, 220, 222-3, 225, 227
standards, flags and horsetails 66, 71-2, 156
standing armies 17, 34, 111
Stephen, King of Bosnia 28
Strangford, Lady 212
Strangford, Lord 212
Sublime Porte 59, 61, 63, 147, 165, 172, 181, 202, 203, 208, 209, 217, 220, 225
Sufi Mehmet Pasha, Grand Vezir 171
Sufis 23, 25, 30, 57, 75, 87, 111, 118, 120, 152, 171, 197, 217, 226, 232
Sufism 28; and fatalism 231-2

Index

Süleyman I, the Magnificent (Kanuni), Ottoman sultan 23, 26, 37, 40, 41, 43, 45, 48, 60–1, 69, 76, 80, 84, 90, 92, 101, 105, 116, 124, 149, 150, 151, 154; death concealed 146; horsetails 72; laws 59, 61; Mohacs and 72, 78, 130–41 *passim*, 166, 175; pessimism of 145; philosopher 143; umbrella 133
Süleyman II, Ottoman sultan 177, 178
Süleyman, brother of Murat IV 163
Süleyman (Solomon), son of Bayezit I 57
Süleyman Pasha, son of Orhan Gazi 27, 43
Süleyman Pasha, Grand Vezir 176
Süleymaniye mosque 39, 58, 70, 86, 208, 212, 217, 225, 226, 231
sultan: ceremonial 57; concept of 55 *et seq.*; fires and 99–100; petitioning stirrup 23
Sultan Ahmet mosque 155, 222, 224, 225
Sultana Sporca (Madame La Quira) 155
Sumatra 80
Sumbullu (Hyacinth), Chief Black Eunuch 169
Sünnet Odası (Circumcision Kiosk) 192, 221
Sunnis 23, 63, 149, 152, 187, 190, 217, 231
superstition 19, 21–2, 28, 102, 198
supply roads 19, 67 *et seq.*, 83–5
Suvarov, Marshal 199, 201
Sweet Waters of Asia 89, 206
Syria 17, 40, 56, 60, 63, 101, 124, 126, 128, 131, 166, 184, 185; Greater Syria 81
Syrmie, island 133
Szeged (Szigeth) 141; fortress 90, 111
Szigeth *see* Szeged

Tabriz 123
tactics: flight 174; improvisation 79; lure and surprise 78
Tartars 21, 28, 29, 32, 67, 83, 119, 121, 136, 147, 191, 195, 226; flaming arrows 80; mounts unshod 77
Taurus mountains 119, 132
taverns and dancing boys 39, 87–9, 198, 211, 218
Tekeli Kiosk 70
Tekfursaray 186
tekkes and *zaviyes* 24, 25
Tenenti, A. 28
tents 74–6
Tersane (Arsenal) 38, 102, 106, 107, 119, 147, 178, 187, 190, 198, 221, 222, 230
Thessalonika *see* Salonika

Index

Thrace 101, 182
Tigris, river 193
timars 41, 65
Timur 25, 30, 33, 45, 56, 75, 91, 122, 148, 168
Timurtaş Bey 62
tobacco banned 101
Tokat 131, 155, 159, 188
Topal Osman Pasha, Grand Vezir 193, 195
topçus 67, 68
Tophane 39, 68, 98, 147, 198, 202, 227
Topkapısaray 23, 39, 43, 52, 72, 99, 158, 205, 220, 222; ceremonial 44, 57, 227; gates stormed 162
Tott, Baron de 92, 99, 107, 197–8, 202
Toulon 17, 103, 107
Trabzon (Trebizond) 46, 83, 131, 188
Transoxiana 21
Transylvania 119, 146, 174
Trebizond *see* Trabzon
Tripoli (North Africa) 192
Tripoli (Syria) 126, 128, 184
Tulip Period (Lala Devri) 186, 190
Tuman Bey, last Mamluk sultan 126–7
Turgut Reis 104
Turhan, Hadıce, Valide Sultan 169, 171–2
Turkey 21, 144, 145, 152, 227
Türkmen 21, 27, 67, 122, 131, 144, 149, 150; bowmen 20, 66
turncoats 33, 35

Üç Şerefeli mosque 150
Ukraine 174, 195
ulema 24–6, 33, 42, 74, 88, 100, 110, 111, 114, 117, 147, 149, 151, 152, 160, 161, 164, 174, 176, 177, 181, 187, 192, 193, 196, 197, 199, 202, 208–12, 216–18, 220–2, 225, 227; conservatism 58; education 58–9; intellectual decline of 60; power of 59; punished by Murat IV 163; rebellion 170, 189–90; rebels 170
Uludağ mountain 186
Urfa 154
Urquhart, David 156
Uskok, pirates 29
Üsküdar (Scutari) 117, 163, 188, 189, 193, 208, 222, 225, 230, 231
Üsküp (Skopje) 60, 130
Uzun Hasan, sultan of White Sheep 79, 83

Index

Uzunçarşılı, I.H. 73

vali 61
Varna 79, 111, 182
Velizade, *şeyhülislam* 203, 204
Venice 38, 90, 104, 116, 119, 120, 122, 169, 179, 197
Versizzi family 178
Vesuvius 103
Vezir of the Dome 61, 70, 72, 86, 184
Vicenza 67, 145; Casa del Capitano 145; Villa Valmarana 146
Vidin 227
Vienna 17, 72, 78, 80, 81, 84, 143, 144, 173, 174, 175, 177, 179, 180
Villa Valmarana, Vicenza 146
Villach 119
Villefranche 103
Villeneuve, Marquis de, ambassador 187
Virginia, slaves in 42
Vlad III Tepes Kazıklı (the younger Dracula) 78
Volga-Don canal 21, 147
voynuks 52

Wallachia 34, 84, 119, 133
Waterloo 69
weapons: arquebus 68, 125, 133, 139 (matchlock 80; miquelet lock 80); battering ram 91; bayonet 94, 199; bombs 68; bow 29, 50, 66, 81-2, 115, 123, 133, 137; cannon 39, 68, 77-80, 83, 85, 90-2, 94, 103-4, 107, 115-16, 119, 123, 125, 127, 134-5, 138, 141, 142, 147, 174-6, 187, 198, 203, 208; catapult 90; dagger 80, 94; dart 80; field gun 212, 221, 223-4; fires 98, 188; flaming faggot 116; grenade 68; halberd 51, 69; hatchet 80; javelin 80; *jerid* 38; lance 66, 80, 94, 137-8 (Holy Lance 118); mace 66, 80, 137; mortar 60; musket 29, 66, 83, 94, 157, 222; noise 82, 115; pikestaff 69, 94; pistol 80, 194; rapier 80; sabre 94, 219, 222; scimitar 66, 80; scythe 80; siege engine 80; stones 161
Wellington, Duke of 150
White Sheep 79, 83
William III, King of England 180
wine 21, 25, 87, 193, 197, 231; and janissaries 197; taxed 202, 211
Wippach, Anna Sophie von 178
Wortley Montagu, Lady Mary 75, 100-1

Yahya Pasha 120
Yalı Kiosk 220

Index

yamaks 67
Yanak, Greek butcher 191
yayas 67
Yedikule (Seven Towers) 92, 158, 160, 219, 220, 226
Yemen 63, 67, 131; control of 153
Yeni Cami (New Mosque) 190
Yeni Odalar (New Barracks) 73–4, 148, 204, 227
Yeni Valide mosque 39
Yeniköy 74
Yerivan *see* Erivan
Yermisekiz Mehmet Seyyit Efendi, ambassador 186
Yıldırım Bayezit *see* Bayezit I
Yozgat 165, 166
Yunus Pasha, cavalry commander 125–6
yürüks 67, 68
Yusuf the Kurd, mutineer 218, 219, 225
Yusuf Pasha, governor of Aleppo 155

Zante 104
zaviyes see tekkes and *zaviyes*
zeamets 65
Zenta 178, 180
Zeynep mosque 225
Ziya Pasha, poet 233
Zoroastrianism 20
Zvecaj 93
Zvornik 105